A Purse of Her Own

Occupations of Women in the Nineteenth Century

Susan L. Nenadic

Published by Susan L. Nenadic
Additional copies available at www.nicholasbooks.com
E-mail: nicolasbooks@tds.net Phone 734-662-0600
2513 Jackson Avenue, Ann Arbor, Michigan 48103

Publisher's Cataloging-in-Publication Data
Nenadic, Susan
    A purse of her own / by Susan L. Nenadic
    Ann Arbor, Mich., Susan L. Nenadic 2013
                    p.   cm.   ill.
        ISBN 978-0-615-80296-1
        1. History–United States.
        2. Women's History

Project Coordination by Bookability of Michigan LLC

Printed and bound in Canada

For my aunt, Dee Delaney,
a working woman of the past
celebrating her 100th birthday in 2013

and

For my grand-daughters, Lily and Elena Nenadic,
the working women of the future

TABLE OF CONTENTS

INTRODUCTION 9

CHAPTER 1: Women in the Sewing Trades 16

           Dressmakers
           Milliners

CHAPTER 2: Working Class Women 41

           Domestics
           Laundresses/ Dyers/ Dry Cleaners
           Carpet Weavers
           Mill and Manufacturing Workers

CHAPTER 3: Fallen Women and Female Felons 68

           Prostitutes
           Thieves and Scam Artists

CHAPTER 4: Wives, Widows and Daughters 76

           Women who ran shops
           Women who farmed
           Misc. occupations

CHAPTER 5: Females as Educators 95

           Rural Schools
           Select Academies
           Public Schools
           Michigan State Normal School
           Michigan Female College
           The Doors Remain Closed at University of Michigan

CHAPTER 6: Women in the Arts 124

           Music teachers
           Artists
           Authors

CHAPTER 7: Emerging Opportunities for Women 138

        Photographers
        Hairdressers
        Kindergarten Teachers
        Canvassers
        Librarians
        Office Workers

CHAPTER 8: Women and Higher Education 158

        The "Dangerous Experiment"
        First Women on the Faculty of the University of Michigan
        Female Faculty Members at Michigan State Normal School

CHAPTER 9: Women Join the Professions 173

        Doctors
        Nurses
        Pharmacists
        Dentists
        Attorneys

CHAPTER 10: Women in Business 204

        Boarding Houses/Rooming Houses
        Inns and Hotels
        Restaurants
        Real Estate
        Flower shops
        Retail Proprietors and Clerks
        Insurance

CHAPTER 11: Women in Communications and Politics 231

        Telegraph and Telephone Operators
        Newspapers and Publishing
        Elected Officials/Political Appointments

CONCLUSION 247

"A woman must have a purse of her own..."

Susan B. Anthony
November 1853 diary entry

*"I think the girl who is able to earn her own living
and pay her own way should be as happy
as anybody on earth. The sense of independence
and security is very sweet."*

Susan B. Anthony
1905 interview

INTRODUCTION

The 1970's advertising slogan," You've come a long way, Baby," is, in so many ways, true. There are opportunities for girls and women today that were non-existent in the 1950's when I was a child. No one can argue with that. 2010 data indicate that more women are graduating from college and doing post-graduate work than are men. Statistics also indicate that younger women in the work force are experiencing less of a wage gap than previously. That is very good news; however, women throughout the United States still earn 75% of what men are paid. A woman's lifetime earnings are even less since it is usually the woman who takes time from her career to raise a family and care for the aged, thus hindering advancement in job status and income. This, in turn, lessens her retirement income, throwing more elderly women than men into poverty. Perhaps the most startling national statistic which emerged in 2009, however, is that, for the first time in history, the majority of paid workers in the United States are female. In fact, 63.3% of all American families are supported by the income of female workers, and 40% of those report being the primary breadwinner for their families.

In contrast to popular perception, women are not new to the work place. They have formed a significant portion of the wage earners in the United States from the earliest colonial days, yet the stereotype persists that women during the nineteenth century did not work outside of the home. That myth has survived because textbooks, novels and films have chosen to portray that image of American women. Yes, we are all familiar with the names of women such as Susan B. Anthony, Clara Barton or Harriet Tubman. These women attained renown, but they are known for their social contributions not for their success in the workforce. How many Americans are familiar with Louise Reed Stowell? Myra Bradwell? Emma Amelia Hall? I suspect less than a handful of readers will recognize their names, yet their careers were seminal within the sphere of women's labor outside of the home.

At the present time there are quite a few books concerning working women during the nineteenth century. Some, like those by Wendy Gamber, focus on specific occupations such as sewing or operating a boarding house; others such as Caroline Bird's *Enterprising Women* are more general. But almost all the statistics either of these approaches utilizes come from the Northeast: New York, Massachusetts and Pennsylvania. With one exception, a book written by Mrs. M.L. Rayne in 1885, there is no volume which focuses on the employment of women of the Midwest – let alone Michigan. One can find very specific books about female lighthouse keepers or women at the University of Michigan, but a survey of the multitude of employment opportunities for women of that era in a typical area of the Midwest simply doesn't exist. This volume, therefore, has narrowed its focus to a single county in Michigan. Other than the fact that Washtenaw County was home to the first mid-western normal school and one of the first universities to accept women, this microcosm represents a typical county in a typical state. It had towns and villages, farmers and merchants. It was settled by families and always has had ethnic diversity. If its schools make it slightly unique, they serve to represent a national trend in women's education. For all these reasons Washtenaw County, Michigan, is ideal for the purpose of illustrating women's employment in the nineteenth century.

Originally Michigan was part of the Northwest Territory, which the British ceded to the United States in 1787. The southern portion of the Territory quickly became the states of Ohio, Indiana and Illinois. Rumors of problems with natives, swampy land and disease delayed settlement in Michigan until a few brave souls discovered its advantages: its oak openings, its rivers, and its natural resources. Until then, Michigan's reputation was so bad that President Monroe once claimed the territory would never achieve sufficient population to become a state. But things were about to change. The lack of interest in Michigan combined with the Panic of 1819 convinced President Monroe to lower both the price of land and the minimum amount of acreage required for purchase. Before that time, one had to buy 320 acres at two dollars per acre. That meant a $640 investment, which today would be over twelve thousand dollars. And that amount did not include any necessary supplies or travel expenses. Such a price would eliminate potential settlers even if Michigan's reputation did not. After May 20, 1820, however, an emigrant could purchase a homestead for a hundred dollars. That was all it took to entice land speculators and families to settle in Michigan. As Harriet Noble wrote years later, the excitement about settling in Michigan in the 1820's and 1830's was comparable to the frenzy of the California gold rush.

"In 1824 there was almost as great an excitement in western New York about going to Michigan as there has been recently in regard to [the gold fields] of California." [1]

Harriet Noble
*Courtesy of the Elk Rapids Historical Society,
Elk Rapid, MI*

The population of Washtenaw County exploded in the 1820's. At the beginning of 1823, when the Woodruff family arrived, there were no residents of European descent living in the county except Gabriel Godfroy, who operated a trading post. Just four years later, the number of settlers in Washtenaw County had increased to 929. When in 1837 Michigan (contrary to President Monroe's predictions) did become a state, 2,994 people lived in Ann Arbor alone and 2,280 more lived in Ypsilanti. The town of Chelsea at that time was just a figment of someone's imagination,[2] but Saline could boast 1,130 inhabitants. Towns of such size could – and did – support a wide variety of employment opportunities for women.

Archival material from the nineteenth century asserts that the proper role for a woman was that of housewife and mother, yet it provides little anecdotal evidence concerning such women's actual lives. Being a wife and mother then was no easy task especially for those who participated in the initial phases of settlement. One Michigan pioneer wife in 1835 traveled four hundred miles with her eight children only to have someone steal the bundle of baby things when her wagon broke down near Ypsilanti. Even then she was still a hundred miles from her husband's newly settled land. Sarah Bryan (Mrs. John), one of the first women to arrive in Washtenaw County, recorded in her journal how her husband left her with her six children, one just newborn, to travel to Maumee in search of work. She ran out of supplies as she awaited his return, not knowing if he were alive or dead. Another pioneering woman, Phoebe Hunt (Mrs. Timothy) experienced a shock when a Native American entered her cabin which had only a blanket for a door. He wanted food and shelter. Mrs. Hunt was alone with her three children, all under the age of four. The Indian stayed the night by the fire while Mrs. Hunt and her children huddled in her bed. Another time it was a huge wolf that imposed himself on the Mrs. Hunt's hospitality. It is hard to tell which unwelcome visitor frightened Mrs. Hunt more. When I think of such pioneering women, I am filled with admiration for their fortitude and courage. Women who were settlers and homemakers have my greatest respect; however, an entirely different volume needs to address their experiences. This volume is limited to women who worked beyond their domestic duties between the date of the first Washtenaw County settlers in 1823 and the beginning of World War I in 1914.

The emerging social viewpoint of that time was that men and women occupied totally different spheres. The male sphere required not just physical strength but unhindered competition in the marketplace resulting in material success. Men developed their cognitive skills and self-reliance to be capable of functioning in an increasingly competitive capitalist world. To balance the equation, women were relegated to home and hearth at the very time when homemaking tasks were being lightened by the production of manufactured goods. A woman's totally dependent role supposedly was sweetened by her being labeled the bastion of morality and philanthropic work. Women were declared to be the heart of society while men comprised the mind. These complementary roles, as the theory would have us believe, made the married couple a microcosm of a "perfectly balanced" society at large. Alexis de Tocqueville commented on such an outlook saying, "They [the Americans] have carefully separated the functions of man and of woman so that the great work of society may be better performed." [3]

This strong division, based on gender, increased as the nineteenth century progressed. Before the industrial revolution, most Americans lived in a rural setting making what they needed themselves. One eighteenth century farmer proudly declared that he had sold $150 worth of produce, but only ten dollars of that profit would buy items for the family. All else was made at home. Certainly this was a patriarchal world; however, women were stout partners of their husbands and were respected for their skills which produced not only the family's food but its clothing, candles, soap etc. These were not delicate ladies of leisure but active, robust women. As the industrial revolution drew men away from the family homestead to work within urban areas, it simultaneously began producing the fabric, bread, candles and soap that women had made at home. Despite the obvious advantages of the new system, the big disadvantage was to women. Their role in society dwindled first in importance and then in respect. For a growing group of middle and upper class women upon whom the stereotype is based, their world shrank to supervising servants and producing children.

The popular press of the day supported this gender division. It extolled the value of the home as a refuge for the hard working men who must deal with the mercenary world of business in order to support their families. But as the men spent more and more time away from home at their places of work and a growing number of available leisure activities, affluent women became increasingly isolated at home with less to do. One mid-century newspaper article "joked" that the proper sphere for women was a hoop skirt. We need to consider seriously all such comments for the implications they convey. What could a woman accomplish wearing the equivalent of a hula-hoop around her legs? The answer is very little. Next, consider the hobble skirt which was introduced in the 1880's and remained the fashion into the early twentieth century. It diminished a woman's stride to tiny shuffling movements much like a Japanese geisha. In such ways, then and now, "fashion" can limit a woman's productivity. Even in the 1970's Lesley Stahl, the first woman hired by CBS, complained that she was required to wear tight skirts and high heels which prevented her from competing with men in the rush for the phone banks in the days before cell phones. Clothing then – and now – can both symbolize and tyrannize.

Modern women also have struggled against the burden of social expectations. Girls of the post-World War II baby boom, like me, were raised in the 1950's in much the same way as girls a century before. Sometimes subtly and sometimes not, society continued to extol the blessings of marriage and of a well-kept home. Media advised wives to be finished with their chores and charities by the time the man of the house returned from work. He, like Mr. Cleaver on the popular television show *Leave it to Beaver*, should find a clean, well-behaved family and a beautifully prepared meal waiting for him. He needed this calm respite from his busy day. This idealized, yet narrow, view of life can be traced to more than a century earlier when the established areas of the United Sates simultaneously began to laud two "cults": the Cult of True Womanhood and the Cult of Leisure.

The nineteenth century's ideal of womanhood was preached from the pulpits and promoted in magazines such as *Godey's Lady's Book*, which in 1860 had 160,000 subscribers. It was so pervasive that the goal of many pioneer women like Harriet Noble of Dexter, Michigan, was to become established enough to be like the ladies of the east coast. They did not recognize the pitfalls. The cults those women emulated were golden traps. Like the corsets fashion decreed women should wear, the Cult of Womanhood and its concomitant Cult of Leisure confined women to a narrow and ultimately unhealthy sphere. The Cult of True Womanhood prescribed purity, domesticity, and submissiveness. All of these values were wrapped in a soft shawl of piety which proclaimed it was God's will. Every sector of society bombarded women with this message. For example, in addition to the Bible, one of the most popular pieces of literature in American homes was John Milton's *Paradise Lost* – a classic, to be sure, but also a stern advocate of male dominance. In it, Adam tells Eve, "...for nothing lovelier can be found/In woman, than to study household good/And good works in her husband to promote."[4] His message epitomizes that of the nineteenth century.

If any woman asked for greater scope for her gifts, the ministers and magazines were sharply critical. Such women were tampering with society, undermining civilization. Female writers such as Mary Wollstonecraft, Frances Wright and Harriet Martineau, who advocated equality of opportunity for women were labeled by one minister named Harrington, as "mental hermaphrodites."[5] Their liberal voices were mocked and muted not only by men but by other women.

The question of female education was primary. How could women expand their lives and use their gifts without education. Neither gender was against the idea of educating women. It was the nature, purpose and source of that education that was debated. Lonely were the voices advocating that women be educated in the same fashion as men so that they could enter the male world of work and influence. Many believed that the goal of a girl's education was to make her a better helpmeet to her spouse or a teacher of children until she married. Sara Josepha Hale, editor of *Godey's* wrote in 1830, "Let the education of women differ ever so much in detail and its end to qualify them to become wives and mothers..." [6] According to Hale, for a woman there is no path that diverges; there is but one path: matrimony. Finding a husband should be every girl's goal. That seems rather hypocritical of Hale since she was a professional business woman, the editor of one of America's most popular magazines. It was Frances Trollope in her book, *Domestic Manners of the Americans*, published in 1832, who went on record about American marriages. She concluded that marriage was no paradise for American women. It was a trap. "It is after marriage," she said, "... that the lamentable insignificance of the American woman appears." [7]

Reinforcing the concept of True Womanhood, the Cult of Leisure became the goal of society at large. As America became wealthier and the number of families in the upper middle class increased, society defined success as a wife who did nothing except the basic guidance of servants. She spent her day in domestic trivialities and social intercourse while an inexpensive servant class cleaned, cooked and ironed. The daughters of these affluent women felt even more trapped in this gilded cage than had their mothers. Amelia Jackson of Boston wrote,"... all we have to do is to pass our time agreeably to ourselves. I think everyone likes to feel the *necessity* of doing something, and I confess that I have sometimes wished I could be poor to have the pleasure of exerting myself." [8] Had any working class woman heard Amelia, she no doubt would have thought the girl crazy. For the poor, employment was part of their obligation to family. They did not work to amuse themselves or to be independent; their meager earnings went immediately to feed and clothe their siblings or children. They could not participate in the Cult of Leisure, but they could – and did – admire it from afar. For them it must have looked like paradise: a world of beautiful homes and clothes, a world of music and books, a world without exhaustion and debt.

Women's history is a palimpsest. Like an existing canvas that has been painted over with a different portrait, its original image remains hidden until interest and technology can make its presence known. In the same manner, women's history exists as a shadowy subtext so faint under the conventional version of history that, until recently, it has gone unnoticed, but it is there peeking through, begging attention. When both of these versions of the past – the traditional and the feminine – are revealed, we receive a contradictory message. In the very midst of the panegyrics praising "true womanhood," some liberal writers and parents asserted the opposite viewpoint. As Mary Livermore, a well-known lecturer of the 1870-1880's,[9] wrote in her volume, *What Shall We Do with our Daughters*, "It is not safe, neither is it wise or kind, to rear our daughters as if marriage were their only legitimate business." [10] The parents of the University of Michigan's illustrious alumna, Alice Freeman (Palmer), obviously would have agreed with Livermore since they told their daughter that they were more concerned that she could support herself than whether or not she married. At the same time as Sarah J. Hale was filling her magazine with encouragement for a traditional life as a homemaker, volumes began to appear advising women of potential careers. As early as 1862 Miss Virginia Penny published her book:

How Women can Make Money, Married or Single. One might find it amusing that such a book would be written by a woman named Penny and conclude that it was a pseudonym. It was not. Miss Penny (1826-1913) was an indefatigable advocate of equity for women in the workplace and of federal legislative action to enforce that equity.

More and more books similar to Miss Penny's appeared as the century progressed: *Money Making for Ladies* by Ella Church, *Occupations for Women* by Frances Willard and *The Ways of Earning Money: A Book for Women* by Cynthia Alden, to name but three. Typically, most of these books focused on examples from the east coast. One, however, *What Can a Woman Do*, written by Martha Louise Rayne, was published in Detroit in 1885. Mrs. Rayne filled her volume with specific details concerning the training required, working experiences and salaries of women who were living in the states carved out of the Northwest Territory.

Some of these books, such as *Money Making for Ladies*, consider only very traditional occupations. In that volume, Miss Church discusses such occupations as needlework, raising and drying flowers, boarding house management, poultry and bee keeping, and writing. Her most innovative idea – personal shopper – sounds very modern indeed to a twenty-first century ear. None of her suggestions, however, violated the limits of the traditional female sphere, and none challenged the domains dominated by men.

Mrs. Rayne, in comparison, has chapters on medicine, law, photography and many other possibilities within the traditionally male sphere. She clearly sought to inspire her female readers with stories such as one about the famous Palmer House in Chicago. [10] Mr. Palmer, upon hiring his first female clerk, quickly discovered that women were better at the job than men. To make sure he kept these wonderful female employees, he paid them the generous salary of $1500 a year, three times what a public school teacher or a nurse would be able to make at the time and almost as much as a professor at the University of Michigan.

Thus, in spite of the pervasive popular view that women should not work outside the home, they did. Need propelled them. For some, it was the need for life's basic substances: food, clothing, shelter. For others, the need was more emotional, spiritual and intellectual. It was the need to fulfill their talents and curiosities. It was the need to follow those inner voices that told them they could do something more significant with their lives. Whatever their motivation, women were in the nineteenth century work force contributing to society in a multitude of ways that have seldom been recognized.

Any study of this sort is hindered, paradoxically, by both the scarcity and the wealth of available information. Census records and city directories provide the names of several thousand women with occupations; however, those public records provide virtually no clue as to the specifics of the women's lives. Why were they working? How did they feel about their work? Why did they stop working? Few working women left journals, diaries or letters to share their thoughts and experiences with future generations. If available, I have used them. If not, I have borrowed the words of similar women who did leave a written record. If possible, these are women in Michigan; if not, they are from elsewhere in the United States. I have also included national statistics and trends to illustrate how Washtenaw County was similar or different from the more established East.

My goal has been to focus on all of Washtenaw County and not just the cities of Ann Arbor and Ypsilanti. That has proven difficult since so much of the available information concerns those two towns. Ann Arbor and Ypsilanti, also appear to have provided a more welcoming environment especially to professional women due, no doubt, to the institutions of higher learning that existed in each. And both of these towns were larger than other settlements in the county. As a result they provided more entrepreneurial opportunities for women. Finally, Ann Arbor and Ypsilanti have preserved quite a bit of information which facilitates research. Sadly, records concerning women in the townships and villages are scant indeed, but I gratefully utilized them whenever I could.

Also, many women, who later became famous, passed through the area but did not stay. Mary Chase Perry Stratton who founded Pewabic Pottery spent only two years as a girl in Ann Arbor, thus she is not included. So many University of Michigan graduates went on to have distinguished careers but not in Washtenaw County. Women such as Marion Parker (Madgwick), the first woman to graduate from the Engineering School; Alice Freeman (Palmer) who became the president of Wellesley College and received the University of Michigan's first honorary doctorate; Alice E. Hamilton (sister of classicist, Edith Hamilton) who was the first woman allowed to join the faculty of Harvard and another recipient of an honorary doctorate from the University of Michigan, and Ida Gray, the first African-American woman to earn a degree in dentistry, were in the area only as students; therefore, their careers, too, have not been included except for comments such women made about their educations.

I am hopeful that this volume will serve not just as a culmination of my research but as an invitation to others to contribute their own findings to create a continually expanding dialogue concerning women's activities. Such a combined effort will do much to provide future generations with a more balanced view of the past. Every woman, as Susan B. Anthony said, needs a purse of her own so that she need not be dependent upon others for her support. But every woman also needs a history of her own. Without a history of her own, she can neither recognize the significant contributions made by women who preceded her nor feel gratitude for their efforts which have allowed modern women lives of virtually unlimited possibilities.

---

[1] Elizabeth Ellet, *Pioneer Women of the West* (Philadelphia: Porter and Coates, 1875), 388.

[2] Chelsea as a town was not platted until 1850.

[3] Alexis de Tocqueville, *Democracy in America*, ed. J.P.Mayer, trans. George Lawrence (New York: Harper Row, 1988), 601

[4] John Milton, *Paradise Lost*, ed. Scott Elledge (New York: W.W. Norton, 1993), 204, L233-234.

[5] Barbara Welter, Cult of True Womanhood, *Our American Sister*, ed. Jane Friedman and William Shade (Boston: Allyn and Bacon, 1973), 114.

[6] Sara Josepha Hale, *Sketches of the American Character* (Boston: Putnam and Hunt, 1830),102.

[7] Frances Trollop, *Domestic Manners of the American* (London: Whittaker, Treacher and Co. 1832), 230.

[8] Carl Degler, *At Odds: Women and Family* (New York: Oxford University Press, 1980), 374.

[9] Mary Livermore spoke in Ypsilanti and Ann Arbor several times.

[10] Sheila Rothman, *A Woman's Proper Place* (New York, Basic Books, 1978), 145.

[11] According to Isabel Ross in her biography of Mrs. Palmer, *Silhouette in Diamonds*, it was Mrs. Palmer's money that financed the construction of the Palmer House.

CHAPTER ONE: THE SEWING TRADES

The two days before Christmas in 1907 were rainy and cold with a slushy snow covering the ground, but that did not stop Florence Smalley Babbitt who remained both afternoons on the main street of Ypsilanti, Michigan, reaching into one of four bushel baskets to hand little packages wrapped in red, white, or blue paper to any child who happened to pass. She had personally wrapped each of the six hundred packages she distributed during those two days. In each was a toy. No, hers was not exactly an early version of Toys for Tots. Hers were very special because each of her gifts was a toy made before the Civil War. Mrs. Babbitt hoped that receiving these priceless gifts might instill in the children an interest and ultimately a love of history similar to her own.

Florence Babbitt
Courtesy of the Ypsilanti
Historical Society

Florence herself was a living embodiment of Michigan history. Her family emigrated from New York as did fully one-fourth of Michigan's nineteenth century population. She and her parents settled in Washtenaw County in 1852 when she was five years old. Avoiding the arduous overland journey, they, like most, had sailed from Buffalo, New York, to Detroit in a boat that serendipitously was built from oak timbered on a farm located near Ypsilanti, the very place where they intended to their new home.

Twelve years later, Florence married the boy next door, John W. Babbitt who was just beginning a legal career that would ultimately make him a judge. The Babbitts raised all four of their daughters at 301 S. Huron, one of the oldest houses in Ypsilanti until it was demolished in 1935. All the while, Mrs. Babbitt was continuing an interest that began when she was just thirteen. She collected old things. By 1901, the year her husband died, she had an extensive collection that included among other things 3,000 pieces of china, 1,500 trays, and hundreds of pre-Civil War toys. In the process of collecting, she became a recognized expert concerning American antiques. It was then, at age fifty-four, that Florence Babbitt turned her hobby into a vocation.

During the next twenty-four years, not only did she give huge parts of her collection to Michigan museums, the Toledo Museum, and Michigan State Normal School, she became the official collector for the State Historical Society. Forty barrels of her vast toy collection found their way to the Grand Rapids' Museum. Henry Ford came to her home to ask her for help in his effort to create Greenfield Village in Dearborn. He did not want glamorous objects but authentic artifacts such as he remembered from his childhood. Theater producer William Brady sought her advice in 1913 concerning the set and props for his production of *Little Women*. Mrs. Babbitt also assisted curators of the Art Institute of Chicago with their American Wing. In fact, they hired her to be their buyer. She visited the great homes of women such as Mrs. Palmer and Mrs. McCormick, looking for treasures that those women might sell or contribute. The Detroit Institute of Arts was less enthusiastic about her ideas for its American Wing, but she finally convinced the curator, Mr. Griffiths, that if he provided a room, she and people she knew would donate enough to fill it.

Florence Babbitt's pitcher collection
Courtesy of the Ypsilanti Historical Society

Though getting along in years, Babbitt remained tenacious in her search and documentation of historic artifacts. Sometimes she transported priceless pieces of china in special pockets she'd sewn into her petticoat. On other occasions her quest might be for something as humble as the iron pot for which she hunted all over Detroit one day. By the time she found the perfect pot and had returned to the interurban trolley stop, she was exhausted. She sat on a bench holding the pot, waiting patiently for the trolley to arrive so that she could begin her hour and a half trip back to Ypsilanti. Basking in the warm sunshine, she soon dozed only to be awakened by the clank of coins dropping into her iron pot. Some charitable soul had passed by and apparently thought she was begging.

No doubt Mrs. Babbitt did not look any different from other elderly ladies either that day or in December 1907 when she played Santa Claus. She probably wrapped herself in a warm but very typical early twentieth century coat and hat. It is unfortunate that she could not have stood there in her famous "Lincoln" costume which is now on display at the Ypsilanti Historical Museum. This entire ensemble, which Mrs. Babbitt enjoyed wearing on special occasions, dates from 1860, the year Abraham Lincoln was elected president. She bought the luxurious green merino wool for the dress at Norris and Follett's. The French embroidered neck piece and elegant under sleeves came from F. K. Rexford's while the hoops and black lace shawl were purchased at Jerome G. Cross'. All of these stores were located in downtown Ypsilanti and were owned and operated by men. The luscious black and purple hat with long satin ties and a feather, however, was made by and purchased from a woman – Olive S. Coe – whose shop was on Huron Street, also in downtown Ypsilanti.

Above, hat made by Olive Coe.
Right, Mrs. Babbitt in her Lincoln outfit.
Courtesy of the Ypsilanti Historical Society

The same year Mrs. Babbitt's Lincoln costume was made, the *Ann Arbor-Ypsilanti City Directory* confidently proclaimed that its "Business Mirror" (the equivalent of twentieth century yellow pages) contained "the name of every business *man* in the City." Perhaps it did, but the statement is misleading because it also included the names of more than two dozen business *women* oneof whom was Miss Coe. Born in Ohio in 1830, Coe was the daughter of Joseph and Sophia Coe. After her father died, the family moved to Ypsilanti where her mother also passed away. Though occasionally referred to as "Mrs.," Olive Coe was unmarried. Her shop remained until at least late November, 1873. She was not a passing fancy. Miss Coe was a reputable business woman for many years, and she was not alone in that role.

This oversight – indeed this slight – was not that of the *Business Mirror* alone. Women's contributions in the world of business and the professions remain a mystery to most Americans. Women's activities have been ignored until recently because they contradicted society's concept of itself as family-based with mothers presiding over the home and children while fathers go out into the competitive, commercial world of work. Such a stereotype has been reinforced in the media and in our schools. American history classes in public schools don't include statistics on women who worked in colonial America. Students don't hear about "Mistress Jenny" of Plymouth whose mill provided the entire colony with grinding and storage of grain in 1644. They do not study Eliza Pinckney who ran her family's plantation introducing indigo into the South Carolina economy. Because such contributions by women are not discussed in schools, the American public is unaware that, in the pre-revolutionary war period, there were women working as silversmiths, woodworkers, leather workers, distillers, print shop owners, and newspaper publishers. Seventeen women practiced medicine in the New England colonies. And one of history's best kept secrets is that Lord Baltimore's cousin, Margaret Brent, an extensive property owner, practiced law for decades and even demanded to vote in the House of Burgesses. In eighteenth century Philadelphia, fully one-third of all shopkeepers were women, and seventeen percent of all tavern licenses were issued to women. And a man may have written the "Declaration of Independence," but it was a woman, Maryland's Katherine Goddard, who first printed it. Despite multitudinous examples such as these, the employment of women still is not taught in American schools except for textile mills and sweatshops. Textbook topics about females tend to fall into three categories: unionism, suffrage and the twentieth century struggle for birth control. Certainly, all of these are important historical concerns, but alone they do not create a complete, let alone an accurate, picture of the daily lives of women.

In addition to being excluded from the historical record, information that is available about working women suffers from two significant limitations. Early works in women's studies circa 1970-1980's simultaneously challenged the public's perceptions but were corrupted by their authors' own preconceived notions. For example, Daniel S. Smith in an article reproduced in Hartman's *Clio's Consciousness Raised*, states unequivocally, "Married American women did not work outside the home until the twentieth century."[1] Smith could not have been more wrong. Married women certainly did work outside the home before the twentieth century as this study will demonstrate. The second limitation to published studies is that their supporting information derives almost exclusively from east coast sources: New York, Philadelphia and Boston. The Northwest Territory, which evolved into the states of Ohio, Indiana, Illinois, Michigan, Wisconsin and Minnesota, has been ignored when it comes to the topic of women's history in general. Yet states like Michigan are representative of the nineteenth century, an era of rapid territorial expansion, immigration and technological change. Our perception of women at that time, however, remains based on stereotypes fostered by novels and movies. Even reputable museums remain dominated by His-story not Her-story. One can only assume that museums perpetuate the stereotype because they do not have sufficient information to change their perceptions about women's activities. But if we could jump in a time machine and return to that by-gone era, even if we limited our journey to a single county such as Washtenaw County, Michigan, we would discover a multitude of women, like Florence Babbitt and Olive Coe, engaged in an amazingly wide variety of occupations.

> The word "stereotype" in the nineteenth century referred to an engraved metal plate used in printing. Not until 1922 did it acquire its current meaning when Walter Lippman wrote "A stereotype may be so consistently and authoritatively transmitted in each generation from parent to child that it seems almost like a biological fact."[2]

Not surprisingly, almost all the females listed in that 1860 City Directory, which is the earliest one available to researchers, were listed as members of the sewing trades: milliners, dressmakers or seamstresses. Nor is it surprising that the first millinery and dressmaking shops in Washtenaw County appeared in the towns of Ypsilanti and Ann Arbor. Woodruff's Grove, which was quickly absorbed into Ypsilanti, was the oldest white settlement in the county; Ann Arbor was settled the following year. They were in the early nineteenth century, as they are now, larger communities than the surrounding ones. Pioneer women such as Mrs. Woodruff, who arrived in Woodruff's Grove in 1823, or Ann Rumsey, who in 1824 spent her first night in the future Ann Arbor sleeping under a sleigh seat, were more concerned with the problems of food, shelter and keeping the ubiquitous wolves at bay than whether or not their attire was of the most stylish mode. But it did not take long for the women of Washtenaw County to recover their interest in the finer things in life.

It took less than a decade for interest in women's apparel to appear. Most local historians have assumed that pioneering settlers were only interested in utilitarian items such as hardware, lumber and leather goods. They most definitely were interested in all of those products; however, there is more to the story if one cares to cast unbiased eyes on newspapers of that period. The proof comes to us in bits and pieces since few records were kept, but there is sufficient fragmentary evidence to confirm the early arrival of shops and services by women. For example, the *Western Emigrant*, the county's earliest newspaper, included in its August 13, 1834 edition an advertisement for a milliner, Mrs. Spencer, who offered to the ladies of the area, "Tuscan Gauze and fancy straw hats" as well as "an assortment of other fancy articles." Her shop was located "two doors north of Maynard and Guiteau's new store" in downtown Ann Arbor.

> Settlers in the first half of the nineteenth century consistently referred to themselves and others as "emigrants." Emigrant means someone who leaves his home and goes to some new place. Perhaps they saw themselves as going forth without anything in the new place to receive them. By mid-century, newcomers, especially those from Europe, always were called "immigrants."

Mrs. Spencer was not the only woman in Ann Arbor who was earning an income in the sewing trades at that time. There was also a Mrs. Beers. We know this because a year later, Miss A. Dewel announced in the *Emigrant* that she had acquired Mrs. Beers' shop on Main Street between Washington and Huron for her own millinery and mantua-making business. The former proprietor, Mrs. Beers, probably was Mary Beers, the wife of Lewis Beers. If this identification is correct, she was born in 1798 and died in Ann Arbor in 1869. A report by John McMath to the Michigan Historical Society indicates that the Beers family emigrated to the Ypsilanti area in 1830 where they remained two years. According to McMath, an Ypsilanti pioneer, a woman named Beers taught at the first school in his neighborhood. [3] If it is the same family, it would mean she arrived in Ann Arbor circa 1832 which would leave three years in which she could have established her sewing business before Miss Dewel took over.

Nor were such shops only in Ann Arbor. In April of 1835, a Mrs. H. Tyler placed notices in the newspaper [4] announcing the opening of her similar shop in Ypsilanti. She offered "millinery, mantua making and tailoring." In addition, she would clean delicate silk dresses at her shop "just three doors south of the Brick School House on the Ypsilanti Road."

By the time of Michigan statehood, when Washtenaw County could boast a population of 21,817, the June 8, 1837 issue of the *Argus*, another early newspaper, contained an advertisement by a Mrs. Love (reproduced on the following page) letting the public know that she had received her new spring articles. Though Mrs. Love's advertisement is from 1837, we can infer that she had been in business for a while since she thanked her readers for "past patronage." Subsequent advertisements tell us that Mrs. Love sold her business to a Mrs. C. Buffington four years later, and if we continue searching the papers, we learn that Mrs. Buffington was still in business in 1855. These early advertisements testify to the existence of women in the sewing trades less than a decade after settlement of Washtenaw County.

For these very first years of women's business efforts, researchers must rely primarily on newspaper advertisements such as these because city directories did not exist and early census records provide little employment data. The Census of 1840 did not include a category for occupation. By 1850 it did provide a space for occupation, but virtually no women were noted as having any. Because of that, it would be easy to assume that women did not have occupations; however, it states that listing an occupation was voluntary. Most males also failed to provide one. A decade later the Census of 1860 did provide information concerning employment. It identified women engaged in millinery, dressmaking and knitting as occupations, but few of those women had shops. Many lived in rural areas where much of the sewing was done at home. In Manchester, for example, Emily Martin, Sophia Nixon and Julie Pease, were wives or daughters of farmers.

> ## NEW GOODS.
> ### Mrs. Love,
> ### Milliner & Dress Maker
>
> Would respectfully inform the Ladies of Ann Arbor and its vicinity, that she has recently received from New York, her spring GOODS, comprising almost all articles in her line, together with the latest Patterns for BONNETS, and DRESSES, she deems it unnecessary to enumerate the several articles, but would merely say, Ladies call and see. She would tender her thanks for past patronage and solicit a continuance of the same. Bonnets cleaned and Whitened in a neat manner.

Another woman involved in the sewing trade was the wife of a cooper. Yet another was a shoemaker's wife, and one was the wife of a druggist. These women were trying to earn a little extra money to help the family without any grand plans of making it a permanent career, nor were they sewing fancy or complicated garments. To find women who did establish themselves as professionals in the sewing trades as a career before 1860, newspapers are the only public source of information. Even so, they are a limited source since many women did not advertise at all, and those that did advertise did so only sporadically.

Miss Dewell, Mrs. Tyler and Mrs. Love, fortunately for us, did use, though sparingly, the local newspapers to promote their work in the 1830's. It is interesting to note what words they chose to describe the variety of services they provided. All three said they were milliners, which means they made ladies' hats. This profession had but recently become available to working women. Before the nineteenth century, only men, such as the ones in plays by Shakespeare or Sheridan, were milliners. The Oxford English Dictionary cites the first usage of the term "lady millineress" in 1802. The label's redundancy only emphasizes the apparent need for clarification in a field that was rapidly changing gender. In addition, Mrs. Spencer included in her notice that she sold an assortment of "fancy articles." Fancy articles such as lace, ribbons or even gloves originally were manufactured in Milan, Italy, from which the term, milliner, derives. Such commodities were a natural fit for women in the millinary trade.

Dewell and Tyler also identified themselves as "mantua-makers." This did not refer to the loose gown known in the seventeenth and eighteenth centuries as a mantua, manteau or mantoa. They probably used that term so that the customer would associate it with the rich silk from Mantua, Italy, which had become available in the early nineteenth century. In this way, they connoted elegance and sophistication. The term indicated to their potential clients that they were very skilled at their trade. Dewel proudly included in her advertisement that she was newly arrived from the East where she had four years experience. That information assured her future customers that she was able to make the most fashionable attire. Mrs. Love, who chronologically came a year later than the other two, is the only one who referred to herself as a "Dress Maker." She might have been living in a newly settled territory, but her use of that particular term identified her as being, literally as well as metaphorically, on the cutting edge.

The word, "dressmaker," did not exist until 1803. Men had dominated this trade since the Renaissance. During the eighteenth century, however, women began making inroads there as they had done in millinery. By the nineteenth century, women had taken over this facet of the sewing trades, too, leaving only a few male couturiers such as the famous Worth of Paris. In America, social mores against males touching females in any sort of intimate way facilitated this transition of dressmaking to a profession exclusively handled by women. Thus Mrs. Love's choice to use the word, "dressmaker," made her appear quite avant-garde to the women of her day.

The sewing trades were a natural choice for women wanting or needing to earn an income. All females were taught to sew. Phebe Crandall's descendant, Gertrude Hiscock Nanry of Ypsilanti, noted that Phebe's aunts began sewing her trousseau as soon as Phebe was born in 1793. Stitching by hand, they made table linens, curtains, sheets and pillow cases, and rolls of lace for dresses and aprons. By age six Phebe was learning fancy needle stitches as well as how to "tat" a lace-like edging. She also learned to "make tree-limb loom blankets having intricate designs" [5] as well as how to dye wool. The Ypsilanti Historical Museum features her recipe for dyeing wool and one of the blankets she made. Phebe Crandall Hiscock (Mrs. Isaac) passed away in 1869, five years after twenty-five year old Sarah Norton (Mrs. Austin) noted in her diary that her mother had purchased some calico for $3.50 but disliked the red in it, so she sold it to Sarah for $2. On December first, Sarah wrote, "I commenced my dress today. I made the skirt and sleeves." [6] She finished it two days later despite the soaring price of thread which had risen to twenty cents the previous fall due to Civil War shortages. No one seriously questions the fact that women sewed clothing and things for the home.

However, there is sewing, and there is Sewing. Louisa McMath Hathaway's family was one of the first to settle in Ypsilanti. Born circa 1808, she described the laborious process of making ordinary clothing for a family in those days. "There was not much effort at style; clothes were just cut, made and put on," [7] Mrs. Hathaway was the daughter of Colonel McMath who settled in Ypsilanti in 1825. Her father died that year leaving her mother to raise nine children and operate the farm. Clothing for such folks was practical. It made no pretense to fashion. As a result, "Observers said they could detect the potato sack-like cut of a homemade garment a mile away, especially next to a tailor-made piece." [8] To obtain style one needed a professional. Seeking the proverbial middle road, it became quite common during the first half of the century for a dressmaker simply to cut a garment for the client who then laboriously sewed it by hand herself at home. As late as 1871, Miss Stebbins of Dexter offered "Ladies and Children's dresses cut and baisted [sic]." [9] This indicated that Stebbins did the planning while the painstaking task of actually sewing the garment was done by the client at home. Thus the client cut costs while still obtaining more stylish clothing.

Fashionable dresses demanded an extremely snug fit, and fabric was far too dear to incur errors. A trained dressmaker was necessary to make sure a gown turned out well. Even trained professionals "found it difficult enough to draft out a pattern from the scaled diagrams supplied by women's journals and dressmaking manuals." [10] It certainly was not something an amateur could complete successfully. Many of these early dressmakers did not need to maintain their own shops but went to homes to do the fitting and cutting and, if desired, the sewing. In such cases, they were not treated as servants but as respected professionals. Clients always referred to them as Miss or Mrs., never by their first names as one might a servant. By 1878 Miss E. Evans of Dexter did maintain a shop in the Exchange Building; however, she still was offering to come to a client's home if that were preferred. Whether such women maintained shops or worked in clients' homes, dressmaking was an excellent occupation for women. As Miss Virginia Penny explained in her 1862 book, *How Women can Make Money*, "Much of the beauty of a dress depends on its tasteful make... In dressmaking a lady has only to establish a reputation as a successful fitter and a fashionable trimmer [to make a profit]." [11]

Downtown Ann Arbor,
circa 1860

Courtesy of the Bentley Historical Library
University of Michigan

A dressmaker, as her skills and the size of the town grew, eventually might open a shop. When she did start her own establishment, she often accepted apprentices or hired others to work with her doing the simpler jobs of sewing seams or trimming. Such was the case for Miss Maycumber, a dressmaker located in the Follett Block in Ypsilanti. She had at least three employees in 1860. These assistants might have been apprentice dressmakers, or they might have been seamstresses. If they were seamstresses, they occupied a lower status because they sewed but never cut or fitted. A dressmaker earned twice as much as a seamstress, and while we in the modern world might be tempted to use the terms synonymously, in the nineteenth century the difference was significant enough that the 1870 United States Census noted them separately. As is true in any field, there were far more of the lesser trained than of the gifted professionals; thus there were far more seamstresses than dressmakers.

Milliners also had a hierarchy of skills. If business were brisk enough, they, too, would hire assistants. Beginners simply shaped the foundations of the hats. More experienced workers trimmed. In 1860 there were several successful shops. Mrs. Britt was on Main Street in Ann Arbor while in Ypsilanti Miss Coe's shop was on South Huron and Mrs. Vincent on Congress. All of these women were milliners with sufficient clientele to support employing more women.

In addition to opening their own stores or working out of their homes, there existed circa 1860 one other option for women in the sewing trades. They could work for an established dry goods store such as Charles Fantle's in Ann Arbor or W.B. Hewitt's in Ypsilanti. Both of these establishments, owned by men, sold millinery and employed women as milliners. Charles Fantle employed four women while Hewitt employed three.

For at least one woman, her sewing skills appear to have evolved into employment for her husband. Mrs. Stanley L. Stevens specialized in undergarments for women. She advertised in the October 3, 1867 *Peninsular Courier* that she would "manufacture to order and repair on short notice, Hoop Skirts, and Corsets according to the latest and most fashionable shapes and has secured the sole agency for Burger's Celebrated FRENCH PATTERN CORSETS." The following year's advertisements indicate that Mr. Stevens had opened a "hoop skirt factory" at 6 East Huron Street in Ann Arbor. Since her advertisements predate his, it suggests that Mr. Stevens' business was an outgrowth of hers rather than the other way around.

In larger cities, dressmaking and millinery existed as two distinctly separate fields of endeavor. More populous areas could sustain such specialization which became popular early in the century. However, women in small towns or villages like Dexter often found it more profitable to provide a variety of services. In the early 1870's, Mrs. Smith obviously felt millinery was her primary objective; however, she also provided dressmaking as well as offering for sale corsets and hoop skirts. She even stocked shoes from New York. Her competitor, Mrs. E. K. Taylor, sold hats for fifty cents to ten dollars. It would be interesting to know how many ten dollar hats she sold because in today's market it would cost $177. Taylor also sold ribbons, flowers, hair goods, and dress trimmings at her shop on the corner of Ann Arbor and Baker Streets. In addition, Mrs. Taylor's ad included a "dress making department" run by a Miss Russ. Mrs. A. M Craine, whose career outlasted both Smith's and Taylor's, managed a similar shop in the Beal Block at that time. She provided yet more in the way of available merchandise including embroidery, hosiery, chignons, collars and hair jewelry. Kid gloves at Mrs. Craine's sold for twenty-five cents in July of 1879, by which time her advertisements included the caveat "dressmaking a specialty." [12] Thus the women of the Dexter area had several shops to patronize.

Downtown Manchester, circa 1883, where the Foster sisters had their shop.

Courtesy of Gerald Swartout

Combining dressmaking and millinery to maximize potential was very common. Eva and Mary Foster, daughters of immigrants from Baden, Germany, [13] maintained a shop in Manchester for about a decade in the 1870's and 1880's. Both were well past the usual age of marriage when they went into business. Eva would have been in her thirties; and Mary in her forties. They advertised that they had a hundred different styles and would sell ostrich tips for only one dollar a bunch.

In a similar fashion, Mary Palmer of Milan advertized in 1883 as both dressmaker and milliner thus doubling her potential clientele. She first hired her sister, Sarah, to do the dressmaking so that she could concentrate her skills on hats. Sarah's presence did not last long, but Mary's did despite a fire that swept through downtown Milan in 1891. By 1894 Mary had added Lucy Clark, the widow with whom Mary boarded, as a partner in what from then on would be called Palmer and Clark. At that time Mary switched to dressmaking while Lucy did the hats. Eventually, as Milan's population grew, they sold only hats. In contrast to the Foster sisters' decade as business women, Mary Palmer was a "downtown fixture" for almost fifty years.

There were other combinations that women could make to enhance their incomes from the sewing trades. Mrs. Uriah B. Wilson did not mix dressmaking with millinery; she sold sewing machines. An advertisement in 1866 notified potential customers that Wheeler and Wilson's was ready to receive customers

Palmer and Clark's building as pictured in the *Milan Area Leader,* January 26, 1983

in Hangsterfer's new building at corner of Washington and Main Streets in Ann Arbor. The name "Wheeler and Wilson," however, does not refer to Mrs. Wilson, the proprietor. It refers to a brand of sewing machine invented at the same time as Singer's model. (Coincidentally both brands were patented on the same day: August 12, 1851.) Some sources believe that Wilson's invention was the more original. Wilson patented improvements such as the first stationary circular disc bobbin which is still used on machines today. Allen Benjamin Wilson, the inventor who lived for a while in the 1840's in Adrian, Michigan, became partners with Mr. Wheeler in order to manufacture the machine. It was this machine that Mrs. Wilson sold.

Mrs. Wilson's husband, Uriah, was born and raised in Michigan. He had sold the sewing machines as early as 1858 and was still in some public records in 1865. I suspect that he died not long after; consequently, Mrs. Wilson simply continued that work since she began advertising using her own name at that time. Her full name was Julia M. Wilson (nee White). She would have been thirty-six years old at the time of the advertisement. She no doubt was in need of some income since she was the mother of four children, three of whom were younger than thirteen and still living at home. But it seems a bit coincidental that both the machine and the agents were both named Wilson. There may have been a kinship element to their becoming the sales agents in Ann Arbor. In any case, Mrs. Wilson disappears from the local record by 1868. She reappears in the 1880 census in Brandon, Wisconsin, living with her brother.

Wheeler and Wilson and Singer were not the only sewing machines available at that time. Another popular manufacturer was Florence. Leander W. Langdon established his factory in Florence, Massachusetts, in 1858. Within a dozen years he had sold 17,600 machines. Then things began to sour for Langdon's company and indeed for the entire national economy.

To maximize profits in a difficult market, Florence ceased sending men around the country in wagons demonstrating the machines, offering free trials and installment buying. Instead Langdon slashed prices by 25% but demanded cash purchases. Despite its financial troubles, the Florence machines were preferred by a great many women. To meet that need, Mrs. Eliza Storms of Ann Arbor became an "agent" or saleswoman for Florence in 1872, and Olive Coe of Ypsilanti added Florence machines to her millinery sales the following year. Other women not in the sewing trades capitalized on the increasing interest in sewing machines. Miss S. A. Carleton of Ypsilanti chose simply to be the sales agent, but she placed her sample machines in Mrs. Martin's shop circa 1871.

That women were actively involved in all facets of the sewing trades is indisputable. Sadly, however, there are virtually no written records to aid us in understanding how these women felt about their work. Did they choose sewing because they enjoyed it, or was it their occupation because they could find no other? The few sources that are available provide a mixed message. One woman in New Hampshire who began a dressmaking and millinery business obviously loved her work. She wrote in 1841 that she and her sister were "happy as pigs in clover; nothing to do but to work and of that we are overrun." [14] A contrasting tale is that of Sarah Rosetta Wakeman of New York. Eldest of nine children, she left home circa 1860 to seek employment. Dismayed at the low wages offered women, she dressed as a male and got a job on a canal boat. No sooner had she settled into that job than she met some Union soldiers and decided to join the army. Miss Wakeman, aka Lyons Wakeman, liked soldiering so much she wrote home that she was considering re-enlisting for five more years. That was not to be, for she died in 1864 still passing as a man and fighting for the Union. She was twenty-one.

> "The scanty reward for female labor in America remains a reproach to the country" [15]
>
> Harriet Martineau 1836

Whether or not Michigan women would agree with the former or latter woman's opinion is a mystery. Anna Howard Shaw, who lived in western Michigan, did comment in her autobiography on her brief sewing career. Her opinion concurs with that of Miss Wakeman. Shaw expressed dismay that the only remunerative employment she could find in 1865 was sewing. "In those days ...in a small pioneer town, the fields open to women were few and unfruitful. The needle at once presented itself, but at first I turned with loathing from it. I would have preferred the digging of ditches [She had, a few years earlier, dug her family's well] or the shoveling of coal; but the needle alone persistently pointed out my way and I was forced to take it."[16] Maybe she should have tried Wakeman's solution of disguising herself as a man. Though such cross-dressing women were widely publicized during the Civil War, Shaw, like most women, never considered trying it.

Shaw was not a skilled dressmaker. She was just a young woman in need of a decent, paying job, and sewing was the best job she could find. As one can infer from both her words and her tone, Anna Shaw did not make sewing her life's work. She actually became the first American female to be ordained a Methodist minister. [17] But many women, for whatever reasons, did create long, sustaining careers in the sewing trades before the time when women's ready-made clothing became widely available. Part of the problem that Miss Wakeman and Miss Shaw encountered was that they were only minimally skilled. Had they remained in the sewing trade, their incomes would have improved though they would never become wealthy. Professional women who opened dressmaking and millinery shops, whether they found the work intrinsically gratifying or not, were, in many ways, to be envied. According to Wendy Gamber's *The Female Economy*, "The custom production of feminine apparel offered advantages that few female occupations could match: skilled work, relatively high wages, and a reasonably respectable social status within the working classes." [18]

Catherine and Hannah Ryan's home at 411 N. Division Street in Ann Arbor.

Milo Ryan preserved in his autobiography a story that illustrates just how comfortable a dressmaker's existence could be. His grandfather, Patrick Ryan, fled the famine in Ireland and came to Ann Arbor in 1848. Patrick's wife died just as they arrived, leaving him with an infant daughter, Hannorah. During that difficult time, both Patrick and Hannorah (Hannah) were financially supported and physically cared for by his younger sister, Catherine Ryan. Catherine and two other sisters had come to America earlier. By the time Patrick arrived, his sister was "a thriving seamstress" though she, herself, was crippled in some way. Catherine taught Hannah (and perhaps several other Ryan girls) the trade. By 1872 Catherine and Hannah were working together. Their income allowed them to purchase a spacious home which is still standing. [19]

A girl was never too young to begin honing her skills. Helen Dodge McArthur, as a young girl, utilized sewing as a way to earn money. Her sewing skills were the result of training by her grandmother, Helen L. Dodge. After the younger Helen's mother died, her grandmother moved in. They spent many hours chatting and sewing together. In fact, as her grandmother treadled away in her sewing room one day, she told Helen how, when she and her own mother, Laura Jane Phelps, first heard about the invention of the sewing machine in the 1850's, they had just laughed and laughed at such a silly idea never imagining how useful it could be. A few years later, Helen put her grandmother's old sewing machine to work mending grain bags for a mill in Whitmore Lake which paid five cents per bag. Helen made $15 which was "a lot of money – and a lot of bags." [20] She used her money to buy white shoes for her graduation party. Her widowed father just shook his head at the impracticality of such a purchase and commented that a fool and his money were soon parted. But the usefulness of the sewing machine was no longer in question.

The prize for the youngest millinery "employee" in Washtenaw County goes, without a doubt, to Katherine Groomes, nee Steeb, whose family lived off Main Street on East Washington in Ann Arbor. At the end of the block just east of her house was a "tiny frame house" where Mrs. Christine Rentschler had her shop. Rentchler's business underwent several changes in name from notions to fancy goods to just millinery, but its location at #16 (later called 124) E. Washington remained the same for over twenty years. An article in the August 17, 1877 edition of the *Ann Arbor Courier* describes what appears to be the very house noting that it had been moved forward on the lot for the "sale of ladies fancy goods." Mrs. Rentschler had a large family: Frederick Jr., Andrew, Magdalene, Lena, Regina and Christian who all lived with their mother in the 1880's. Her son, Frederick Jr., became quite well known in Ann Arbor as a photographer. In any case, it was the widow Rentschler who in 1894 hired eight-year-old Katherine Groomes for ten cents a week. Katherine's job was to come in after the store closed to sort and arrange the day's jumble of hats which came in various sizes and shapes. Customers would try on the untrimmed hats until they found the one that fit best. The rejected hats would pile up in total disorder. The next day, thanks to Katherine, Mrs. Rentschler's shop would be neat and tidy, and she could commence decorating her customers' selections to suit their individual tastes. Katherine recalled that the money she earned was taken immediately to her mother; it was never spent on any frivolities. She did not, however, make millinery her life's work.

For a wide variety of females of all ages, the sewing trades offered excellent entrepreneurial opportunities throughout the nineteenth century. An 1864 study by the Bureau of Labor and Industry shows millinery to be the highest paid of twenty-six occupations commonly held by women. That study states that milliners earned slightly more than a dollar an hour in contrast to dressmakers/seamstresses/tailoresses who averaged seventy-eight cents. Those statistics may be slightly high for Washtenaw County Michigan since they derive from east coast cities, but they certainly demonstrate how lucrative the sewing trades could be. Little wonder then that women flocked to the sewing trades which by 1870 were exclusively a female domain. The United States Census of that year ranked those trades third and fourth in the number of American women employed. Washtenaw County had hundreds of female dressmakers and milliners, and not just in the larger towns of Ann Arbor and Ypsilanti. By 1874 every village of Washtenaw County also offered its ladies such skilled assistance with their wardrobes. Dexter boasted at least eight milliners and/or dressmakers; Saline had at least six; Manchester, four; and Chelsea, three.

It is impossible, however, to generalize about these women. Some worked out of their homes; others were employed in shops, and some operated their own establishments. They could be in their late teens or middle-aged. Some were single; others married. Some were widowed; others divorced. Some had short careers; others long and prosperous ones. A brief look at a few of the women with long careers will suffice to demonstrate the wide variety of backgrounds they had.

In Ypsilanti, two dressmakers who had long careers were unmarried women. One of these was Emily A. Remington. She was the daughter of Josephus and Ellen Remington. Her family experienced the tragedy of losing three of her four brothers within two weeks in 1872. Emily Remington survived to begin her career in the late 1870's working as a dress and cloak maker. Later she offered cleaning services for laces, feathers, and fine wools. Her shop on the southwest corner of Congress and Chicago, sustained significant financial losses when a cyclone struck Ypsilanti in 1893, but she continued working until her death on April 21, 1906. That would indicate a career of approximately three decades. The other long-time Ypsilanti dressmaker was Arvilla L. Williams. Miss Williams began in the mid 1880's and did not retire until 1913. Her success is indicated both by her longevity and by the fact that she needed to hire several assistants.

Looking east in 1859, Congress Street in Ypsilanti, Michigan.

Courtesy of the Ypsilanti Historical Society

In Ann Arbor, one of the most successful women was not only a married woman but an African-American named Hannah Jane Graves. Mrs. Graves, according to Chapman's *History of Washtenaw County*, was the first female child of African descent to be born in Washtenaw County. Her father, Ephraim Williamson, was among the first settlers in the county coming to Ann Arbor in 1824. Census data only confirms that she was born circa 1831. Hannah began her career out of her home soon after marrying William Graves in 1866. William was a former slave who escaped during the Civil War. He was fortunate in that he had been taught to read and write by a northern lady who was visiting her family in the south. He was not only literate, he was also a skilled blacksmith employed by Ann Arbor Agricultural Works. His steady, skilled employment presents the question of what motivated Hannah to work at a time when that was an unusual choice. Perhaps they had financial needs or maybe they simply were ambitious. They do not appear to have had any living children which possibly was a motivation for her working. Whatever the reason, Hannah found sufficient clientèle to remain in the dressmaking business for over twenty years and even hire assistants such as Carrie Lewis, who was also African-American. Mrs. Graves' business was located at #27 South Main Street until the mid 1890's while her home was on Wall Street. She appears to be the only African-American who was a consistent presence in the field of dressmaking.

Some milliners were equally successful. In addition to the long career of Mary Palmer in Milan, Matilda L. Forbes, the second wife of Jortin Forbes, established herself in Saline above W. H Davenport's store in the 1870's and 1880's. The 1870 Census lists her as "keeping home" for her husband and two daughters, aged seven and ten. Her husband was fifty-four years old, so she probably was a widow by the time she opened her millinery shop. Mrs. Forbes appears to have retired in the early 1890's when she was about seventy years old, but she lived until the early twentieth century.

Saline had another milliner, Mrs. Minerva J. Bacon. The fire of 1881 that swept through part of Saline destroyed her first shop. She lost almost $200 in stock. That amount does not seem significant today, but in 1881, it represented $4,350, an enormous sum in a time when a skilled male worker would make about two dollars per day. Fortunately Bacon had fire insurance which helped her re-establish herself quickly in the Union Block. Her place in Saline's business community eventually was taken by Mrs. Ella A. Glasier (also spelled Glazier) whose

millinery shop is the one captured in the above photograph of the southeast corner of Saline's "four corners." The brick block of buildings in which Bacon and Glazier had their shops was constructed in 1887 to replace the block of wooden buildings which had burned. Theirs was the darker building second left from corner.

Fire was a huge concern throughout nineteenth century America since most buildings were made of wood. In Ann Arbor, a fire in March of 1858 consumed the Exchange Block where two sisters named Peterson had their millinery shop. Since their losses totaled $600 and they had no insurance, it was a tragedy for those ladies.

In the village of Chelsea, the name Hooker was synonymous with millinery for almost five decades. The milliner's name was Hooker, however, it does not refer to a single woman but to a mother and then her daughter. Phoebe Ann Oxtoby Hooker, wife of Fisher M. Hooker was the mother. She and her husband originally came from Ypsilanti in 1857. Their family included three daughters with Kathryn being born sometime after their move to Chelsea. Phoebe began her millinery shop in the 1870's. Daughter Kathryn, called Kate, started her career as a trimmer in her mother's shop in 1894. The next year, when Phoebe passed away, Kate assumed management of the millinery shop which she continued until 1923.

Phoebe Oxtoby Hooker, left, and Kathryn Hooker, right.

Courtesy of the Bentley Historical Library, University of Michigan

In Ypsilanti one woman, Esther Curtis, achieved the same amazing longevity all by herself. Esther, born circa 1843, married Henry Matthew Curtis in the early 1870's. From then on, she always referred to herself professionally as Mrs. H. M. Curtis. She never used her own first name. The young couple spent the first years of their marriage and businesses boarding at the Hawkin's House. It was not unusual for young couples to do so thus avoiding the expense and effort needed to maintain their own home. Later in the 1880's when they had no children of their own, they adopted two daughters, Florence and Jess, and moved into an apartment above the Curtis Carriage Works which Henry owned and operated.

As with any career, Mrs. Curtis' experienced a tenuous beginning. She began before her marriage working with a Miss Reno who was an established milliner in Ypsilanti. In 1871 Curtis took over Reno's shop on Huron Street. She moved in April 1872 to a shop in the Worden Block previously owned by a Mrs. Kellogg. Business was brisk enough to require Mrs. Curtis to advertize for five extra milliners to help fill orders. Then the nationwide financial panic of 1873 hit. Curtis cut back, lowering her prices and doing her own trimming. As the economy settled down, her business improved. By 1880 it provided steady work. She expanded her millinery to include "fancy goods." In 1883 she regularly employed at least four other women to assist her in her shop as well as at least one domestic, Annie Adair, at her home.

Tornado damage to Mr. Curtis' shop.

Courtesy of the Ypsilanti Historical Society

Mrs. Curtis probably was feeling financially secure for the next decade. Then a tornado struck Ypsilanti in 1893 destroying both her home and her husband's carriage works. The Curtis family sustained a $7500 loss. It was such a massive loss that by April 22 Mr. Curtis was forced to sell all undamaged carriages to raise money with the hope of rebuilding. Mrs. Curtis' nearby millinery shop was also damaged. A brick wall in the rear collapsed, and the glass window in the front shattered. Her inventory also suffered damage. The *Ypsilanti Commercial* on April 13, 1893 stated, "...not a dollar of insurance [was] available for anyone." Despite these significant setbacks, she soon was back in business declaring that she had the "Finest Patterns to be found in the East." [21] She continued her career for a total of forty years. Mrs. Curtis retired circa 1904. She died in Ypsilanti in 1931 at the age of eighty-eight having survived her husband by almost twenty years.

Most of these women who owned shops, despite their longevity, left little personal information for us to know about them. One of the few who has entered local lore is Mrs. Henrietta Wagner. She is well known not because she had a long and influential career but because she had the misfortune to be murdered in October 1871. Mrs. Wagner, a recent immigrant from

Germany, partnered with Mary F. Miley to open a millinery and fancy goods shop located at #4 Washington Street in Ann Arbor. Mrs. Wagner and her son Oscar, age three, lived behind the shop. She was a widow who soon married her first husband's brother, Henry Wagner. Their relationship, according to Mary Miley was stormy at best. Just months after marrying, Henry killed both his wife and the child by bashing their skulls with the dull side of a hatchet. Local newspapers reported that Mrs. Wagner was found in their apartment behind the millinery shop. Blood and gore covered the floor and her nightdress. The murder weapon lay soiled nearby. It was only then that the officer heard a slight noise and found the boy, Oscar, barely alive in the bed. He died soon after. According to Mary Miley, Mr. Wagner was insanely jealous of his wife. His wife was heard telling him to get out. "I cannot live with a crazy man." [21] Others testified that he wanted the money his brother had left her. Whatever his motivation, it was so heinous a crime that it provoked threats of lynching. Instead he was convicted of murder and sent to the state prison in Jackson for life. Mary Miley continued the business after her partner's death, proving herself to be a resilient and successful businesswoman. She provided art, embroidery, and stamping as well as selling fancy goods in her millinery shop which employed several clerks and assistants until the mid 1890's.

Despite the long careers some women enjoyed, others in the sewing trades went out of business fairly quickly. Statistics indicate that one out of every three shops closed within a year. Of the shops which remained, only twenty-five percent lasted a decade or longer. The average time in business was six years. The question, of course, is why did so many shops not last. Were they "business failures?" Was there not enough clientele? Did the owner have poor management skills? It is also possible that the women closed their shops because they married. They also might have become ill or even died.

The Shadford girls of Ann Arbor illustrate those statistics and suggest some possible answers. Jennie Shadford, her sisters Lizzie, Louisa and Lucy, and her two brothers all lived with their widowed mother, Mary A. Shadford, at 53 Broadway in Ann Arbor. The Shadford parents had immigrated from England, but all of the children were born in Michigan. When Jennie was twenty-one, she and her business partner, Mollie Corson, opened a millinery, dressmaking and fancy goods shop. They called their new endeavor simply "Shadford and Corson."

Jennie Shadford and Mollie Corson had much in common. They were both born in 1864. Both were the oldest of six children in the family. Both young women had lost their fathers. Both lived with their widowed mothers and siblings. And both had a sibling less than eight years old at the time they began their shop. Jennie's family lived on Broadway across the Huron River in Lower Town while Mollie's family lived on east Washington Street. That might sound like quite a distance, but in reality it is at most a mile. We are probably safe assuming both girls' families were struggling financially since there were many children with no father to support them. So Jennie and Mollie open their shop at 10 E. Washington Street circa 1885. Jennie's younger sister, Lucy, worked for them as a trimmer, and so did Mollie's younger sister, Mabel. Lucy was seventeen; Mabel, nineteen.

Two years later their shop was gone. At that time Jennie became the book-keeper for Ann Arbor's newspaper, the *Argus*. She remained in the job until she married William H. Morton in December, 1892. In Jennie's case, the shop probably closed because they were not making sufficient money. Book-keeping paid more. Her sister Elizabeth, who was called Lizzie, apparently

thought she could do better. After a year or two of working as a trimmer, she opened her own shop. The photograph above taken circa 1901 shows twenty-three year old Lizzy Shadford standing proudly in front of her lovely shop. Lizzie remained a milliner for the rest of her life, but her shop, like her sister's, only lasted two to three years. She is not listed anywhere in the City Directory for 1904. That was the year her mother died, so she may have closed the shop to stay at home caring for her. After that Lizzie moved to her brother's house and lived with his family. Though she stated she was a milliner between 1905 and 1909, there is no indication of where. She may have worked for some other milliner, or she may have made hats for previous clients at home. Even that career was cut short when Lizzie Shadford died in 1910. She was thirty-three.

Information about seamstresses and milliners is even scarcer when it comes to employees rather than owners of shops; however, Miss Julia Stevens who worked for Mary E. Martin (Mrs. H. D.) of Ypsilanti is an exception. Miss Stevens lived to be over one hundred years old. On her hundredth birthday, she was featured in an article for the local paper. She was boarding at Miss Ethelyn MacKenzie's. She assured the reporter that her eyesight and hearing were fine for a woman her age. Miss Stevens also told the reporter that she had been born in Vermont on September 9, 1843, the daughter of Asaph and Hannah Stevens. In 1857 the family came to Ypsilanti where she had lived ever since. She probably trained with Olive Coe with whom she also boarded; however, when Mary E. Martin (Mrs. H. D. Martin) opened her shop in Ypsilanti just a few years before Miss Coe vanishes from the local record, she began working there.

Miss Julia Stevens
Courtesy of the Ypsilanti Historical Society

Stevens was a real asset to Mrs. Martin's shop. She not only created exquisite embroideries, but "her wit and culture and cheerfulness won for her hosts of friends." Miss Stevens worked for Mrs. Martin for almost thirty years. When Mrs. Martin closed her shop on Congress Street circa 1900, Miss Stevens continued to crochet and embroider for others in her home where she could care for her aging mother. As Miss Stevens neared the end of her own life, her loyal clientele kept her room bedecked with flowers and gave her $100 to celebrate her birthday.

Milliners and especially dressmakers were forced to experiment with innovative ways to maintain their businesses in an increasingly difficult market. Two dressmakers in Ann Arbor in the 1870's tried to enhance their advertising by assuring potential customers that their gowns were cut in the latest mode using full-scale paper patterns. Before that time a dressmaker had to be very skilled to look at a fashion plate in a magazine or a tiny pattern and convert that to full size. Misses Soules and Jenkins used "celebrated Taylor imported patterns"[22] while Mrs. Electra F. Todd in the Huron Block extolled her training with Madame Demorest in New York.

Madame Nell Demorest was famous. *Godey's Lady's Book* featured her patterns as early as 1860. Unfortunately Mdm. Demorest never patented her paper patterns, so the idea was taken in 1867 by Butterick who ultimately made it a household word. [23] At first, full-scale paper patterns were not intended to be used at home; they were meant for professional dressmakers. In *Waste Not, Want Not*, Susan Strasser states that patterns were used primarily to update the style of a gown not to help make a dress from scratch. Labor at that time was relatively inexpensive; fabric was not. Popular ladies' magazines, of which there were over a hundred different publications, encouraged women to reuse worn fabric by turning it or even switching left and right sleeves so that the worn part would not show. Such recycling of material was not limited to the less affluent; wealthy women also reconfigured their designer dresses. Thus an important element of a dressmaker's job was altering, re-trimming, or completely remaking existing apparel. Indeed the era's fondness for trimmings was not just a reflection of its aesthetic sensitivities. Braid, ribbon, lace etc. camouflaged old seams or damaged areas in the fabric. Catherine Broughton in her 1896 book, *Suggestions for Dressmakers*, claimed that while one could earn more money making new frocks, anyone who had skill in remaking dresses was a "rarity" and would do well in business since "making over is an ever present burden of the feminine mind." [24] It is quite possible, therefore, that this was the important selling point Mrs. Todd was trying to convey with her Demorest pattern claims.

> Mrs. Charles Root was working out of her home at the time Mrs. Todd was beginning her Ann Arbor career, simply called herself in 1874 a "Clothes Renovator."

Such pattern claims did not make Soules and Jenkins successful; however, Mrs. Todd's career, according to Chapman's *History of Washtenaw County*, spanned twenty-five years. Since that history was published in 1881, it would suggest that her career began elsewhere. She did not appear in Ann Arbor until circa 1873. Mrs. Todd lived alone on Miller Street and gained some notoriety as the president of the local chapter of the Women's Christian Temperance Union, which was active in reducing the number of saloons in Ann Arbor from eighty to thirty-five.

The 1890's brought challenges and changes especially for dressmakers. The rise of department stores and mail order catalogs selling ready-made clothing posed a significant threat to their profession. Ready-made clothing had been available for men for decades but only started being sold for women at the end of the century. By 1913, however, it had become a billion dollar industry surpassing the profits of men's clothing which had leveled off at twenty million. In the 1910 United States Census, the occupations of dressmaker and seamstress, for the first time, were lumped together into a single category. Even with the combining of two categories into one, the trade slipped from third to fifth place in the Census' ranking of most common occupations. A partial explanation for this radical change may be found in a special note included in the Census identifying the category as women sewing independently, thus excluding the vast numbers of women sewing in factories. This only reinforces the fact that the growing trend was factory-made rather than custom-made clothing.

As ready-made clothing and sewing machines in homes became more available, some dressmakers appear to have tried to adapt with the times. Following the advice of the 1876 *Ladies Treasury* which stated unequivocally, "It is almost impossible to learn dressmaking without taking lessons," [25] a few dressmakers began offering lessons in the difficult art of cutting and fitting. The village of Dexter was home to three different programs of sewing instruction to enhance women's ability to cope with the more difficult aspects of dressmaking. As early as 1886, R. J. Langdon began classes in "the art of dress cutting" for $5 which included all supplies. Six years later Miss Bertha Spooner, newly arrived from Detroit, offered instruction in the New York A.B.C. of cutting and fitting dresses. For a fee of $10, she provided two days of instruction.[26]

Dressmakers Wanted
TO INVESTIGATE THE

**KELLOGG
Magic Tailor System
OF DRESS CUTTING**

Ypsilanti Commercial
12/16/1887

Courtesy of the Ypsilanti Historical Society

The most famous system for cutting and fitting clothing was invented in France in 1868 and was promoted by Martha Kellogg of Battle Creek, Michigan. Born Martha Kennie of Detroit, she was the first wife of Frank Jonas Kellogg of Battle Creek. After their marriage circa 1874, they toured Europe and vowed to bring fashion to the United States through the French method that changed the way women's clothes were measured. Calling herself Madame Kellogg, Martha patented in 1880 and 1883 her version of the method which she called the French Tailor System. Men's clothes for years had been tailored according to precise measurements and a mathematical system which used a tailor's square (an "L" square) and precise scales. Women's clothing derived from patterns or plates was imprecise thus requiring far more skill to avoid irregular results. The desired tight fit was not just a matter of unwanted looseness but of the garment conforming to the individual body's proportions. Mrs. Kellogg claimed that to obtain accurate cutting for ladies' dresses, one should use a tailor's square as was done for gentlemen's clothing. Mrs. Rayne's *What Can a Woman Do?,* published in 1885, maintained that the system was the" best now in use" because it allowed a dressmaker to accomplish "four times the amount of work " since the system eliminated endless time refitting garments.   Mrs. Rayne also told her readers that the system could be learned by any "good plain sewer." [27]

There were instruction books available for approximately seven dollars; however, some women obviously preferred to be instructed in person. That created another employment niche for several women in Washtenaw County who latched onto this new system not only to make clothing themselves but to teach the skill to others. Louesa or Louisa P. Rowley or Row Lay (pictured above) taught the Kellogg system in Ypsilanti at #32 Washington St. She charged $2-3 per day; however, students paid nothing until they could cut and baste dresses "without refitting." Almost a decade later, Mrs. Charles Nub and and Miss Bertha Ferris opened dressmaking rooms in Mrs. Nub's home in Dexter. They, too, taught the Madame Kellogg system.

Latest Styles in Everything
IN
Millinery
and
Dressmaking
AT
MARY E. BELL'S
127 MAIN ST. N.,
ANN ARBOR,   ·   ·   MICH.
[29]

To attract women who still preferred and were willing to pay for a custom dressmaker, Ratie E. Cory and Mary E. Bell in Ann Arbor tried a different tack by referring to themselves in 1898 as "modistes." A modiste was the highest level in the dressmaking hierarchy. It suggested someone who is extremely skilled in cutting and fitting ladies' clothing. Obviously Cory and Bell were endeavoring to enhance their reputations by utilizing that elite term. It does not appear to have been a successful ploy since that was the only year they described themselves as such. Perhaps they simply were not skilled enough for such a claim. Modistes were usually in their thirties or forties because it required years of training. Cory was thirty-five when they began; Bell was only twenty-eight.

Also Miss Cory, whose real name was Rachel, left the partnership in less than two years. She and her parents returned to Nankin Township. [28] It is highly possible that she did so to take care of her parents who were becoming quite elderly. Her father died in 1902 followed by her mother nine years later. Ratie Cory passed away in 1912. But Miss Bell remained in the sewing trades for nine more years at her shop at 127 Main. She returned to calling herself simply a dressmaker and hired Miss Jennie Cory, Ratie's niece. Eventually she switched to doing exclusively millinery work.

Also during the last two decades of the century a "new" term began to appear: "tailoress." This label actually was not new; it had been commonly used before the word "dressmaker" became popular. Previously it simply meant a woman who sewed for men, women and children. Louisa McMath Hathaway, born in the first decade of the nineteenth century, remembered when fabrics were produced at home. The family's womenfolk performed the laborious soaking, carding, spinning and weaving, but "when all was ready the important tailoress came in." [30] The term, tailoress, was also used in the 1860 Census to describe many rural ladies who worked out of their homes. By 1868 in the more urban areas only three women, Helen Farmer and Sara Hope in Ann Arbor and Mrs. Silena Miller in Ypsilanti still identified themselves as tailoresses. These women did not advertise in the Business Mirror and were working out of their homes rather than shops. It would appear that by 1860 the term tailoress connoted an adequate but not highly trained garment maker while "dressmaker," which suggested more skill, was far more popular with women who had shops.

By the end of the century, however the word "tailoress" reappeared. There are several possible explanations. Dictionaries define tailoress simply as "a female tailor." It was indeed the preferred term used by women working in men's clothing stores doing alterations or custom work. Sarah Cosgrove of Ypsilanti worked in this capacity for Alban and Crane, a gentleman's clothier located at 16 Congress Street, beginning circa 1883 and continuing into the twentieth century. J. J. Raftrey, a tailor in Chelsea, also hired women as tailoresses but not until the 1890's. Raftrey's staff included Myrta Fenn and Mrs. Jane Geddes who remained there throughout the decade. Thus they were, as the dictionary says, female tailors.

By 1906, the "ess" had been dropped by Mary A. Fingerle of Ann Arbor. Others followed suit. They referred to themselves as tailors, using the same term as men in their field. Then in 1914 yet another variation appeared: "Ladies Tailor." That is what Elizabeth Maegle of Ypsilanti called herself. Her use of the word tailor may refer to how the clothes were measured and cut indicating that the seamstress was using a system like that of Mdm. Kellogg.

The sewing trades were a mainstay for women who, for whatever reason, worked. In addition to married, widowed or single women, some like Madame Kellogg were divorced. In such a case, a woman needed skills with which to earn a living. The fragments of Blanche Cole Palmer's story demonstrate just how important such skills and opportunities could be for a woman. Blanche was born in 1879 in Eaton Rapids, Michigan, and came with her family to Chelsea when she was nine. One fragment of her story tells of how she was partially deaf due to childhood illness. Despite that handicap, she attended Chelsea High School while also studying violin and oil painting. Another fragment shows her marrying Henry Wood, the son of a Chelsea merchant, with whom she had a daughter named Maurene. A year after her daughter's birth, however, she divorced Henry. At that time she turned to millinery, opening a shop first in Chelsea and then in Bronson, Michigan, where she later married George Davis. Unfortunately he died of tuberculosis, which she also contracted while nursing him. She, luckily, recovered and returned to Chelsea where she opened first a needlework shop and then a millinery shop. Her third marriage to Ray Sanborn in 1916 was also brief. It lasted only two years before he, too, passed away. The final fragment of her story records that in 1922 she sold her shop to the Miller sisters and married Dr. Faye Palmer, a dentist. It was then that her creative endeavors turned from sewing to literature. She wrote poems which were published by Edwards Brothers, Ann Arbor, though no extant copy resides in any library or archive in the area. She wrote greeting card verses and a novel, which she finally finished at the age of eighty-three, five years before her death in 1966. Millinery may have come to her rescue when she found herself without male support, but clearly she had other talents seeking expression.

Madame Kellogg's and Blanche's divorces might be surprising. Most Americans' impression is that divorce is a modern phenomenon. Actually divorce was not an uncommon feature of nineteenth century life in America. By the turn of the century, when both of these women divorced, the United States led the western world in the number of divorces which is why it provoked such a strong backlash in the early twentieth century. This, in turn, resulted in much tighter laws and stronger social stigma until recent times.

Almost ten thousand marriages (9701 to be exact), were performed in Washtenaw County between 1834 and 1880. That created an average of approximately 180 marriages per year. During the same time period, 513 divorces were granted in the county. This is the number of *approved* divorces. The number of *requested* divorces would have been higher. "In the U.S.," wrote Captain Marryat in his 1839 *Diary of America*, "divorces are obtained without expense and without it being necessary to commit a crime...a divorce is granted upon any grounds which may be considered a just and reasonable cause." [30] Harriet Martineau in her analysis of society in America reported her opinion that, although she found marriages in America "more tranquil and more fortunate than in England," marriages were still "subject to the troubles which arise from the inequality of the parties in mind and occupation." She believed marriage in America was "safer" due to the fact that American women possessed the freedom to divorce. [31] That freedom was denied to women in England. In England before 1858 nothing short of an act of Parliament could grant a divorce. Even after that date, in England the only cause for divorce was adultery.

Quick divorce rulings were seen in nineteenth century America as a legal necessity since married women had no legal rights. In most states, a married woman could not own property, be legal guardian to her children, initiate legal proceedings, or manage her own money. In Michigan, she was somewhat better off as she could own her own property and engage in business without a husband's approval. In at least one case, that of Lucy and Allen Stephens, the husband was so provoked by his wife's teaching school against his will that he requested a legal separation. Whether a man deserted the woman or she left him, which she often did, it was imperative that she regain her legal rights by being pronounced legally single again. That fact, as well as the prevalent social attitude requiring the protection of women who were "weak and defenseless," resulted in divorce laws being broadly interpreted allowing for a fairly quick and easy ruling.

A woman could obtain a divorce for something as simple as the fact that her husband could support her, but he did not. This certainly would be the case if he deserted her. But a greater number of divorces were the result of physical abuse and/or alcoholism. Sadly, even when women filed for divorce under nineteenth century law, they were not necessarily "safe" as Miss Martineau suggested. On February 28, 1860 Mrs. Lucy Washburn of Ypsilanti filed for divorce on the grounds of her husband's drunkenness and adultery. Three months later in May, her estranged spouse, George, murdered her when she refused to retract her suit. He apparently suffocated her with a pillow and then threw her body down the cellar stairs in the hope of making it look like an accident. Mrs. Washburn's body was discovered by her children when they returned from school. At his trial, the Washburn sons, ages eight and six, were two of the thirty witnesses called to testify. It must have been difficult for them, yet the situation apparently had been even worse, for both Washburn boys testified against their father who was sent to the Michigan State Prison in Jackson.

Mrs. Washburn, unfortunately, was not the only unhappy wife in Washtenaw County. Extant issues of the *Western Emigrant* newspaper from the 1830's include many notices of "elopement." In today's usage that term, of course, means running toward a marriage. In the nineteenth century, however, it meant running away. Husbands, such as Rueben Barnes, had to swallow their pride and notify the community of their wives' "desertion" so that they would not be legally bound to pay any debts their wives might incur in the women's efforts to survive on their own. The notices used specific legal language stating, "This is to forbid all persons harboring or trusting her on my account..." Leonard Morse of Lodi tried to skirt the embarrassing issue in February of 1835 by not referring specifically to his wife. He simply warned against trusting "any person." James Maroney of Northfield tried a different ploy to project a better public image. He used that same language in a notice which announced that his wife and two-year-old daughter had been "stolen." He offered a ten dollar reward for the return of his daughter. There is no mention of a reward for his wife, who had obviously eloped. In most cases, the term "elope" referred to a woman who left her husband in order to be with another man as would appear to be Mrs. Maroney's case. There is no record, however, of whether or not that relationship lasted. Nor is there any information regarding the fate of Margaret Dougherty of Dexter who left her husband in April, 1869. Mr. Dougherty did not use the term "elopement," but the language of his notice remained the same as that in the earlier examples.

In addition to these cases of elopement, *The Ann Arbor Courier* of May 4, 1877 provides an article concerning Fannie Johnson who decided to "live apart" from her husband, Harrington. She apparently had been the one who purchased "the outfit with which her husband carried on business." After the Johnsons' separation, Fannie leased "them" to a man named Blackburn who opened his own business. Since she had purchased the horses and the wagon, she obviously was using that investment to earn some income through renting them out to Blackburn.

> The divorce rate in America doubled from two to four per thousand between 1870 and 1900. Between 1900 and 1920 it doubled again reaching 7.7 per thousand.[33]

In such cases where women, for whatever reasons, left their marriages without finding security in a new relationship or legally divorcing their husbands, some method for generating income had be found in order for them to survive and provide for any family they might have. For some, the sewing trades offered the required occupational haven. There they joined young and old women, married and unmarried women, Caucasian and African-American women who had found it an attractive option when they needed or wanted a purse of their own. Sewing was a clean, respectable job that provided a decent income especially for women with a certain skill level. Millinery was especially popular perhaps because the training was less demanding than dressmaking which required years of experience to become a modiste. Millinery also remained a viable option as custom dressmaking declined in popularity.

---

[1] Daniel Smith, "Family Limitation, Sexual Control and Domestic Feminism in Victorian America," in *Clio's Consciousness Raised: New Perspectives on the History of Women*, ed. Mary Hartmann and Lois Banner (New York: Harper Row, 1974), 120.

[2] *Oxford English Dictionary*, 2nd edition.

[3] "The Willow Run Settlement," *Michigan Pioneer and Historical Collection*, Vol 14 (Lansing, MI: W.S. George and Co., State Printers and Binders, 1884), 482-3.

[4] It was customary for people to advertisements for several weeks, usually three.

[5] Gertrude Hiscock Nanry, *Lest it be Forgotten* (1987), III 5.

[6] Sarah Norton, *Sarah Jane Knapp Norton Diary* in "Norton Collection," Ypsilanti Archives, Ypsilanti, Michigan, March 30, 1864.

[7] Susan A. D'Ambrosio, "Genealogy" in "McMath Collection," Ypsilanti Archives, Ypsilanti, Michigan, 4.

[8] Marc McCutcheon, *Writer's Guide to Everyday Life in the 1800's* (Cincinnati: Writer's Digest Books, 1993), 105.

[9] *Dexter Leader*, May 6, 1871.

[10] Norah Waugh and Margaret Woodward. *The Cut of Women's Clothes, 1600-1930* (NewYork: Theatre Arts Books, 1968), 185.

[11] Virginia Penny, *The Employment of Women* (Boston: Walker and Co., 1863). 324.

[12] *Dexter Leader*, July 4, 1879.

[13] There was no unified country called Germany until later in the 19th Century. I have added it only for clarity.

[14] Virginia Drachman, *Enterprising Women* (Cambridge, MA: President and Fellows of Harvard College, 2002), 47.

[15] Harriet Martineau, *Society in America,* Vol. 3 (London: Saunders and Otley, 1837), 150.

[16] Anna Howard Shaw, *Story of a Pioneer* (New York: Harper and Brothers. 1915), 55.

[17] The first woman ordained as a Protestant minister was Antoinette Brown Blackwell. She was the sister-in-law of Lucy Stone and Dr. Elizabeth Blackwell. She was ordained in 1853; Shaw in 1880.

[18] Wendy Gamber, *The Female Economy* (Champaign, IL, University of Illinois Press, 1997), 39.

[19] Milo Ryan, *View of the Universe* (Ann Arbor: McNaughton and Gunn, 1985), 20.

[20] Thomas Hennings, *Looking Back* (Whitmore Lake, MI: Northfield Township Historical Society, 1985), 201.

[21] *Ypsilanti City Directory* (1901), 123.

[22] *History of Washtenaw County, Michigan* (Chicago: Charles C. Chapman Co., 1881), 233.

[23] It won't surprise any reader that the idea for paper patterns was Mrs. Butterick's inspiration and design.

[24] Catherine Broughton, *Suggestions for Dressmakers* (New York,: Morse-Broughton Co., 1896), 14.

[25] Waugh, 185.

[26] *Dexter Leader*, August, 1892.

[27] Martha Louise Rayne, *What Can a Woman Do* (Detroit: R.B. Dickerson and Co., 1885), 214.

[28] Nankin Township included a huge area between the city of Detroit and Washtenaw County.

[29] *Ann Arbor City Directory* (1899), 261.

[30] D'Ambrosio, 3.

[31] Frederick Marryat, *Diary in America* (London: Longman, Orme, Brown, Green, and Longmans, 1839), 428.

[32] Martineau, 119.

[33] Another source indicated one in twelve marriages by 1900 ended in divorce. That would be 8.3%.

CHAPTER TWO: WORKING CLASS WOMEN

Married or single, widowed or divorced, the nineteenth century witnessed more females working outside the home than ever before. Some chose to work in order to be independent or to add to the quality of their lives. Some were only working until they could marry. Others did not have a choice. They worked because they needed an income to support themselves and often other family members. These women tended to be less educated since they usually came from a working class background, but a destitute widow or divorced woman might find herself in this group as well.

With the sewing trades ranking third and fourth in 1870, what was the most common occupation performed by women? The answer, not surprisingly, is domestic labor. In that year six out of every ten working women in the United States worked in someone else's home or business. Domestic labor remained the largest group of working women until 1940 though it fell to less than one sixth of the national labor force by 1920.

The issue of domestic labor was a major theme in nineteenth century ladies' magazines such as *Godey's Lady's Book*, but the message was mixed. On the one hand, articles idealized and promoted homemaking as, not only the appropriate sphere for woman, but as the preferred area of concern for "true" ladies. A real woman should be a domestic goddess perfectly capable of taking care of her own home. Servants, to some Americans, signaled a lack of skill and self-reliance. One University of Michigan faculty wife, Elizabeth DuBois, gossiped in an 1864 letter to Mrs. Andrew White, another faculty wife. She wrote that she had heard that Mrs. Haven, the current University President's wife, criticized the former President's wife for hiring two young women to work in her home saying, "Mrs. Tappan must have been a very lazy woman to keep *two* girls!" [1] One can only infer that a single girl as help was acceptable, since it suggested Mrs. Tappan was doing some of the chores. But to have two? Oh my, that was the height of indolence.

The statistics, however, indicate that the majority of public opinion did not agree with Mrs. DuBois' supposed statement. Not only was there sufficient work in every home at that time for a wife and at least one helper, there was a growing recognition that a "middle class lifestyle required servants whether for the comforts servants provided or as an indication of the family's status in the community." [2] Most households, therefore, were anxious to acquire and keep domestic help. An advertisement, dated August 18, 1846, sought, "A girl to do household work in a small family, to whom liberal wages will be paid." Mr. Jas. E. Platt who placed the advertisement, appears very anxious to locate such an employee. [3] Similar want ads continued throughout the century. All were phrased to make the work appear enticing. Mrs. A. Griffiths in the October 2, 1869 issue of the *Ypsilanti Commercial* was willing to pay "high wages" for "light work." Nor was it just urban dwellers who advertised. Another ad in the *Commercial* the summer of 1887 wanted "a strong and willing girl to go into the country." The advertisement ran for three months which suggests few applicants were interested in the position. Whether the job was eventually filled or the prospective employer simple gave up and stopped advertising is unclear, but such advertisements illustrate the widespread desire to obtain domestic help.

> A woman in Saline wrote a letter to her mother on December 14, 1845 announcing the birth of her daughter two weeks earlier. "We have now been keeping house about 8 weeks have been obliged to keep a girl all the time am in hopes soon to be able to do my work with the help of a little girl who is going to board with us and go to school." [4]

All of the previously mentioned advertisements specifically asked for "a girl." This was not just a condescending label; it was the reality. The 1860 Michigan Census clearly indicates that most servants indeed did come from the sixteen to twenty year age group. In Northfield, a rural area north of Ann Arbor, seventeen of the twenty-two domestics were between those ages. In Saline, just south of Ann Arbor and one of the larger villages, two-thirds of the eighty-six servants were in the sixteen to twenty year age group while in Ann Arbor, for the First Ward alone, the census enumerators tallied sixty-eight domestics with slightly over half in that age group. Domestic service was, therefore, a job filled by predominantly young, unmarried women.

Annie Paton

Courtesy of Eastern Michigan University

Annie Paton, whose family immigrated from Scotland circa 1849, was just such a teen-ager when she began working out. When she was younger, her family had a hired girl for a year or two. That girl was paid only fifty cents a week, yet Annie had marveled at the wonderful things she bought with that money. So it seemed natural for her, when she became a teenager, to begin working out as a servant for a storekeeper in Romeo, Michigan. She earned $1.75 per week plus board circa 1864 as the second girl in the home of the shopkeeper. Either the girls or the housewife divided the domestic duties. The girl with whom Annie worked did the baking, laundry and sewing. Annie's tasks included washing the dishes, making the beds, preparing meals and scrubbing floors. It sounds like a lot of work, and it was, but Annie had been toiling since the age of six when her parents removed her from school to help at home. "Life," she recalled, "was a great heap of dishes and babies to be washed." [5] In her memoir, she confessed how working in town resulted in a much higher standard of cleanliness than what her family maintained on the farm. She did not use her wages for ribbons and dresses as she had once planned; she usually bought things needed to improve her family's hygiene and standard of living.

There were, of course, a few older women who worked as domestic servants. The most extreme case I found of an older female domestic is that of Martha Bliss. Bliss identified herself to the 1860 census enumerator as a "servant, age eighty-one." I suspect that Bliss was more of a charity case than a servant; however, pride may have motivated her to think of herself as employed in exchange for her board. When seeking to hire an older woman, potential employers usually referred to the position as that of "housekeeper." Naturally there were no age specifications mentioned, but there was an implied level of maturity and experience. Olive Parson, who died in Saline in May of 1873 at the age of twenty-eight, was identified as a housekeeper. She was native to the area having been born in Lodi Township, which is adjacent to Saline. Also she probably was a widow since her maiden name was Eddy. Employers would have regarded a married woman or widow as more mature and experienced even if she were in her mid-twenties. Another factor in distinguishing between a "hired girl" and a "housekeeper" would have been the required duties and whether or not this employee would be working without further supervision. Advertisements for a housekeeper might or might not identify for whom they would be working; however, one often can make educated guesses. For example, in January of 1889 the *Ypsilanti Commercial* published an advertisement that said, "Wanted, immediately, a good housekeeper to have entire charge." That could have been a wealthy woman who shunned domestic work but, to me, it sounds more like a man. He needed help; he needed it ASAP, and once hired, he wanted to be left free to pursue his other concerns. Another advertisement in March of 1871 asked for a housekeeper and nurse for Mrs. Blanchard of Rawsonville. For such specific employment, one would not want a semi-skilled or unskilled girl.

Another widespread perception is that most domestic servants were immigrants. It is true that many immigrants filled such positions as they adapted to their new surroundings. In fact, many employers favored them. Because of the dearth of local domestic help, people scrambled to be the first to locate newcomers. As early as the 1830's, Harriet Martineau in her book, *Society in America*, described "A country lady [who] traveled thirty miles to a town where she might intercept some Irish coming down from Canada into the States and supply herself with domestics from among them." [6] Such a claim might sound odd; however, before the 1850's many Irish immigrants did come through Canada because the fares were less expensive to Canada than the United States. When the White Star Line established competitive ticket prices to New York and Boston, potential employers or their representatives met the new arrivals at the dock of those cities.

The Ten Brook home as portrayed in the 1874 *Atlas of Washtenaw County.*

University of Michigan's Professor Ten Brook and his first wife, Sarah, solved their servant problem in an unusual way. They had routinely employed two "hired girls" in their Ann Arbor home; however, when they returned to the United States in 1862 after a six year stay in Munich, Germany, they brought with them a servant named Margaret Schnapp. She may have been working for them in Germany. Mrs. Ten Brook obviously valued Schnapp because, when she died only five years later, she bequeathed $50 to Margaret. It was not uncommon to leave one's servant some money; however, $50 was generous when one considers Schnapp's annual income might be only $150. By importing their own servant, the Ten Brooks assured themselves of high quality domestic help.

Some employers had more mercenary motives for hiring immigrants. They viewed the immigrant worker as being more docile than a native-born American. Because European society had an established servant class and an immigrant worker would be uncertain of American customs, it was assumed that she would be less likely to complain about her situation. Whatever the reasons, domestic service was definitely a job often filled by recently arrived immigrants. By mid-century, 74% of New York City's domestics were Irish girls. By 1900 40% of the 322,000 foreign born servants were Irish. But New York and Boston were wealthy urban areas which after 1850 served as entry points for immigrants. That helps explain the predominance of immigrant domestic labor in those cities and the surrounding areas.

In Michigan, Washtenaw County, too, was home to many immigrants, predominantly German or Irish. Many of them worked as domestic help. In Ann Arbor's fashionable Fourth Ward seventy percent of the domestics were immigrants. The 1860 Census lists twenty women as domestics. Of those seven were German, five were Irish, one was English and one Scottish. In the Second Ward, twenty-seven women worked as domestics; half of them were German. Those statistics certainly make it seem like immigrants dominated this area. Once one leaves those two neighborhoods, however, the statistics begin to offer a different scenario. Ann Arbor's First Ward counted sixty-four domestic servants: twenty of German origin, thirteen Irish, five English and three Canadian for a total of forty-one. The remaining twenty-three were born in the United States with over half of that number from Michigan. Thus thirty-six percent of First Ward servants were native born. And the numbers continue to climb as one leaves Ann Arbor.

Though the 1860 Michigan Census indicates that twenty percent of the population was foreign born, it also demonstrates that in Washtenaw County the majority of domestics were not foreigners but girls born in the United States and most often in the state of Michigan. For example, thirty percent of Saline's servant population at that time was native to Michigan. Others were American-born but in other states, and despite that community's strong German influence, only four domestics were from Germany. Nearby Bridgewater had only seven German servants out of a total of thirty-three. Sarah Barret would be a more typical Bridgewater domestic. She was the eldest of six children born to a local farmer. Young women, like Sarah, comprised eighty percent of the domestics in her area. She helps us recalibrate our perceptions. Yes, foreign women did work in Washtenaw County homes, but that conclusion must be balanced with the fact that a great many American women did as well.

A third popular perception is that poverty drove these young women into service. Again that was the case for some, but not all. Indeed, the 1860 Census also provides some rather amazing figures which disprove that stereotype. In Saline, Sayell Tower, a forty-year-old farmer, claimed to have $5,000 in real estate and $1,500 in personal property which was a considerable amount in 1860; however, his two eldest daughters Julia (age twenty) and Sarah (age seventeen) both worked as domestics. The Lindsey sisters, Margaret and Theresa, also from Saline, experienced much the same situation as did the oldest daughters of Zalmon Church, who listed himself as a "gentleman" with $8,000 worth of property. The Tower sisters and the Church sisters certainly do not seem to have needed the income.

Sending these daughters to "live out" was a significant change from just twenty years earlier. Caroline Kirkland states in her autobiographical novel, *My New Home – Who'll Follow*, that upon arriving in the Pinkney area in 1836, "My first care was to inquire when I might be able to procure a domestic." Having only recently arrived in Michigan from the east coast, she was shocked by the response she received. Few girls were willing to "live out." Michigan families at that time needed every member to do the arduous work demanded by their own land. Oh, they might "chore round" as a favor to an ill neighbor who was unable to care for her family. Or a girl or woman might work to raise the cash for a doctor's bill or fabric for a new dress, but such efforts were always considered temporary. Mrs. Kirkland, a refined, educated woman who could speak four languages, had six children and was ill prepared for the rigors of pioneer life. Fortunately, she was able to find a temporary employee to help her get settled, but it required a slight change in attitude. "I take it [the help] as a favor and this point, once conceded, all goes well."[7] In other words, she would have to treat the help not as a servant but as a friend.

By 1860, however, things in rural Michigan were more settled. Farm families could spare "eldest" daughters to go into service since there were younger siblings left at home to do the chores. In fact, sending daughters to "live out" and "help" in another family was a long standing tradition dating back to the Puritans. Since older girls in the family tended to help their mothers with chores and childcare, once those requirements were no longer necessary, the adolescent daughter was available for some other housewife in need of help. It was considered a reciprocal experience which developed rural community ties and aided those most in need. It also provided a type of apprenticeship for girls in art of homemaking. They would have learned much from their mothers, but it is a well known truth that teenagers often learn better from someone other than their own parents. A more formal mistress/servant relationship suggests a more rigorous discipline and obedience than what might be found at home. Such an experience provided a transition to independent adulthood and ultimately marriage. The era readily supported the virtue of self-reliance. It is also possible that despite significant assets, the families were cash poor at the very time when more and more manufactured goods were becoming readily available. If this were the case, their daughter's wages, though minimal, would help.

The fourth prevalent stereotype concerns the African-American servant. The 1860 Census showed that for Ypsilanti's African-American women, it was virtually the only employment available. Eighteen women were counted as employed. Except for two who will be discussed later in the book, the remaining sixteen women all worked as domestic servants. Ranging in age from seventeen to thirty, all were single though two had a child each. Almost half of those African- American women were under twenty which conforms to the national average of sixteen to twenty year olds predominating. In the post Civil War era, a significant portion of Ypsilanti's African-American population came from Canada where runaway slaves had found refuge from the Fugitive Slave Law in the United States. Many had found their way to Canada via the Underground Railroad stations in southeastern Michigan. When Genevieve Ward Williams wrote an account of her mother's experiences, she did not say if she or her family were slave or free. The very fact that they came from Canada suggests they were slave, but even free African-Americans lived in fear both before and during the Civil War. Whichever they were, her mother, Rebecca Luvenia came to Ypsilanti because her brother, James, had settled there before her. Rebecca married Archibald Ward, and with the income earned by both husband

and wife, the family was able to buy a modest house at 722 Norris Street. Mrs. Ward earned her share working as a domestic for Helen Swift, a wealthy widow, whose house was at 203 Huron Street in Ypsilanti.

Statistics from Ypsilanti seem to support the stereotype; however, the situation in Ann Arbor appears quite different because as few as two African-American women worked as domestics in 1860. Years later, Emiline White worked for James Simpson in the 1870's, and two sisters, Ora A. and Mary R. Green, worked together for Professor Stanley in his home at #21 S. Ingalls in the 1890's; however, the African-American domestic did not form a prominent part of the local domestic scene until the early twentieth century when waves of African-Americans came north in search of a better life. With many seeking work and often poorly educated or skilled, domestic service was where they found employment.

Mrs. Ward was lucky to have a daughter who preserved even a tiny morsel of her story. If most women in the sewing trades went unnoticed as individuals, the problem is even more severe for women who were domestics. Their private lives have passed into history in virtual silence. Without a family to memorialize a woman's life, no one noted what these women were doing. We know of Aurilla Cook, only because bits of her story are revealed in a letter by George B. Goodell who lived east of Ypsilanti where his own grandmother had been employed as domestic help when she arrived from New York in 1824. George wrote that when he was a boy after the Civil War, his father's cousin, Aurilla Cook, worked for them as a "hired girl." She was born in April of 1849. Having just finished school, she worked for the Goodells before marrying Amsi Dunlap. Perhaps because she was a distant relation or perhaps because of fond regard or proximity, Mr. Goodell remained close to Aurilla Cook Dunlap who lived in nearby Denton. She "has been and now is well acquainted with and about all our family." At the time of Mr. Goodell's 1939 letter, Mrs. Dunlap was still alive and well at age ninety, living her final years in Kalamazoo, Michigan. Her story, however, illustrates several significant points. She came from a family secure enough financially to allow her to finish school. She was in the eighteen or nineteen year old age category so typical of domestic help. And she didn't work as a domestic very long before marrying. [8]

Emily Hollister mentions in her diary a very atypical situation. Mrs. Hollister was a nurse who often spent weeks in someone's home tending to the ill. Her entry for January 8, 1894 is about Miss Hannah Gregory. This atypical situation may derive somewhat from Miss Gregory's age. She was seventy-six but still "thinks she has a chance at matrimony." Miss Gregory had an African-American maid named Nellie Bly "a witty black eyed tease" said Hollister. Nellie and Miss Hanna were good friends after sixteen years of coexistence. There was also a domestic named Frances whom Hollister describes as "a dull Polish girl." Nellie and Frances somehow managed to take care of Miss Gregory and her brother, "a fossil of a ruined life." [9]

Without a diary like Mrs. Hollister's or a memoir or letter, a domestic employee's specific experiences would be known only if she gained some notoriety. At least two interesting cases of Washtenaw County domestics made it into the public record. Newly married, Mrs. John Layton found herself in much the same situation as did Henrietta Wagner in the previous chapter. Mr. Layton, according to the May 30, 1877 *Ann Arbor Register*, was of a "jealous disposition." His wife refused to continue living with him. She then lived in the Ypsilanti home of her employer, W. F. Halleck. In the middle of the night of May 28, Mr. Layton, crawled through a window of the Halleck home. Like Mr. Wagner, Layton had armed himself with a hatchet. And just for good measure he also carried a large rock. He woke his wife and told her he was going to kill her. She screamed. Mr. Halleck awoke and grabbed a pistol with which he shot Mr. Layton. Then Mr. Halleck went to his neighbor's house and asked Professor Pease of the Michigan State Normal School to assist him in taking Mr. Layton to the jail.

The unfortunate story of Mrs. Layton did not get as much press as that of Martha Miner, a domestic for Charles Gadd in Manchester. Considering the attitudes of the era, the fact that Mr. and Mrs. Layton were African-American might have had something to do with it. A more likely explanation, however, would be that, since no one was actually murdered, it was not sufficiently gruesome to be recalled. Miss Martha Miner's story gained her a dubious place in local lore. In the wee hours of July 17, 1879, the residents of the Gadd household were abruptly awakened by two gunshots. Searching the house, they found their servant, Martha Miner, mortally wounded and a man, named Niles James, dead. Forensic science did not exist then, so it remains unproven as to which one killed the other and then turned the gun on himself or herself. The *Manchester Enterprise* readily assumed, or at least printed the fact, that Mr. James killed Miss Miner and then himself. That assumption later found its way into Chapman's *History of Washtenaw County* thus firmly fixing in people's memory the idea that Niles James was the guilty one. Looking back, however, I cannot help but wonder why James would kill himself. Clearly the two had a relationship. He should not have been in her room in the Gadd house. Such things were strictly prohibited. If they were having a lovers' spat, all he had to do was walk away from the relationship. Was he the jealous type like Mr. Layton? That, too, seems unlikely. Miss Minor, as a live-in domestic, would have had very little time to juggle one dalliance, let alone several, at once. She would have had, however, a great deal to lose were she perhaps pregnant and he unwilling to accept that responsibility. Did a doctor even examine her? Even if one did and found her to be with child, the newspaper would never have publish it and certainly wouldn't have speculated that she had been the one who had fired the shots. Since imagination had to compensate for a lack of facts, this shocking case captured the public's notice.

More typical of female domestic servants are the passing references to Lana Harra, Bertha Wiederhoft, or Lena Schaeffer. Lana worked in Ann Arbor for Mayor William S. Maynard. History has preserved her name, but not what she looked like or how she felt about her work. We know a bit more about Bertha Wiederhoft who worked for Henry P. Glover in Ypsilanti. Her widowed mother had eight living children, three were domestic servants. Bertha could read and write. She had a dormer room in the Glover home until she married. Next to what we know about Lana Harra, that is a treasure trove of information though it doesn't tell us much about Bertha's mindset. Milo Ryan also recalled that his family, though far from rich, needed help and his mother saying that hired girls were "difficult to find and expensive." [10] In his memoir, *View of the Universe*, Ryan mentions, in particular, one such girl, Lena Schaeffer. She worked for his family for three or four years before she left to marry. She "lived in," he recalled and earned $2 a week during the first decade of the twentieth century. But those were Mr. Ryan's only memories of Miss Schaeffer. Again, they provide a glimpse into domestic service but no real clues to Miss Schaeffer's thoughts or feelings.

The sparse personal comments that have survived from domestics elsewhere, however, are consistent. As the century progressed, it was a job no one really wanted. Unlike alternative areas of employment, the domestic servant usually lived in her employer's home. She was on call 24-7. She did not go home at the end of the day or experience virtually any free time. She was not supposed to entertain friends, let alone lovers, since she roomed where she worked. Her duties also were less defined than those of a young woman working in a shop or factory. That left her assigned chores to the whim of her employer. Sheila Rothman, in her book, *A Woman's Place*, noted one young woman who worked in a private home and claimed, "Better the ten hour discipline of the sewing machine than the 24 hour oversight of a middle class housewife." [11] Carl Degler's *At Odds* confirms that domestic work was "shunned like the plague" primarily due to the loss of personal freedom. Domestics also were not paid well. Most made less than five dollars per week when milliners could make twice that amount. [12] Employers justified the low pay scale by asserting that part of a hired girl's salary was her room and board. In addition, since virtually all were young and single, females were often at risk of being sexually harassed by the men of the house. If that were not bad enough, a domestic was not only socially stigmatized in her employer's home by her uniform and the custom of addressing her by her first name but ostracized by workers in other fields for not having enough gumption to do something better. As the century progressed, it became a job taken only temporarily or as a last resort.

John Morrison in his unpublished history tells of the fate of a girl who went to rural school with him in the 1880's. She was the daughter of a prosperous farmer who sent her to Michigan State Normal School to prepare for a teaching career. Then she married a banker with whom she had eleven children. Thus far her life had been a success story. But years later the bank failed, and her husband disappeared. She was left to support the family and "*had* to go to work doing housework." [13] Morrison's use of the verb "had" suggests just how undesirable such employment was.

Not only were women employed as domestics in private homes but in public lodgings. Frequently, like residences, these hotels provided room and board to employees as a supplement to their modest wages. Hotels such as the St. James Hotel and Cook's Hotel in Ann Arbor and the Hawkins House in Ypsilanti needed chambermaids as well as waiters and cooks. The Palace Hotel in Milan, Harmon House in Saline, and Chelsea House in Chelsea also offered employment opportunities. Manchester House of the 1870's boasted running water which flowed from a third-floor water tank. That surely saved its employees significant time and effort, but the hotels of the era needed a host of employees to provide myriad services.

Every town and village provided some temporary housing for travelers, but it was Whitmore Lake which became a summer vacation mecca during the last quarter of the nineteenth century. During the summer season, four trains a day stopped in Whitmore Lake, and on weekends extra coaches were added to trains to accommodate the hordes of visitors. The *Ann Arbor Register* of July 30, 1885 labeled the area "Washtenaw's Saratoga," thus enhancing its reputation by linking it to New York's famous resort area. Such activity was a bonanza for young women looking for summer jobs. In addition to all the cottages being built, Whitmore Lake possessed two grand hotels, one of which was called the Lake House. In fact, the strangest extant story about a domestic comes from that hotel. It concerns a Miss Lena Schlemmer. Miss Schlemmer probably was Lana Schlimmer, one of six the daughters born to Carl and Lucette Schlimmer. (The era was not at all consistent in its spelling of names.) In any case, Lena was working as a maid in the Lake House on May 2, 1877 when lightning suddenly struck the building. The impact propelled poor Miss Schlemmer out a window. Though the accident induced convulsions, she apparently soon recovered, as did a baby who suffered a similar lightning-caused defenestration while taking his nap near a window.

Greetings from Lake House, Whitmore Lake, Mich.

Lake House postcard

Courtesy of the Bentley
Historical Library,
University of Michigan

In this microcosm of the domestic servant, there were a few who had jobs of a slightly different nature from the average. Mrs. James Burns identified herself as the janitress for the Third Ward School in Ann Arbor where she also lived with her husband and son circa 1883. Mrs. Margaret Cross did the same job at Ypsilanti's Fourth Ward School. Even more interesting might be Louisa Aldrich's job. She cleaned the county jail in Ann Arbor. Hospitals also needed support personnel. Ellen Cunningham in 1890 was the cook for the Homeopathic Hospital at the University of Michigan where she also had her living quarters.

A university town like Ann Arbor provided one more possibility for employment: fraternity house mothers and domestics. Unfortunately most of the local fraternities had terrible reputations. Pi Kappa Psi could not keep a housekeeper for long due to the behavior of its members. One young woman, who had begun working there, fled the house early in the morning seeking sanctuary at a neighbor's home. Some drunken fellows had tried to assault her. She never returned even for her clothes. Another fraternity, finding itself without domestic labor, inquired of a prominent resident where it could find someone who was "not too d---d particular" [14] about their having women in the chapter house at night. The previous housekeeper had quit over such scandalous behavior. None of these stories circulating in the 1890's would entice a respectable woman to work at a fraternity.

There is, however, one recorded example of an exception. She was exceptional for three reasons. First, the fraternity was Psi Upsilon at State Street and South University, one of only two chapters with spotless reputations. Second, the job was not as a domestic servant but as "matron" or housemother which put it at a more supervisory level. The final reason for its uniqueness is that the woman in question was none other than Mrs. Emma Ten Brook.

What makes this woman's employment so intriguing is that she was the second wife of Professor Andrew Ten Brook, librarian for the University of Michigan, whom she married in 1868. At the time of her marriage, Emma Smallwood Smoot was a forty-four year old widow with a nine-year- old daughter and an eleven year old son. As a widow, Mrs. Smoot brought to the marriage assets of her own. When Mary, the professor's own daughter, married, it was her step-mother, Emma, who "expended some four hundred dollars of her own money" [15] to give Mary a suitable wedding. Professor Ten Brook, who apparently was a fine librarian but a poor businessman, lost most of Emma's money in an ill-fated land development scheme. He also lost the land which he had inherited from the first Mrs. Ten Brook. Finally he also lost his position at the University. The Professor quickly returned to his natal state, New York, but Mrs. Ten Brook continued living in Ann Arbor with her children as well as caring for the Professor's mentally unstable son.

Until her children married and Ten Brook's son died, Emma supported herself first by taking in students as boarders. Then she became house mother at Psi Upsilon. What makes her job at the fraternity so deliciously ironic is that one of the many controversies in which Andrew Ten Brook had been involved was the question of secret societies. In the late 1840's any student who joined a secret society, that is a fraternity, would be expelled from the University. Some sources claim that Mr. Ten Brook used to skulk around the woods hoping to catch members of these secret societies. By the 1880's things had changed considerably, yet one cannot help but wonder if Mrs. Ten Brook took the job as house matron because it was the only one she could find or because it would have been particularly unsettling to her estranged husband. Her job also may have been the final blow to an already strained relationship because in 1887 Mr. Ten Brook sued for divorce on the grounds of his wife's deserting him. The court case was acrimonious with considerable evidence to support Emma's claims; however, a Detroit judge ruled in favor of Mr. Ten Brook. The judge even denied Emma the $5 per week support she had requested. She then left Ann Arbor to live with her children. In 1900, at age seventy-six, she was residing in Washington D.C. with her daughter.

Psi Upsilon House

Courtesy of the Bentley Historical Library
University of Michigan

The negative impression of domestic labor in the latter part of the nineteenth century, however, belies an earlier time when domestic labor was a more valued and honored occupation because it represented a skilled trade. The housewife and the employee worked side by side more as equals than mistress and servant. That was an era when candles and soap were still made in the home; bread, butter, cheese and beer were produced at home, and the family's clothing was created not by a factory but by the family itself. Everything had to be sewn of home-woven cloth made from flax or wool which had to be processed as well. In 1810 Secretary of the Treasury, Albert Gallatin, estimated that two thirds of all fabric in the U.S. was made at home. He went on to say that if one considered only the rural portions of the country, all fabric was the "product of family manufactures." [16] Born in 1808, Mrs. Laura Ripley Wallace of Saline remembered learning to spin and weave when she was a child. She came from a family of fourteen, so it was a full time job to produce sufficient material "as nearly all garments were "home made." [17]   The practice of wearing homespun clothing continued until the eve of the Civil War. Making one's own fabric was a long and laborious process that began with raising the sheep or a crop of flax. Then there was shearing and carding or soaking and pounding to do. Next one had to spin the fibers. Spinning was an art form in and of itself. It took years of practice to become a consistent spinner. Only after the fibers had been spun, could one begin the weaving. So many young unmarried women earned a living spinning that the word soon evolved into the term "spinster" to indicate a woman's unwed status.

So it is not surprising that early Michigan pioneers such as Mrs. Woodruff and Mrs. Grant each brought a hired woman with them when they settled Woodruff's Grove. A Mrs. Snow came with Woodruffs in 1823, and Jane Johnson came with the Grants in 1824. That same year, when twenty-one year-old, sandy haired, and freckled Aurilla Stevens arrived in Woodruff's Grove, the Woodruff's were very glad to be able to hire her to help with the domestic chores. Her job was to card and spin. Aurilla would have been respected as a skilled and valuable employee. She did not stay more than two years with the Woodruffs, but it was not because she was unhappy. It was because she abandoned her "spinster" status by marrying Jothan Goodell, a widower with three children. They moved nearby where she lived until 1880. Aurilla provides history with not only a picture of a woman who worked early in the century as a domestic but also a splendid example of the courageous sort of women who immigrated to the Michigan Territory. She was the eldest of four children whose family resided in Painted Post, New York. Seeking opportunity, she left her family and

Aurilla Stevens Goodell
Courtesy of the Ypsilanti Historical Society

traveled with some New York neighbors to the newly settled Woodruff's Grove. She must have had an adventurous spirit.

Roccena Norris
Courtesy of the Ypsilanti Historical Society

The experience of Rachel Horner Watt is even more indicative of the close personal connection between employer and domestic employee that exemplified the early nineteenth century pioneers but was lost by the end of the century. When Rachel arrived in Woodruff's Grove with her husband, William, and their nine children, she was immediately given a job by Roccena Norris (Mrs. Mark). William wrote to his in-laws in England assuring them by saying, "Her missis is very fond of her. She giver [sic] 2 shillings per week and have bought her a handsome dress for the winter." [18] In fact, when Rachel's health failed after giving birth to her tenth child, Roccena Norris took her and the baby as well as one of her daughters into the Norris home where "Mrs. Mark Norris waited on my wife herself and nursed her as she would her own Child [sic]. She had everything that could be thought of for her comfort but all in vain…" [19] Rachel Watt died and was buried on Christmas

Day 1836, yet her story is important in that it reminds us of a time when the relationship between the domestic servant and the mistress of the house was more collegial.

Another particularly common domestic occupation that has always offered women employment is that of laundress. Domestic servant and laundress actually formed the largest category of female workers well into the twentieth century. The number of private laundresses peaked in 1910 when labor was still relatively inexpensive and society's increasing fastidiousness demanded cleanliness for all who strove to be socially acceptable. Being a laundress, however, was not the future every little girl dreamed of having when she was growing up. It was strenuous work. Sarah Grimke wrote in 1837, "A woman who goes out to wash works as hard in proportion as a wood sawyer or a coal havier, but she is not generally able to make more than half as much." [20] Another author equated a day as laundress to walking twenty miles. It was not only exhausting; it took a heavy toll on any woman's body. It made a woman like Milo Ryan's grandmother, Joanna, "back-bent" with "fiery red hands." [21] Yet a government study in 1911 unquestionably demonstrated that being a laundress, despite the exhausting labor it required, was preferred over domestic service. The only explanation for this is that a laundress, whether she came to her employer's home to work or took the laundry home to do, was more independent than someone working as a live-in domestic servant. In addition, unlike the predominantly young and single domestics, laundresses were often wives and mothers who could thus earn money without leaving home.

One of the earliest recorded examples of a local laundress is Mrs. F. Thompson, who lived on Ballard Street in Ypsilanti in the 1860's. She called herself a "washerwoman." Common sense tells us there were many, many more such women in all the towns and villages. Their efforts simply were not noted in public documents. In the 1870's, several women can be found who worked independently as laundresses. The care with which Mrs. Emily Townsend, Mrs. Riley Sweaney and Mrs. Nancy Williams listed their addresses in the Ann Arbor City Directory indicates that they, like Mrs. Thompson, expected people to come to them. Mrs. Townsend described her address as the west side of Pitcher, south of River. Mrs. Sweaney lived nearby. Mrs. Williams lived at 8 Maiden Lane. Both Townsend and Williams are labeled "col'd" in the Directory, thus they were "people of color" [22] ie. African-Americans. Similarly in Ypsilanti, fifteen of the sixteen laundresses in 1878 were married or widows, and six were African-American. Mrs. Eliza Stewart, a widow with five children, was one of those fifteen women. She had worked as a laundress as early as 1860.

These women must have been kept quite busy, because according to Susan Strasser in her history of housework, *Never Done*, laundry was the "most hated task." Whether it was the lady of house or the unfortunate lone domestic servant who performed all tasks from baking to cleaning, she considered herself "unlucky" if she also had to be washer-woman and ironer.[23] *The Manual of Domestic Economy*, published in 1840, shows why this was a hated task. Washing was a two day process, requiring thirty to sixty gallons of water which had to be hauled in by the bucketful. Whites had to be boiled in order to be sure they were clean. To get things dry, one had to watch the weather carefully. And then there was the ironing which required using a hot 4-12 pound iron which easily could scorch a fabric if one were not very careful. If women, as soon as they had any discretionary money, "jettisoned laundry" as Strasser asserts, [24] other women who were willing to do that laundry found a way to support themselves and their families. One woman's burden was another woman's opportunity.

By the 1870's, however, things began to change. Professional laundries were becoming more common. The first steam powered laundry had opened in Troy, New York, in the 1830's. Such commercial laundries, though, were virtually unknown until after the Civil War, when they started appearing in larger cities. It took until 1909 for factory styled laundries to become a major employer of women. At that time ninety thousand women in the United States worked as starchers, ironers, dryers, or menders. M. M. Seabolt's City Laundry in Ann Arbor started in the early 1870's with Annie Sechrist working for him. His laundry was probably typical for its day specializing in "flat work": collars, cuffs, sheets and table linens. Women such as Katie Maynard, Mrs. Minnie McIntyre and probably Mrs. H. E Johnson, a woman "of color," who earlier had worked independently, pressed, folded and stacked for Seabolt in the 1880's.

Several other women at that time worked as laundresses in local hotels. Anna Bank was employed at the St. James Hotel, Mrs. William Parker at Leonard House, and Sarah McLeod at Cook's Hotel in Ann Arbor. Ypsilanti offered the same type of employment at the Hawkins House. Both of its laundresses in 1883 were African-American: Frankie Johnston and Mrs. Wealthy Andrews. [25] More impressive were the three women, all married, who operated their own laundries in the 1880's in Ypsilanti: Mrs. Rachel Ayres, Mrs. Norris and Mrs. Potter. By 1892 nine women, seven of whom were African-American, were employed in Ypsilanti as laundresses. At that time, the villages of Washtenaw County still relied on individual laundresses such as Mrs. Frances Davis of Manchester while the larger towns began offering commercial laundries of which Ypsilanti had two and Ann Arbor, six. By 1900 over 320,000 women in the United States earned their living as laundresses. Since only 82,000 of those were employed in steam powered laundries, the remaining 238,000 still worked in homes or hand laundries.

Varsity Laundry of Ann Arbor

Courtesy of the Bentley Historical Library, University of Michigan

Although a large percentage of laundry employees, were women, as the photograph above indicates, the vast majority of laundries were owned and managed by men. A few women did own their only laundries in the 1880's; however, by the 1890's and early twentieth century only one of the laundries in Washtenaw County was owned and operated by a woman. That woman's name was Sophie Allmendinger. Miss Allmendinger took this humble form of employment and turned it into a profitable business.

The story of Sophie and her family is an interesting one because in some ways they are representative of so many foreign-born families in the area, yet in other ways they differ sharply from the stereotype of such families. Ann Arbor was home to many Allmendingers. Various Allmendingers, such as Sophie's paternal grandfather, were some of the first immigrants to arrive from Germany. Grandfather Allmendinger was a farmer. His son, George, born in Michigan, was also a farmer. When it came time to marry, George chose for his wife a woman named Barbara. She had been born in Wurtemburg, Germany. This scenario of a second generation immigrant marrying a woman from the old country was very typical.

In any case, this particular family of Allmendingers had four children. Frederick was the oldest child while Sophie was the eldest of three daughters. Sophie was born in 1860, Marie in 1868 and Amanda in 1870. Sophie's family lived quite close to a John Allmendinger. John probably was George's brother because John chose family names for his own children: George, Sophia and Mary. Thus far the Allmendinger clan exemplifies our perception that families in the past were large, extended, and multi-generational families. If we toss in the fact that Sophie's grandparents lived with George's family, we only confirm that perception.

Because we imagine that most families were like the Allmendingers, many people find modern families formed of step-children as well as children born to a later marriage a disappointing change from an imagined past. The truth is that families have always been cobbled together in odd ways, combined and recombined to compensate for deaths, divorces, abandonments etc. In such situations people always have responded in the most practical way. The story of Sophie's parents may fit our stereotype, but the lives of the Allmendinger children challenge that illusion.

First, one would expect Frederick to take over his father's farm as his father had done before him, but Frederick trained as a carpenter, not a farmer. He probably learned his carpentry skills from John. Then Frederick left Michigan to seek his own fortune in Illinois. By 1880 George had passed away, and the Allmendinger women were living in Ann Arbor. Sophie began working as a milliner circa 1880. By the time she began as an ironer for M. M. Seabolt, at # 4 North Fourth Avenue, however, she was an unmarried twenty-five year old trying to support her widowed mother and two younger sisters.

Sophie's sister Marie/Mary married a man named Baur who had a daughter from an earlier marriage. Marie had not been married very long when her husband died leaving her to support her step-daughter. So Marie joined Sophie and began working at M. M. Seabolt's laundry. Sisters frequently worked, if not side by side, at least in the same occupation. By 1894, however, they had gained sufficient knowledge about the laundry business to open their own laundry at #1 E. Liberty. Because most of the linens brought to a professional laundry were flat work such as collars, cuffs and sheets, they called their shop the White Laundry. Business went well for four years until Marie married Charles Petrie, who also had a daughter from a previous marriage. At that time Sophie bought Marie's share in the business. Thus Sophie, at age thirty-eight, became the sole owner and manager of the White Laundry, and the new Mrs. Petrie found herself, at age thirty, to be the step-mother to two little girls, Ruth Baur, eleven, and Olive Petrie, seven.

Some time after Marie married, their mother died, so Amanda, the youngest of the sisters, moved in with Sophie. Sophie put Amanda in charge of the White Laundry while she began another one which she called the White Star Laundry. That situation did not last. In a short time, the White Laundry disappeared. History has not left us any record of what exactly happened. Had Amanda mismanaged the White Laundry? Had she disliked the work? Though Amanda remained single, she does not appear to have had another job in 1900. Instead she was living with her sister Marie's family. Was Amanda ill? Was Marie? Had there been a falling out with Sophie? Was Amanda "helping" Mrs. Petrie to avoid her having to hire a domestic? The family dynamics are intriguing but too elusive to draw any conclusions. Whatever the reason, Amanda had not moved very far because Marie Petrie lived next door to her sister, Sophie Allmendinger.

Meanwhile Sophie's White Star Laundry remained in business until 1914 when its owner would have been fifty-three. Sophie listed no profession after that time until resurfacing as a seamstress at Varsity Laundry. Laundries usually hired their own seamstresses to mend tears or replace buttons lest customers claim the damage was done by the laundry. But what, one wonders, was Sophie doing in the meantime? Again history is silent. Was it illness that curtailed Sophie's laundry business? Or was she caring for Marie? Whatever the specific circumstances, she proved herself a resilient and capable business woman for more than two decades.

If it is difficult to obtain personal information about early Caucasian working class women like the Allmendingers, it is almost impossible to learn anything about African-American women even though there were quite a few such women in the county. The 1850 Census indicates that of the 2,095 residents of African descent living in Michigan, 231 lived in Washtenaw County. Thus Washtenaw was second only to Wayne County (which includes Detroit) in African-American population. Ann Arbor alone had more than eighty African-American residents in 1860. Few details, however, remain concerning these people. In addition to the women "of color" working in the sewing trades and as laundresses or domestics, the directories and censuses do tell the fragmentary story of an Ann Arbor woman named Elsie Madary. Mrs. Madary first appears in the late 1870's as the wife of Richard. She had one daughter named Eva or Evaline born circa 1870 and another, Mina, born circa 1874. Mrs. Madary's parents were from New York, but Eva was born in Canada, so we may safely assume that her family, like so many African-American families had fled to Canada before the Civil War. The Fugitive Slave Law made the ante bellum north no safe haven for African-Americans. Men hunting escaped slaves often cared little if the person they caught were the correct slave or even a slave at all. Many free individuals finding themselves in jeopardy and left the United States preferring the safety of Canada. After the Civil War, they frequently returned as it would seem Mrs. Madary did.

Mrs. Madary, by the 1880's, was a widow living at the northeast corner of Liberty and Fifth. Later she moved to North Fifth Avenue, but for twenty years, she consistently earned her income as a "dyer/scourer/clothes cleaner." Though listed in the City Directory as a dyer/scourer, Mrs. Madary told the 1880 Census enumerator she" cleaned clothes." It is unclear what she exactly meant. If she meant a laundress, she probably would have said so. On the other hand, she did not say that she was a "dry scourer" let alone a "dry cleaner," but she might have been. Both of those processes were available at the time. It would be so fitting if she, as an African-American, were a "dry scourer" because that process was the first United States patent received by someone of her race. Thomas L. Jennings, a free citizen of New York City, who earned his living as a tailor, obtained Patent # 3306x on March 3, 1821 when he was only thirty years old. The profits from his process allowed him to purchase the freedom of other family members and generously support the abolitionist cause. He died in 1856, the year after Jean Baptiste Jolly, a French dye works owner, introduced a similar process he called "dry cleaning" which meant that clothing was washed in solvents such as kerosene, benzene, turpentine and the like. Dry cleaning was extremely labor intensive and dangerous since the chemicals involved were volatile. [26]

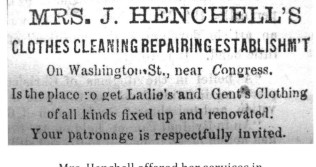

Mrs. Henchell offered her services in
Ypsilanti circa 1867-1873

Courtesy of the Ypsilanti Historical Society

Whatever service Mrs. Madary was providing, it foreshadowed a business that would become increasingly popular. By the early twentieth century, Mrs. Mary Godfrey and Mrs. Lucy Crane of Ypsilanti offered dry cleaning. Mrs. Crane, age forty-six in 1910, lived and worked at #8 Washington Street adjacent to Crane's Printing, owned and operated by her husband, John Crane. Crane and Godfrey also included dyeing of cloth as one of the services they provided. Clothing at that time was not colorfast, thus the dyes faded long before the fabric wore out. This also may suggest what Mrs. Madary was doing since she said she was a "dyer." Dry cleaning and dyeing clearly provided yet another entrepreneurial opportunity for enterprising women in Washtenaw County.

Rug making, like doing laundry, was a job which housewives willingly delegated. Eighteenth century American homes generally did not have rugs or carpets. Their popularity began to rise in the East in the second and third decades of the nineteenth century. Soon several styles of rugs were often advertised. There were actually three techniques used to manufacture rugs at that time. One was braiding which created round or oval rugs. These are still popular, and I recall my own German-born grandmother braiding rugs for her home in the mid-twentieth century. Another method was hooking, which allowed for highly original and artistic patterns. This latter method is less practical since it is very time consuming. The third kind of rug was made by weaving fabric on a large loom. It resulted in the striped, rectangular rugs still sold in stores. No matter what kind of rug was being created, it took a good deal of time to produce, but time alone was not the defining factor for the nineteenth century woman who wanted a rug. By mid-century when rugs became popular, few women possessed the large looms needed to produce the woven rugs which were in such demand, hence the need for professional rug weavers.

Just as dressmakers might rework an old garment, rug making was a form of recycling since the final product usually was made from strips of old wool or cotton. Families would collect fabric scraps, tear them into strips and deliver them to a weaver. Mrs. Austin Norton noted in her 1864 diary that on Feb 6, "Eve Vansaltenberg came here this afternoon. I sold her my carpet rags." Also an 1874 journal, owned by Dorothy Laughlin and believed to be the diary of J. M. Wagner's daughter, contains a January first entry stating, "Mary is tearing rags." On February 11, the writer recorded that her mother took the rags for the stair carpet to Mrs. Stoll who would deliver the finished rug on March 5. Because the client provided the material, there was no overhead for the weaver herself except her loom. Later, as silk became more available, "genteel" women would collect it in order to have a weaver turn it into portieres (curtains hung in doorways) or table coverings.

This combination of need, tedium and lack of appropriate tools created a niche of entrepreneurial opportunity. In Europe, rug making was an occupation of men. Several males in the Spathelf family were rug weavers, a skill they brought with them from Germany to Washtenaw County. John and George Spathelf may have emigrated together in 1855. Both were carpet weavers. In America, however, men often found other work, such as farming, more remunerative thus allowing women to enter the trade. John Spathelf, who settled in Freedom Township, brought his two daughters, Henricke and Louisa, into the trade by 1880. George's daughter, Anna, was only ten then. If she ever helped her father in the workshop behind his home on Pontiac Trail in Ann Arbor, there is no record of it. When she matured, she made her living operating a store.

Map of Barnegat (on right)

Courtesy of the Saline Historical Society

Carpet weavers, such as the Spathelfs, existed throughout the county as early as the 1850's. Even a tiny village such as Barnegat [27] had a carpet weaver. Never heard of Barnegat? Few have. It sat on the west bank of the Saline River until Saline absorbed it. Perched on a bank far steeper than that which is there today, 1855 Barnegat consisted primarily of an ashery, a saw mill, a cooper's shop and a blacksmith's. On a side street, however, was a carpet weaver who was probably a woman. The only known reference to this individual is by a male contemporary, John McKinnon. What indicates to me that the weaver was a woman is that McKinnon carefully mentions the working men of Barnegat by name but only says there was also a carpet weaver. Such omissions frequently indicate a working woman. Mr. McKinnon does say that the weaver "enjoyed a prosperous business, as everyone seemed bent on possessing such a luxury." [28]

By the 1870's and 1880's demand had risen to a level sufficient to provide incomes for quite a few women in this field. Mrs. Susan Way was the first to advertise in the *City Directory* in 1874. She was joined in the trade four years later by Mrs. C. Greenman, also of Ann Arbor. It must have been an occupation with enough clientele because twelve years later Eliza Felch employed an assistant, Mrs. Betsy Lee. Mrs. Felch, like so many Michigan residents, was born in New York circa 1840. She and her husband, Newton, had eight children, so for many years she balanced housekeeping and motherhood with rug making. Newton died in 1906, and she retired by 1910 when she was seventy. Like dressmaking, carpet weaving was an area in which married women and widows were able to find sufficient clientele to support themselves. And it was also an occupation available to African-Americans, such as Frances Johnson.

Less than a dozen weavers were able to continue into the early twentieth century when large scale manufacturing and catalog shopping doomed local carpet weavers to obsolescence. By 1906 the Ann Arbor Fluff Rug Company was hiring weavers such as Minnie and Edith Steffen. Few self-employed weavers could compete though Eliza Felch was still advertising in 1912 as were three women in Ypsilanti, one in Saline and one in Salem Township. By that time Mrs. Felch would have been in the weaving business for twenty-six years.

In addition to sewing, domestic labor, laundry and rug weaving, the option of factory-work provided local opportunities. Thousands of working class women on the east coast had found factory work paid better than their other options. And such jobs did exist in Washtenaw County but on a much smaller scale. The Huron River made Washtenaw County ideal for milling. No less than twenty-two mills lined the river between Dexter and Ann Arbor, and more hugged the banks between Ann Arbor and Ypsilanti. Well-known locations of a hundred years ago –Geddesburg, Delhi and Foster's Station – are now unknown to most Washtenaw County residents. Delhi, today hardly even a ghost town, was in the 1860's a bustling hive of activity. The river there has an eight foot fall which provided excellent power for the mills. At its 1860 peak, Delhi supported two large flour mills, a woolen mill, a saw mill and a plaster mill. Between Delhi and Ann Arbor, there was the Cornwell Woolen Mill at Foster's Station where the photograph on page 59 was taken circa 1874. It clearly indicates women working at the mill. In the back row are Delia Warren Reader with Adeline Gates, Libby Warren Snyder and Eva Curtis. Sandy Kerr stands in the middle row.

By the time the Chapman Company published its *History of Washtenaw County* in 1881, almost a thousand persons in the county were in the manufacturing trade. Though the text does not explicitly list women, it is clear that they participated in local manufacturing. It is important to recognize that Chapman's history was not written by Chapman. The book is a compilation of articles and records written by various local authors which were then published

The mill at
Foster's Station

Courtesy of the Bentley Historical
Library, University of Michigan

in a single volume by the Chapman Company. Exact authors are generally unknown but who-ever wrote the piece about mills on page 361 carefully itemized the number of men in various fields. He documented twelve "men" working at three breweries and sixty "men" working for twenty-two coopers (i.e. barrel makers). When it came to the four tanneries, two textile facto-ries, and a woolen mill, however, it mentions "persons" or "hands." At first a reader, if he or she notices at all, assumes that the author simply is changing his word choice to provide variety, but this clearly is not the case. Whether intentionally or subconsciously chosen, the words in Chapman's compilation camouflage the fact that many of those workers were women.

That author is not alone in this obfuscation of the facts unless the same person wrote several articles. On page 833, another entry discusses Palmer and Son Woolen Mill which again employed six to twelve "hands" as did the knitting factories described on page 944. And there is a boot and shoe manufacturer on page 829 who also employed fourteen "hands." A significant portion of those employees itemized by the Chapman book in gender neutral terms were women though it is very difficult to pinpoint just how many. Unlike Mrs. John Hill, who worked at a woolen mill circa 1875, most did not include their occupations in census records or city directories. But common sense and the above photo of Foster Station make me confident that Mrs. Hill was not alone in working in local mills.

As the century progressed, more manufacturing companies offered employment. Compa-nies like Ann Arbor's Union Shade Pull Company, which produced brass products, hired women as operators and clerks, but Ann Arbor never developed a strong industrial base. Miss Cora B. Randall began the Randall Skirt and Corset Company circa 1899. Her competition was a firmly established corset company, Crescent Works, located at 306-308 S Main. For whatever reason, Miss Randall's company lasted only five years. Despite Ann Arbor's concerted effort to woe man-ufacturing, the turn of the century found the majority of Ann Arbor women working in white collar office jobs. It was Ypsilanti that developed the most employment opportunities in factories for women. Morrison in his unpublished history of the Washtenaw County asserts, "The city of Ypsilanti had the name of the best industries in Washtenaw of the 1880's and 1890's." [29]

Milling came to Ypsilanti early in its history. The Huron River was a major reason why people settled in that area. The river there has a strong current and back then ran approximately five feet higher than it does today. One of the early mill owners was Abraham Larzelere who began his career by buying out his Uncle Jacob's Ypsilanti property. (Uncle Jacob, by the way, built Ypsilanti's first brick home.) Abraham used the property for a saw mill. Unfortunately Abraham died rather young, but he had a son, John, who inherited the mill in 1841. John converted it the next year into a woolen mill. His decision was a sound one as times were changing. Early settlers needed wood and flour, but by the 1840's Michigan was on its way to become a major wool producing state, and Washtenaw County was its top producer of Spanish merino wool. With more and more sheep to shear and "clips" to process, the county was ready for woolen mills. Again Chapman's *History of Washtenaw County* skirts the issue of female workers in such mills by failing to mention them explicitly. "This [woolen milling] was an important industry of the times employing from 15-20 hands." [30]

John Larzelere also died young, so his widow, Harriet W. Larzelere, began running the woolen mill in 1847. Harriet was one of five children of Daniel Waldo "a family of education and refinement" from New York. She had no children of her own but adopted a daughter named Hattie. After managing the woolen mill for eight years, she traded the mill and its water rights to Cornelius Cornwell for shares in his new paper mill. This mill was the first large scale paper producer in the county. It used a combination of water and steam power to produce wrapping paper for local businesses. It was enormously successful which made it a shrewd investment for Mrs. Larzelere who later in 1863 sold her share of that mill. The 1874 map of Ypsilanti pictured above reflects Harriet's sense of herself as a woman. She did not identify herself as Mrs. John Larzelere. She gave her own name, Mrs. H. W. Larzelere, ie. Harriet Waldo Larzelere, as the property owner. It was quite uncommon for a woman to choose to use her own name or even her initials rather than those of her husband whether he was alive or dead.

1894 map indicating Mrs. Lazelere's property, just to the left of the darker square.

Another early manufacturing company was Peninsular Paper. Unlike Cornwell, Peninsular Paper obtained in 1867 the contract to be the sole supplier of rag newsprint to the *Chicago Tribune*. Peninsular also supplied the *Detroit Post* and *Detroit Tribune*, and it manufactured fine book paper as well. In the 1870's the company expanded by building a second mill as a safeguard against the first plant's potential destruction by fire. (Cornwell's other solution to the threat of fire was to purchase Ypsilanti's first fire engine affectionately called "Cornwell Number One.") Ironically it was this second Peninsular Paper Mill that ultimately burned. Peninsular Paper employed 110 persons of which about half were female. Circa 1883 quite of few of its employees were sisters such as Katie and Mary Rigney, Rosa and Theresa Sanders, and Kate and Maggie Shaff. Peninsular Paper remained in business until 1974 when it was absorbed by the James River Company.

Peninsular Paper Co. remains in Ypsilanti.

Much of the paper, which the early mills, like Peninsular, produced was made from rags. These could be sold directly to the mill or to a local middleman. Snow and Fisk Booksellers in Detroit advertised the need for twenty-five tons - yes, tons- of rags as early as 1835. Washtenaw County also had its demand for rags. On January 2, 1839, J. Jones and Sons, a purveyor of groceries, domestic goods and shoes, located at #2 Exchange Building in Lower Town, Ann Arbor, advertised that it would pay "in goods or cash" three cents a pound for rags. Three cents sounds like such a pittance, but if one does a few simple calculations, one realizes that three cents a pound means $60 per ton and the twenty-five tons Snow and Fisk sought would have cost them $1500. That is a significant amount which, at that time, would have purchased a thousand acres of farm land in Michigan. The demand for rags continued for many decades because Laflin Butler and Co. advertised in the *Dexter Leader* in 1869 that it "paid cash for rags." This provided enterprising souls with an opportunity to earn money. In Ypsilanti, Mary Madigan, Mary Moore and Johanna Sheehan collected and sold rags to Bradley and Damon circa 1878. Bradley and Damon, a store on Huron Street, specialized in crockery and glassware. They, like Laflin Butler and Co., also functioned as a collection point which then sold the rags in large quantities to others. The paper mills of Ypsilanti would have been perfect buyers.

As Susan Strasser states in *Waste and Want*, "The history of paper was, in one sense, a history of rag gathering." [31] Not only did women and girls collect and sell rags to the mills, but rags defined the nature of the work many women performed within the mill. First came the job of the dusters. These women had to shake the rags vigorously to remove the dust. Other women then sorted the rags by fiber, coarseness, color and cleanliness. Yet a third group of women cut off seams, buttons, patches. They removed any areas that were rotten or badly stained. Finally the rags had to be cut into two to four inch squares using a scythe that was attached to the work table. Needless to say it was a dirty and dangerous way to earn a living. Not only could one easily be cut by the scythe, which before the days of antibiotics could be life-threatening, but dust contaminated the air. Fear of infectious diseases on the rags was so strong that it resulted in an 1884 national embargo on the importation of rags from foreign countries. The final stage of the rags-to-paper process was for the rags to be beaten into a pulp in a liquid laced with lime. Fortunately water power performed that part of the operation.

As rags became more difficult and more expensive to obtain, manufacturers began making paper out of wood pulp. Wood pulp paper cost half as much as rag paper. It is very easy today to notice the difference between these two kinds of paper. An old newspaper made from wood pulp paper will crumble in your hands while a rag sheet, though over a hundred years old, remains as soft and pliable like as old pillowcase. In 1885, however, when the Cornwell brothers built their seventh mill at Geddesburg, they did not care if their paper survived a century or more. They were looking for a cheap and efficient mode of production. Wood pulp was cheaper and more easily processed thanks to a technology which evolved circa 1870. The Cornwell mill utilized 90,000 pounds of wood pulp daily and employed ten "hands." Peninsular, however, continued to utilize only rags and turned its attention towards the production of high grade, specialty papers in many colors. Workers in such factories in 1872 would have earned about fifty cents for a very long day's work. That would amount to a meager annual income of approximately $130.

Elvira Norris Follett

Courtesy of the Ypsilanti Historical Society

Not all mills were as successful as Cornwell's and Peninsular's. Manufacturing could be a financially volatile business. Seven investors contributed a total of $100,000 to build a new mill in 1865. One of these investors was Mrs. Elvira Follett, oldest daughter of Mark and Roccena Norris. It was not a good time for Mrs. Follett. Her husband, Benjamin Follett, a prominent Ypsilanti businessman would die on December 26, 1865 only a month after the death of their daughter, Lucy.

Unfortunately for Mrs. Follett the timing of her investment was wrong. The company, called the Ypsilanti Woolen Manufacturing Company, hoped to capitalize on the demand for blankets due to the Civil War. During the war, wool blanket material sold for $2 a yard. The price dropped to half that after Lee's surrender at Appomattox signaled the end of the Civil War thus making the mill impractical to operate. Mrs. Follett was fortunate to be a woman of some means for whom the loss of such an investment did not signal bankruptcy which would have been disastrous for so many widows with five children to raise. Fifteen years later when she was fifty-nine, she still had four children at home. Though it seems logical in all that time that Mrs. Follett, as a wealthy citizen of Ypsilanti, must have made other significant investments, her memorial booklet provided pages describing her benevolent charitable activities without any mention of any business concerns.

The mill in which Mrs. Follett lost investment money sat unused for a decade, but its location was too valuable not to be used. Finally it was purchased by Frank Hay and William Todd for their company that produced fine yarns and knitted goods such as long underwear. The Hay and Todd Company was so successful that it established a second mill in Ann Arbor on Detroit Street in the building previously owned by Moses Rogers. They also had a third mill in Detroit, Michigan. By 1889, Hay and Todd was marketing its products with little jingles such as:

> *"If love grows cold, do not despair. / There is always Ypsi underwear"* [32]

The dress reform movement and the 1893 Chicago Exposition helped make Ypsilanti underwear a household word. Soon nationally recognized stores such as Marshall Field and Co. of Chicago were buying the bulk of Hay and Todd's inventory which sold in its stores and mail order business. Wool "union suits" sold for $8 while silk ones cost $25. Like so many popular products today such as Kleenex and Xerox, the word "Ypsilantis" entered the language to refer

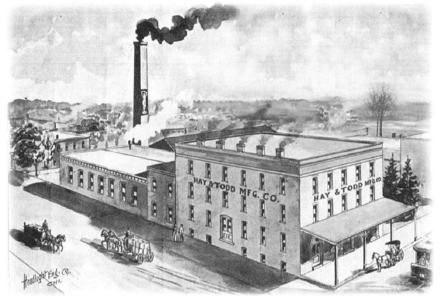

The Hay and Todd
Building in Ann Arbor

Courtesy of the Bentley
Historical Library,
University of Michigan

to any suit of underwear even if it were made by some other company. Perhaps that is why circa 1905, Hay and Todd renamed their company the Ypsilanti Underwear Company.

The mill itself was equally famous. It had always been a landmark in Ypsilanti; however, once the owners painted a fifteen-foot lady wearing a union suit on the side of the mill, everyone began talking about it. The painting was an inspired piece of advertising which foreshadowed modern advertising practices. It was a bit salacious for its time. A few critics condemned it for its overt sexuality. But it worked. It caught the eye of anyone riding the train through Ypsilanti. In fact, Ypsilanti was quite well known for a while. As Julian Street wrote in his 1914 *Abroad at Home*, Ypsilanti had "attained fame entirely disproportionate to" its size. Ann Arbor might be the "seat of learning," but Ypsilanti was "a seat of underwear." [33]

The mill offered more than a hundred women employment. At one time it was the single largest employer of women in Ypsilanti and was obviously a place that also produced long-term friendships. Throughout the 1940's, former employees attended an annual picnic reunion. As late as the 1960's, the *Ypsilanti Press* noted that forty-three former employees – then in their eighties or more – were having a reunion in Ypsilanti.

Someone, perhaps a transient, perhaps a local familiar with the advertising jingles, graffitied the following limerick on the depot wall:

"A sculptor of Nymphs and Bacchantes
Omitted the coats and the panties
A kindhearted madame
Who knew that she had 'em
Supplied them with warm Ypsilantis." [34]

Knitting Mills, Ypsilanti, Mich.

Meanwhile, Enoch Bowling of Ypsilanti had patented a perspiration proof dress stay which was composed of a strip of steel encased in rubber covered with satin. They were very light weighing just a sixth of an ounce each. He partnered with Henry P. Glover in the creation of the Ypsilanti Dress Stay Manufacturing Company, which challenged the Ypsilanti Underwear Company for its spot as the largest manufacturing company. In 1899 Ypsilanti Dress Stay employed 170 women. One hundred seventy may not sound like so many, but it was three percent of the town's entire population of Ypsilanti at that time. These women worked as tippers, pinkers, creasers, stampers and counters. Ypsilanti Dress Stay was one of the few places where men and women worked at similar jobs since males were also listed at tippers. Though not as famous as the Ypsilanti Underwear Company, Beakes' *Past and Present in Washtenaw County* extols Ypsilanti Dress Stay as "one of the most successful factories ever started in Michigan." [35]

The situation at Ypsilanti Dress Stay was similar to that at Scharf Tag, Label and Box Company which employed many women as well as men as box makers, tag makers, and operators. The Scharf Company also printed books such as Daniel Putnam's *History of Michigan State Normal School*. The company moved to Ypsilanti from Toledo in 1891, the very year that it published Mr. Putnam's book. Mrs. Belle Imes served as the fore-lady there, a job Mrs. Lenora Chapman had at that time at Hay and Todd.

Ypsilanti Canning Factory

Courtesy of the
Ypsilanti Historical Society

One of the most elusive manufacturing groups is that of cigar makers. Cigars became exceedingly popular in the mid-nineteenth century. Between 1850 and 1862 per capita cigar consumption in the United States increased 150%. By 1900 cigars were the most popular tobacco product in America with 6.7 billion produced in United States alone. And Michigan was one of nine states which produced 90% of those cigars. In 1868 there were no such manufacturers listed in Washtenaw County though there were establishments such as Hangsterfer's in Ann Arbor that sold cigars. By the early 1880's, however, there were half a dozen manufacturers such as Benham, established in Ann Arbor in 1872 and Schemmeld and Cook, established the following year in Ypsilanti. By the mid-1890's that number increased to four manufacturers in Ann Arbor and six in Ypsilanti. Guild and Son in Ypsilanti produced thirty thousand cigars a month. Schemmeld and Cook, which had half the work force of Guild and Son, produced sixteen thousand cigars a month; Schemmeld and Cook remained in business longer than any other cigar manufacturer in those towns. But Chelsea and Milan both had their own cigar manufacturing businesses. Eisenman was in Chelsea, and Hinkley in Milan

While this may not at first appear to be an area that would employ females, by the early 1880's a conservative estimate of the number of women employed in various occupations cited almost two thousand female cigar makers in the United States. By 1910 it had developed into "a woman's industry" with all the negatives that connotes. This job, like that of the rag sorters, was neither remunerative nor safe. Manufacturers particularly liked to hire women as stemmers. Stemmers stripped away the midrib of the tobacco leaves. It was "dirty, dead end, low wage work" [36] which paid women by the number of pieces produced. Often work areas had no open windows, and there was a high rate of tuberculosis among the workers who sometimes were just young girls. A few skillful women like Mamie Wade, who worked for Eisenman's circa 1894, rose above leaf stripping to become cigar rollers. This work involved rolling loose filler tobacco within the binder leaf so that the end to be lit was tapered while the opposite end was round and cleanly finished.

Boston Poultry House,
215 W. Congress Street,
Ypsilanti, Michigan,
owned by George H. Morse

Courtesy of the
Ypsilanti Historical Society

*(Notice the feathers clinging
to their clothing and the
chicken the man on the
far right is holding.)*

Such were the more traditional opportunities available to working class women in Washtenaw County and throughout the United States in the century prior to World War I. Virtually all domestic servants, laundresses, rug weavers and factory workers appear to have been working outside of the home because of financial need. Neither the jobs nor their remuneration were enticing enough to attract anyone who absolutely did not need the wages. No one would choose backbreaking physical labor of a laundress or the demeaning status of a servant or the unhealthy work in a rag or cigar factory if other options were available. But manual labor jobs such as these, though common enough, do not come close to telling the whole story about women's working lives.

[1] Russell Bidlack, "Andrew Ten Brook: Forgotten Figure in Ann Arbor History," *Impressions* (Ann Arbor, Washtenaw County Historical Society, December 1989), 5.

[2] David Katzman, *Seven Days a Week* (New York: Oxford University Press, 1978), 149.

[3] "Lucy Chapin Collection," at Bentley Historical Library, University of Michigan.

[4] "Lucy Ann Smith Papers" at Bentley Historical Library, University of Michigan.

[5] "The Oral History of Annie Allan Paton", as told to Kathryn Stephen Wright, 1930, at Eastern Michigan University Archives, 23.

[6] Harriet Martineau, *Society in America*, Vol 3 (London: Saunders and Otley, 1837), 140.

[7] Mary Clavers, aka Caroline Kirkland, *A New Home – Who'll Follow?* 5th ed. (New York: C.S. Franses and Co., 1855), 63.

[8] "Goodell Collection," at Ypsilanti Historical Archives, Ypsilanti, Michigan.

[9] Emily Hollister, *Emily Hollister Diary* in "Richard Teall Hollister Collection," at Bentley Historical Library, University of Michigan), 20.

[10] Milo Ryan, *View of a Universe* (Ann Arbor: McNaughton and Gunn, 1985), 50.

[11] Sheila Rothman, *A Woman's Proper Place* (New York: Basic Books, 1978), 92.

[12] Carl Deglar, *At Odds: Women and Family* (New York: Oxford University Press, 1980), 372.

[13] John Morrison, "Memories of Washtenaw County" (unpublished memoir, Bentley Historical Library, University of Michigan), 47.

[14] *The Voice*, (New York, June 9, 1898).

[15] Russell E. Bidlack, "Andrew Ten Brook: Forgotten Figure in Ann Arbor History," *Impressions* (Ann Arbor Washtenaw County Historical Society, February 1990), 6.

[16] Susan Strasser, *Waste and Want: A Social History of Trash* (New York: Metropolitan Books, 1999), 126.

[17] *Saline Observer*, September 19, 1890.

[18] "Pioneers of the Ypsilanti Area," *Ypsilanti Gleanings* (Ypsilanti: Ypsilanti Historical Society, December 1973), 4.

[19] "Pioneers," 8-9.

[20] Gerda Lerner, *The Woman in American History* (Menlo Park, CA: Addison Wesley 1971), 52.

[21] Ryan, 23.

[22] "People of color" was what African-Americans were called as early as 1801.

[23] Susan Strasser, *Never Done* (New York: Pantheon, 1982), 105.

[24] Wealthy Andrews was born in Canada in 1852. She is predominantly remembered for her efforts to help build the African Methodist Church in Ypsilanti. She collected discards and castoffs which she either donated or sold for cash to buy building materials. Her efforts were recognized at a testimonial dinner on June 23, 1937. She died in 1942.

[25] *Ypsilanti Commercial*, April 12, 1873.

[26] Sarah Norton, *Sarah Jane Knapp Norton Diary*, in "Austin Norton Collection," at Ypsilanti Historical Archives, Ypsilanti, Michigan), March 30, 1864.

[27] Schuyler Haywood came to Michigan in 1845. He was from Barnegat, NJ, hence the name Barnegat.

[28] John McKinnon, "Pioneer Times," *Saline Observer*, January 19, 1939.

[29] Morrison, 62.

[30] *History of Washtenaw County Michigan* (Chicago: Charles C. Chapman Co, 1881), 1129.

[31] Strasser, 82.

[32] James Mann, *Ypsilanti: A History in Pictures* (Chicago: Arcadia Press, 2002), 83.

[33] Street, Julian, *Abroad at Home* (New York: The Century Company, 1914), 108.

[34] Mann, 28.

[35] Samuel Beakes, *Past and Present Washtenaw County, Michigan* (Chicago,: St. Clarke Publishing Co.,1906), 754.

[36] Patricia Cooper, *Once a Cigar Maker* (Urbana: University of Illinois Press, 1987), 15.

CHAPTER THREE: FALLEN WOMEN AND FEMALE FELONS

In the early decades of the nineteenth century women comprised only a fraction of the documented criminals. More often women were the victims rather than perpetrators of crime. Before 1861 Michigan judges were somewhat at a loss as to what to do with the women convicted in their courts. The only option then was the state prison in Jackson which most people agreed was no fit place for women. Sometimes judges simply let them go or suspended the sentence if the crime were insignificant, which frequently was the case since women tended to be arrested for lesser crimes such as drunkenness, lewd behavior, public disorder, vagrancy or petty theft. The female murderer existed but was rare.

Arrests of women increased in the 1850's and skyrocketed in the 1860's during the years of the Civil War. Most experts suggest that it was the result of a change in social patterns. Certainly social changes affected women in particular. Urbanization cut them off from the support and control of their families and communities. For women, it marginalized them economically. A by-product of industrialization and urbanization was the shift from a family to a market economy which deprived women of traditional work and status. Some women mid-century worked a full week for less than a dollar. Few made more than three dollars per week. "The limited opportunities for wage earning and the lower salaries paid working women placed them in the most marginal economic position in the society," states Estelle B Freedman in *Their Sisters' Keeper.* [1] Susan B. Anthony in her speech "Social Purity" said much the same thing. Anthony was emphatic that the only solution to the rising crime rate was to provide women with a way to earn a living and provide adequate remuneration for that work. They needed a purse of their own.

What worried many observers in the crucial decade of 1850-1860 was less the rise in the rate of arrests as it was the type of activity for which women were arrested. Many working, but underpaid, women were becoming "temporary" or "episodic" prostitutes when they needed or wanted extra money. They were not, strictly speaking, members of the world's oldest profession. They were not professionals who worked in brothels or walked the streets. They were women who granted their favors to a few for some financial consideration. As early as 1858, when Dr. William Sanger of New York published his evaluation of prostitution in the United States, he, too, warned that working women were paid so little that they lived on the edge of destitution. In the anonymity of a larger town or city, women found that their sexual favors could earn in a day what a seamstress made in a week, and seamstresses made more than unskilled female laborers. When Dr. Sanger interviewed women circa 1855, 75% said they had fallen into prostitution due to poverty.

Amazingly, prostitution itself was not a crime until the twentieth century. Such behavior instead was covered by statutes against lewd behavior or public disorder. It was operating a house of prostitution that was singled out as a crime. The fine distinction between these two activities brought two young women into a Manchester, Michigan, courtroom in February of 1872. They were neither young innocents nor poor unprotected women as they wanted the judge to believe. These women, who did not actually live in Manchester, were undoubtedly members of the 25% Dr. Sanger interviewed who claimed they worked as "ladies of negotiable affections" because it was an easier way to earn a living or because of an alcohol or drug addiction.

The *Manchester Enterprise* reported that the women had been seen consuming alcohol and "introducing themselves in a familiar way to everyone they chanced to meet." Apparently they were doing quite a business in the town. This overt behavior in public would seem to be sufficient to get them in trouble, but it appears that what finally brought the law down on them was the fact that the girls were entertaining men in a house, hence it was a brothel. The authorities raided the house arresting the girls while most of the men escaped. Originally fined $20 each, the young women were able to negotiate a reduction to $10. The newspaper suggested that townspeople "chipped in" to pay the fine and rid Manchester of such disreputable women which the good citizens convinced themselves were an anomaly. They may have rid themselves of those two, but the problem never truly went away as every town in the county had such women most of whom had sufficient sense to not be so obvious.

Prostitution is, understandably, difficult to quantify. Such "fallen women" do not label themselves in a census or city directory, yet the social problem was clearly evident. Dr. Sanger in his study of prostitutes in ten cities, such as Philadelphia, Boston and New York, concluded that there was an average of one prostitute for every fifty-two men in any locale. Later national estimates circa 1900 concluded the ratio was one prostitute for every seventy-two males. The two estimates are not inconsistent with each other. Whether or not these statistical conclusions held true for Washtenaw County remains to be seen; however, common sense and historical evidence clearly indicate that the gals in Manchester were not the only women engaged in prostitution in the county.

John Morrison in both of his unpublished histories of the county mentions two such women. One was a "southern belle" whose husband supposedly died in the Civil War. She bought an eighty acre farm about a mile outside of Dexter Village and established a house of "ill fame." Mr. Morrison recounts that once, when she was called upon to testify in court, the lawyer pressed her for her occupation. She kept evading the question. "When she could not avoid answering any longer, …she pulled a gun on the lawyer and said, 'If you ask me another question, I will drill you full of holes.'" [2] She may have been a southern "belle," but she clearly was no Melanie Wilkes. Circa 1880, she sold the farm and moved her "resort" to Saginaw, Michigan, which was a boom town due to lumber money. Saginaw in the 1870's had 360 saloons and "sporting houses." Local men who stopped to see her there commented that she had portraits of prominent Washtenaw County men on her walls.

The *Dexter Leader* in 1873 reported a story similar to Morrison's identifying the woman as Mrs. Rapalje. At the time of the news account, there was a Mrs. Rapalje but she was living in Ann Arbor. Were there two Mrs. Rapaljes? According to an 1878 *Ann Arbor Democrat* article, Mrs. Rapalje and her "husband" arrived in Ann Arbor in 1866. At first they appeared respectable enough, but the town decided that though he ran a livery, Mr. Rapalje was a "good for nothing." He soon left town, and Mrs. Rapalje purchased a house on Second Street between Ann and Miller. The "character of [the] house" said the *Democrat*, "would not stand close scrutiny," and indeed any boarding house that catered only to women was assumed to be a brothel. On the night of October 31, 1878 over five hundred University of Michigan students congregated outside Mrs. Rapalje's "boarding" house demanding she leave town. One of their fellow students, Howard K. Williams, had committed suicide because of unrequited love for one of the girls in the house. When Mrs. Rapalje refused to agree to leave, rocks began breaking windows in the house. Rapalje and her girls responded by firing at the crowd. Fortunately only one person received a flesh wound. It took a half hour for Sheriff Case to disperse the crowd. That bit of mayhem which the Sheriff referred to as Ann Arbor's biggest mob was hardly unique. According to Ruth Rosen, author of *The Lost Sisterhood*, "Unorganized spontaneous and violent outbursts called 'whorehouse riots' were a common occurrence in urban areas." [3] And Mrs. Rapalje saw the wisdom of leaving Ann Arbor soon after.

But that was 1878, so how could Mrs. Rapalje be in Dexter at the same time? If she were in Ann Arbor between 1866 and 1878, how could she also be in Dexter in 1873? The unusual surname certainly invites speculation. The primary sources may refer to the same person - or they may not. It is quite possible that sources simply confused two individuals attaching the same name to both. It seems improbable that two women in the same profession could have the same unusual name. That improbability diminishes as soon as one learns that, when Rapalje's "husband" left Ann Arbor, he moved to none other than Dexter where he opened another livery in 1869 with man named William Stephens. The *Ann Arbor Democrat* article questioned whether or not the Rapaljes of Ann Arbor were even really married. Whether they were or not, it remains feasible that Mr. Rapalje left Ann Arbor and went to Dexter where he took up with another "wife" whose occupation was similar to that of the woman in Ann Arbor with whom he had been living, thus there could have been two "Mrs." Rapaljes. Such discrepancies will probably never be resolved. The seedy underbelly of society then, as now, did not like to include itself in public records if it could be avoided.

The background for the other woman's story that John Morrison relates came in part from a local man, John Roberts, who was born in 1829 and died 101 years later. The facts behind this account are equally elusive. It was common at that time for people to "adopt" orphans. Unfortunately these children were often treated as slaves rather than members of the family. The situation could be so bad that in one case in 1875 a boy named Lyman Burkhardt was convicted of killing the Scio Township farmer who had taken Lyman in and, some asserted, abused him. The little girl Morrison describes ran away instead. Her name was Lillian Robinson. That may not be her birth name, but it was the name she gave herself. When she fled, she was sixteen years old and completely without education, friends or resources. She turned to the only thing she saw as a possibility; she became a prostitute. Years later in the 1890's when Mr. Morrison was boarding in Ypsilanti, a fellow roomer pointed out a large brick house "near the Lake Shore and Michigan Southern Railroad." "That is Queen Sill's place!" [4] Queen Sill was a large, blond woman who liked to ride in her open carriage to the horse races in Ypsilanti. When Morrison finally saw her in person, he claimed he recognized her. She was the runaway, Lillian Robinson.

Eventually, according to Morrison, Lillian married and moved to Ann Arbor where she and her husband opened a saloon on West Washington Street. Upstairs she (or others in her employ) continued to ply their trade. By 1912 she purchased a dairy farm between Ann Arbor and Ypsilanti. Upon her death three years later, many men boasted of their friendship with her. "She was known from one end of Washtenaw to the other," [5] and her estate was valued, according to Mr. Morrison, at $20,000. That amount would be equivalent to an estate of $426,000 today. Not bad, for a girl who started out with nothing.

In striking ways this scenario fits a woman whose name was Lillian W. Brillinger. She and her husband, Marshall, came to Ann Arbor and occupied a building at 206 W. Washington Street which had been a saloon. There they operated the Horseman's Club circa 1906. The couple then purchased a farm, and Mrs. Brillinger died shortly thereafter at the age of forty-seven. There were no notices of her death except a brief one in the *Ypsilanti Press*. She was buried in Detroit.

Then again, Lillian Brillinger may not be Lillian Robinson. The story may be a composite of several separate stories with a whole lot of rumor tossed in. There is simply no way to tell. It is true that the building at 206 W. Washington in Ann Arbor had a notorious reputation. It had been owned by John Schneider and his wife, Barbara M. Schneider. Schneider's, as the place was called, specialized in homemade wines, liquors, and cigars as well as offering a lunch room. In the 1890's the place was frequented, according to a newspaper article, almost exclusively by students. The "old woman who keeps the joint does not see anything." [6] She operated what was called the "Sunday Club" whereby males purchased a key. Then members were free to use the rooms on the upper floors to entertain the women "of questionable character" who frequented the place. Schneider's closed in 1903 after seven years as a "student resort." It does seem a perfect location for Lillian and Marshal to purchase if she were Queen Sill, but that bit of evidence does not prove she was.

Women such as Mrs. Rapalje and Queen Sill, no matter how well known they might have been in their day, were not, needless to say, among the prominent citizens discussed in Chapman's 1881 *History of Washtenaw County* or Beake's 1906 *Past and Present of Washtenaw County*. And such employment as theirs definitely wasn't mentioned in any of the "how to make money" books written by nineteenth century ladies – but prostitution did exist. It always has existed as one of the ways women earned their livings.

The social problems caused by the potent combination of alcohol and prostitution provoked a widespread clamor demanding better controls. It was no secret that a "significant amount of prostitution centered around the saloon." [7] The University of Michigan tried in the 1860's to avoid such problems by issuing its policy which said that no student was allowed to frequent gaming houses or play at cards. "...drinking in saloons was off limits" as was keeping "company with persons of ill repute." [8] In Ypsilanti, the situation became so problematic that on January 15, 1877, the city passed an ordinance "to prevent vice and immorality." Section three of that ordinance prohibited any female except a wife or daughter of the proprietor from acting as "clerk, servant, agent or waiter" in any place within the city of Ypsilanti that served alcohol. Likewise in Ann Arbor, a self-appointed Citizens' League during the 1880's demanded that officials actually enforce the laws concerning saloons and bawdy houses. Each town wanted to improve its reputation.

Other than prostitutes, women comprised only a tiny number of those convicted of crimes in the nineteenth century. If a woman were arrested, it was usually for something like petty larceny. Such was the case of Sophie Lyons. Sophie was a pickpocket. In 1882 she stole a gold watch from Mrs. Cornwell. She was caught and sentenced to almost five years. Was Lyons a career pick-pocket or just a desperate young woman? I'll leave that for you to decide. Washtenaw County did have other female felons who are interesting simply because they do not fit any stereotype. One of these women was Esther Fuller whose criminal activities came to light one day in May 1858 when Mr. Campion was standing outside his Clothing and Tailoring Emporium enjoying the spring weather. Things were looking up. Mr. Campion, and other shop keepers, had experienced a difficult winter. Ann Arbor had been plagued with burglaries. Someone had broken into his store and stolen $500 worth of clothing. (I suspect Mr. Campion may have exaggerated a bit because that was an enormous sum.) But on that beautiful day in May, Campion came abruptly to attention when he noticed some of his stolen goods walking down the street on the back of Mrs. Fuller's son, James. Campion notified the Marshall who obtained a search warrant and went to the Fuller home.

We don't know much about Mrs. Fuller. She is not in the census. Whether she did not want to be counted or whether the enumerators did not want to count her and her family is unclear, but she left no paper trail except in the local newspapers. She had two sons, Robert and James, and a daughter named Anna. When Deputy Marshalls J. B. Ganson and Lemuel Root arrived at the Fuller house with the warrant, son Robert pointed a loaded pistol at them. The deputies were acquainted with Thomas since he and his friend, Frank Walker, had spent a month in jail the previous January for disrupting religious services at the Methodist Church. Ganson managed to talk Robert into surrendering his weapon, which Mr. Sutherland identified as one of the guns stolen from his shop earlier in the year. By the time the search was over, deputies had uncovered clothing and linens sewn into mattresses and pillows as well as tools, guns and even a violin case unearthed in the cellar. They arrested the whole family. End of the story? Not by a long shot. Because she was a woman, Mrs. Fuller was placed in the "debtor's room" which was not a cell with iron bars. She managed to escape in August by tearing through the ceiling, climbing through an attic window and using the classic bed sheet as a rope trick. Two weeks later she was arrested by N B. Nye in Milwaukee and returned to Ann Arbor for trial.

As her jail break suggests, Mrs. Fuller was neither a passive agent nor innocent dupe. She, in actuality, was the ringleader of the gang. She and her daughter, Anna, were two examples of women who engaged in the popular nineteenth century past-time of cross-dressing. Though it was against the law for women to wear pants in public, many have found it more convenient for farm work. Other girls in all-girl schools would don male attire for dances etc. And some women, finding women's work paid so little, would disguise themselves as men to get a better job. Thousands fought in the Civil War as men. For whatever reason, Esther and Anna apparently not only dressed in men's clothing but donned false mustaches and sideburns to add to their disguises when they went out to commit burglaries. There is no record of what happened to Anna. I suspect she was released; however, Esther received ten years of hard labor for her part in the burglary spree. This time, she did not manage to escape. Her son James also was sent to the state penitentiary.

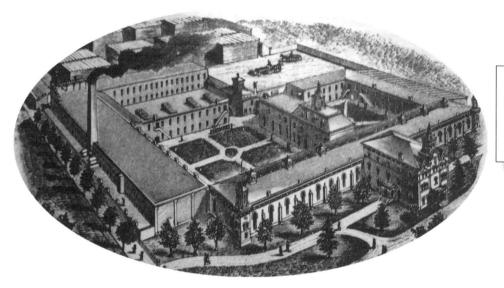

Postcard of Michigan State Prison in Jackson, Michigan

Courtesy of the Bentley Historical Library, University of Michigan

Esther also was a defendant in a second trial that year. In this case, the charge was murder. Her son, Robert, and his friend, Frank Walker, were charged with robbing and killing S. M. Holden in August of the previous year. In early December 1858 the court sentenced Robert and Frank to life imprisonment. The jury did not convict Mrs. Fuller. There is a fascinating epilogue to this trial. Mrs. Holden, the victim's widow, was the beneficiary of $29,000 in life insurance which her husband had taken out just before his death. *The Chicago Press and Tribune* ran an article in October of that year stating that the three insurance companies refused to pay. They accused Mrs. Holden of being a participant in insurance fraud. They claimed that Holden had arranged his own death so that his wife would receive the insurance money. Considering the value of that amount of money, one should not be surprised. In 1858, $29,000 is the equivalent of over $700,000 in today's currency. No wonder the insurance companies shouted fraud.

Fraud was rife in nineteenth century America. Rapid urbanization and improved transportation brought people together in unprecedented numbers. Previously, rural people tended to stay in one place and knew their neighbors. They became comfortable with a handshake and a verbal promise. It was harder for a person to lie when everyone knew him, his parents and maybe his grandparents. Because of this, people tended to be amazingly gullible. They took things at face value and would accept someone with decent clothing and manners as a respectable citizen. Mark Twain immortalized this attribute in the characters populating *The*

Adventures of Huckleberry Finn. Every reader remembers the scams perpetrated on innocent and gullible people by the King and Duke. And don't forget, Huck, though still a boy, was a con artist par excellence.

Ann Arbor and the rest of Washtenaw County were no exceptions to this scenario. *The Ann Arbor Courier* of March 16, 1877 called the area "a rich field." Continuing the metaphor the article stated, "...the crop is fully ripened ready for the sickle of the harvester, all they have to do is to gather the crop." And it did not require an adult worker to do the job. A girl named Ada told her sad story to any lady of apparent means who would listen. She claimed she was an orphan bereft of parental guidance and support needing a Christian home in which she could find affection and protection. How could a charitable soul refuse such a pathetic "child." Mr. and Mrs. Thomas Martyn/Martin who lived at 3 North State Street, took her in - much to their regret. A few days later having cased the house for valuables, Ada absconded with whatever she could carry and sell. The police searched for her, but she was long gone seeking fresher fields for her confidence scheme.

Washtenaw County's most famous female felon was Olive Howard Friend of Milan, Michigan. In the 1880's, Olive, her parents and her first husband, "Professor" Friend, went to New York where they convinced people to invest in their amazing, electric sugar refining machine. The second half of the nineteenth century marked the beginning of the industrialized processing of food. Processed foods were more durable and thus more portable. The Friends were capitalizing on this as well as the new technology of electricity. Edison opened the first American electrical generation station in New York in 1882. By 1888 Westinghouse, who had been operating his own plant in Massachusetts, incorporated the patents of Nikola Tesla to improve his system. Conversations were abuzz with the amazing power of electricity. The only problem was that Olive and the Professor's machine did not do anything. In fact, it did not even exist which is why potential investors were not allowed to see this incredible invention actually work.

The Friends (a rather ironic name for a couple of con artists) said secrecy was necessary "for fear of imitators." The Friends and their gang invited potential investors into a room. There on a platform shrouded in cloth was the machine and bags of raw sugar. But then the investors were asked to step out. They heard lots of grinding and whirring noises. When it stopped, investors entered to find refined sugar. What was truly mindboggling was not the nonexistent machine and nonexistent factory but the fact that people fell for it. In a wild rush to get rich quick, American as well as foreign investors jumped at the opportunity to buy shares in the company. The Friends took in the equivalent of millions of dollars. By 1888, however, the boom was going bust for Olive Friend. Her husband died, some say by suicide. Olive returned to Milan, Michigan, where she had a house already under con-

Hack House in Milan
Courtesy of the Milan Historical Society

struction. She hardly had moved into her grand new home when allegations started to fly and investigations into the Electric Sugar Refining Company began.

Had it been earlier in the century, Olive would never have been arrested in the first place. In the early nineteenth century, a wife could not be held accountable for her husband's crimes even if she aided and abetted them. Consistent with the laws that prohibited married women from owning property or entering into contracts, the courts considered a woman to have been "coerced" by her husband. He would have been at fault, not she. After the Civil War, however, this attitude and the legal codes that reflected it gradually were modified. By 1889 she could no longer plead not-guilty as "the widow of the inventor."

The melodrama opened when William Cotterill, president of the Electric Sugar Refining Company, made statements in January 1889 that he was investigating the fraud. Olive, with equal bombast, sued him for $20,000 in damages to her reputation. In the midst of this free-for-all, a grand jury issued indictments against Olive, her parents and other gang members, and put an injunction on all property owned by them. They were all incarcerated in the Ann Arbor jail awaiting extradition to New York.

By December of that year, Olive Friend was pleading guilty to grand larceny in a court-room in New York. She was thirty-seven years old when she and her whole gang were sent to the New York prison called the "Tombs." It appears that, despite her obvious guilt, she was never actually convicted of any crime. Authorities ultimately released her from jail. Then she married George Halstead, a member of the Milan gang, and moved to Detroit where she died in 1902. Her uncle, Henry Hack, bought her house in Milan. In this way Olive Friend's house, a home built on the ill-gotten proceeds of a truly sweet scam while it lasted, became known as Hack House and today is a museum.

Why these women chose to obtain money through such nefarious ways, no one knows. Their reasons were probably the same as those of today's criminals: need, greed and opportunity. There were plenty of available jobs though admittedly the jobs did not pay very well. But these women could have found legitimate employment if they had wanted to do so. Obviously they did not.

---

[1] Estelle B. Freedman, *Their Sister's Keepers: Women's Prison Reform in America 1830-1930* (Ann Arbor: University of Michigan Press, 1981), 14.

[2] John Morrison *"Memories of Washtenaw County,"* in "John Morrison Papers" at Bentley Historical Library, University of Michigan, 76.

[3] Ruth Rosen, *The Lost Sisterhood: Prostitution in America, 1900-1918* (Baltimore: Johns Hopkins University Press, 1982),

[4] Morrison, "Memories," 70-71.

[5] Morrison, "Local History 1," in "John Morrison Papers" at Bentley Historical Library Univeristy of Michigan, 51-2.

[6] *The Voice* (New York:.June 9, 1898).

[7] Rosen, 184.

[8] Howard Peckham, *The Making of the University of Michigan* (Ann Arbor: University of Michigan Press, 1967), 68.

CHAPTER FOUR: WIVES, WIDOWS AND DAUGHTERS

Many of the women mentioned thus far have been unmarried. It is true that single women predominated in the work force. The stereotype is that married women retired from the employment world in order to dedicate themselves to home and family. And there is a great deal of truth to that generalization Being a homemaker in the nineteenth century, especially the early nineteenth century, was more than a full time job especially if one lived on the frontier which Michigan definitely was. Pioneer women found domestic help extremely scarce at the very time when everything needed to be made at home. As one foreign visitor, Frederick Marryat, wrote in his 1837 *Diary in America*, "The duties of a wife in America are from circumstances very onerous." [1]

Onerous or not, the fact remained that, when a woman married, she surrendered not only her legal right to property and her ability to enter into contracts but her very identity. Symbolic of this is the fact that virtually all women took their husbands' names. Once married, the hypothetical Jane Doe ceased to exist. She became Mrs. John Doe. Etiquette books, even today, encourage this by maintaining that there is no such person as Mrs. Jane Doe. Before the option of the modern title, "Ms.," it was considered polite to address a woman by her status, Mrs., and her husband's name even if he had been dead for decades. Her identity from the time of her marriage resulted from her relationship to him. Only the most ardent feminists, such as Lucy Stone, refused this tradition and kept their own names. Thus, whatever the family's accomplish-

ments, they tended to be attributed to the husband with no reference to the contributions of his wife other than as mother of his children. As a result history has overlooked many women who were working side by side with their spouses in family operated businesses.

This was clearly the case for Mrs. Jacob Aprill, who came to Ann Arbor with her husband, Jacob, soon after their marriage in 1832. Both Magdalena Schnyder and Jacob Aprill

The Aprill family farm as depicted in the
Portrait and Biographical Album

were born in Germany; she in1805, and he in 1808. They met in New York, where he was doing his apprenticeship in shoe making and she was a domestic. Still in their twenties, they arrived with the first wave of German immigrants to Ann Arbor in the early 1830's. Their entire net worth at that time was $200, half of which Magdalena had saved from "wages during her time of service." [2] Considering she only made seventy-five cents a week, that amount is pretty impressive. At the time of their arrival, her husband was the only shoemaker in the area. People traveled ten or fifteen miles to get their shoes resoled, so he had more work than he could do by himself. Magdalena assisted him for fifteen years. This husband and wife partnership in shoemaking was fairly common. The husband usually made the shoe bottoms which required heavier materials, punches and needles. The wife would sew the upper part of the shoe. Magdalena's assistance and frugality helped the family purchase 340 acres of farm land in Scio Township. The couple lived on the farm until 1889 when Magdalena died just nine weeks before her husband. Their grandson, William Aprill, continued operating the farm, and their descendants still live in the area. Aprill Road serves as a reminder of their contribution to the development of the county.

Magdalena Aprill's contemporary, Nancy A. Parsons, worked with not only her first husband but her second husband as well. Miss Parsons, who was born in Massachusetts in 1807, came with her family to Michigan. Her first job was as the teacher at Webster Township's Boyden School. She then married. As Mrs. Eamons (also spelled Eman), she became one of the earliest women in the county to begin a business with her spouse. She and her husband opened a general merchandise store in Dexter in 1836. During the time the Eamons operated their store, Nancy delivered and was raising two children, John born in 1837 and Mary A. in 1839. Sadly, her husband died a year after Mary's birth. Mrs. Eamons ultimately sold the business. In 1851 at age forty-four, Nancy married Professor Rufus Nutting, head of the Lodi Academy which he had established in 1847. Nutting had been widowed in March 1851; therefore he remarried quickly. The second Mrs. Nutting moved into his home and school on the southeast corner of Textile and Ann Arbor-Saline Road. At that time the four corners was called Lodi Plains. Residents had dreams of making it into a town. That never happened since Saline just a few miles south developed more quickly. One of the Academy's buildings still stands but has been divided into apartments.

After her second marriage, Mrs. Nutting served as matron as well as instructor of Latin, Greek and French. Her daughter, Mary, taught music at the Academy before leaving the area to teach in Detroit. Mary went south after the Civil War to educate former slaves. As Professor Nutting approached his eightieth birthday on July 28, he retired and moved with Mrs. Nutting to Detroit. The Professor died just two weeks short of his birthday. His widow and her children continued living in Detroit until Mary married. At that time Mrs. Nutting joined her daughter's household where she lived the rest of her life.

Wives and daughters throughout the nineteenth century worked in family owned businesses. At the turn of the century, Zingerman's, the now famous Ann Arbor destination, was the Disderide (Diz der RI Dee) neighborhood grocery store and residence. Located at 422 Detroit Street, the store was built in 1902. The Disderides who immigrated from Italy in 1881 operated their business until 1921.

Rocco Disderide, when interviewed on his one hundredth birthday in 1957, claimed that the key to his longevity was never to "work very hard." Apparently it was his wife, Katherine, who made sure their store opened early and closed late. According to Milo Ryan, who grew up in the neighborhood and shopped there often, Mrs. Disderide never mastered English but was highly skilled in counting money. Mr. Ryan described her as a "long suffering and over-worked wife."[3] She died in 1940 at age eighty. Even the Disderide daughters – Theresa, Rosa and Henrietta – regularly put their time and energy into maintain-

The Disderide's store which is now Zingerman's

ing the family business. Theirs is one of the most explicit examples of women doing a good deal of the work for which their husbands were getting most of the credit.

Helen Dodge McArthur offered posterity a personal testimony of just how important women were in maintaining family-owned businesses. Her mother, Almira "Allie" Pray, and father, Henry Phelps Dodge, married in December 1891. They then took over a store on Main Street in Whitmore Lake previously owned and operated by Mr. Dodge's mother, Helen L. Dodge. Perhaps because of the ideal location of the store, Mr. Dodge also accepted the duties of postmaster. Later, he decided to expand into the ice business. McArthur recalled, "Our mother helped in the store because Dad had become involved in a second business..."[4] Just how much Allie helped her husband became tragically clear in 1903 when, at age thirty-three, she died suddenly from complications surrounding a miscarriage. "Our father must

The Dodge's store in Whitmore Lake

Courtesy of the Bentley Historical Library, University of Michigan

have had a very bad time during the next few years. He was unable to handle the store, post office and ice house without our mother's assistance. So in 1906, he closed the store, gave up the post office and moved ..."[5]

Women's knowledge of family business affairs did receive quiet legal validation in the sheer number of women whose husbands named them as administratrices for their estates. When Leonard Miller died in 1830, his widow, Rachel, posted notices of her legal role in the

Western Emigrant as the law required. Other men died intestate which meant that the Court had to choose an executor. This was certainly the case for Ephraim Carpenter. On July 23, 1834, the Court appointed Cynthia Carpenter, Ephraim's widow, to serve in that capacity for her late husband. Cynthia, too, had to provide a public notice of that decision. Early newspapers are full of such announcements. Through these notices, we can ascertain that a woman's ability to manage a family's affairs was recognized by both their spouses and by the courts.

Administering a man's estate would not have been that difficult if, as so often was the case, the wife had been working side by side with her husband and thus was well acquainted with his business affairs. According to historian Carl Degler, "That widows did take over their husbands' businesses... certainly attests to the acceptance of women in such roles when necessity required it. But then most people recognized that in such small businesses wives were often as much a part of their husbands' enterprises as farm women were of their husbands'... [such transfer of leadership] was silent but effective testimony to their familiarity with their husbands' enterprises." [6] A century and a half ago most people recognized the fact that wives shared the business, but that is not how the story has been told since.

Despite all the propaganda about the appropriate feminine sphere, the process of women's involvement in business only accelerated mid-century due to the Civil War. Every war has offered women opportunities for fuller participation in life outside of the home. The Civil War of 1861-1865 was no exception. Of the more than 90,000 Michigan men (one fourth of the entire male population) who served in that conflict, most left wives and families behind to carry on with farms and businesses in their absence. Some men, like Taylor Pierce, apologized to their wives in letters saying that their duty to their country had taken precedence over their duty to their wives and children and that for a least a while - and maybe permanently if they were killed- the wife would have to be solely responsible for their affairs. They told their wives they trusted them to do as they saw fit. Pierce owned a sawmill, yet he was confident his wife could use her own judgment about the business. And that is exactly what she and most of the women did.

In towns like Ann Arbor and Ypsilanti where more extensive historical records exist, it is quite obvious that, especially in the post-Civil War period, there was a significant number of wives sufficiently involved in their husband's or father's or even brother's business affairs to be able quickly and efficiently to assume responsibility if their relative died or was unable to manage on his own. Mrs. Catherine Barklay Hangsterfer was one of those wives.

Hangsterfer Hall on the corner of Main and Liberty in Ann Arbor.

Courtesy of the Bentley Historical Library, University of Michigan

After marrying in Pennsylvania in 1849, the Hangsterfers came to Ann Arbor in1853. Catherine's husband, Jacob, immediately began his confectionary business and built Hangsterfer Hall at Main and Washington Streets in 1860. The Hangsterfers sold cigars, ice cream and other goodies on the lower level. The upper story was a ballroom used for meetings and presentations including the 1863 Sanitary Fair which raised money to support the troops. For a decade Hangsterfer's was the preferred venue for musical and theatrical performances until Hill's new Opera House created serious competition.

At the time of Jacob's death at age fifty-two on December 18, 1873, he and his son, Jacob William, were listed as proprietors of Hangsterfer and Son on Main Street. At that time Catherine was forty-seven and the mother of seven children the youngest of whom (Edwin/Edward) was twelve. It would be wonderful to know exactly how she felt at the time, but whatever her personal feelings she took charge of the Main Street business while her son, Jacob William, began a similar business at 36/38 State Street. In a very short time the company's name changed to "Mrs. Jacob Hangsterfer and Son." The "son" seems to have referred not to Jacob William but to another son, Albert Frank, who at eighteen was too young at the time of his father's death to take over the business thus the job fell to his mother. During Mrs. Hangsterfer's time as proprietor, the Hangsterfers expanded the business to include a restaurant which served oysters. It was not until five years later that the name of the company changed again. This time it was "A. Frank Hangsterfer and Co." Even then both his mother and sister, Elizabeth, age thirty, were listed as co-owners. Mrs. Hangsterfer appears to have held together the family business which continued until the early twentieth century.

In a similar fashion, Mrs. Hangsterfer's contemporary Christine Gerstner, despite being a mother of five children, worked side by side with her husband, Louis, in their bakery cum confectionary at 3 Detroit Street, Ann Arbor, from 1868 until he died in the late 1880's. At that time she took charge. The bakery was truly a family affair. Both sons, Fred and William C., baked while daughters, Louisa and Christine M, clerked. By the end of the 1890's Mrs. Gerstner retired. Since she was born in 1829, she worked until she was almost seventy. She was able, at that time, to buy a spacious home at 214 N. Fifth in Ann Arbor where she lived with her daughters: Katherine M.; Louise, a clerk at Mack and Co; and Christine M. who continued clerking at the bakery.

The Bigalke store is on the left in this photo.

Courtesy of the Bentley Historical Library, University of Michigan

Not all widows worked for as long as Mrs. Gerstner. Mary A. Bigalke (1844-1926), the wife of Theodore Bigalke, assumed responsibility for only a few years, but they were critical years. Mr. Bigalke moved to Ann Arbor circa 1868. By 1883 he had progressed from being a laborer to becoming the owner of a grocery, flour and feed store at 29 E. Washington Street. When Mr. Bigalke died in 1886, his son, Frank, was running the store. For some unknown reason, Frank left the store and began working as a butcher for a neighbor, M. Weinmann, whose shop was only a block away at the corner of Fifth and Washington Streets. Whether he did this to make extra money or to learn the butchering trade is not known, but while he was busy with that, Mary ran the grocery store for about four years.

Sometimes it was not the widow but a daughter who assumed command. In each of the following cases, the daughter had established a career of her own which she abandoned upon the death of her father in order to maintain the father's business.

Katie Rogers

Katie Rogers was born in Ann Arbor in 1849, the daughter of Moses and Letitia Rogers. Her only sibling, an older sister, died at age seventeen. Katie, however, graduated from Ann Arbor High School and then in 1876 was first in her class at the Chicago Academy of Design. She returned to Ann Arbor advertising herself as a portrait painter and teacher of drawing. She painted portraits of many local dignitaries including one of James Kingsley, which is now owned by the Washtenaw County Historical Society. Miss Rogers came by her artistic skills quite naturally since her paternal uncle was the nationally recognized sculptor, Randolph Rogers, who created the bronze doors for the Capitol building in Washington D.C. Some of his sculptures are on display at the University of Michigan's Museum of Art. Randolph's brother, Katie's father, had a no less successful career. He began as an employee of Mr. Chapin, a dealer in agricultural implements but soon opened his own

store in 1843. He had a showroom on Catherine Street between Fourth Avenue and Detroit St. After losing his inventory to fire, he moved to 417 Detroit Street. When Moses died in 1888, Katie abandoned her art and took charge of her father's extensive business concerns. For seven years she managed the business. Then in 1895 she sold the company in order to return to her chosen career in art. She died in 1901 at the age of fifty-two. The Rogers home at 121 N. Division still stands as a reminder of the family's accomplishments.

The Rogers home at 121 N. Division St., Ann Arbor, Michigan.

Nellie A. Keal, like Katie Rogers, was a very intelligent and talented young woman. Born in Dexter in 1871, a generation after Rogers, Nellie Keal graduated from Dexter High School in 1890 with a 96% average. As a student, Nellie studied German and Latin as well as history and math - an excellent education for the time. She then opened a millinery shop above her father's novelty store in January, 1898. She hired Nellie Staley as a trimmer. Within two years she was advertising sofa pillow covers and many products such as doilies made of lace. She handled Armenian, Battenberg and Duchess lace.

Within three years she was successful enough to require two assistants, both were married women. After eleven years of steadily expanding her own business, she abruptly abandoned it in order to move downstairs to operate the Novelty Store when her father died in February 1907. The store sold medicines and toilet articles as well as books. The *Dexter Leader* not only ran the advertisements for Miss Keal, it joyfully announced her marriage to Mr. G. Francisco on September 1, 1910. The paper referred to the couple as "two of Dexter's best known young people."

Nor was it always a biological daughter to whom a man or woman left a business. Upon at least one occasion, it was an adopted "daughter." In Ypsilanti, Leopold Shade (also spelled Schade) built the Shade Block in 1871 at Congress and Park His growing businesses included a bakery, confectionery, grocery, hotel and saloon. The grocery occupied the first floor, west side, while a saloon existed on the east side. On the second floor was the Shade residence as well as rooms for tran-

The Keal Family

Courtesy of the Bentley Historical Library,
University of Michigan

sients. These travelers often brought herds of cattle or other animals on their way to market. Others were peddlers and salesmen. The third floor, like Hangsterfer Hall in Ann Arbor, was a dance hall. That part of the building was closed in 1904. Probably the most exciting thing at the Shade's was Leopold's bear. No, it was not a stuffed bear. It was quite alive, much to the fascination of visitors and the terror of the other animals.

The Shade Block in Ypsilanti, Michigan

Courtesy of the Ypsilanti Historical Society

Within seven years Leopold's wife, Kunigunda, was operating the business though Leopold was still alive. In her sixties, Kunigunda received help from two "Miss Shades." They were not Mrs. Shade's daughters but her nieces. Mrs. Shade had brought the girls, their mother and two other siblings from Ohio when their father died. Though Rosa and Lena's real maiden surname was Brooker, the 1880 Census records both young women using the last name of Shade. What happened to Lena and the rest of the family is unclear, but when Mrs. Shade passed away in 1888, it was Rosa who inherited the business. Rosa Brooker Shade later married a man named Smith; however, she continued to manage the Shade Block which under her leadership remained much the same as it had always been – except for the bear. According to her obituary in the *Ypsilanti Press*, July 1935, she "gained a well deserved reputation for business acumen and enterprise." The year Rosa died, the Shade Block was demolished.

In other situations a new owner might have been not a daughter or niece but a daughter-in-law which is what happened in the case of the Lodholz family. The Lodholzes were a German family that came to Washtenaw County and established a business that, thanks to the women of the family, lasted for several generations. Goetlieb Lodholz and his wife Henrica, nee Spathelf, arrived in Ann Arbor in 1854. Mr. Lodholz opened a bakery at #4 Broadway. Their son, William, was seventeen and a student at Ann Arbor High School when his father suddenly died at age forty-six. William quit school in order to help his mother by clerking in the bakery. But it was Mrs. Lodholz who operated the business from 1877 until much later when William took over expanding the store to include #6 Broadway and adding groceries. For many years he remained a bachelor liv-

Rosa Brooker Shade Smith

Courtesy of the Ypsilanti Historical Society

ing with his mother. There is no record of how he met Mary A. Moses of Lansing, Michigan. He married her and brought her to Ann Arbor. In a replication of the parents' experiences, Mary and William had one child, a son named Raymond, who was but ten at the time of his own father's death in 1904.

Lodholz Business Card

Courtesy of the Bentley Historical Library, University of Michigan

Mary, newly widowed, took over management of the store and bakery. She maintained a large factory near the Huron River in what Ann Arborites called Lower Town. She devised an efficient delivery system and utilized new telephone technology to enhance her service to customers. Mary Lodholz seems to have not just duplicated her mother-in-law's experience but to have outdone her, achieving "gratifying success" as a business woman. [7]

Stories of these women and others like them are simultaneously a part and not a part of our history. One has to be terribly patient and observant. Women's history has been lying hidden and relatively dormant for centuries. During all that time no one was interested in looking carefully enough to discover the truth. Sometimes social perceptions and stereotypes hindered the process.

A quick glance at the documentary record as found in the City Directories would suggest that Christian Roth was a bachelor. The existence of Caroline Roth, Christian's wife, was hidden by the fact that she was not mentioned in the City Directories which indicated that her husband, who was a mason in the 1880's expanded his interests by purchasing a saloon circa

1890. Christian and his businesses are listed in all the City Directories of that time. But there is not one mention of Caroline which is unusual since it was customary to note a wife's name at least in parentheses. She, of course, is identified in census records so we know that she was born circa 1856; thus she was three years younger than her husband with whom she bore four children. Then in November 1891 Christian Roth died. Suddenly Caroline's name appears in the City Directory, and for the next six years, she was listed as the proprietor of the saloon at 9 E. Liberty in Ann Arbor.

The Victorian stereotype suggests that no "respectable" women would not enter such a saloon, let alone own and manage it. While mores did change in the nineteenth century, if we look beneath the surface, history tells us that women have been involved with taverns both as patrons and proprietors throughout American history. This is one area of women's employment that is well documented because all taverns back to the colonial era had to have a license. Thus we know that in Boston 30-40% of the tavern licenses were given to women. Portsmouth, N. H., had a similar situation with 38% of its taverns owned and operated by women. Portsmouth's earliest documented example would be Mrs. Thomas Harvey, a widow, whose tavern, established in 1697, was used for town and General Assembly meetings as well as a postal center. Her daughter-in-law, Ann, took charge when the elder Mrs. Harvey died. We should not assume that these women were disreputable in any way. Just the opposite is true. In order to apply for a license, they would have to have had the approval of their communities and the government. They were required to post a bond guaranteeing the "orderliness" of the place. Their licenses could be revoked if they ran a "disorderly house." This is why people used the term "disorderly house" when they meant a brothel. Due to that threat or just because they were women with a greater affinity towards cooking and cleaning, female owners tended to run good clean taverns which, in turn, made them very successful in a competitive business.

Laws had changed somewhat by the time when Mrs. Roth assumed command of her husband's business in 1892, but I suspect a woman who owned and operated a tavern/saloon still had to be very circumspect about the reputation of herself and her establishment. Any suggestion of riotous behavior or sexual impropriety occurring there would have been duly noted by the community as it was in several cases mentioned in Chapter 3. So we should not be surprised to find Mrs. Roth in such a business endeavor. Nor was she alone. Her contemporary, Catherine Girbach, a widow, had a similar establishment in Chelsea. Two decades earlier in the 1870's, Catherine Schumacher ran one of the eighty saloons in Ann Arbor. There is no mention of a Mr. Schumacher. And Mrs. Schumacher was not alone in her tavern trade at that time. Mrs. Anna Vogel in Ypsilanti, Mrs. Catherine Traub in Manchester and Mrs. May Golden in Chelsea also operated saloons.

Another case of stereotyping skewing the public record concerns Mrs. Catherine Caspary. In her situation, her husband was very much alive; however, according to their daughter, theirs was not a harmonious marriage, which made working together difficult. After ten years of operating together a grocery and bakery at 15 Ann Street, Ann Arbor, William started a saloon nearby at Fourth and Ann in 1886. Catherine remained at the bakery. Three years later Mrs. Caspary was operating a restaurant in addition to the bakery. Meanwhile her husband, having failed at the saloon business, moved to Chelsea where he, too, set up a bakery and restaurant. Then in 1898 William and his wife were together again temporarily running the business in Ann Arbor while daughter, Kate was a seamstress; daughter, Frances, a vocal music performer and teacher; and their youngest daughter, a stenographer. They had, in addition, two sons both named William, like their father; however, only the younger one survived to adulthood. Apparently the business partnership again did not prove harmonious. Husband William returned to Chelsea while Mrs. Caspary continued living and working in Ann Arbor with her four unmarried children.

The Caspary home.
424 N. State Street in Ann Arbor, MI

Louis Doll's family moved next door to the Caspary's house in the early twentieth century when he was a boy. In his recollection written many years later, Doll unintentionally sent a slanted, yet very typical, message to posterity. He mentions that Mrs. Caspary "ran the Ann Arbor Shop" when Mr. Caspary moved to Chelsea. He also tells us that Mrs. Caspary bought the house on State Street. He even notes that the family had a cottage on Whitmore Lake, and that Frances' music education was costly. In addition he claims, "The only time they [Mr. and Mrs. Caspary] saw each other was when Mrs. Caspary went to Chelsea to get money to run the Ann Arbor household." [8] All of those statements are true. The problem is that his article makes it sound like Mr. Caspary was the hard working, primary bread winner for the family. In a way, even that has some truth to it – at least for a few years. Mrs. Caspary appears to have retired circa 1906 while Mr. Caspary continued to work in Chelsea until his death circa 1913. For those seven years, during which Doll lived next door, she may have gone to her estranged husband for support. But what Mr. Doll does not discuss is how Mr. Caspary's business failures affected the family. He also does not give sufficient credit to Mrs. Caspary for her years of toil which contributed significantly to the financial security upon which the family of seven relied for its comfortable lifestyle. Mr. Doll's omissions, I am sure, were not calculated distortions. They simply reflect the bias of his era concerning the activities of women outside the home. His was a sin of omission more than one of commission, but since his article was published, it became part of the historical record thus helping to perpetuate the stereotype.

Though some might claim that farming does not qualify as working "outside the home," a study such as this would be remiss not to mention the multitude of farmers' wives who worked side-by-side with their husbands and frequently carried on after their spouses' deaths. Few farmers saw fit to credit in print the vast contributions their wives made to their success. Squire Price was an exception. The Prices owned 120 acres in Ypsilanti Township where they raised three children. Mr. Price proudly announced in the *Portrait and Biographical Album* that he couldn't have done it without his wife. Maria Waterford Price was "a woman of unusual managerial qualities, prudent and industrious who has been to him a most able helpmate." [9] Most farmers' wives had to wait for their husbands to die before they received any credit for their labors.

The earliest case of a husband passing away and his wife assuming responsibility for the property was the death of Samuel McMath. Colonel McMath came to Ypsilanti area in 1825. He purchased land and returned to New York to buy seed. He again traveled to Ypsilanti in 1825 with his two oldest sons to begin the clearing and planting and building of a log cabin. Before his wife and their other seven children could arrive, however, he died. Mrs. McMath emigrated anyway, maintained the farm and raised her nine children to adulthood. In this way she perfectly illustrates Frederick Marryat's 1837 comment about American women. "The independence and spirit of an American woman who is left a widow without resources, is immediately shown; she does not sit and lament but applies herself to some employment so that she may maintain herself and her children, and seldom fails in so doing." [10]

Colonel McMath was the second recorded death in Ypsilanti and Washtenaw County. Nathan Brundage was Northfield Township's first. Brundage died soon after purchasing a farm there in 1829. His death left his wife with four children and a farm to run. Just a few years later the 1834 cholera epidemic took George Sessions, another resident of Northfield Township. He had arrived the previous year at which time he purchased 480 acres. He and his wife, Eunice Mather Sessions, a descendant of Cotton Mather, had eight children to support. She, too, must have been successful keeping the farm going because their oldest son, Hanson, later inherited it from her.

Such stories were not uncommon. The 1850 Census indicates that in Dexter alone four women, in their thirties and forties, declared themselves to be farmers without any spouses. Their property values ranged from $400 to $7,000. One female head-of-household, Abigail Boyden, probably was a second wife because she was only nine years older than the eldest of her six "sons." Unfortunately for posterity, few women who found themselves in such circumstances had sufficient leisure time to leave any written account of their experiences.

Laura Haviland, abolitionist.

Courtesy of the Bentley Historical Library,
University of Michigan

Laura Smith Haviland, a Quaker woman who settled near Adrian, was the proverbial exception to that generalization. She published an autobiography in 1881. Her story, called *A Woman's Life Work*, went into three editions. Though Adrian is just west of Washtenaw County, her voice surely represents the experiences of women a few miles away.

Mrs. Haviland's mother, sister, husband and baby all died in 1845 leaving her with seven remaining children and $700 indebtedness. She calmly took stock of the farm assets and the family's debts. Then she went to see each creditor to arrange for future payment. One man told her, "You do not think of taking your husband's business and carrying it forward, do you?" She replied, "I thought of trying to do the best I could with it." "With a look of surprise, he said firmly, 'You are very much mistaken, Mrs. Haviland; you cannot do any such thing; you had much better appoint some man in whom you have confidence to transact your business for you.' " [11] Naturally, she ignored his advice and continued with her efforts until she was successful.

Mrs. Haviland had married at sixteen and traveled with her husband in 1829 to Michigan "to share in the privations of a new country as well as advantages of cheap land."[12] She was an altruistic person who helped organize Michigan's first anti-slavery society and maintained a principal stop on the Underground Railroad. She also began a school for indigent children which she funded herself. Later Mrs. Haviland expanded her efforts into a higher level school on the Oberlin plan; that is a school which does not discriminate on the basis of gender, religion or race. During the Civil War, she traveled extensively collecting and distributing supplies, inspecting hospitals, and generally taking care of whatever needed to be done even if it were making sure three thousand soldiers imprisoned for petty offenses on Jail Island, Lousiana, were freed to return to the battlefield. The man who told her she "could do no such thing" obviously underestimated Mrs. Haviland's character.

Though most farming women did not leave any personal accounts such as that written by Mrs. Haviland, many were left with large Washtenaw County farms after their husbands' deaths. Some found the challenge more than they could or wanted to handle. Others were very successful. Both John Morrison and Chapman relate the story of Mrs. Mary Ann Wilcox. Born in Ireland in 1825, her family came to Scio Township in 1833. She married Jason Wilcox with whom she had three sons: Henry, Edward and David. There is some confusion as to whether Mr. Wilcox died or they divorced. Local memoirs say he died; however, the 1880 U.S. Census states that Mrs. Wilcox is divorced. In any case, she was without a spouse for many years. Son Henry died, and Edward moved away, but David, the youngest, stayed home. He and Mrs. Wilcox continued operating the 160 acre farm. John Morrison makes it clear, however, that it was Mrs. Wilcox, not David, who was in charge. According to Morrison, she ruled "with a rod of iron." Morrison also described their home in 1898 as the most modern dwelling on the Ann Arbor-Dexter Road, one that was filled with "fine furnishings" suggesting that she was pretty successful at farming. [13] Mrs. Wilcox died at the home of her son Edward in Emmett, Michigan, in 1912.

A contemporary of Mrs. Wilcox's was Betsey A. McComber of New York. She was born in 1814, the daughter of Zebadee and Rebecca McComber. In 1836 Betsey married a farmer, Charles Treadwell, who later would be remembered eponymously for the development of a strain of wheat named for him. Together they had five children; three survived. After her husband's death in 1892, Mrs. Treadwell continued operating "one of the finest farms in the community." Her efforts made her widely known as "a woman of unusual ability in the line of business"[14] Mrs. Treadwell died in 1899 in Saginaw, but both she and her husband are buried in Ann Arbor.

There was even a farming widow whose name was Farmer. Julia arrived in Ann Arbor in 1831 at the age of eleven. There she met and married her husband, William Farmer. Together they worked 120 acres and had two children. Mr. Farmer, however, died in 1859, leaving the farm in the charge of his wife. It may have become too much of a burden, for fifteen years later she was living in Ann Arbor working as a laundress. Being a laundress seems equally exhausting. Perhaps she just wanted to be closer to her daughter who was living there since her marriage to James Davis in 1864. Then in the early 1880's, Mrs. Farmer converted her home at #37 Broadway into a boarding house. Three years later she moved a few doors down the street to #41 where she again operated a boarding house. In 1886 she had six boarders: five females and one male. She died nine years later in Ann Arbor.

Mrs. Louisa Douglas Ticknor's husband was alive but never at home; hence, the full responsibility fell to her. Her family was one of the first in Pittsfield Township. They arrived in 1826, the same year as her birth. Eighteen years later she married Giles W. Ticknor with whom she had two surviving children: Luther and Louise. Giles doesn't appear to have been around the farm much. First he taught school, and then he spent fifteen years in California. Three of those years were with the army. He did not return to Pittsfield until 1867, five years before his death. So it would appear that Mrs. Ticknor maintained the dairy farm and raised the children. "The pleasant home now occupied by Mrs. Ticknor is the result of her own industry and energy ... she was engaged in dairying business in which she was successful." [15] Though at one time four generations of Ticknors lived at her house, it was her grandson Frank, Luther's son, born in 1867 who, with several hired hands, helped her work the farm.

Susan C. Cox's career was the most varied of any of these Washtenaw County farming women. She was born in 1831 in Batavia, New York. Before she married in 1858, she studied at Oberlin College, one of the earliest institutions of higher learning open to women. She remained in Ohio working as the principal of a high school. At age twenty-seven, she married Philander Chandler, also a graduate of Oberlin as well as Medina College where he received a law degree. For a while they maintained 700 acres of land even though Mr. Chandler was working as a traveling salesman. They sold that land and came to Ann Arbor where she managed an inn called Chandler House. They exchanged the inn a year later for the 148 acre Booth farm in Pittsfield Township. Philander passed away in 1888, but she continued the farm demonstrating to everyone that Mrs. Chandler was "a thorough and active business woman." [16]

It was not only wives who assumed the responsibility for family farms. It was daughters, too. Misses Jeanette and Elvira/Alvira Waterbury were the daughters of Ira Waterbury. Their parents came to Washtenaw County in 1854 from New York and bought a 116 acre farm in Ypsilanti Township. First their mother died in 1879, and then their father in 1886. Usually a son would take control of the farm, and Jeanette and Elvira did have an older brother, John. John, however, either before or after his marriage, moved to Dekalb, Illinois, where he had his own farm thus leaving the property in Washtenaw County to his sisters. Since both women were in their thirties when their father died, they would have been considered spinsters. That would not mean they could not marry but that it looked less likely. The sisters were listed as joint proprietors in one source while another states that it was the younger, Jeanette, who ran the farm. The two statements are not necessarily contradictory. They both probably owned it, but Jeanette handled the business of farming. Elvira passed away in 1899, so Jeanette, age sixty-six, continued operating the farm. Her obituary adds that Jeanette "superintended the affairs of the place until coming to Ypsilanti" [17] where she lived the rest of her life. Jeanette lived until the 1930's which means she was in her late nineties or even early hundreds when she died. She is buried in Ypsilanti's Highland Cemetery.

These women were part of Michigan's most important industry in the nineteenth century. Its produce was far more valuable than that of mining or lumber. As late as 1900, sixty percent of Michigan's population remained agrarian. In the United States Census of that year, almost 300,000 women throughout the United States were counted as farmers, planters or overseers. Some established farms without any male support; most were widows. Virginia Penny did not know any of these facts when she wrote her book, *How Women Can Make Money,*

Married or Single, yet in it she exclaimed, "With industry and enterprise what may not woman accomplish! We have heard of women in Ohio and Michigan that not only carry on farms, but do the outdoor work."[18] Miss Penny wrote her book in 1862.

> Michigan State University was originally Michigan Agricultural School. Classes for men only began in 1857. Women were not accepted as students until 1870.

What may not women accomplish indeed! Wives, widows and daughters not only performed traditional domestic services and taught and farmed, but had, in some cases, highly unusual and quite unexpected occupations. Throughout the United States women worked as bakers, and bankers, clockmakers and clergywomen, agents and auctioneers. It is true that men and women, unless they were a husband and wife team, normally labored in quite separate realms. This would be particularly true when it came to heavy physical labor, but even then exceptions existed. One Washtenaw County woman earned her living in the 1880's as a whitewasher. Painting fences and barns certainly placed her well outside the "proper sphere" for a woman. And Martha Drew Smith from Dexter trained as a blacksmith, a trade she practiced after her marriage and removal to New York. Another Dexter woman cleaned barns and stables for a living circa 1893. An article in the *Ypsilanti Commercial* states this was no passing fancy but her "regular" work. Mrs. Julie Macoby of Ann Arbor was a forty-five year old widow in 1860 with two daughters to support. She made specialty papers. And Serena Becraft, widow of H.L. Becraft also lived in Ann Arbor with her teenage son. She was a taxidermist.

So we should not be surprised to learn about Ora Cooley (or Celley in some computerized records) who identified herself to the 1850 census enumerator as a female, aged forty-six with her occupation as "brickmaker." Ora at the time lived with sixty-eight year old Irena Cooley. Irena was probably her mother-in-law since Ora was born in Germany while Irena said she was born in Massachusetts. No male existed in the household suggesting that the women were on their own thus in need of income. Just below their names is that of John Magee. Magee was probably a neighbor because the census enumerators went by neighborhood. Magee's occupation is also listed as "brickmaker." It is highly probable, therefore, that Ora worked with or for him. If this scenario is correct, as it certainly seems to be, Ora would not be as unique as she might seem. *Popular Science Monthly* in an 1880 article concerning women's employment listed seventy-four female bricklayers in the United States. That number was probably quite conservative since the numbers cited for other occupations were significantly low when compared to other sources. If a woman could lay a brick, she certainly could make a brick.

Neither did Amelia Volz Muehlig, wife of John, subscribe to the cult of leisure so popular at that time. Instead she contributed her efforts toward the family's income in three realms during the early 1880's. She is listed as an upholsterer, a dealer in furniture, and an undertaker. All of these endeavors took place at the same address as her husband's carpentry business address at 37 S. Main. How long she participated in the business is unclear. Since she and her husband had five children (Florian, Bertha, Edward, Ernest and Walter), she may have excused herself from the business as soon as it was sufficiently successful to allow her to focus her energies on the home since her children were still young.

Finally, such a study as this would not be complete without mentioning Mary McCormick and her husband, Charles, who ran the County Poor House or Poor Farm, which had been established in 1836-7. In 1860 the facility changed to the Washtenaw County Poor House and Insane Asylum. Many of its residents were aged or senile. It was actually Charles whom the county appointed in 1887, but Mrs. McCormick truly functioned his partner in all things. Mrs. McCormick was born Marian/Mary Ann Minton. She married Charles in 1851. A few days after her death in June, 1910, the Pioneer Society met in Saline, Michigan, and paid tribute

County Poor Farm as portrayed in the 1874
Atlas of Washtenaw County

to her contributions to Washtenaw County. Not only did Mrs. McCormick supervise the work of the inmates, she was responsible for producing all their clothing. The McCormicks' leadership resulted in a more comfortable situation for the inmates while simultaneously reducing the county's financial burden for their support. The speaker in Saline described Mary as always kind and sympathetic towards the unfortunates in her care and praised her garden as a thing of wonder to anyone who passed by the County Farm. The Poor Farm buildings were razed in 1917; however, Mrs. McCormick would, no doubt, be very pleased to know that the property, which is on Platt Road just south of Washtenaw Avenue in Ann Arbor, is now a county park.

The prize for the most unusual combination of occupations with which a woman sought to support herself and her family would go, without a doubt, to Sophia M. Pierce (Mrs. Nathan) whose husband died in 1862. Mrs. Pierce, born in 1828 in New York, was nineteen when she married Nathan Pierce, who served as Ann Arbor's city marshal. They had five children, three of whom survived. While busy raising her family in Ann Arbor's Lower Town, she served within various philanthropic groups and was an active member in the Pioneer Society. Chapman claims she "probably has done more work and toiled longer for the benefit of that organization than any other of its lady members." [19]

In addition to publishing her poetry and volunteering with the fledgling historical society, she served as an enumerator for the fifth (where she lived) and sixth wards in the 1880 U.S. Census. According to Chapman, She was "probably the only lady to be engaged in that business throughout the state of Michigan." [20] Mrs. Pierce's most interesting career, however, was as a magnetic healer and clairvoyant physician which she practiced in her home on Pontiac Trail.[21]

Tracing its lineage back to the Greeks, magnetic healing's nineteenth century incarnation began with Franz Anton Mesmer who coined the term, "animal magnetism," which he said was a combination of gravitational and magnetic forces. Louis XIV of France established a Royal Commission to investigate Mesmer's claims. The commissioners, one of whom was Benjamin Franklin, reported that they could find no such biophysical powers. Thomas Jefferson, who had just arrived in France in 1784, wrote in his journal, "Animal magnetism is dead." That certainly was one of several issues about which Jefferson was mistaken. Magnetic healing was wildly popular in the United States after the Civil War (but then so were séances) even though the American Medical Association labeled it a hoax. It remained popular particularly in the Midwest. Traveling salesmen and catalogues purveyed a host of magnetic products including insoles, waistcoats, and corsets. C.J. Thatcher, who established the Chicago Magnetic Company, offered circa 1886 an entire outfit with more than seven hundred magnets and claimed it could cure anything. In fact, Emily A. Remington, a dressmaker in Ypsilanti at that time, became the agent for Dr. George Scott's Electric Corsets. Scott, an Englishman, patented his "electro-magnetic" products in the 1880's and 1890's. His advertisements in *Harpers Weekly, Century* and other magazines extolled the curative power of magnetism (not electricity). "Their therapeutic value is unquestioned." He even sold electric curry combs for ailing or weak horses. Whatever the problem, he assured readers that his products would cure it. [22]

On the other side of Mesmerism lay the beginnings of the science of hypnosis. Some scientists suggested that it was not the magnets but the hypnotic suggestion that had a "curative" value. At first simply a performance of putting people into trances, it was used later by healers. Others believed that, an "operator" could go into such a trance and see the diseased areas of the patient's body. Mrs. Pierce may have trained with Dr. Albert C. Kellogg to whom she referred as "a clairvoyant physician of considerable skill." [23] Dr. Kellogg, like his father, practiced traditional medicine as well but found clairvoyant medicine took most of his time. His father had claimed that during hypnotic sleep he would discover remedies for diseases and could see a patient's organs in color.

Mrs. Pierce remained a practitioner for about a decade. In a petition to the Ann Arbor City Council May 23, 1890, she declares herself to be a "registered physician" who was severely injured when she left the home of Eli Moore where she was attending a patient. It was late at night and very dark. Mrs. Pierce fell down a steep embankment which had been dug by the city but which had no protective fence. She fell twenty-five feet, breaking several ribs, spraining her ankle and being knocked unconscious. Her injuries prevented her from working for several weeks; therefore, she sought damages from the city.

Mrs. Pierce clearly was a formidable woman of great energy and ingenuity, but the most adventurous wife was Julia Silk. Despite the fact that census information shows her family in Canton, Michigan, when the Civil War began, Mrs. Silk continually stated she was from Ann Arbor which is where her mother lived. Julia was a working class wife and mother, who accompanied her husband when he left to fight in the Civil War. The Silks had two children at the time: Julia, 8, and Charles, two. She left both children with her sixty-five year old mother, Mary Goritte [sic].

Julia was not the only woman from Michigan to participate in the war. The most famous was – and still is – Sarah Emma Edmunds from Detroit, who had donned men's clothing and was selling religious books throughout the Midwest before enlisting as Frank Flint Thompson to fight beside the male soldiers. Edmunds/Thompson also served as a spy and a nurse. In a more conventional manner, Hannah Glover Carlisle from Buchanan, Michigan, and Jennie Fyfe from Lansing each volunteered as nurses and were stationed at Kentucky hospitals in Columbus and Paducah, respectively. Mrs. Carlisle's reason for volunteering was patriotism. Because she later taught in a school for newly freed African-Americans, Miss Fyfe may have been one of the many who toiled out of a sense of Christian duty which was a very common reason. Julia Silk's stated rationale for going to the war, however, was to be with her husband, Thomas, and do whatever she could to bring him home alive.

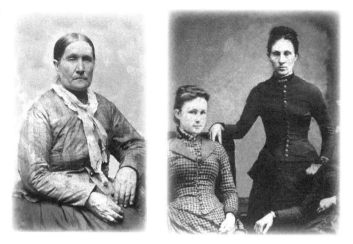

Julia Silk, left, and her daughters; battlefield-born Jennie, right, and Mattie.

Courtesy of the Sweeny Family

Silk's first husband, Gilbert Anderson, had headed west in search of gold and never returned. Julia did not intend to lose her second spouse. Thomas Silk, age thirty-eight, enlisted on March 1862 in an Illinois regiment which was recruiting in Detroit. He probably chose this regiment instead of a Michigan one because its men were primarily Irish Catholics led by Colonel James A. Mulligan of Illinois. Mulligan recruited men from Ohio as well for his 23rd Illinois Volunteers. Originally Thomas was performing guard duty in Chicago, but when his regiment was ordered east where the real war raged, Julia, age thirty-two, decided to go too.

"God must have sent you," exclaimed the Colonel when she arrived. "We are in need of nurses." [24] So she nursed and cooked and laundered and even stood guard duty proving herself so useful that upon one occasion, when the other women were left behind, Colonel Mulligan smuggled her to the front lines in a supply wagon. Another time she appropriated an abandoned home only to be surprised when the family suddenly returned. They were angry, assuming they had been robbed in their absence. Mrs. Silk calmed their fears showing them where she had buried their silver in the back yard and how she had cared for their animals and even baked bread. And then Mrs. Silk walked away, leaving their house to its owners. After that experience, she served at some of the most ferocious battles such as Gettysburg and Petersburg. In the midst of all of that, she delivered a baby girl, Jennie, whom she tucked under her arm as she roamed the battlefields with water for the wounded.

Mrs. Silk was quite willing to do whatever needed doing but, as she says in her memoir, her "circumstances in life were very moderate." [25] In other words, she had no supporting income arriving from family back home. She told the military, "I was willing to lend my assistance as far as lay in my power for whatever remuneration might be judged sufficient recompense for my services." Nowhere in her fairly short autobiography does she ever mention being paid in cash. She did receive, however, compensation in the form of government transportation and rations. And she and Thomas returned home safe and sound just in time to be honored at the big Fourth of July celebration in 1865. "I was invited," recalled Mrs. Silk, "by William S. Maynard, mayor of Ann Arbor, to sit as his table and was crowned queen of the occasion, being the only lady present who had been to the war." [26]

The Silks moved to Windsor, Ontario, circa 1870. Their third daughter Martha/Mattie was born in Michigan 1868 while their son George was born in Canada 1873. Thomas passed away circa 1893. Julia died in January 1901, one week after the death of her battlefield-born daughter, Jennie.

Nineteenth century social conventions have camouflaged the true role of women. Primary sources, such as city directories, newspapers etc., did not value their activities; therefore, they did not include much information about them. If one truly looks, however, one finds evidence which clearly demonstrates that women, whether they were wives or daughters, very often functioned as silent, invisible partners in "male" enterprises. Their efforts not only helped support themselves and their families; they provided the necessary training for the women to assume total responsibility in the case of the husband's or father's disability or death. The stereotype of nineteenth century women which maintains that only single women or widows worked is obviously flawed. Married women may have sacrificed their own names and their legal rights when they married, but they were actively involved in their families' business affairs.

---

[1] Frederick Marryat, *Diary in America* (London: Longman, Orme, Brown, Green and Longmans, 1839), 420.

[2] *Portrait and Biographical Album of Washtenaw County* (Chicago: Biographical Publishing Co., 1891),537.

[3] Milo Ryan, *View of a Universe* (Ann Arbor, McNaughton and Gunn, 1985), 137.

[4] Thomas Hennings, *Looking Back* (Whitmore Lake, MI: Northfield Township Historical Society, 1985), 194.

[5] Hennings, 197.

[6] Carl Deglar, *At Odds: Women and Family* (New York: Oxford University Press, 1980), 360.

[7] Samuel Beakes, *Past and Present Washtenaw County, Michigan* (Chicago: St. Clarke Publishing Co.,1906), 305.

[8] Louis Doll, "Frances Caspary, Soprano," *Impressions* (Ann Arbor,: Washtenaw County Historical Society, April 2000), 1-2.

[9] *Portrait*, 280.

[10] Marryat, 420.

[11] Laura Smith Haviland, *A Woman's Life Work* (Grand Rapids, MI: S .B. Shaw, 188), 47.

[12] Haviland, 29.

[13] John Morrison, "Local History 1," in "John Morrison Papers" at Bentley Historical Library, University of Michigan, 17.

[14] *Portrait*, 246.

[15] *Portrait*, 290.

[16] *Portrait*, 604.

[17] *Portrait*, 276.

[18] Virginia Penny, *The Employment of Women* (Boston: Walker, Wise and Co., 1863), 136.

[19] *History of Washtenaw County, Michigan* (Chicago: Charles C. Chapman Co., 1881), 1033.

[20] History, 1033.

[21] Mrs. John V. Cook of Ypsilanti advertised in the March 14, 1875 *Ypsilanti Chronicle* as a "clairvoyant and electrician."

[22] Before you start shaking your head over the naiveté of such beliefs, try googling "magnetic healing" and see all the products and opinions concerning this alternative approach. Magnetic healing is alive and well in the twenty-first century.

[23] History, 436.

[24] Julia Silk, *The Campaign of Julia Silk* (Ann Arbor: Courier, 1892), 7.

[25] Silk, 1.

[26] Silk, 40.

CHAPTER FIVE: WOMEN WHO TAUGHT

Certainly an educated, middle class woman would not want to be a domestic servant, laundress or dyer/scourer. Nor would she choose to work in a mill or factory, let alone be a prostitute. And, unlike Olive Friend, few women of this class chose crime as a way of life. Most middle class women who did work became teachers. Until the nineteenth century, teaching had been a profession dominated by men. Various historical factors converged to change that. The population of the United States was exploding while social and financial advancement demanded a more educated populace. Thus there was a shortage of teachers at the very time that demand for them was high. Another influence was that teaching never paid very well. A man could make a lot more money in some other employment. The century was chock full of opportunities for a man to make his fortune. Meanwhile the strident voices of women such as Emma Willard and Catherine Beecher were advocating improved education for women to prepare them for careers in education. Teaching was appealing to women of a certain class because there was no negativity associated with it. According to Caroline Bird in *Enterprising Women*, "Teaching was an occupation that enhanced a woman's femininity. Her contribution was to extend one of the functions of a traditional mother beyond the home to paid employment..." This rationale "was eventually applied to social work, nursing, secretarial work and even library work. Anything that can be interpreted as helping people has automatically become woman's work- and underpaid- because women were expected to work, in part at least, 'for love.' " [1]

Education was clearly an important element of Washtenaw County's pioneer existence. Despite the arduous work of building a cabin, clearing the land and planting crops, early settlers immediately wanted to provide schools for their children. Only a few families comprised the township of Pitt (now called Pittsfield), but they were large families that wanted schooling for their children. So anxious were they that classes began before the township could finish erecting its first log schoolhouse. Miss Elsada Fairbrother taught that summer session under a big oak tree beside Mallett's Creek. The site of that tree and the school house is located just south of Packard Road and east of Platt Road on Pittsview Drive. The residents of Pitt then hired Miss Harriet Parsons, daughter of local pioneers, Roswell and Agnes Parsons, to teach at the new school in 1825. Miss Parsons was twenty-one years old. She moved to Ann Arbor in 1829 to replace Miss Monroe, Ann Arbor's first teacher who had died. Unfortunately Miss Parson's health was not strong either. In both 1829 and 1830 she found herself too ill to finish either school year.

Harriet Parsons Mills

Courtesy of the Bentley Historical Library,
University of Michigan

Parsons' stay in Ann Arbor, however, did lead to her marriage to Lorin Mills. Mills, his parents and his siblings came to Ann Arbor in 1825 as the result of a serendipitous encounter with John Allen, one of Ann Arbor's founders. Allen had come to Mills' tailor shop in Buffalo, New York, to have his jacket mended. While Allen waited, he raved about the beauties and opportunities of the Michigan Territory. Mills was hooked. He moved to Ann Arbor opening the first tailor shop west of Detroit just a few years before Harriet Parsons arrived in town. He also built the first brick house in Ann Arbor at Main and Liberty Streets for his growing family. Harriet Parsons Mills, despite bouts of ill health, became the mother of four children, two boys and two girls and lived in Ann Arbor until she died in 1860. She was buried in Forest Hill Cemetery.

The Ypsilanti Historical Society has retained the most complete record of teachers during those early days of settlement. Those records illustrate a fairly typical scenario. The first pioneers to the area settled in Woodruff's Grove on the east bank of the Huron River in 1823. Just a year later, Mark Norris hired Mrs. Ruth Freeman to teach school using his own home since there was no separate school building. Other settlers, however, bought land on the west side of the river. The Huron River was, therefore, a mixed blessing to the area's residents. It offered water, transportation and energy but also divided the two tiny settlements. The story of its first teachers mirrors the evolution of the city itself. [2]

Miss Olive Gorton was one of the west side settlers. She came from New York with her parents, Job and Sarah Gorton. They traveled on the Lake Erie Schooner "Red Jacket," transferring in Detroit to a barge plying the Huron River. This was a very common way early emigrants arrived. Many may have originated in New England, but New York was the jumping off point for even those pioneers. Miss Gorton, who had taught in New York since she was fifteen, established her Washtenaw County school immediately after arriving in 1825. Since the Huron River separated potential students from her school and there was as yet no bridge, she personally rowed east-side children across in order to attend class and then rowed them back home after school dismissed. Miss Gorton taught only one year before marrying Lyman Graves, but she lived within three miles of her little school until her death in 1880. She was eighty-two.

Hope Johnson grabbed the educational baton immediately. She, too, was newly arrived in the area. Miss Johnson came to Michigan with Sylvanus and Nathan Noble and their families because her sister was married to Sylvanus. Unlike Olive, Hope opened her school on the east side of the Huron River in Woodruff's Grove. That school also did not last long since the Nobles continued moving westward ultimately settling in Dexter. Hope eventually married a Noble cousin from Cleveland.

During the interim between her teaching in Ypsilanti and her marriage, however, Hope Johnson's career intertwined with that of Harriet Parsons, for it was Hope who replaced Miss Parsons for the 1829 and 1830 terms. According to Elizabeth Allen, the mother of John Allen, Miss Johnson was "obliged to walk quite a distance from down the river. The exposure in all weathers with but indifferent protection against the cold and wet, injured her health, and one day she informed the school she would not be able to teach any longer. James, one of Elizabeth's grandchildren, ran home begging her to allow the teacher to live with her. Mrs. Allen immediately said, "Yes." [3] In this way, Ann Arbor's school continued to provide itself with a good teacher.

Teacher shortages continued well past the period of initial settlement in the 1820's. Any qualified new arrival was put immediately to work. Such was the case for sixteen-year-old-Fidelia D. Randall who came to Bridgewater with her parents and seven siblings in the fall of 1836. It took them two and a half days to make the journey from Detroit to their new home. No sooner had the family arrived than she agreed to teach at the local school. Fidelia did so both that fall and the next summer in the first schoolhouse in that township. Miss Randall later married another teacher, David Palmer, and was still a Bridgewater resident in 1881.

Most of the teachers in those little schools were young women, like Fidelia, who tantalize us with their presence but have passed on with little if any fanfare or notice though their names are frequently noted. The fact that many of the earliest schools did not remain for long and most teachers stayed as little as a term exacerbates the problem for researchers. Mary Davis Harris of Clinton recalled only one teacher she had as a child circa 1872 in Tecumseh, Michigan. Harris remembered Miss Sarah L. Train only because she had remained longer than most. Mrs.

Bridgewater School circa 1900.

Courtesy of the Kinsvater family

Harris' school experienced a turnover of twenty two teachers in fifteen years. It is difficult to imagine such a situation in education today.

The modern world tends to romanticize these little one room, rural schools in comparison to modern ones. We envision sturdy farm children unencumbered with our modern materialism and technology walking joyfully to a nearby school. Even though we recognize that these schools were uncomfortable, we translate that into a sign of students' (and teachers') fortitude. Such settings developed strong characters. Some of that stereotype is based on truth, but much is just nostalgia; however, rural schools must be given credit for turning out thousands of functionally literate students so necessary to a rapidly evolving democratic society. As a teacher myself, I have nothing but admiration for the class management skills of any woman with so many diverse students to instruct, but one must recognize also the limitations of such schools. Resources were meager. When a thief stole the tiny supply of books from Maribelle McMath's school just east of Ypsilanti in 1831, she must have panicked. Fortunately, he was apprehended, and the books returned. Since books were rare, the curriculum was exceedingly limited. Most learning was by rote memorization; higher level thinking skills were not stressed as they are in today's schools.

Thus unlike modern schools, the quality of nineteenth century rural schools depended entirely on the skill and academic background of the single teacher in charge. That single teacher was, more often than not, just a teenager herself with all the limitations in knowledge and maturity that age implies. Thomas Henning, in his history of Northfield Township, recognized the limitations of many teachers' backgrounds. "When a student mastered proper fractions, he had, as a rule, exhausted his teacher's knowledge of mathematics and thereby completed his study of arithmetic." [4]

Nor did it require any exceptional training to become a rural school teacher. All one had to do was convince the local school board that she was of good moral character and had sufficient learning to teach young children. Mrs. Edward Nordman of Freedom Township, by then a mother of twin girls and a son, recounted how she became a teacher at the Dresselhouse School circa 1846. Mrs. Nordman was born Irene Smith, daughter of Henry Smith, a resident of Freedom Township. Her aunt was actually the one Mr. Dresselhouse asked to be the teacher, but her aunt had already committed herself to the spring term elsewhere. The future Mrs. Nordman said jokingly that she would take the job. Her aunt believed her to be fully capable, so "when they [the members of the school board] asked me how old I was, I told them I wasn't yet seventeen." [5] Indeed she was not; Irene was not yet fourteen. But she was hired and apparently did a fine job.

At the very time Irene Smith was beginning her career, prominent Michigan citizens were demanding improvements in education. Michigan Governor, Alpheus Felch, said the "chief deficiency" of the educational system in the state was a lack of qualified teachers. A decade later J. M. Gregory, editor of the *Michigan Journal of Education* concurred with the Governor with one caveat. At a conference held in Ann Arbor in April of 1855, Gregory stated that more than half of the children in the state had woefully inadequate teachers. For that reason, Gregory urged schools to hire well-trained teachers *and be willing to pay them.* [6] Then, as now, it was problematic both to find an excellent teacher and obtain sufficient funds to pay his or her salary no matter how meager. Teaching simply did not pay well. It did not pay much per week, and the number of weeks were limited. Anna Howard Shaw, who turned so reluctantly to needle work explained in her autobiography that she did so because she could not make sufficient income as a teacher. The problem in part was that the school terms were only for a portion of a year. In Shaw's case, the school "year" lasted twenty-six weeks. That schedule technically left her unemployed for the other half of the year. As a result, a rural teacher's income was at best modest compared to other occupations.

Some communities could not even pay their teachers in cash; they relied on barter in the early days of settlement. Cash, said Annette English of Manchester, was reserved for postage and taxes. According to English, "trade or barter was the custom." [7] That was why Eusebia Minor (Alvord), who taught at a school between Clinton and Tecumseh was paid with a load of apples and a heifer calf. To earn cash, Eusebia worked after school for a shoemaker sewing shoes for "six pence an hour." [8] Today that would be about $1.50 per hour. Miss Minor eventually married but remained in the community. Years later she donated a half acre of land for Manchester's District Nine School where Emma Dickerson became its first teacher. Fortunately for Miss Dickerson, she *was* paid in cash.

In those communities that had cash, early salaries varied considerably. Miss Miranda

Leland (Hurd), sister of Judge Leland, taught at the newly constructed Sutton School in North-field. Her salary in 1828 was $4 per week. Four dollars a week may not sound like much, but it was amazingly generous for the time. Land in Michigan was selling for $1.25 per acre, so she was hypothetically earning the equivalent of three acres of land or $90 each week in today's currency. Parmelia Pattison (Frost) who taught in 1827 in Superior Township made only a dol-lar a week, yet it must have been seen as sufficient because, when she left to marry, her sister, Delight, replaced her.

There could be several reasons for this discrepancy in remuneration. It could reflect something as simple as supply and demand; however, the demand was high in the 1820's and the supply rather limited. It might also demonstrate a common practice in the early days called "rate-bill." This method of determining salary was based upon each parent paying according to the number of children sent to the school. The more children taught, the greater the salary. A third possible explanation for Miss Leland's princely salary of $4 versus Misses Pattison's one dollar is that that the Pattisons may have "boarded out." In other words, they lived in students' homes moving each week or so. This was particularly common for female teachers for whom it was considered not only a salary supplement but chaperoned housing. One of the characters in a story by Ann Arbor's Cornelia Corselius explains, "The school ma'am is boarding here. She has to stay three weeks because we send three [children to school]." [9] In this way boarding became part of the rate-bill. Mary A. Rice (Fairbanks), who was born in 1825 and taught in rural Michigan schools, suggests in her brief memoir that through boarding in student's homes, a young teacher "becomes without knowing it, deeply versed in human nature." [10]

> The *Saline Observer* reported on September 9, 1837 that the teacher at Gleason School, who was being paid seventy-five cents per six day week plus board with students' families, had the effrontery to request a Saturday off.

Yet no matter how it was calculated, everyone agrees that all teachers were underpaid and female teachers were paid considerably less than male teachers. According to the unpub-lished report entitled *History of Ann Arbor Public Schools*, "...the salaries listed for these pioneer educators prove ...that women teachers in particular were paid practically nothing for their la-bors." [11] The report continues by citing salaries in Districts Nine and Eleven for the year 1843. In District Nine, Mr. William Branigan was paid a dollar a day for 78 days. Miss Ann Irons' salary was $1.50 per week for fifteen weeks. That indicates that Mr. Branigan earned $78 for thirteen weeks' work while Miss Irons received only $22.50 for fifteen weeks. Miss Irons worked two weeks longer but earned $55.50 less. Simultaneously in District Sixteen, Mr. Glover earned $12 per month which was exactly twice what Miss Jones earned. Nor can it be claimed that such a situation only occurred in the first half of the century.

Almost forty years later when the Chapman Company compiled its *History of Wash-tenaw County*, the question of pay inequity remained. The book lists wages paid to teachers by the various Washtenaw County districts for the 1879-80 school year. The table indicates that two males taught a combined total of eight months while ten females taught forty-eight months in Ann Arbor schools. Each of the males was paid $737 while the ten females earned $198 each. In Bridgewater, where the supply of teachers was more limited, salaries were a bit more equitable but still discriminatory. Nine males taught twenty-seven months while ten females taught thirty-nine months. The total salary paid to the males was $663 which when divided by nine for the number of months they worked equals $73.66 paid each male teacher. In contrast the women's total was $476 which meant they each received only $47.60 even though they taught twelve weeks more than the men did. Thus the males in Bridgewater earned 64.6% more than the females.

The fact that women earned less than men is not disputed. The question is why. Was it just that women were supposed to work "for love"? The *Chelsea 125th Anniversary Booklet*, states that Harriet Wines, the first teacher at Sylvan School #7, earned $10 while Mr. Arnold Bell earned $36. The rationale given for such a discrepancy in salaries was that Harriet's salary was for the summer while Arnold's was for the winter when the older boys came to school and thus, not only were there more students but more discipline problems in the winter.

There appears be quite a bit of credence to the discipline problems in winter when boys older than ten came to school. Young men, as old as twenty-one, might attend a one room school for the three months of midwinter. Four Merrill School students, ages twenty and twenty-one, left school to enlist when the Civil War began. It is easy to imagine the difficulties in managing a large group of such diverse ages in a confined space. Toss into that a group of assertive "adult" male students who may or may not have really wanted to be there, and problems could easily arise especially for a beginning teacher still in her teens. Flora Saley Bauer who attended school in Manchester shared her experience. "When I was a small girl and Miss [Ella] Wellwood was the teacher, the big boys locked her outside one cold winter noon while inside they danced to the music of a mouth organ and Jew's harp. My father... saw the teacher walking around and around the schoolhouse. So down he came to investigate. It did not take long for the dancing to end and the teacher to come in." [12] One wonders if the bigger boys were being truly mean-spirited or simply testing or possibly even flirting with the young teacher.

Whatever the motivation, the result of such problems meant that "male teachers for the older boys became the rule." And, therefore, as the rationale went, they were paid more than the female teachers." Gottlob Schmid, from Dixboro, confirmed that it was "customary to hire men teachers for winter term... Because there was a greater need for discipline and there were more pupils to teach, the male teachers received higher wages." [13] It is also important to remember that men often received far better educations than women. Also men were not needed on farms as much during the winter, which made them available – and willing – to take another job. Such was the case for James and Susan Fair in the 1840's. Mrs. Fair taught in the fall. She would put both of her children as well as herself on a horse to travel to the little school on Earhart Road in Ann Arbor. When winter came, however, Mr. Fair became the teacher.

Entire extended families dedicated their lives to teaching. One of those families was the Wines family. Mahlon Wines, a teacher himself in Vermont, settled in Sylvan Township in 1834. His daughter, Harriet became the first teacher in that area. In fact, she hardly had time to unpack before she was contracted to teach the summer session. Harriet later married D. Warner and passed away in 1847. Her brother Charles, after the death of his first wife, married Fanny Emmett, a widow with a long career as a teacher. Fanny had attended Michigan State Normal School and taught in Wisconsin. She also served as principal of a high school before her marriage to Wines. Finally Charles' older brother, William, was an educator all his life.

Returning from Tennessee, he was first a teacher and then principal of Chelsea Union School where his wife, Elizabeth Woodworth Wines, also taught. Mrs. William Wines, sadly, was killed on September 15, 1867 at the age of forty-eight when she was struck by a train while crossing the tracks. One of her young students witnessed the accident. There may be a morbid irony to her death since Charles and William Wines had helped build Michigan Central Railroad in 1842. Tragedy, however, did not curtail William's career. He later moved to Washington D.C. to be near his son, but he continued teaching.

The 1850 Merrill School now a residence.

Another teaching family focused its attention on one particular school; as a result, the family's impressive reputation rubbed off on the school itself. In Webster Township, Winthrop Merrill organized a school in 1834 or 1836 on Barker Road. It was appropriately called Merrill School since he was director for two decades and many of his eleven children attended the school. His daughters: Susan, Julia, Emily/Emma and Francis, all taught at the school. The original building was a log cabin. That was replaced in 1850 with the frame building seen at the right. A century later, it was moved to a different location and became a private residence.

Fifty-two of the 289 students for all eight schools in Webster Township in 1859 were lucky enough to attend Merrill School. It had an annual operating budget of $24.18. Parents were required to furnish firewood; one cord per child. Resources may have been in short supply, but the quality of teaching at the Merrill School distinguished it. According to Winthrop Merrill's son, Herbert, "This school for many years had the reputation of being the best district school in Washtenaw County. Not only were the common branches taught but also algebra, geometry, physics, physiology and United States history. Believe me the teachers had to know their stuff." [14] Its reputation was so excellent that its students, unlike those from other rural schools, were accepted at the University of Michigan without having to take an entrance examination. Merrills were still teaching at the school in 1940 when Mercedes Merrill was in charge. Indeed, according to Professor David L. Angus, there were as many one room schools – and teachers – in 1950 as there had been a hundred years earlier.

The most controversial debate of the period, however, was not pay equity. It was educational equity. It was the question of whether or not girls should be educated beyond elementary school. This is one debate that has been put to rest once and for all since women, according President Obama's "Report on the Status of Women," have achieved not only parity, but majority, in graduate schools throughout the United States. In the first half of the nineteenth century, however, a truly academic education for girls was practically unknown unless a girl was allowed to be tutored at home with her brothers. The first school of higher education for women was established in Philadelphia in 1787. The Young Ladies Academy of Philadelphia did not teach music, foreign languages or art. It did not aspire to make girls "cultured." But neither was it designed to train girls to enter the workforce. It was a private school established by upper class men, such as Benjamin Rush, to train girls to be better wives and mothers by instructing them in useful knowledge such as mathematics. But its very existence and popularity (a hundred girls enrolled the first year) set a precedent in women's education.

> Rev. Dr. Chapin spoke out in favor of women's education in the February 8, 1859 issue of *Ann Arbor Local News*. So far, he said, women have been either man's slave or his empress, and they needed deliverance from both scenarios. Chapin strongly asserted that education would not hurt her role as wife. In fact, "The true way to find the sphere of anything is to educate it to its highest capacity."

History of the Ann Arbor Public Schools blames the society of the era, not the lack of schools for young women's woeful ignorance. Franklin Sawyer Jr., Superintendent of Public Instruction for the State of Michigan in 1841, reported "an entire generation is growing up alarmingly destitute of cultivation, without knowledge and with woefully obscure and feeble moral principles." [15] He did not say so; however, I could add that without an education, women did not have a chance of participating fully in the society. Without advanced education, a woman's life, both personally and professionally, was limited. Roccena Norris, a founding settler of Ypsilanti, wrote to her son, Lyman, in 1848: "If ever I regret my want of education, and I often do, it is when in the society of such minds. No one but those who so long from the heart to explore the depth of science now hidden, and forever so, from their view, can have any idea of the regret and disappointment which is buried in many a human heart." [16]

Mrs. Norris was one of the wealthiest and most prominent women in the county. She made sure her daughters, Elvira and Helen, attended the finest school which existed in the area at the time. She sent them to a select school in Detroit. Select schools were private academies. These were very popular until public high schools began to emerge mid-century. The schools that did exist for females too frequently were like the one a Miss Thomas advertised in Ypsilanti describing the curriculum as one that included French, music, drawing and three styles of painting. The intent of such a school as hers was not to educate a woman intellectually but to make her genteel. Was that the sort of education the editor of the Ann Arbor *Argus* preferred for young women when he wrote on Sept 3, 1835: "How many of the females who strut about our streets be-essenced, be-jeweled, and be-millinered, with posies in their hands and ribbons floating from their hats, are capable of writing their own names legibly? For the sake of a few shillings, their daughters are left to grow up unfit to mingle in the society in which they wish to move."

Others desired gentility but also demanded an education for girls that would prepare them intellectually to participate fully in a wider world. Emma Willard was a giant in the early nineteenth century education of women. When she failed to convince the New York State Legislature to sponsor an academic school for girls, she started her own in Troy, New York, in 1821. There girls learned mathematics, geography, natural science and physiology. Graduates such as Elizabeth Cady Stanton praised Willard's work, but at least one New York journalist responded petulantly in print, "We'll be educating the cows next!" [17]

That certainly was not the opinion of Ann Arbor's Reverend Clark. He sent his three oldest daughters to Miss Willard's seminary where they received excellent educations and totally accepted Mrs. Willard's second objective which was to have her graduates go forth and do likewise. Establish your own schools, Mrs. Willard advocated. And that is exactly what the Clark sisters did. They returned to Ann Arbor and began in 1839 the Misses Clark's School for Young Ladies. Thus, only fifteen years after Ann Arbor had been settled and only two years after Michigan became a state, the Clarks introduced to that raw frontier existence a school that would not only teach girls to be genteel but would teach them to think.

Mary Clark was the driving force behind the school; however, her sister Chloe was described as not only more artistic but possessing more wit. Later their other sister, Rhoby, taught the younger students though she, herself, would only have been ten when the school opened. Rhoby also provided music instruction. The youngest of the Clark girls was Jessie, who was born only four years before the school opened. She became one of their students and eventually taught at the school before she married and moved to California. Chloe and Mary used Emma Willard's school as their model and often quoted her to their students. Their teaching methods obviously worked because in less than a decade students were traveling from New York to Michigan to attend the Clark School. In fact, by 1849, 37% of the student body was not from Ann Arbor.

Mary Clark

Miss Mary Clark was a recognized expert in botany. She may have developed that interest due to the influence of Almira Lincoln Phelps, Emma Willard's sister, who taught at Troy Female Seminary and published a botany text. If the source of Clark's interest is not clearly known, the effects are. Twice each week, Clark took her girls into the countryside to collect and classify flora. They increased the identified species of Michigan wildflowers from 100 to 1,000. It is no wonder they called their monthly periodical, published to encourage good writing, "The Wildflower." In addition, under Miss Mary's tutelage as well as her 400 volume library, they studied rigorous academic subjects including Latin, French, theology, astronomy, philosophy, geometry and history. Cornelia Corselius wrote in her unpublished history of select schools in Ann Arbor, "As I look back upon that school room, it reminds me of the Marconi system, Miss Clark being the center. Sparks of knowledge were flying all about and sure to hit." Corselius goes on to say that, when anyone in the village had questions about anything, he or she would go to Miss Clark who was bound to know the answer.

It was not so much the curriculum which gained the school such a reputation for excellence as the approach to education the Clark School employed. Mr. Van Buren, the principal of the high school in Battle Creek, once commented that Misses Clark's School was one of the finest institutions of learning found anywhere because it taught its students to analyze and think independently rather than just memorize and recite. Martha Ladd, daughter of Ann Arbor pioneer, Doctor David E. Ladd, was, in 1841, one of the first graduates of the Misses Clark's

The fourth and final building to house the Clark School for Young Ladies remains at 505 N. Division Street, Ann Arbor, MI

school. She would have been sixteen at the time of her graduation. Miss Ladd went on to become the principal of Ann Arbor's fifth ward school. That would have pleased the Clarks very much.

Mary and Chloe Clark are two of only a handful of women who proudly listed their occupations in the 1850 Census. The Clark School existed for twenty-five years more, for a total of thirty-seven years. During that time, it moved to four different locations. The final move was caused by the 1865 Fourth of July celebration going awry, causing a fire that reduced their school to a pile of ashes. Fire insurance was sufficient to purchase a new lot while friends and former students made donations to build the final edifice, which still stands on the northwest corner of Division and Kingsley Streets.

Mrs. Collina H. Johnston was twelve years old in 1872 when she began as a student at the Clark School. Her memories of the school in its final three years contrast strongly to those of earlier students. She remembered how few students were boarding. Like so many private academies, the opening of public schools presented a real challenge. Ann Arbor Union School competed with the Clark sisters for students. The Clark School's most prosperous year apparently was 1855, the year before the Ann Arbor Union School opened. It must have been discouraging for the Clarks to see the daughters of former students attending the public - and co-educational - Union School. Despite those challenges, Mary Clark's personal income in 1866, according to Dr. George W. Pray was $627, an amount equal to his own.

The school ultimately closed in 1875 when Mary Clark died suddenly following University of Michigan commencement exercises to which she always took her students. Mary was sixty-two. She was buried in Brighton, Michigan, where her two brothers John and Benjamin resided. Chloe died only five years after her sister at age sixty-four and was buried beside her sister. Their former student, Miss Cornelia Corselius, collected contributions to purchase a simple, gray granite stone. Engraved on it are Mary and Chloe's names, dates and an inscription: "A memorial from their scholars."

The Misses Clarks' was not the only academic school for girls in Washtenaw County. O.W. Stephenson's *Ann Arbor First Hundred Years* itemized several dozen privately operated schools open to girls though most did not stand the test of time. One such school called the Teacher's Seminary was opened by Mr. and Mrs. Henry O. Griffin in 1835 at the north-west corner of Main and Ann streets. Their advertisement in the December 31, 1835 in the *Michigan State Journal* indicates that their objective was "to qualify youth of both sexes to become teachers,"[19] but they offered only one class about actual teaching. Apparently they subscribed to the common fallacy that anyone who knew the subject matter could teach. The Griffins did stress that their school was open to both boys and girls regardless of religious preference, and they had an impressive curriculum. It included astronomy, surveying, civil engineering, book-keeping as well as the usual reading, writing, and mathematics. The following year, they let the county know that they had hired a young woman from the East who had been in charge of a female seminary there. Beginning in the autumn of 1836, she would be in charge of the primary department [six to ten year olds] at his school. A decade later the Griffin's daughter established another school. This time it was for girls only. Though she offered Latin, her curriculum was decidedly less academic than the Clarks'. Miss Griffin stressed languages, music and art.

One of the schools that lasted quite a few years was run by Mrs. Julia Ann Gott who had graduated from the Albany Female Seminary and served as Superintendent of the Jonesville Female Seminary in Saratoga, N.Y. circa 1834. She then married James B. Gott who had a seminary for boys in Ann Arbor. He abandoned that school in order to devote his time to Mrs. Gott's female seminary which was located in their home at Fourth Avenue and Ann Street in Ann Arbor. In 1841 Mrs. Gott advertised her sixth term of classes which cost $2.50 for students in her "introductory department", $3 for juniors and $4 for seniors. Mrs. Gott also provided board for $1.75 per week. At the time of that advertisement, Mrs. Gott would have been twenty-three years old and the mother of a two-year-old daughter. While the details of Mrs. Gott's life have been lost, what details remain portray a very busy woman juggling family and occupational responsibilities in the years following Michigan statehood.

There was an even earlier school than Mrs. Gott's. It was operated by the daughters of David Page. Mary M. Page first opened the school circa 1828 in her home. That was just four years after Ann Arbor was founded. John and Ann Allen sent their daughter, Sarah to the Page School. Later Eliza and Melanie Page operated the school. "They were fine women and good teachers, so the school was deservedly popular." [20] To those who felt higher education was impractical, Eliza affirmed that she believed a woman was neither less interesting nor less useful because she had become well educated. An advertisement from September 18, 1834, included an announcement that a younger sister, Miss S. H. Page, also would be offering her own small classes in "Reading, Spelling and Sewing for the modest price of $2 per quarter." Eliza taught the secondary level students while Melanie taught the primary. That same advertisement declared that a Monsieur Fasquelle, who had studied at the Universities of Paris and Milan, would be teaching French and Italian at the Page School.

In 1837, Melanie abandoned teaching in order to marry Timothy Paige. Thus she became Melanie Page Paige, and Eliza was left without a business partner. Soon after that, Miss Levina Moore joined Eliza. Moore took charge of teaching the younger children. Miss Moore was the niece of Mary Lyon, the founder of Mount Holyoke Female Seminary which is now Mt. Holyoke College. By all accounts, she, like her aunt, did not tolerate any nonsense in her classes. The little girls who were her students sat on high benches, feet dangling in the air. Each seat had a number on the back. The girls were supposed to keep their heads touching their numbers. And Miss Moore literally would drop a pin on the floor to see if they were quiet enough to begin lessons. One former student said she remembered her number for the rest of her life. She was number six.

This new incarnation of the Page School was sufficiently successful that more staff had to be hired. The school's 1845-6 catalog lists a male Latin and math teacher named Adonijah Welch, Mrs. Saunders who taught French and music; Miss Georgiana West, piano; and Mrs. Hughes, drawing and painting. Tuition that year ranged from $6 for primary to $12 for seniors per 22-week session. They had as many as 127 students at one time spanning ages from six to nineteen. It was an impressive curriculum and student body.

The highlight of the school year was the annual spring exhibition for the parents and community which was held in the Presbyterian Church. Apparently the entire town turned out to hear the girls recite. All the students looked angelic in their white muslin frocks with light blue sashes over their left shoulders and tied in a bow in back. Unfortunately in 1846 at the end of a performance, one little girl (yes, it was number six) made an "impish" response to the audience. She scandalously responded to applause in the gallery by dropping her book, joyously clapping her hands and laughing out loud. Miss Moore was in a "mighty wrath" as she "quelled the tumult." [21] Some sources say that Miss Moore quit that very night because of the embarrassment of such an outrageous breach of etiquette, but Lucy Chapin claims Moore already had secured another position and chose unkindly to announce her resignation at the end of that exhibition. Eliza carried on briefly by herself and then left town. She passed away years later in Paw Paw, Michigan. Thus ended the career of the Page School but not the careers of its graduates.

One such lucky young woman was Lettice Smith, pronounced in those days like lettuce; however, she seems to have gone by Lettie. Whatever her preferred name, her family left New York on her first birthday. Her father, Asa L. Smith, literally carried her to newly established Ann Arbor where she was the "bright particular star" of the settlement since she was, for a time, the only child. Her mother and Mrs. Rumsey were the only white women there. The Smiths were welcomed into the Rumsey's home. The first settlers always shared their modest cabins with newcomers until another cabin could be built. Mrs. Smith provided not only an extra set of hands to help with the work but much missed companionship. Soon Lettie's brother arrived becoming the first child born in the settlement. Lettice's story, in many ways, is the story of Ann Arbor; unfortunately, little of her story has been preserved. Of her early years, all that remains is an incident when she was chased by wolves while picking strawberries.

She must have enjoyed school, however. After attending the Page School, she went on to graduate from Oberlin College in Ohio which was one of the few institutions of higher education at that time which would accept women. She firmly declined Oberlin's shortened course for women and took instead the full classical program. Her future husband, Rev. Thomas Holmes, later eulogized her saying that she was "spurred on by a lofty and noble ambition, at a time when the ability of a woman to cope with men in classic strife was doubted, and under circumstances superlatively adverse and discouraging." [22] Lettie shared her experience at Oberlin with future feminist, Lucinda Stone. How Lettice felt about Stone's "eccentric activities" (a description given by Stone's future sister-in-law, friend and fellow feminist student, Antoinette Brown) is not known. After graduation, Lettie married; she was twenty-four. Marriage, however, did not deter the new Mrs. Holmes. Three years later she finished her Master of Arts Degree, also at Oberlin. She then joined her husband for an extended stay in Europe. Returning to the United States, Lettice accepted a professorship of modern languages at Union Christian College in Indiana where she remained for nine years. In 1875 when Mr. Holmes became minister at a Congregational Church, she and her husband returned to Washtenaw County to spend the rest of their lives in Chelsea. As for Lettie's parents, Mr. Smith passed on in 1844. He did not live to see his daughter graduate. His wife, knowing her daughter was safely married and on her way, left Washtenaw County for Kalamazoo, Michigan, four years later.

Education has been a defining element in Washtenaw County making it special in the history of Michigan and the United States. Since the mid-nineteenth century, Ann Arbor and Ypsilanti have been known not only for their select schools but for their institutions of higher learning. What many people do not realize is that students coming from most small, rural, one-room schools were ill prepared for university work. They needed an academic high school to prepare them for classes at a university. In the first half of the century this service was provided by private academies and select schools. Then public union schools began to open.

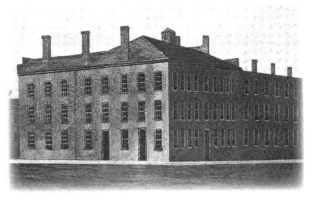

Union Seminary Building

Courtesy of the Ypsilanti Historical Society

The first union school in Washtenaw County began in Ypsilanti. It was called Union Seminary. A union school was graded. At first, all grades, primary through high school were in the same building. At Ypsilanti's new school, (which originally had been a hotel) the upper story of the new facility was converted to a dormitory for female students who lived too far away to return home each day. The majority of female students in 1851 came from Ypsilanti; however, 26% lived elsewhere. A few came from as far away as Eaton Rapids and Lansing, Michigan; Tremont, Illinois; and New York. During the first years of Ypsilanti Seminary, board cost $1.50 per week. The Seminary's bulletin also announced that "Young gentlemen can procure good accommodations in the village." [23] While the boarding policy favored the female students, its tuition policy did not. Boys paid $8 per semester; girls paid $10.

The Seminary's preceptress was Miss Abigail C. Rogers. Preceptress, a term now obsolete, was a role similar to a dean of women/assistant principal. In fact, the entire Seminary faculty except for two was female. In 1853 Miss Rogers resigned and was replaced by Harriet Cutcheon, a graduate of Mt. Holyoke Female Seminary which Mary Lyon had established in Massachusetts in 1837. In addition to her duties as Preceptress, Miss Cutcheon also taught French, botany, and rhetoric. Early teachers had to be Renaissance women. She remained in Ypsilanti for seven years until she accepted a similar position in Monroe, Michigan. After that, she became head of the Women's Department at the University of Wisconsin.

When Harriet resigned as Preceptress in Ypsilanti, her sister, Anna, assumed her position. Anna had graduated from Union Seminary, in 1857. Anna Cutcheon's career thus began in Ypsilanti, but it later took her to Illinois and Tennessee before she returned to teach art at Michigan State Normal School between 1872 and 1876. She then taught at the University of Minnesota. Finally in 1897 she returned to Michigan again to become principal at the Detroit Seminary where she offered her students the opportunity to travel in Europe each summer. At that time, she also began the Pope and Cutcheon Art School with Harriet Bissell Pope, another Detroit art teacher. Though her career took her to many other cities, Anna returned to Ypsilanti by 1899 to live with her sister, Harriet, who also had returned to Ypsilanti circa 1878. They purchased a home at 209 Normal Street where they lived for the rest of their lives. [24]

Mrs. Emma Williams, who was born in Van Buren Township, attended the Seminary while Miss Rogers was Preceptress. Later, the future Mrs. Williams must have experienced some exciting times when she taught in Kentucky and Tennessee during the Civil War. She returned to teach three years at Willow Run, Michigan, where she said her salary was $25 per month. Her teaching career ended when she married in 1867, but she lived to the ripe old age of eighty-seven, serving for most of those years as a rural correspondent for the *Ypsilanti Daily Press*.

Turnover in the faculties of union schools was almost as rapid as that in rural schools. Of all the women who taught in the early years of Ypsilanti's Union School, only Miss Louisa M. Waldron remained for any length of time. Miss Waldron, came to Michigan as a child. She never married. She spent her entire life with other members of her family: her mother, Eliza; her aunt, Nancy; and her brothers, William, James and Thomas. Miss Waldron began her career as a teacher in the preparatory department in 1851 and became the teacher in the grammar department in 1860. That meant that she was teaching at the school when it burned in March 1857 forcing the classes to find other venues until a new building could be constructed. She was also alive, though not teaching, when that second building burned twenty years later. She died at the home of her brother, James, in 1888, so she missed the excitement of May 1893 when the third Ypsilanti Union School also suffered damage especially on the third floor due to a fire.

Fire damage at Ypsilanti Union School, May 3, 1893

Courtesy of the Ypsilanti Historical Society

Two of the girls attending Ypsilanti's Union Seminary in 1851-2 when Miss Waldron was teaching there were Mary Cook and Sarah Newton of Ann Arbor. Why, you wonder, would girls from Ann Arbor go to Ypsilanti to school? They went to Ypsilanti because Ann Arbor, at that time, did not have a union school. Eventually, as communities grew and established primary schools in other buildings, secondary buildings became high schools. Mary Cook and Sarah Newton probably were at the secondary level. The fact that Ann Arbor lacked such a school in 1851-1852 is not really surprising since there were few public secondary or high schools in the

United States. As late as the 1860's, there were only about forty such schools, thus Ypsilanti was in the vanguard of public education. Ann Arbor and Dexter quickly followed suit establishing their own schools in the 1856 and 1857 respectively. Manchester and Saline each built a school in 1867 and 1868 respectively. Thus Washtenaw County could boast a total of five of the forty public high schools in the entire United States.

After Ann Arbor's Union School opened its rather elegant Italianate doors in 1856, students from beyond Washtenaw County attended. In fact, sixty percent of Ann Arbor's first graduating classes were not residents of the city. Most were young men preparing for the University of Michigan. Their presence swelled the ranks of the junior and senior classes which far outnumbered the under classmen who were predominantly local children. There were also girls from as far away as "London." That probably referred to London, Michigan, which was south of Milan, but it could refer to the London in Ohio or in Kentucky or even in Ontario. As did students in Ypsilanti, female students often traveled far to obtain the best preparatory educations available even though there were very few institutions of higher learning at that time that would accept women. Naturally, such non-residents were charged extra. It would appear that there were some people who tried to save tuition money by having their out-of-town children live with relatives in Ann Arbor. The problem must have been significant because the July 21, 1857, *News and Advertiser* provided an article about the school stressing free tuition to "bona fide residents." For non-residents, the grammar school charged $3.50 per term or $4.75 if the child wanted Latin or French. The High School cost $4.50 per term for the English program; $6 for the Classical.

Ann Arbor's Union School
Courtesy of the Bentley Historical Library, University of Michigan

It might seem odd to modern readers that teenagers, especially girls, were sent away from home to live in towns with family friends or, even more startling, in boarding houses, in order to attend high school. It was, however, a relatively common practice 175 years ago. Miss Ruth Parker (Worthington), who opened a select school for young ladies above Mr. Vanderbilt's Shop in Ypsilanti in 1834, also strove to find places for her students to live while they were at her school. She advertised that she would find places with "respectable families" for students in need of "board." [25] Many girls who lived on isolated farms but had parents supportive of their education, therefore, resorted to boarding in nearby cities. Some, like Bertha Van Hoosen of Rochester, Michigan, were forced to lodge in public boarding houses when she studied at Pontiac High School. Abby Warner Hayes (Smith) from Dixboro was lucky. She lived with the

Allens for a time and later with Marcus Lane and his sister (the future Mrs. Robert Geddes) so that she could attend the Page School. Abby recalled the harrowing times she experienced fording the swollen Huron River which was necessary in order to reach her home in Dixboro for the holidays.

To the social mind of the mid-nineteenth century, boarding out was of less concern than the idea of co-education. There is a rumor that the very word was coined in Ann Arbor at an 1855 conference on education held in that city. But since the word was used in the *Pennsylvania School Journal* three years prior to the Ann Arbor conference, such a claim must be dismissed. Who coined the term is far less important than the fact that in the middle of the century a wide variety of concerned and educated people were debating the concept of having males and females taught together.

While most select schools accepted only a single gender, co-educational select schools did exist from the very earliest days of the county. O.C. Thompson opened "The Academy" in 1832 in Ann Arbor's original Presbyterian Church. Girls and boys learned together. According to Stephenson, Mr. Thompson had over a hundred students the first winter term with some coming from as far away as Detroit. That school moved its location several times but remained a local institution for over two decades.

The Clark sisters adamantly were opposed to the idea of co-education. Cornelia Corselius said that Chloe thought coeducation "demoralizing;" [27] however, Elizabeth Cady Stanton, who also attended Mrs. Willard's school, believed that school's biggest failing was the fact that it was an all-female academy. "My own experience proves to me," stated Stanton in her autobiography, that it is a grave mistake to send boys and girls to separate institutions of learning, especially at the most impressionable age. The stimulus of sex [i.e both genders] promotes alike a healthy condition of the intellectual and the moral faculties and give to both a development they never can acquire alone." [28] Stanton found the back and forth discussions and play with males to be stimulating while simultaneously creating a restraint to socially unacceptable behaviors.

One of the prominent concerns conservatives had about co-education was the intrinsic problem of competition between boys and girls. They asserted that, since the appropriate sphere for females was that of home and morality, such competition would stunt their development in those prescribed social areas. In contrast, males were educated to enter the dog eat dog world of business and finance where competition was an integral part. One cannot help but wonder if the real problem were that the girls too often won in school competitions thus making, if not the boys, the boys' parents unhappy. For example, Ann Arbor Union School's brochure from 1856 listed all the prizes won that year. Not surprisingly boys did win the three prizes for rhetoric. Public speaking was still considered inappropriate for females. When Lucinda Stone won the ultimate prize by graduating valedictorian from Oberlin College, she was told she could write the speech but a male would deliver it. She declined. Even with the boys winning in rhetoric, more female than male students took home prizes that year despite the fact that girls then, like girls in the twentieth century, were encouraged by society to hide their excellence.

Lucy Osband, who later taught at Michigan State Normal School graduated valedictorian at Genessee College in New York. According to her daughter, Marna, she declined the award for fear of hurting the feelings of her fiancé who happened to be a member of the same graduating class. Such sacrifices were so common that nineteenth century poet John Greenleaf Whittier wrote a poem about it. In "School Days," though he ignores the impact such values had on girls, he captures perfectly the effect it had on boys. Whittier's poem perfectly reflects society's viewpoint. Boys need to learn life's hard lessons early so they could contend with a tough world; a girl's kindly spirit should be filled with self-sacrificing love.

> ## School Days
>
> *He saw her lift her eyes; he felt*
> *The soft hand's light caressing*
> *As if a fault confessing,*
> *And hard the tremble of her voice;*
>
> *"I'm sorry that I spelt the word.*
> *I hate to go above you*
> *Because," –the brown eyes lower fell–*
> *"Because, you see, I love you!"...*
>
> *He lives to learn in life's hard school,*
> *How few who pass above him*
> *Lament their triumph and his loss,*
> *Like her, because they love him.*

Michigan's public schools, however, were by law co-educational. Whether male or female, not all who tested for admission to the high schools were sufficiently prepared to be allowed to attend. Of the thirty-eight candidates examined on July 15, 1859, only twenty-five were admitted to Ann Arbor's school. Of those, sixteen or 64% were girls. It would be very interesting to know the gender of the thirteen who did not pass, but that information was not preserved. Like Ypsilanti, Ann Arbor's school offered "a male and female department, in which young gentlemen may be prepared for admission to the University and young ladies may receive such instruction as usually is afforded in the highest female Seminaries."[29] Technically, therefore, there were separate departments for males and females just as rural schools had separate doors for each gender. In practice, however, at least in Ann Arbor, only the study rooms were truly segregated so that the female students could speak there with the Preceptress should they need counseling. The fact that boys and girls took the same classes meant that girls received the same college preparatory education as boys even though there were very few colleges or universities that would accept the girls after graduation.

Yet for a girl or young woman who had been educated in the sheltered confines of an all-female school, the transition to co-education may have been a bit daunting. Perhaps the boys felt the same though the situation was quite different for them. A girl in Ann Arbor (the signature sheet has been lost) wrote to a friend named Mary in Peru, New York, expressing her excited anticipation of attending the new high school. "I am well," she said, "enjoying myself vastly and what is better than all, intend to commence school next week. Our 'Union High School' opens at that time, the building being completed and every thing [sic] in readiness. It is a splendid structure, costing $24,000, and presents a fine Appearance from my window. It is now two years since I left school, and I fear I shall really make an awkward appearance in the schoolroom. It will seem strange to me, to enter a school with gentlemen, having been under the supervision of lady instructors since I left the old district school in Peru."[30]

Many were less than overjoyed with these expanded educational opportunities for women. William Edward Baxter, who toured America, published his impressions in his book, *America and the Americans* in 1855. His opinion of American girls was that they were far too "voluble" in public and lazy at home. "It appears to me that the system of education encourages this prevalent folly. The proficiency of young misses in algebra, moral philosophy and physics is being published far and wide and exhibited before audiences, whilst the humbler but far more important engagements of domestic life seem to be entirely forgotten." [31]

The development of public high schools had the added advantage of providing women not only with preparatory educations but with the opportunity for careers as teachers beyond the elementary level. By 1870 over a hundred thousand women were employed as public elementary and secondary teachers in the United States. Sarah Merrylees was one of the first women hired to teach at the new high school in Ann Arbor. She later married T.C. Abbot, who served as principal of the Union School beginning in 1860. In his diary he chronicles his four year courtship of Miss Merrylees. Lest anyone question the integrity of this arrangement, Mr. Abbot never referred to her even in his diary as anything but Miss Merrylees until after they married. Then he felt free to call her Sarah. Sarah was born in the islands north of Scotland and educated in Edinburgh. Her future husband, not surprisingly, described her as "fine looking." She taught French and English grammar, rhetoric, botany and history.

One of the women listed with Miss Merrylees in 1857 was Eliza Botsford who is a perfect example of the difficulties involved in researching women of this era. Unlike so many women of that era who have left few artifacts to provide information for researchers, Eliza Botsford's name appears in several sources. Such a wealth of information should make research much easier, but that is not what has occurred in Botsford's case because, as often happens, the sources disagree concerning the essential facts concerning this woman.

Bodsford Monument

Primary sources are generally better than secondary, so we turn first to those. Since we have the 1857 school catalog, we are certain there was a woman named Eliza Botsford who taught in the Ann Arbor schools. Further investigation revealed that she taught at the Old North School until 1868 when she became principal of the new Fourth Ward School where she oversaw a faculty of four. And there is a wedding license dated April 1825 in the Washtenaw County Historical Society's collection. So far so good, but there is also a tombstone, located in the southeast corner of Botsford Cemetery off Earhart Road in Ann Arbor, inscribed with the name Eliza Botsford who died at the age of forty-four in 1847. Clearly this Eliza Botsford could not be the same woman as the teacher. Furthermore the Eliza Botsford of the tombstone was born in New York. She was a school teacher who, on the day of her wedding, in 1825, taught all day and then tidied the school before going home to be married to Elnathan Botsford, a merchant and farmer. They departed the very next morning for Michigan. She and her husband had three sons and five daughters, one of whom died young.

The 1902 obituary for Eliza Botsford, the teacher, at first only adds to the confusion. It states that she was born in 1818 in Ireland. Her father, a surgeon for the British navy, brought her to America at the age of three and educated her himself. While still in her teens, she began teaching in New York. A cousin encouraged her to come to Michigan where she met and married a prominent merchant named "Binathan? Botsford." Unfortunately he died soon after their marriage leaving her to support their infant daughter, Ada, who was born in 1852. She then returned to teaching for a total career in education of thirty-five years. In 1881 she moved to California where she lived for the last twenty-one years of her life with her daughter.

This obituary presents several problems. First, the writer was uncertain of the name of Eliza's husband. There was no one named Binathan Botsford, but one can see how an "El" might look like a "Bi" on an old document. The writer of the obituary clearly was in doubt about the name since a question mark was included. Second, if the name truly is Elnathan, the marriage date, 1856, cannot be correct because Elnathan Botsford died in 1853 and Ada was born the year before that. Elnathan's death date is literally carved in stone in the Botsford Cemetery, and Ada was eight when the 1860 Census was taken. What is one to make of this historical conundrum? Primary sources, valuable as they might be, are the products of human memory which is often flawed in its facts. The obituary was written in 1902 probably by Ada or another relative. Over half a century and thousands of miles separated this writer from the events described. Ada never knew her father since she was only a few months old when he died. Despite these contradictions, all the evidence available seems to point to the fact that, indeed, Elnathan Botsford had two wives, both named Eliza. It was a very popular name at the time. His first wife was Eliza *Smith* Botsford and his second, Eliza *Copeland* Botsford.

Eliza Copeland Botsford, his second wife, was unfortunate to become a widow so soon after her marriage, but she was quite fortunate that she was educated and could support herself as a teacher. She was also fortunate that she returned to teaching when she did. Within a decade or two, married women would find it difficult, if not impossible, to get teaching jobs in many communities no matter how qualified they were. As it was, Mrs. Botsford was the only married woman in the faculty of ten for Ann Arbor's Union School. By 1878 there were less than a handful of married teachers in Washtenaw County. They were tolerated because, like Botsford, they had begun their careers earlier when married women as teachers were more acceptable. In 1879 the Michigan Board of Education openly expressed its bias against married teachers in its "Code of Ethics for Teachers" This code explicitly states that any female teachers "who marry or *engage in unseemly conduct* [the italics are mine] will be dismissed." [32] This bias slanted later histories, such as *A History of Ann Arbor Public Schools*. It consistently refers to Mrs. Botsford, a widow, as "Miss." I seriously doubt that she, a mother using her married name, would refer to herself as "Miss." I suspect the author of that document just assumed she was single since women who taught at that time, virtually always were. And the list of those unmarried female teachers is lengthy indeed. A quick sampling of Ann Arbor teachers, however, provides a pretty impressive picture of the caliber of those women.

Anyone who has read closely the 1881 *History of Washtenaw County, Michigan,* probably has noticed a chapter concerning the county's flora written by a familiar Ann Arbor family name: Allmendinger. This particular Allmendinger refers to Elizabeth C. Allmendinger who was born in Ann Arbor in 1837. Miss Allmendinger never married but had a very long and full life. For two years she taught a freedman's school in the south after the Civil War and then returned to Ann Arbor where she taught botany at the high school. Botany was both her vocation and her avocation. She assisted Professor Harrington in constructing the University of Michigan's herbarium and clearly was the spiritual heir to Mary Clark. Clark had catalogued wildflowers while Miss Allmendinger became a local expert on 850 species which she claimed was a complete list of all flora within four miles of Ann Arbor. Miss Allmendinger lived with her widowed sister, Mary Fisher, and helped raise her fatherless nephew, George Frank Allmendinger. He continued to live with his Aunt Elizabeth well into the twentieth century long after he had become a successful businessman and leader of the community.

Irving K. Pond, who attended Ann Arbor High School in the 1870's, extolled Miss Allmendinger's colleague, Miss Anna Eastman. Eastman taught algebra as well as geology. Pond especially recalled how she would send her geology class out to find specimens. One day he put a piece of slag from a locomotive in the collection. Later as Miss Eastman was demonstrating her expertise by identifying what the students had found, she saved the slag for last. Picking up Pond's contribution by two fingers as if she were holding someone's dirty underwear, she said, "And this – this is a piece of impertinence." [33]

Lela Duff, in her book, *Pioneer School*, eulogizes five Ann Arbor High School teachers she knew when she began her own teaching career. Four of them – Gertrude Breed, Mary Ella Bennnett, Cora A. Robison and Sara G. O'Brien – began teaching in the late 1890's, but one, Alice Porter, was a contemporary of Miss Eastman. Miss Porter was a Latin teacher.

Alice Porter

Courtesy of the Bentley Historical Library
University of Michigan

Born in 1853, she lived her entire life in Ann Arbor. Her father, Charles Porter, was a dentist. She did not graduate from the high school until she was in her early twenties. Miss Duff attributes this tardiness to extremely poor eyesight. When young Miss Porter finally was fitted with glasses, she was ecstatic to be able to identify a plaid dress on a woman walking across the street.

She began her forty-two year career at Ann Arbor High School in 1879. Apparently many found her quite intimidating. She knew the commentaries of Caesar by heart. Her dignity, said Duff, "set up a cool barrier" [34] with colleagues and students who were shocked to hear Mr. Wines call her by her first name one day. They were even more shocked, no doubt, when she revealed an underlying playful nature by allowing herself be cast as the Walrus in a rendition of *Alice in Wonderland*. Beginning in 1927, six years after her retirement, the school awarded the Alice Porter gold medal for outstanding citizenship to a girl in each graduating class. Miss Porter was proud of the award but less enthused about the unattractive image of her on the medal. Miss Porter was ninety-five years old at the time of her death in 1948.

Porter's forty-two year career was only five less than that of Anna L. Clinton. Miss Clinton's grandparents, William and Mary Kearns, settled in Ann Arbor in 1834 when Clinton's mother was just a toddler. Miss Clinton was born in 1870 and died ninety years later. No one can doubt her hardiness when he/she hears the story of how she was hired at age twenty-two and the conditions under which she worked at the Fifth Ward School. Miss Clinton was first hired in 1892 to replace another teacher, Hattie Haviland, who had been hit by a male student. The incident resulted in Miss Haviland's resigning her job. Clearly the school needed someone with sufficient presence to control the students. As if such a rowdy group were not bad enough, there was, according to Miss Clinton, standing water beneath her room. It created dampness and condensation on the walls. During spring rains, class had to be canceled while the water was pumped out. Fortunately for the final thirty years of her career, that school was replaced by the Donovan School. Ann Arbor Public Schools paid tribute to Miss Clinton by naming an elementary school for her. Today that school is home to the Jewish Community Center of Washtenaw County on Birch Hollow Drive.

Ypsilanti also had a few women with long careers. The photograph to the right is the Ypsilanti High School Faculty in 1885. The woman sitting on the right is Frances/Fanny E. Gray who taught German, Greek, history, rhetoric and English literature between 1877 and 1893. Miss Gray was born in Detroit to Horace and Mary Gray. She had no family in Ypsilanti and boarded with Louisa Alexander. Miss Gray died in 1911.

Her contemporary on the left is Ada Norton. Unlike Gray, Miss Norton spent her entire life in Ypsilanti living with her parents and brothers. She taught eighth grade and high school math. Miss Norton was the daughter of Russell and Lucy Norton who came to Ypsilanti, like so many others, from New York. By 1892 she was teaching math at the Michigan State Normal School. Her mother died fairly young, but her father lived until circa 1907. Ada continued to live in the family home until her own death in 1939.

1885 Ypsilanti High School Faculty

Courtesy of the Ypsilanti Historical Society

Women not only had long careers as teachers, some became principals although more frequently it was a male who ran a school with female teachers beneath him. That certainly was not the case for Marie Kirchhofer of Manchester. The second of five children, Marie was born in 1869 in Chicago. Her family came to Manchester, Michigan, after the devastating Chicago fire of 1871. She graduated from Manchester High School in 1886. In 1892 she began teaching at her alma mater where she remained as principal until 1918. At that time her sister-in-law suddenly died leaving her brother, Hugo, to raise their two young daughters. Marie moved to California to manage her brother's household and help raise his daughters, Margaret (age three) and Dorothy (age five). It was in Dorothy's home that Miss Kirchhofer passed away in 1956.

The biggest problem most women, like Marie Kirchofer, faced when trying to step up the teaching ladder was the lack of university educations. Marie Kirchofer most certainly must have spent the time after high school and before beginning her teaching career, doing advanced studying at some educational institution. There is no record of where. She may have attended Michigan State Normal School (now Eastern Michigan University), established more than three decades earlier in Ypsilanti for the express purpose of training teachers. When it opened its doors on March 9, 1853, Michigan State Normal School was one of only five normal schools in the entire country and the first of its kind west of Albany, NY. Students were required to be eighteen years of age if male and sixteen if female. A written "declaration of intention" to teach in a school in Michigan after graduation was mandatory for admittance. That is why everyone who graduated from there taught at least for a few years.

Marie, Margaret and Dorothy Kirchofer.

Courtesy of the Manchester District Library

Ever wonder why it is called a normal school? The term was first used in France for the Ecole Normal which was instituted to regularize or "normalize" instruction so that all children received the same education based on the best methods.

Though teaching was still a male-dominated field at that time, two of the three students who graduated first from Michigan State Normal School were female: Alzina Morton and Helen Norris. Alzina, born 1828, was the daughter of Almira and Jonathan G. Morton. She taught for a decade until ill health required her to retire. She spent the rest of her life with her sister, Mrs. James Holmes and died on her birthday in 1898. Perhaps it is uncharitable, but since she lived seventy years, one wonders just how ill she really was. The other graduate was Miss Helen C. Norris, younger daughter of Roccena and Mark Norris. She taught at Ypsilanti Seminary before attending the Normal School. After graduation, Miss Norris taught at Ann Arbor High School. In addition to the graduates, the photograph at left includes Miss Abigail Rogers who was the Preceptress at Union Seminary in Ypsilanti before becoming the first Preceptress at the Michigan State Normal School.

First graduates of Michigan State Normal School: Alzina Morton, bottom row, Helen Norris, top row and Abigail Rogers, center row left.

Courtesy of Eastern Michigan University Archives

Roccena Norris, Helen's mother, wrote a letter to her friend, Mrs. Payson, in the spring of 1853 discussing her daughter's admission to Michigan State Normal School. "I find that an academic department has been added under the supervision of Miss Rogers, who in all departments is one of the best teachers of my acquaintance." [35] Rogers was not only a fine teacher but a strong proponent of women's higher education. She was born in Avon, New York, in 1818. By age nineteen she was in charge of the Ladies Seminary in Coburg, Canada. Before becoming Preceptress at Ypsilanti Seminary, she spent several years as Preceptress at White Plains Seminary and Genesee Wesleyan Seminary. Both were in New York. Rogers came to Michigan in 1847 to become Preceptress at Albion College. Such movement within the profession was not a sign of inadequacy, but rather it indicated her growing reputation in the field of education.

Miss Rogers believed that the Normal School alone was insufficient to meet the educational needs of Michigan women; therefore, "discouraged over the failure of efforts to open the University of Michigan to women," [36] she resigned her position at the Normal School in 1855 in order to open her own college. She and her sister, Delia, moved to Lansing where they established the Michigan Female College. Rogers requested from the Legislature a $100,000 endowment and $50,000 building fund. It never happened. She had to struggle on her own to finance her female college.

Portrait of Abigail Rogers
Courtesy of Eastern Michigan University

Rogers' request was denied because she found herself in the middle of a political standoff. It is difficult to tell where Governor Kinsley Bingham stood on the question. Using passive voice, which is so favored by politicians who are skirting the issue, he told the Michigan Legislature in 1855, "A want is seriously felt for seminaries in the highest grade for the education of young ladies." [37] Where was that want going to be satisfied? That was the question. The proponents of co-education in the Legislature felt their objectives would be weakened if Rogers' female college were subsidized. They argued that the University of Michigan instead should become co-educational. Such an objective was consistent with Abigail's own beliefs. According to Frank M. Turner's *Historic Michigan*, "Her great work, the work on which she spent her whole life was the admission of women into the University of Michigan... on an equal basis with men." [38] But at the time that goal seemed quixotic. Neither the University nor the Legislature appeared at all inclined to accept women. An 1859 report from the Michigan Legislature asserted, "Many of the studies pursued at the University are not only unnecessary to the proper education of woman [sic] for the appropriate and destined sphere, but are absolutely incompatible..." Yet the very same document continues by contradicting itself. "Women as a class have in no instance been found inferior in intellect...nor have they lost any of that delicacy of sentiment or refinement" [39] in other co-educational schools, BUT "the highest institution of learning in the state" can only have students who are "the most accomplished masters." [40] In other words, the dignity or reputation of the institution would be lessened if women attended.

In the meantime, Miss Rogers remained undaunted and continued to lobby for state support for her school. In 1867 she reported to the Superintendent of Public Instruction that both she and her sister were determined "to keep before the public mind as constantly as they could, the duty of the State to provide for the education of its daughters as it has already provided for the education of its sons." In June of 1868 *Godey's* featured a lengthy article about the Michigan Female College which included a letter from Miss Rogers in its "Editor's Table" section. Hoping to capitalize on the strong emotions that followed the end of the Civil War, Rogers claimed that surely the women "of loyal states" had proven themselves worthy of such funding. No financial support was forthcoming; however, Miss Rogers managed to keep the college open until her death in 1869.

Michigan Female College campus,
later the State School for the Blind.
Courtesy of the Bentley Historical Library, University of Michigan

Abigail Rogers' Michigan Female College campus became the Michigan School for the Blind on September 29, 1880. Seven years later it expanded its curriculum to teach the deaf as well. Another Washtenaw County woman, Nettie Latson was Preceptress at the School for the Blind before moving to Tecumseh, Michigan were she continued her career. Her family had settled in Webster Township in the 1830's. Nettie who was born in 1853 was one of twelve children. She graduated from Ann Arbor High School circa 1870.

The lives of many female educators often intertwined before veering off in different directions. Hannah Keziah Clapp, born in New York in 1824, taught history and math at Union Seminary in Ypsilanti beginning in 1849 when Abigail Rogers was the Preceptress. Not only did they work together, Miss Clapp and Miss Rogers both boarded at the home of fellow teacher Louisa Waldron and her family. In 1856 Clapp was in charge of Michigan State Normal School's Model School before moving to Lansing where she became principal of Lansing's Female Seminary; however, when Abigail and Delia Rogers opened the Michigan Female College, Hannah quickly joined the faculty there.

Eventually Clapp's experiences diverged from Rogers' because she decided to move west in 1859 with her brother and his family. Passing through Utah, Hannah attended a Mormon service. It is hard to say who was more shocked: the Mormons because she wore a bloomer costume with revolver at her side or Hannah who felt that Mormon women were "miserable slaves" and Mormon men, "licentious knaves." [42] The Clapps went on to California. She taught there briefly before returning to Carson City, Nevada, where she opened a school. Mark Twain, while he was "roughing it," stopped by twice and used Miss Clapp's examination night as the inspiration for Chapter XXI of *The Adventures of Tom Sawyer*. Clapp later became preceptress, professor of history and English and librarian at the University of Nevada in Reno. She also won the position of committee clerk of the state assembly in 1883. In 1901 at age seventy-seven, she returned to California to spend her final four years.

Where Rogers and Clapp acquired their extensive knowledge remains a mystery. There are no local records that indicated their attendance or graduation from any institution of higher learning. They may have been lucky enough to attend a seminary like that of Mrs. Willard in Troy, New York. They may have taught themselves or shared a tutor with siblings. That certainly was not uncommon. However they gained their educations, they were part of a growing chorus of men and women demanding higher education for women in general and access to male-only universities in particular.

Hannah Clapp, far right, with some pupils
outside of her Sierra Seminary.

Courtesy of the Nevada State Museum
Carson City, Nevada

The experience of Anna Howard Shaw, which she recounted in her autobiography, was probably similar to many girls of the era. She lived in rural western Michigan. One incident stood out in her memory. Anna's father had berated her severely for "idling away" reading when there was "real work" to be done. She had finished all of her chores, so she answered him, somewhat angrily, saying, "Father, some day I am going to college!" Later she admitted, "So far as I knew, no woman had ever gone to college. But now I had put my secret hopes into words."[43] Shaw did not know women like Rogers and Clapp. She did not have any role models, but she knew what she wanted. From then on, she worked steadily both academically and financially to achieve that goal. Obtaining money to pay for college was one of the reasons she abandoned rural school teaching in favor of sewing which paid more.

Regarding educational opportunities for the women of Washtenaw County, there is a delightful and true story about a young woman from Ann Arbor who also wanted an education. Her name was Sarah E. Burger. Sarah felt it was unfair that only men could attend the University of Michigan. In 1853, though still only a child, she had witnessed the Fourth National Women's Rights Convention in Cleveland, Ohio. The experience of participating in such an important event with more than 1500 other participants including William Lloyd Garrison, Lucy Stone, Antoinette Brown Blackwell, and Lucretia Mott, no doubt had a profound impact on Sarah. Five years later, having studied very hard at Ann Arbor High School, eighteen-year-old Sarah Burger led a dozen qualified young women to a University of Michigan Board of Regents' meeting telling the all-male Board that not only should the University open its doors to women but that she and the others intended to apply for admission the following year. Sara did apply – twice. And they turned her down – twice. She finally went to Michigan State Normal School from which she graduated in 1862. One cannot but admire her spunk. She married Ozora Stearns, who graduated in the first class of the University of Michigan's Law School in 1860. After his service in the Union Army, they moved to Duluth, Minnesota.

Sarah Burger Stearn's rejection from Michigan did not stop her from developing a life of service to her family, her state and her country. During the Civil War, she collected supplies

Sarah Burger Stearns

and money throughout Michigan and its adjoining states to support Union troops. For the rest of her life she wrote and lectured advocating university educations for women while also serving as National Vice President of Woman's Suffrage Associations. As a resident of Duluth, Minnesota, she served on the Duluth School Board and founded a home for needy women and children. She did all this and raised three children as well. She certainly would have been a credit to the University of Michigan had it chosen to admit her. Harriet Ada Patton who applied at the same time and was refused at the same time went on to become the second woman to graduate from the University of Michigan School of Law in the class of 1872.

When Sarah Burger and Harriet Patton applied for admission in 1858, Regents McIntyre, Parsons and Baxter prepared a lengthy report against the admittance of women which they presented at the Regents when they met the following fall. Their report objected not to the idea of educating women but to idea of co-education. They felt it was an overwhelming problem to have males and females in close proximity "unrestrained by parental influence." As a result, the Regents passed a resolution at that meeting in September of 1858 declaring it "inexpedient" to include women in the University. Nine months later, they received a petition with 1,476 signatures asking them to re-evaluate their decision and admit women to the University of Michigan.

> On Tuesday, February 8, 1859, Ann Arbor's *Local News and Advertiser* included an article by Rev. Dr. Chapin entitled "Woman and her Work." Chapin maintained that woman "has been man's slave and his empress," and she needed deliverance from both roles. The solution, he said, was to educate her. "The true way to find the sphere of anything is to educate it to its highest capacity."

Only one young woman, Alice Boise, was able to circumvent the University's refusal to admit women. Alice was intelligent, but she was also lucky in several ways. First, she lived in Ann Arbor which provided an excellent preparatory high school. She also had a father who not only supported her goals but who was a professor at the University of Michigan. She described her unique experiences in a letter thirty years after the events. On the final day of examinations in the spring of 1866, Alice's father, Professor James R. Boise, met with her teacher, Mr. Lawton. University President Erastus O. Haven and his son were also there because young Haven was a classmate of Alice's. Both young people had received outstanding scores on their examinations. "My father," wrote Alice, "laid one hand on young Haven's shoulder and one on mine, and said in impassioned tones to President Haven, 'Your son can go on, and my daughter, because she is a girl, cannot.' " President Haven, she said, was adamantly opposed to women entering the University. By September, Professor Boise had decided to let his daughter audit his class. "I remember," said Alice, "I stole hurriedly down the path in the hillside, trembling. In a little room beside my father's classroom, I left my shawl and my hat, and waited for the roar of the advancing tread of my dreaded classmates. Would they hiss, or would they howl? They entered. [From] Some, there was a little murmur, and for the rest, they were silent." Alice later audited Professor Adams' class studying Livy and Professor Frieze's studying Horace. By the time she wrote the letter which described these events, she was convinced that her experiences had contributed to the ultimate acceptance of women to the University of Michigan. Providence had given her an opportunity "to lift from within the latch of its [the University's] door..." [44] And perhaps she had been somewhat instrumental, but it took, according to Boise, the resignation of President Haven three years later and the appointment of "dear Professor Frieze" as interim president to actually open the door.

Alice's reminiscence, like all personal memory, tells only her part of the story. In 1855, Dr. Haven, then a professor not president, maintained that he advocated at the State Education Convention in Ann Arbor that women be admitted. In his autobiography, he claimed "...it was regarded as rather a dangerous joke on my part." [45] But Andrew McLaughlin's 1891 *History of Higher Education in Michigan* only says that Haven was in favor of women's higher education. That should not be confused with co-education at the University of Michigan. Elizabeth Farrand supported Alice Boise's statements about Haven. In her 1885 *History of the University of Michigan* Farrand stated that Haven was "decidedly opposed" to co-education, but he succumbed to public pressure and in 1868 "mildly recommended the admission [of women]." His recommendation was so mild, the Regents ignored it. Haven also said that allowing women into the University would "infallibly" lessen its "prosperity and success." [46] That is the old argument that the University's reputation would be diminished. The following year, however, Regent Willard upped the ante when he publically declared, "No rule exists in any of the University statutes which excludes women from admission the University." [47] The original statute of the University when it was established in 1837 declared "The University shall be open to all persons who possess the requisite literary and moral qualifications." [48] His resolution remained on the table until after President Haven's resignation in June of 1869. Alice Boise was not present when the final decision was made to open the University of Michigan's doors to women. She and her family had moved to Chicago where she ultimately graduated in 1872 - not from the University of Michigan but from the University of Chicago.

Women's suffrage has long been heralded as the great reform movement for women of the nineteenth century. I suggest we all rethink that assumption. Without the dramatic improvements in the area of women's education, the suffrage movement would have died stillborn. Elizabeth Cady Stanton attended Mrs. Willard's school in Troy, New York. Susan B. Anthony was not as lucky since her family suffered financial reverses in the panic of 1837 which curtailed her formal education. But any woman, like Anthony, who learned to read and write at the age of three and left a local school because the teacher would not instruct a girl in long division, would have no trouble being an autodidact. Michigan's feminist leader, Lucy Stone attended Mt. Holyoke before graduating from Oberlin. Educational opportunities such as Michigan Female College and Michigan State Normal School trained women so that they could expand their opportunities beyond the family and home environment. With a better education, women could write more persuasively and speak more eloquently in public forums. And they could be more effective teaching in rural schools. They even could establish select schools and teach at public high schools.

[1] Caroline Bird, *Enterprising Women* (New York: W. W. Norton and Co., 1976), 72.

[2] The east west division in Ypsilanti ultimately created quite a rivalry enhanced by the fact that the railroad located its depot on the east side while the post office was on the west. Jealousy peaked in the 1850's when the east side seceded creating its own town. Not until 1858 did the two sides rejoin to incorporate as the City of Ypsilanti. Ann Arbor had a similar rivalry between Lower Town and Upper Town. Anson Brown the founder of Lower Town wanted to make it the center of activity, but a cholera epidemic in 1834 gave the advantage to Upper Town which is now the center of City of Ann Arbor.

[3] O.W. Stephenson, *Ann Arbor: The First Hundred Years* (Ann Arbor: Ann Arbor Chamber of Commerce,1927), 78.

[4] Thomas Hennings, *Looking Back* (Whitmore Lake, MI: Northfield Township Historical Society,1985), 118.

[5] Julius Haab, "Developments in Rural Education in Washtenaw County," *Impressions, #4* (Ann Arbor: Washtenaw County Historical Society, 1943), 4.

[6] "History of the Ann Arbor Public Schools" (unpublished, Ann Arbor Public Library), 125.

Two years after this conference, on February 23, 1857, the newly formed Washtenaw County Teachers Association met at Professor Nutting's Lodi Academy.

[7] Annette English, "History of Manchester Township" (unpublished manuscript, Manchester Public Library, 1930), 149.

[8] Jane Palmer, "A History of Manchester" (Unpublished, Manchester Public Library), 105.

[9] Cornelia Corselius, *Financie* (Ann Arbor: Register Publishing Co., 1885), 32-33.

[10] Mary Rice Fairbank,"A Sketch of the Life of Mrs. Mary Rice Fairbank (memorial booklet, 1907), 10.

[11] "History of the Ann Arbor Public Schools" (unpublished, Ann Arbor public Library), 86.

[12] Palmer, 106.

[13] Carol W. Freeman, *Of Dixboro*, (1979), 35-36.

[14] Haab, 10.

[15] "History," 30.

[16] Sister Marie Hayda, "The Urban Dimension and the Midwestern Frontier" (unpublished dissertation, University of Michigan, 1966), 106.

[17] Glenda Riley, *Inventing the American Woman, An Inclusive History* (Wheeling, IL: Harlan Davidson Inc., 1995), 78.

[18] Cornelia Corselius,"Ann Arbor's Earliest Select Schools" (unpublished in Lucy Chapin Papers, Bentley Historical Library, University of Michigan), 17-18.

[19] Corselius, 4.

[20] Corselius, 5.

[21] Corselius, 9.

[22] Chapman 781.

[23] "Ypsilanti Seminary," in "Education Collection: Ypsilanti Union School and Seminary 1834-79," at Ypsilanti Historical Archives, Ypsilanti, MI.

[24] Harriet and Anna were the daughters of James and Hanna Cutcheon. They had eight other siblings. Hanna was born in 1817 and died in 1908. Anna was twenty-three years younger and died in 1921.

[25] Sources do not agree about this woman's name. Chapman calls her Palmer; however, a talk given by one of her contemporaries calls her Parker. I have used Parker because that is what was in the advertisement in the Emigrant in September 1834. Miss parker married and was succeeded by Miss Granger (future wife of Dr. Smith. Miss Clarke (no relation to the Ann Arbor Clarkes) followed Granger. She ultimately married Rev. Murdock. Thus we can see that the school lasted for a while.

[26] "Lucy Chapin Scrapbook" in "Lucy Chapin Papers," at Bentley Historical Library, University of Michigan.

[27] Corselius, 14.

[28] Elizabeth Cady Stanton, *Eighty Years and More: Reminiscences 1815-1897* (New York: T. Fisher Unwin, 1898), 35.

[29] Stephenson, 129.

[30] Courtesy of Wystan Stevens.

[31] William E. Baxter, *America and the American* (G. Routledge and Co., 1855), 94

[32] "History of Chelsea," *Impressions* (Ann Arbor: Washtenaw County Historical Society, February 2002), 8.

[33] "History of the Ann Arbor Public Schools,"130.

[34] Lela Duff, *Pioneer School* (Ann Arbor: Ann Arbor Board of Education, 1958), 19.

[35] Roccena Norris, "Memories of Roccena Norris" in "Norris Family Collection" at Ypsilanti Historical Archives, 10.

[36] Egbert Isbell, *A History of Eastern Michigan University* (Ypsilanti: Eastern Michigan University Press, 1971), 306.

[37] Justin Kestenbaum, ed., *A Pioneer Anthology: the Making of Michigan* (Detroit: Wayne State University Press, 1999), 288.

[38] Frank N. Turner, ed. "An Account of Ingham County From its Organization," in *Historic Michigan*, Vol 3 (Dayton, Ohio, National History Association, 1924), 134.

[39] Kestenbaum, 293.

[40] Kestenbaum, 289.

[41] *Nevada History Society*, Quarterly XX, no.3: 168.

[42] Anna Howard Shaw, *The Story of a Pioneer* (New York: Harper and Brothers 1915), 44.

When Lucy Stone said much the same thing, she received "a deluge of ridicule" from her family

[43] Mrs. J. Leslie French, "Looking Backward - The Status of Women in University Life," *Impressions* (Ann Arbor: Washtenaw County Historical Society, December 1968), 11-12.

[44] Elizabeth Farrand, *History of the University of Michigan* (Ann Arbor: Register Publishing House, 1885) 188.

[45] Farrand, 191.

[46] Farrand, 192.

[47] Dorothy McGuigan, *Dangerous Experiment* (Ann Arbor: Center for the Continuing Education of Women, 1970), 15.

CHAPTER SIX: WOMEN IN THE ARTS

Sarah Burger, since she was older than Alice Boise and attuned to the feminist message, may have heard Lucinda Stone, a western Michigan contemporary, speak when Miss Stone delivered a lecture in Ann Arbor in March of 1855. According to a letter written to the *Argus* on March 23 of that year, there was a good deal of heckling, stamping and whistling that disturbed Stone's talk. The letter writer may have been a woman because he/she chose to remain anonymous and found such behavior juvenile, disrespectful and embarrassing. On a separate occasion, Lucy Stone summed up the frustration many well-educated women in Washtenaw County no doubt felt when she wrote: "I seemed to be shut out of everything I wanted to do. I might teach school... I might go out dressmaking or tailoring or trim bonnets or I might work in a factory or go into domestic service; there the mights ended and the might nots began." Lucy Stone and the women of nineteenth century Washtenaw County were constrained by many impediments. Primarily they were confined by the middle class standards of their day which believed that women should not work and, if they did need to work, they should work in respectable "feminine" jobs which would have included cultural endeavors such as music, art and literature.

The availability of music instruction, like millinery, was erratic at first; however, soon women in every town and village in Washtenaw County offered some form of instruction in music. Much of that instruction was provided in select schools and academies which charged extra for musical instruction. For example, the Clark School for Young Ladies' academic tuition in its earlier days was only $5 for senior classes, but it asked $8 for piano instruction and "use of the Instrument." Any parent who was disposed to send a daughter to the Clark School would certainly want her to learn piano as a sign of refinement. Providing music instruction for additional tuition was also a fairly standard practice in public schools. Ann Arbor Union School in 1859 charged the same price, $8 per term, for piano instruction.

In the days before radio, CD's or MP3's, learning to produce music for the entertainment of oneself and others was an important part of a child's education. Not only was such a skill a sign of refinement, having a piano indicated a family's level of affluence. Such social standards provided many young women with opportunities to earn income by teaching music. One of the earliest private teachers who has left a record of herself appears to be Rosette Andrews. Miss Andrews was nineteen when she indicated to the 1860 Census enumerator that she was a music teacher living in Saline. What form of music she taught was not noted. Most of the early teachers taught voice, piano or violin. Jennie Wood was somewhat unusual because she offered harp as well as piano lessons in Ann Arbor the 1860's. Her advertisement in the September 1,

1865 *Argus* states that she was continuing to provide these lesson thus suggesting that she had been doing so previously.

Magoffin Monument

Unlike Rosette Andrews and Jennie Wood, Mrs. James Magoffin was a mature woman. She was the wife of the rector of St. James Episcopal Church in Dexter. The Magoffins had three children, but only the middle child, a daughter named Mary C., called Carrie, survived. Mrs. Eliza Ann Foster Magoffin taught both piano and organ in the 1870's. Her advertisements in the *Dexter Leader* offered lessons to beginners as well as advanced students with the caveat that "she can teach successfully if she is allowed her way to do it." [1] History has not preserved what her style of teaching was, but she clearly had confidence in it. Mrs. Magoffin became a widow in 1883. She spent her final years in Saginaw, Michigan, with her married daughter, Mary C. Humphrey. After her own death, she was buried in Ann Arbor. The Magoffin monument is located on the far east side of Forest Hills Cemetery.

In addition to Miss Andrews, whose career was brief, Saline benefited from the presence of three women with long careers in music. The earliest of the three was Mrs. Samantha Wood Hall, wife of Dr. Daniel Hall, who began teaching music in Saline when she arrived with her husband from Hillsdale County in 1862. According to Saline historian, Bob Lane, she had been educated at Professor Nutting's Lodi Academy, a school noted for its music and language curriculum. Nutting also officiated at her wedding. [2] In addition to giving lessons, Mrs. Hall played the organ for several churches in the area. She was for the second half of the nineteenth century "Saline's music teacher."

That designation transferred to Vesta Mills late in the century. Miss Mills lived her entire life in her family's home on the corner of Michigan Avenue and Mills Street. The American Legion now occupies the site, but the street name remains as a silent tribute to her father, Ruel Mills, and herself. Miss Mills graduated from the University School of Music in 1896. She appears to have begun teaching while still a student and continued teaching until the year before her death. That adds up to an impressive career of more than fifty years. Wayne Clements of Saline recalled taking lessons from her during the last years of her life. Despite the fact that she was quiet and never overbearing, there was an element of intimidation felt by students such as Clements. "She was," he said, "well respected. There was a status to taking lessons from her."[3] He especially remembers, as every student does, the ordeal of giving a recital. Miss Mills held recitals for her students in her home. Everyone would walk up the long tree lined drive and congregate in the room where her big, black, grand piano sat. It was a memorable experience for everyone involved.

Vesta Mills never married. She devoted her life to her music. When she died, she left a sizable part – if not all – of her estate to the University of Michigan's School of Music. As a result, there is a room in the Music School named for her. It houses part of the Stearns Collection of musical instruments. I am sure that would have pleased her immensely. Less encouraging is the fact that there is no indication in the gallery of either who she was or why the room was named for her. Even more discouraging is that no one at the School of Music seems to know how that room got its name. As so often has happened, history preserved the name but forgot the woman.

The third musical woman from Saline was a contemporary of Vesta Mills. Born in 1866, Fannie Caldwell Unterkircher was the daughter of William Caldwell, pastor of the Presbyterian Church in Lodi Plains, which was what residents hoped would become a town. It never did. Today Lodi Township lies to the north of Saline. Her mother, Sarah Whiting Caldwell, was an accomplished organist in Boston; therefore, her parents sent Fannie to Boston to study organ at the New England Conservatory of Music. She was fourteen. When she returned three years later, her father was serving as chaplain in the Ionia House of Correction. She taught music and played for services in the prison chapel as well as providing organ music for the Presbyterian Church. She continued in that capacity until her marriage to Harry D. Heller. Sadly, Harry died five years later at which time she not only began teaching school but also taught piano and organ. Her second marriage was to Dr. C.F. Unterkircher. It was as Mrs. Unterkircher that Fannie organized one

Vesta Mills

Courtesy of the Saline Historical Society

of the first junior choirs in Michigan. She made her influence felt throughout Saline. A true educator, she helped establish the Saline Public Library and in her will, designated $10,000 (the price of a very nice home in 1956, the year she died) to create a scholarship in her husband's name. By doing so, she, like so many women, unselfishly ensured that his name, rather than hers, would be remembered.

Music has always played a prominent role in the Saline area. Because of its size and proximity to the University of Michigan, however, it was Ann Arbor which contained the greatest number of female music teachers. Some were local women while others came to town in order to teach at the Ann Arbor School of Music. That school, which opened in 1880, became in 1892 the University School of Music; however, it was not until 1940 that this school officially became part of the University of Michigan. Teaching the pianoforte at the school was Elsa Von Grave, who had played for the Bavarian royal family before immigrating to the United States in the 1890's. Her colleague, Alice Griswold Bailey, born in Boston, received her entree into the Ann Arbor music scene when she first appeared with the Choral Union as a last minute substitute for an ailing diva. Finally Miss Charlotte Eleonore Jaffe and Miss Francis Taylor also were faculty members in the 1890's. Not only were they pictured in the *Headlight* of 1892, their names are listed in faculty concert programs during that decade.

In addition to the University School of Music, Michigan State Normal School established a music department in 1854. Jessie Gibbes taught there after graduating from the University School of Music. She simultaneously taught in Ann Arbor before moving to New York to establish her own school of music. Her contemporary, Miss Clyde Estelle Foster, however, stayed in the area for thirty-five years serving as a training supervisor in the music department of the Normal School. Miss Foster was called "a pioneer in the field of public school music." [4] She began her teaching career in Fargo, North Dakota in 1889. Ten years later she returned to the Normal School in Ypsilanti. Foster did not even take her summers to rest. Instead she taught at both the University of Minnesota and Northwestern University. She retired in 1935, three years before her death at age seventy.

Clyde E. Foster

Courtesy of the Ypsilanti Historical Society

The most locally famous Ann Arbor female vocal music teacher is, unquestionably, Pauline Widenmann Kempf. Pauline was born in Ann Arbor just in time for Christmas 1860. She attended local public schools and sang in the Episcopal choir. At the age of fourteen she made her first public appearance in "The Naiad Queen." Lifelong Ann Arbor resident, Marie Rominger, recalled how the schools were closed on that January day because everyone was either on stage or in the audience. Two years later University of Michigan Professor Henry Frieze helped to organize a concert to raise money to send the talented Miss Widenmann to the Cincinnati Conservatory of Music, an opportunity her family could not afford. She studied there until age eighteen when she joined her widowed mother at the Somerville School for Girls in St. Clair, Michigan. Mrs. Widenmann had been forced to sell the family home and seek employment at the school. Pauline also taught there until her marriage to Reuben Kempf of Ann Arbor in 1883.

Pauline Widenmann in 1874

Courtesy of the Bentley Historical Library,
University of Michigan

By the end of the century, the Kempfs were proud parents of daughter Elsa and son Paul as well as the equally proud owners of a Greek Revival house at 312 S. Division which soon was dubbed, "the little school of music on Division Street." [5] Mrs. Kempf served as choir director at the Congregational Church as well as a soloist at the St. Andrew's Episcopal Church. She also worked as the voice coach for artists performing at Hill Auditorium. Except for one winter during which she joined Metropolitan stars in studying with Oscar Saenger in New York, she taught private pupils in her home. Mrs. Kempf did not retire until she was eighty-five years old, seven years before her death in 1953.

Considerably less well-known locally but more famous nationally were several other Washtenaw County women. One was Frances E. Caspary/Caspari. Born in Ann Arbor in 1879, she was the daughter of William and Catherine Caspary. Her mother ran a bakery and restaurant in Ann Arbor while her father did the same in Chelsea. In fact, Frances worked for her father in Chelsea circa 1894 before going to Pittsburgh to study with John Dennis Mehan. Frances began her music training at the St. Thomas School in Ann Arbor. When she was twelve, she attended St. Mary's Academy in Monroe, Michigan. Returning to Ann Arbor, she became a pupil of Dr. Willis and starred as the Choral Union's lead soprano before she even had begun her training at the University School of Music. On the very day of her graduation exercises, June 12, 1903, Caspary and six other graduates met and formed Sigma Alpha Iota, the international professional music sorority to complement Phi Mu Alpha which only inducted men. Frances was elected first secretary-treasurer of this new organization, which still exists today.

Her big career opportunity occurred at the 1907 May Festival in Ann Arbor, when Madame Schumann-Heink shared the stage with Caspary At that time Madame Schumann-Heink urged Caspary to go to New York City. Frances took her advice and studied with Harriet Ware. It was during the nine years that she taught and performed in New York that Frances changed the spelling of her name to Caspari with an "i" not a "y." Perhaps she thought it made her appear more exotic. She certainly was not some obscure individual wandering the streets of the great metropolis. At one point the street cars of New York were festooned with banners announcing: "Caspari sings Tonight!" The venue was Carnegie Hall. She was, at least for a little while, famous. Eventually Caspari (still with an "i") returned to Ann Arbor in 1916 where she maintained a studio, in addition to one in Detroit, until 1929. Then ill health forced her to retire. Local historian, Louis Doll, suggested Caspari's ill health was the result of obesity. It is true that she was what the nineteenth century would call "fleshy." Miss Caspari died in 1948.

Frances Casperi

Courtesy of the Sigma Alpha Iota

Minnie Davis Sherrill

Courtesy of Sigma Alpha Iota

Frances Caspari's fellow musical Ann Arborite was Minnie Minton Davis who served as the first president of Sigma Alpha Iota. In fact, it was Minnie who was instrumental in encouraging the others to form the sorority though Davis herself gives the credit to Mrs. Howland, whose husband was a music professor. Davis like Caspari was born in Ann Arbor. Her father was a builder while her mother, Lizzie Smith Davis, achieved some success as a writer for newspapers and periodicals. Minnie, who began her piano studies in 1877 at age five, had her public debut at the tender age of seven. F. H. Pease from the Normal School and Professor F. L Yorke from the Detroit Conservatory of Music both guided her development. Graduating from the University School of Music in 1901, Minnie remained in Ann Arbor to teach piano at her alma mater. While at the School of Music, she not only gave her own recitals and concerts but was a favored accompanist for others as well as for May Festival and the Choral Union, a three hundred voice choir. She did her graduate work in Paris with Harold Baurer. In 1909, Miss Davis married Dr. Edwin Sherrill. They lived in Detroit, yet Mrs. Sherrill remained active in the wider musical world lecturing and giving recitals throughout Michigan. She continued to accompany and coach vocalists for the rest of her life. Mrs. Sherrill celebrated her one hundredth birthday by playing selections by Offenbach and Rubinstein for some friends. She died in 1972.

Elsa Stanley succeeded Minnie Davis as president of Sigma Alpha Iota. Elsa came to Ann Arbor as a girl when her father replaced Calvin Cady as the director of the University Musical Society in 1888. Mr. Stanley also became a professor of music in 1890. He later headed the Music School for many years. His profession, no doubt, exposed Elsa to the best the music world had to offer; however, before making music her career, she earned a degree in literature from the University of Michigan. Following graduation she studied for two years in Paris, returning to Ann Arbor in 1908. Then she taught at the School of Music until her untimely death in May 1910. She was thirty-one.

Elizabeth Campbell, daughter of Robert and Lavina Childs Campbell, was yet another one of the seven founders of Sigma Alpha Iota. Born 1873, she spent her early childhood on her parents' farm near Ann Arbor. Elizabeth's parents, both of whom were college educated, left the farm and moved into town so that their children could have the best educations possible. Elizabeth graduated from the University of Michigan in 1895. She then taught for a year in Wyandotte, Michigan, before returning to graduate from the University School of Music. Between 1903 and 1910, she taught voice. As has happened to so many women, she sacrificed her musical career in order to care for her dying mother. After her mother died, Elizabeth became recorder of transcripts for the School of Engineering at the University of Michigan. She remained at that job for more than twenty-five years during which time she also supervised Sigma Alpha Iota's finances. Elizabeth Campbell died in Ann Arbor in September, 1949.

Elizabeth Campbell
Courtesy of Sigma Alpha Iota

Nora Crane Hunt
Courtesy of Sigma Alpha Iota

Two months after the death of Elizabeth Campbell, another woman important to the local music scene also passed away. Nora Crane Hunt was born in Jackson, Michigan, in 1874. She graduated first from Jackson High School and then University School of Music in 1903. She immediately joined the faculty of University School of Music where she remained for thirty-eight years. Until 1912 Nora continued to live in Jackson, commuting twice a week to Ann Arbor. She and her mother moved to Ann Arbor permanently in 1912 no doubt as a result of the harrowing experiences Nora experienced commuting. Hunt recalled one stormy winter night when the trolley derailed. She and her fellow passengers remained in the trolley car all night as the blizzard raged outside. She did not reach her home until the following afternoon. That seemed as good reason as any to move closer to her work. For over twenty-five years she directed the University Girls' Glee Club. Nora Crane Hunt died in 1949. Her contributions were commemorated in 1958 when one of the units of Mary Markley Hall at the University of Michigan was named for her.

Recitation and oral reading, like music, were also common forms of social entertainment in the nineteenth century. Since public speaking is not something most people naturally and comfortably do, lessons were required. Miss M. A. Kelsey advertised in the *Ann Arbor Courier* in February of 1877 as an elocution teacher

In addition to music and elocution, a "respectable" lady also could engage in artistic pursuits. Art was a perfectly acceptable female hobby which might be turned into a vocation within the narrow parameters of nineteenth century society. Miss Anna Robinson taught art as well as music in 1859 at Ann Arbor Union School. The school charged $3 per term for watercolor and $8 for oil painting instruction. One also could provide private lessons. Miss E. A. Horan of Ann Arbor offered lessons in wax fruit and flower making as well as other branches of "ornamental work" in the September of 1865 issues of the *Argus*. Similarly, Mrs. Alice J. Whitaker of Chelsea offered instruction in crayon and pastels as well as oil and water color painting. A dozen lessons cost $5. That certainly wasn't going to make Mrs. Whitaker wealthy since each lesson in today's purchasing power cost only seven dollars. But neither was it to be scoffed at, especially if she did the lessons for groups.

Or a woman could put her talents to use as an independent artist. In addition to Katie Rogers whose artistic career was put on hold for seven years when she assumed the management of her deceased father's business[6], her contemporary, Roccena "Roccie" B. Norris, niece of Ypsilanti pioneers, Mark and Roccena Norris, aspired to earn a living as a painter. Miss Norris was raised with a strong sense of her place in one of Ypsilanti's most prominent families. In addition to philanthropic efforts, she supported women's suffrage and higher education. What made her slightly unusual among her social peers was that she advertised herself as a portrait painter in the City Directories of 1878 and 1883. And she was not alone in her aspirations. Gibson's *Early Artists of Michigan* reveals nine more Washtenaw County women who sought to take their art beyond an amateur pastime: Almira Spaford of Manchester, Harriet Hyde and Hilda Lodeman of Ypsilanti and three ladies from Ann Arbor: Lillie Nichols, Matie Cornwell, and Sarah Gardner (daughter of Nanette Gardner). None of those additional ladies, however, appears to have been successful on a long term basis.

Two Michigan women who did become fairly well known in the art world have connections to Washtenaw County although they did not achieve their reputations there. They never established themselves in any one place but traveled and studied and exhibited in many cities around the world. One of the women was Jane Mahon Stanley, daughter-in-law of well-known artist, John Mix Stanley. She painted primarily watercolors and retired in Ann Arbor, passing away in 1940 at the age of seventy-seven.

In similar fashion the village of Dexter became home to Della Garretson and her twin sister, Lillie. The sisters were born in Logan, Ohio, in 1860 and studied art in Detroit, Bruges and Paris but decided to spend their later years in Dexter. Though they studied art together and both won prizes in competitions, it was Della whose painting, "Portrait of Miss G," is part of the permanent collection of the Detroit Institute of Arts. The ambiguous title makes it unclear whether the portrait is of Lillie G. or a self-portrait of Della G. Most believe it is Lillie. There is no record of whether or not they were identical twins. Remaining a team to the very end, they both died in 1940, four months apart, at age eighty.

Mary Shaw

By the end of the century, at least one woman found, for a few years, a more commercial outlet for her artistic talents. Mary L. Shaw worked for the Chelsea Manufacturing Company which originally made gadgets such as tea strainers and knife sharpeners but which became Washtenaw County's first automobile works. This wasn't the career she expected to find. Born in Chelsea in 1874, the daughter of Dr. Thomas and Mary Shaw, she graduated from Michigan State Normal School in the mid 1890's and worked for a while as music teacher. She probably also taught school after graduation, but there is no record of where. Nor is there any record of how she was hired by A.R. Welch to draw pictures of automotive parts for his company. We can speculate, however, that her employment resulted from close family ties in Chelsea. Though her parents had moved to Ypsilanti, Mary's maternal grandparents, Fisher and Phoebe Hooker as well as her aunt, Katheryn Hooker, remained active members of the Chelsea community.

Mr. Welch who owned the Chelsea Manufacturing Company produced an automobile called the Welch Tourist, which he took to the 1903 Chicago Auto Show. Chelsea Manufacturing apparently did not make all the parts; it subcontracted some. That was where Mary's skills became important. It was her drawings that Mr. Welch sent to other manufacturers. Mary once told Nina Belle Wurster that "She was always afraid the drawings might be wrong, but they never were." [7] Mr. Welch moved his company to Pontiac, Michigan in 1904. When he died only eight years later, General Motors absorbed the business.

Mary then turned to a variety of related careers. She did not, however, return to teaching. She worked for a time as a bookkeeper. In 1922, Ypsilanti's First National Bank hired her as the safe deposit box custodian after which she became a bank teller. And, according to an anonymous primary source, she ran a "haberdashery" in her home. During the depression, Miss Shaw worked at "Ford's" which probably meant the Ford Motor Company. This source also indicated that Mary did not retire until she was seventy-one years old. For all of her life until just prior to her death in 1969, she continued residing in the family home at 106 N. Adams in Ypsilanti.

Mary Shaw
Courtesy of the Ypsilanti Historical Society

The anonymous source, unfortunately, presents several problems for researchers. It contains many contradictions. The writer indicated a birth date for Miss Shaw of 1892 yet said Shaw was seventy-one in 1945. The latter age and date coincide with the 1874 birth date found in the census. Second, the anonymous source in the "106 N Adams" file at the Ypsilanti Archives also said Shaw graduated from Michigan State Normal School in 1888. Since she was born in 1874, Shaw would have been only fourteen in 1888. Michigan State Normal School would not have accepted her at that age. Sixteen was the minimum age. Despite these inaccuracies, the anonymous source offers potentially valuable information about Mary's later life. It may be that the writer only knew Mary Shaw as a mature adult since the inaccuracies all derive from Mary's childhood years.

At least one woman in Washtenaw County turned her hobby of drawing and painting into a career as an illustrator. Charlotte Doty, fourth daughter of Samuel and Hannah Doty of Ann Arbor, might have remained just an amateur artist had she not had a sister named Clara, who was three years older. Clara Doty was a poetess who so impressed the male editor of *Graham's Magazine*, one of the most popular national magazines before the Civil War, that he published her poems on many occasions with his own commentary. In an 1858 issue, he said Miss Doty, then age twenty, had a "clear yet sensitive mind" and had obviously "appreciated the sweetest lyrics of Heine" [8]

Clara Doty portrait
by Katie Rogers

Courtesy of the Bentley Historical Library,
University of Michigan

Both Doty daughters married, Clara to a man named

> *With Grandmother Cricket on washing day*
> *Was always the mischief and all to pay.*
> *If sunny and fair, then that rogue of a Tim*
> *(Her little grandson,) had the witches in him,*
> *And played her such pranks, and such tricks,*
> *that she said,*
> *T'was a wonder she had a wit in her head.*
> *But ah! If it rained, woe to everyone there,*
> *For their Granny herself was as cross as a bear.*

Bates and Charlotte to a man named Finley, but that did not stop their artistic efforts. In fact, they joined forces to create a book for children *Songs for Gold Locks* published by E. B. Smith and Co. of Detroit. The "gold locks" presumably referred to Charlotte's daughter, Flora. A few of the poems are retellings of famous stories such as the "Three Billy Goats Gruff." Most, such as "Grandmother Cricket's Washing Day," are original.

Clara continued her poetic career, publishing three more children's books through D. Lothrop and Co. of Boston. A copy of *Songs for Goldlocks* is being preserved in the Bentley Historical Library while the University of Michigan Special Collections has a copy of *Classics of Baby-Land*. Charlotte designed but did not execute the drawings for the later books.

Clara Doty was not, however, the only woman in Washtenaw County who published poetry. Though busy raising her family and active in community endeavors as well as her own career as a magnetic physician, Sophia M. Pierce (Mrs. Nathan) continued an interest in writing that began when she was just sixteen. Since that time she wrote articles and poems for "leading papers of Michigan" and magazines with national circulation. She published sentimental poems which were so popular at the time using her own name, but she also composed biting social criticism which no doubt caused quite a stir since by doing so she was overstepping the appropriate bounds for female behavior.

In the 1870's Mrs. Pierce composed a series called "Ann Arbor in Slices" for the *Ann Arbor Courier* using a pseudonym. Mrs. Pierce clearly received her initial inspiration from George Foster, a New York journalist who published extremely popular accounts of life in that burgeoning metropolis in the 1840's. He called his series, *New York in Slices*. It was compiled and published in book form in 1849. Following suit, Mrs. Pierce began each of her poems with the following:

> This beautiful city, its virtues and vices,
> Its art and its science, I'll serve you in slices;
> Besides I will give, for sake of variety,
> Occasional views of its scenes and society.

Once having appropriated the idea and title, however, Mrs. Pierce's poems were entirely her own. She utilized her poems to comment on local events such as the 1874 explosion in the store of A. Hertz in which twenty people were injured. On the front page of the June 16 1876 issue, however, her poem took a slice out of the medical profession:

> The nurse and the doctor were checkmates-
> Their dupes the old man and his wife,
> Whom thus they had cornered adroitly
> By moves in professions so rife.

By August 4, Pierce's thoughts had mellowed or else she was trying to mollify local physicians who, no doubt, took umbrage at her previous comments.

> The medicine given brought soothing repose
> And rest that bore signs of improving
> And softly caressed was the babe's little form
> By father and mother so loving.
> The long hours passed, and the doctor still sat,
> His vigil so faithfully keeping
> Watching the pulses and breathing so low
> Of the baby still quietly sleeping.

Since her material was trenchant and controversial, it is easy to see why she used a pen name. The nom de plume, she chose was "Soph." Several possible reasons for choosing that pseudonym come to mind. Clearly it is a shortened version of her name which derives from the Greek word for wisdom. She may also have seen herself as a reflection of the sophist tradition from ancient Greece. Sophists were rhetoricians who taught their students to utilize cogent and effective argumentation. In either case, it conveyed a subtle message of authority to her readers.

In addition to poets, Ann Arbor produced published prose writers of widely different styles and themes. The earliest was Daphne S. Giles who authored a temperance novel in 1856. Called *East and West*, it denounced drink as "the engine of destruction." [9] The temperance issue, a very popular reform topic in the nineteenth century, eventually led to the passage of the eighteenth amendment prohibiting alcohol from being made or sold in the United States. According to David Reynolds, author of *Waking Giant*, the average American in 1830 drank four gallons of hard liquor per year. By 1845 that had diminished to 1.8 gallons. That statistic does not indicate the problem of drunkenness went away since the beer industry was expanding at that time. In 1850 Americans drank 36 million gallons of beer; by 1890 consumption had risen to 855 million gallons.

Thus temperance was still a serious issue and would remain so the rest of the century, prompting civic groups such as the Women's Christian Temperance Union, which had 150,000 members, to advocate reform. There were even temperance hotels for tee-totaling travelers. Some local historians claim that the reason women's suffrage was voted down twice by Ann Arbor voters was that the men feared women would use their votes to shut down the saloons; hence they did not want to extend the vote to include women. Jack London says much the same thing in the *John Barleycorn: Alcoholic Memoirs of Jack London*; however for London, it was a positive statement. "The moment women get the vote in any community, the first thing they [will] proceed to do is close the saloons." And if the saloons were closed, London reasoned, then he would have to stop drinking which he was unable to do when liquor was readily available. I suspect that even then London would have managed to find bootlegged alcohol. Daniel Okrent in *Last Call: The Rise and Fall of Prohibition*, however, asserts that the notion that women would vote for prohibition was "incontrovertible." [10]

By 1871 communities were demanding that their leaders do something to limit the effects of alcohol. Silas Douglas successfully campaigned for mayor of Ann Arbor on a platform of strict enforcement of a law banning saloons from being open on Sundays. The problem of drunkenness was so ubiquitous that, when Jesse Brayman died of a broken neck near Manchester, the same year as Douglas' election, the members of the jury at the inquest – with straight faces – returned a verdict saying that Brayman was murdered and the culprit was alcohol. With that as the social backdrop, it is little wonder that Daphne Giles chose the evils of drink as the theme for her fiction. Nor did she discriminate by gender. Chapter Six is entitled "The Inebriate Wife" while another subplot describes a brother who, under the influenced by alcohol distributes counterfeit money. This causes his father to die of shock when he learns of his son's misdeeds. But this is fiction, you might say. Yes, however, in the preface Giles states that she was not a reader or writer of novels. In other words, these situations, bad as they sounded, were based on real incidents.

Another fiction writer was Cornelia E. Corselius, daughter of George and Clementia Corselius. Cornelia's father was one of the first pioneers of Ann Arbor. He is best known as the editor of the *Western Emigrant*, established in 1829. Mr. Corselius died at sea on his way to the gold fields of California in 1849 when Cornelia was only eleven; however, his unconventional attitude towards women must have influenced his four daughters. Mr. Corselius, according to Jonathan Marwil's *History of Ann Arbor*, was "more at ease with 'the ladies of Ann Arbor,' whom he regarded as 'more intelligent and of a more dignified tone of character, than the men.'" [11] That alone in Marwil's opinion made Cornelia's father a true pioneer. After her father's death, Cornelia's widowed mother earned a living teaching in Ann Arbor at the primary school. Cornelia followed in her mother's footsteps and began teaching at the same school.

The 1830's home on Ann Street in Ann Arbor where Cornelia Corselius lived as a child.

Miss Corselius' book, *Financie and Stories from Real Life*, is a collection of short stories based on children she knew. Similar to *The Adventures of Tom Sawyer*, which was published in 1876, *Financie*, describes the harmless trouble children manage to get into and the warm supportive adults who rescue them. "Little Tommy Bright," for example, decides one morning to pick nuts. Without telling a soul, he walks nine miles to his uncle's farm in Dexter. Seeing how late it has become, he doesn't even tell his uncle he is there but heads back home. Darkness overwhelms him, and he becomes lost. Somewhere near Foster's Mill, he is rescued by kind Mr. and Mrs.

Herbert. The next day Tommy returns home to his frantic parents.

Financie, like Twain's novels, also includes historically significant vignettes of nineteenth century life and attitudes. When ten-year-old Susie Chilton finds a friend at her Young Ladies' Seminary (Misses Clark's?) in Ann Arbor, Susie goes home with her friend to visit. Her friend's farm is ten miles "out," and Susie is appalled that the girls in the family help in the fields. She, too, is expected to "watch the gap." This is a place where the fence came down, and she is to keep the animals out of the fields. She is equally shocked to learn that her friend's little sister was named Financie. The father tells her that his younger daughter is "uncommonly smart" so he has invested $500 in her name which she will get when she reaches age twenty-one. "I'm going to have her taught how to take care of her money, so I named her Financie." [12] Quietly tucked into these charming stories are revealing bits of social commentary. Nellie Bright and her friend, Libbie, discuss fashion one day as they search for Nellie's lost cow. Nellie describes a woman "with her waist all squeezed in so that looks sickly." Her friend tells her frankly that she would not "want to be so slim that I'd be in danger of breaking in two." [13] Historians can glean splendid details about the era from Miss Corselius' fiction which is probably one reason the book is still available. [14]

Miss Corselius' book was published in 1885 the same year as Elizabeth Farrand's *History of the University of Michigan*. Both women were descendants of original settlers. Elizabeth Martha Farrand's paternal grandfather was Bethuel Farrand, Washtenaw County's first probate judge. Her parents were Lucius and Frances Shaw Farrand. Born in 1852, Elizabeth graduated from Ann Arbor High School and attended the University of Michigan in the Literature Department. In 1877 she became the assistant to the University librarian. Her salary as assistant librarian was $600 in 1883. That was about what a high school teacher would make. It was during her fourteen year career as assistant librarian that she wrote her "controversial" history.

Corselius' book was perfectly acceptable by the standards of the day. As a fictional work about children, it fell into the feminine genre of moralistic fiction. Elizabeth Farrand's was far less acceptable since hers was non-fiction intended for an adult audience. Though it is definitely not a panegyric to the University, it is difficult today to understand why it was considered controversial. Her text is well documented and not unlike more modern volumes regarding the same subject. It certainly wasn't her discussion of the acceptance of women to the University that was the criticism. She presents a balanced tone discussing both sides of that controversial issue; however her revelations, such as the one that male students had drilled holes in the floor of the President's office so they could ease-drop, certainly might have embarrassed the University. And it is easy to see how her candidness might have offended conservatives. For example, she meticulously details a financial scandal that involved Dr. Douglass and Dr. Rose. The University and its supporters probably would have preferred not to have such matters known by the general public.

Miss Farrand, however, was just beginning her professional life when she wrote her *History of the University of Michigan*. Two years after its publication, she graduated from the University of Michigan's School of Medicine. Her practice took her first to Detroit, but by 1890 she was living in Port Huron, Michigan. In addition to attending to her growing number of patients, she served as president of the Northeastern Medical Association. Her fascinating life was cut short in 1900. Forty-eight year old Dr. Elizabeth Farrand died of cancer that year. She was buried in Forest Hill Cemetery, Ann Arbor.

Not until 1907 did another female author create such a stir at the University of Michigan even though her book was fiction. That debate concerned *Road to Damascus*, a novel by Mrs. Hersilia Keays. Mrs. Keays was a widow in 1902 when she lived in Ann Arbor while her two sons attended school there. The entire family left town circa 1905 so they were not around for the brouhaha the novel caused. The plot focuses on a young wife who adopts her husband's illegitimate son but never tells her husband or the boy who the child really is. The novel created such a furor that the University withdrew it from its collection because the "librarian and assistants made inquiries among other members of the faculty and found considerable antipathy against it though it was not declared harmful." According to a newspaper article dated January 3, "Students of the university do not welcome its withdrawal. Hundreds were eager to read it, and every copy owned by the library was kept in constant circulation while many people were on the waiting list." [15]

The University apparently took umbrage with the novel's character, Professor Maxwell. Maxwell closely resembled one of the faculty members at the time, a Professor Robert Mark Wenley, who began teaching philosophy in 1896. The fictional character, Professor Maxwell, is a cynic, a nihilist and a misogynist who, according to the heroine of the novel, has a profoundly negative impact on students like her adopted son. The character, Professor Maxwell, suggests to her that he, at least, has honestly expressed what he perceives at truth, while she has left her "son" to wander his personal road to Damascus not knowing who he really is. But there is nothing like controversy to stimulate book sales. The news article cited above concluded, "Now that the book is withdrawn, the book stores are preparing to lay in a larger supply." The book's appeal appears never to have waned since it is still available both in the original publication and a reprinted edition.

As with teachers, what separated these women of the arts from those who were domestic servants or factory workers or even dressmakers was their social backgrounds, their educations and their skills. Remaining safely within the prescribed parameters of their "appropriate" sphere, artistic women could instruct others in music or art. They could perform vocally or instrumentally. And they could write though this was more questionable especially if such women stepped beyond the demarcation line of inspirational feminine fiction. Nathaniel Hawthorne once expressed his frustration that there were so many "scribbling women." His real problem was that they were enjoying more success than he was.

---

1 *Dexter Leader*, July 4 1879.

2 Bob Lane, interviewed by Susan Nenadic,

3 Wayne Clements, interviewed by Susan Nenadic

4 Obituary in "Clyde Foster File," at Eastern Michigan University Archives, Ypsilanti, MI.

5 "Ann Arbor Lyra Male Chorus," *Impressions* (Ann Arbor: Washtenaw County Historical Society, April 1989), p2.

6 See Chapter Four

7 "Shaw Collection," at Ypsilanti Historical Archives, Ypsilanti, MI.

8 *History of Washtenaw County Michigan* (Chicago: Charles C. Chapman Co., 1881), 468.

9 Daphne Giles, *East and West* (Ann Arbor: Davis and Cole, 1856), 71.

10 Daniel Okrent, *Last Call: The Rise and Fall of Prohibition* (New York: Scribner, 2010), 63.

11 Jonathan Marwil, *History of Ann Arbor* (Ann Arbor: Ann Arbor Observer Co., 1987), 6.

12 Cornelia Corselius, *Financie* (Ann Arbor: Register Publishing Co., 1885),102.

13 Corselius, 26.

14 *Financie* was republished in 2009. It is also the title story in the *Cairns Collection of American Women Writers*, 2011,

15 This article has the by-line "Ann Arbor" and is glued to the inside of the cover of the novel at the Bentley Historical Record. Obviously it is from a paper outside of Washtenaw County.

CHAPTER SEVEN: EMERGING OPPORTUNITIES FOR WOMEN

The Civil War was one of the most significant events in the history of the United States. Just as the War cleaved the nation in half, it formed a bold line of demarcation between the country as it was before and the country as it became after. Before the Civil War, 80% of Americans were farmers living in rural areas. They wore home-made clothing. The region known as "the west" referred to what now would be labeled the midwest. Government, business and industry were modest in scope and influence. After the war, American expansionism reached new proportions doubling the size of the continental United States in 1860 and even stretching to foreign lands. Improvements in transportation and communication connected these diverse regions as they never had before. Americans by the thousands began moving into cities to capitalize on the new manufacturing power of the country. The Civil War formed the crucible from which so many of these changes emerged. Harbingers of these radical changes certainly existed before the War, but they only bore fruit in the final decades of the century.

Jennie Fyfe, one of the many Michigan women who nursed during the Civil War, wrote that, of course, she had been changed by experience, how could it be otherwise? She had, as the people then said, "seen the elephant." Most Americans thought the war would be quickly over. They were shocked when the casualties at Shiloh announced that the war would be long and bloody and costly. For the first time in history people did not have to volunteer to fight or nurse to see the elephant. They could experience the grandeur and grotesqueness of war through the art of photography. Matthew Brady and Alexander Gardner took vivid – indeed shocking – photographs of wartime activities: battlefields, hospitals and burial details which they put on display for the folks behind the lines. They also immortalized significant public figures such as Lincoln, Grant and Lee. But photography was not just for the famous. For the first time in history even humble families could possess a likeness of a loved one who left to fight and possibly die. [1] Before the invention of the daguerreotype in France in 1839, one had to be quite wealthy to preserve one's image in a painting. Monsieur Louis Daguerre, a commercial artist, changed all that.

Samuel Morse, having become friends with Daguerre in France, wrote to his brothers about Daguerre's technique. Morse's brothers sent the letter to the *New York Observer* which published it on April 20, 1839. When Samuel Morse returned to the United States, he partnered with a chemistry professor, named William Draper, to perfect Daguerre's system. In 1840 they opened America's first photographic studio. As with any new invention, people quickly utilized it to earn an income. The availability of the process spread like wildfire across the United States because there was no licensing process involved as there was in England. Within a few years,

New York City offered no less than seventy photographers. Anyone who could master the complex and labor intensive process could become a daguerreotype artist. And that is exactly what such people considered themselves – artists. "Many early daguerreotypists considered their craft as art as much as mere commercial reproduction service. In kind, the subjects considered this an art session also, posing as they would for a grand painting." [2] In fact, Miss Susan Speechly used that very word "artist" to describe herself on the back of her portraits. As an art form, photography thus became a viable employment option for middle class women. It was such an appealing form of employment that by 1885 almost a thousand women in the United States were engaged in that occupation. Washtenaw County was home to a dozen women working as professional photographers; however, only five of them remained in business for any length of time.

Speechly colophon
Courtesy of Gerald Swartout

The earliest known female photographer in Washtenaw County, surprisingly, did not work in either of the larger towns. Instead she established herself in Saline where she had settled with her parents, Gershom and Mary Gillett, in 1858. Two years after arriving, at age forty, Lucretia Gillett opened her daguerrotype studio at 203 Adrian Street (now Ann Arbor-Saline Road). She, no doubt, was influenced by George C. Gillett, also a daguerreotype artist. George was three years younger in the census records and would appear to have been her brother.

Lucretia Gillett
Courtesy of the Saline Historical Society

By 1867 Lucretia had switched from daguerreotypes to the new wet plate process. The daguerreotype process went out of fashion for several reasons. It was a difficult and laborious technique which produced only a single print. The wet plate process was equally difficult, but it required a shorter exposure time and could make multiple copies. Ambrotype or tintype photographs resulted from the process. Miss Gillett was wisely moving along with technological improvements. She must have been successful because she remained in business for thirty years. By the time she retired, George Eastman had perfected the use of camera film which further revolutionized the field.

Many years after Miss Gillett retired, Mrs. L. A. Catey recalled how, when she was a child, Miss Gillett took photographs in her second floor studio across from Saline's Union School. "Here I remember, as do many others, sitting in the old fringed chair, with a prop behind my neck, watching Mrs. [sic] Gillett move slowly about adjusting shades and backgrounds and finally duck under the big black cloth." [3] Gillett sold her business to George Waterman of Ypsilanti in 1890. Her reputation was obviously well known since Waterman continued to advertise his business as "Miss Gillett's Old Stand." After that, she and her sister, Anne, moved to California.

Osbourne colophon

Courtesy of Gerald Swartout

It is interesting to note that Mrs. Catey referred to Lucretia as *Mrs.* Gillett despite the fact that all evidence indicates that Lucretia never married. It may have just been a simple mistake or, due to Gillett's maturity, a sign of respect. Unlike today, it was fairly common to find older spinsters addressed as "Mrs." in the nineteenth century. The same situation arises with another female photographer who established herself in the 1860's in Manchester rather than Saline. Colophons on the backs of her photographs confirm her existence at that time as an artistic photographer, but some colophons say "Miss" and others "Mrs."

Just to complicate things further, some spell her "Osborn," and others have "Osborne." Despite these variations, they are clearly referring to the same woman.

The problem arises when one tries to discover exactly who she really was. One source from nineteenth century Manchester states that she was the unmarried daughter of William Osborne. Another Manchester source says, she is the daughter of Hassel Van Riper and wife of a man named Osborn who served in the Civil War. Both William Osborne and Hassel VanRiper lived in Hillsdale County, Michigan, which is about forty miles southwest of Manchester. Since the primary documents from the 1860's are so sparse, it is impossible to know if either of these Harriet/Hattie Osborn/Osbornes are the photographer since there are quite a few women with some form of that name. No matter who she was, the discrepancies on the colophons may have been just printing errors which were too expensive to change. Yet another possibility could be the printer was simply using the era's polite convention of respectful address as Mrs. Catey had done for Miss/Mrs. Lucretia Gillett – who also spelled her name "Gillet."

Manchester at that time had another photographer, Mr. E. A. Graham, who had his studio in the Graham and Goodyear Block. He decided to retire and sold his business to Susan T. Speechly of Ann Arbor. According to the October 28, 1869 issue of the *Manchester Enterprise*, "E. A Graham has concluded to stay at home and 'mind his own business' and would say to those wishing a good photograph, that he has secured the services of Miss S. T. Speechly of Ann Arbor in his photograph room. Miss S. [sic] comes recommended as a first class artist."

"Miss S." was the daughter of Robert and Elizabeth Speechly who came to Ann Arbor in 1838. Since Susan was born in 1844, she would have been twenty-five at the time she replaced Graham in Manchester. She operated a second studio in Ann Arbor in the early 1870's. Her Ann Arbor studio at 72 S. Main (ground floor) offered its clients the "instantaneous process "while her Manchester studio assured patrons that "particular attention [will be] paid to children and copying old pictures." [4] Speechly also offered gilt and rosewood molding for framing which was done at the studio as well. She must have been an ambitious, hardworking woman to assume the extra work and responsibility of two studios. Miss Speechly married Converse G. Cook, a printer from Dundee, Michigan in December 1886. By 1910 they had left Michigan to spend their remaining years in the sunshine of Biloxi, Mississippi.

Susan Speechly

Courtesy of the Bentley Historical Library, University of Michigan

An Ypsilanti photographer was living proof that women often worked side by side with their husbands in a business. A photographic studio is a complex business, yet when her husband died, she was able to assume full responsibility for it. This clearly suggests that she was an active partner before his death. She confirmed that assumption when she later wrote to Martha Louise Rayne, author of *What Can a Woman Do*, saying that her husband, "took up photography and I learned printing from him and afterwards as his health failed, I assisted." [5] That woman was Mrs. J. H. Parsons. Mary Elizabeth Parsons, nee Jacobs, and her husband, John, lived during the Civil War in Ohio where they both taught. He taught at a commercial school from which the war took so many of its students that he was out of a job. Soon they settled in Ypsilanti where they purchased the equipment of J. A. Crane, a photographer who was retiring. Their two older sons were born in Ohio in 1860 and 1865, but their daughters were born in Ypsilanti in 1866 and 1869. Mrs. Parsons' third son and her husband both died in the early spring of 1871. From then on Mary supported her four children by maintaining the family's photography business located above the post office. In memory of her husband, she always referred to her professional self as Mrs. J. H. Parsons, never as Mary E. Parsons.

Mary Elizabeth Parsons
Courtesy of the ypsilanti
Historical Society

The trials she weathered, as a single parent trying to maintain a career, resonate with any working mother today. For example, only a year after her husband's death, not only did a severe summer storm destroy her photographic studio's skylight, but her three year old daughter fell from a second story balcony breaking her collar bone. Despite these problems, Parsons' business had prospered sufficiently by 1883 that she needed to hire extra help. George Davis joined her as a photographer. George took charge of the "operating room" where the photographs were taken while Mary performed all the finishing and printing tasks. Parsons was responsible for many of the extant photographs of Michigan Normal School faculty, buildings and students. The same year that Mr. Davis began doing all the photography, Mary remarried. Her second husband was Erastus Samson, a local businessman. Mary survived him by thirteen years passing away in 1918 at the age of eighty. For Mrs. Parsons a career in photography had been a life-saver. It prevented her family from falling into destitution and provided her with much gratification and social contact. It is little wonder that she wrote to Mrs. Rayne who was researching for her 1885 book, advocating photography as a career opportunity for women. "I hope," Mrs. Parsons wrote, "you will ... [give] encouragement to our sex compelled by adverse circumstances to support themselves for all cannot be teachers, clerks or seamstresses." [6]

The final woman who entered the photographic profession was the youngest of the five. Miss May Clark, daughter of John H. Clark of Ypsilanti. May Clark began her working life circa 1883 as a teacher. She was twenty years old. Like so many young women, May appears to have abandoned teaching right after that time and obtained training in clerical work at Cleary College. Such a change was extremely popular since office work paid considerably more than teaching did and was emerging as a perfectly respectable occupation for middle class women. In May Clark's case, it turned out to be a truly life changing decision.

By 1886 she was working for Jefferson Gibson as his book-keeper. Mr. Gibson, a native of

London, Canada, had recently moved his photography business to Ann Arbor. May became proficient enough in photographic techniques to become Gibson's assistant. Finally in 1889 they married. After their marriage, they were exceptional in that they always listed themselves as joint proprietors of the Gibson Gallery which had sufficient business then to hire yet another female assistant, Miss Carrie Shultz. May also began a second photography studio in Ypsilanti with Fred M. Robbins, but that business expansion was cut short when her husband became the official photographer for the 1893 Columbian Exposition in Chicago.

Mary Clark Gibson
Courtesy of Cleary University

The couple left Ann Arbor placing John J. Clark in charge of the Ann Arbor studio. John was May's younger brother who recently had begun working as their printer. The Gibsons' move to Chicago was fortunate, for Mr. Gibson not only became quite famous as a popular photographer of the upper classes but also as the originator of photographic studios in department stores in New York and Pittsburg as well as Chicago. It is unclear how much May was involved in her husband's business once they moved to Chicago; however, when he died a decade later, she, like Mary Parsons, assumed the management of all the businesses for the following decade.

> Miss E.C. Foster briefly combined photography with a very different type of sales. She was the official agent for Vose Pianos. Potential patrons could see and play a Vose piano when they were in her rooms in the Exchange Block in Ann Arbor to get their pictures taken.

Another acceptably feminine entrepreneurial opportunity that evolved during the mid-nineteenth century was hair care. Unlike some occupations, this clearly was an area that was wide open to married women. By the 1880's literally thousands of women were involved in the field. It was especially popular option for African-American wives, probably because barbering was an occupation handled by quite a few African-American men. Thomas Jefferson arranged to have Robert Hemings, his son by slave woman Sally Hemings, trained as a barber. He did so because barbering "...was considered a high status occupation for men of African descent during and even after slavery."[7] The roll of Washtenaw County's earliest settlers included a few free "men of color." Among those African-American settlers in Washtenaw County were the Freemans of Ann Arbor who immediately established themselves as barbers.

Likewise African-American women were trained to do hair. Louise Hayes of Ypsilanti is a good example. When her husband died circa 1890 she turned to hair care in order to support herself and her daughter, Mayme/Mamie who quit Ypsilanti High School to assist her mother. Louise, had been raised by Pennsylvania Quakers who taught her to do hair. She was especially skilled, Mayme said, in making wigs. It was to this training Louise and Mayme turned when they needed to earn a living. Mayme eventually moved to Chicago where she married. She lived to be 105 years-old, thus being one of very few Americans to be alive not only for the nation's centennial but its bicentennial as well. African-Americans dominated the hair care field until the twentieth century.

Erastus W. Basom's unpublished "History of Ypsilanti" claims a Mrs. Wells in Ypsilanti worked with her husband in his barber shop on the north side of Congress Street as early as the 1830's. The Census does not confirm this until 1860 when a Mr. and Mrs. Wells both are listed as barbers. Other sources identify Mr. Wells as one of the most prominent African-American citizens of the city. The Census of 1850, however, does list another African-American barber in Ypsilanti. His name was William Pattison, age forty-nine. He had a twenty-four year old wife named Clarissa. Perhaps Mr. Basom, because he was a boy in the 1830's, confused this earlier couple with Mr. and Mrs. Wells who were so prominent two decades later. Another anonymous primary source states that a Mrs. Pattison was working as a barber in 1850; however, that source refers to her as "Mary" but does mention she was twenty-four years old at the time, which would coincide with the Census data for Clarissa Pattison. It is possible that Clarissa went by the name of Mary. Then again, the source may have confused her first name with another Mary Pattison who lived in Ypsilanti until 1866. It is difficult to draw conclusions since the historical record is so contradictory, yet even these conflicting pieces of evidence clearly indicate that some African-American women were working as barbers before 1860.

Barber shops today cater to a predominantly masculine clientele, but in the days before ladies' beauty salons became popular, women might patronize a barber shop. It is doubtful they did so to have their hair cut though Caroline Kirkland's 1839 book *My New Home – Who'll Follow* assures us that early female settlers often cut their hair short as a matter of practicality and hygiene. This was a common nineteenth century practice for girls, so it is not surprising that settler women might see the advantages for themselves. Those women, however, probably just cut their hair at home. An advertisement from the 1850's, however, does offer a tantalizing piece to the puzzle. T.B. and J.A. Freeman, barbers in Ann Arbor, advertised "To the Ladies." The Freemans stated that they had in stock hair fronts and curls straight from New York for their female customers.

One of the most fondly remembered African-American hairdressers had both male and female clients. Her name was Mrs. Mary Roper. Mrs. Roper was born a slave probably in Alabama and would recall how hard she was forced to work then lest she be beaten. She came to Dexter in 1864 with her husband, Benjamin. For many years they and a man named Samuel Johnson, whom she called her brother though it may just have been an honorific, were the only African-Americans in Dexter. Mr. and Mrs. Roper established "Ben's Tonsorial Emporium" and worked together for almost three decades until Ben died in 1894. Mary continued the business and even made house calls. The *Dexter Leader* called her "an artist at her business" because she used soft rain water which she collected in a cistern and also did hair dyeing. As early as 1874, while still partnering with her husband, she ran her own advertisement in the *Dexter Leader* soliciting female patrons: "Mrs. Mary Roper would respectfully announce to the ladies of Dexter and vicinity that she has a choicer variety of hair work such as switches, curls and frizzes. A good variety of shades and values which she will sell on the most reasonable terms." [8]

Her shop in 1904 was described as having several arm chairs and a magazine rack; two barber chairs; two mirrors; a shelf for soap, bay rum, brushes and combs. There was also a glass door cabinet with shaving mugs owned by regular customers. Mrs. Roper passed away in

Ann Arbor at the age of eighty-nine – thirty-eight years after her husband's death. Sadly, while she purchased an elegant tombstone for her husband and smaller ones for their lost children, there was no one left when she died to add her name.

The Roper monument in Dexter's
Forest Lawn Cemetery

In December of 1953 Minnie Steinbach shared a childhood remembrance with the Washtenaw County Historical Society. Because African-Americans were so rare in Dexter during her childhood, a silly rumor spread among the children when Mr. Roper died. The rumor claimed that African-Americans turned white when they died. So curious were the children that about a dozen of them stole into the room to view Mr. Roper's body. They were disappointed to discover he was the same color dead as he had been when alive. [9]

Mrs. Roper's contemporary was Elizabeth A. Shewcraft. Shewcraft, like Roper, was an African-American widow who had an equally long career. Before her husband, Micagy Shewcraft, died in the late 1870's, he had managed a shaving parlor on Huron Street near the Post Office. Perhaps Mrs. Shewcraft had been working with him all the time. At his passing, Elizabeth took over in order to support herself and her son. She moved the shop to 22 S. State Street near the University of Michigan campus but continued residing on Kingsley Street. Finally in 1894 she began working as a barber out of her home resurfacing in the early twentieth century transformed into a ladies' hairdresser. Mrs. Shewcraft remained in business until 1918 for a total career in hair care of forty years.

Mrs. Shewcraft's career exemplifies the evolution from barber shop to beauty salon though she appears a little tardy in that transition. It was in the 1870's that women's hair care began leaving the predominantly male barber shop and quickly became a popular feminine entity of its own. Mrs. Elizabeth West, also African-American, was one of the first, if not the first, woman to advertise as someone offering hair care exclusively for ladies. Mrs. West appears to have been a widow with three grown sons, two of whom were blacksmiths and one, not surprisingly, a barber. Considering the earlier pattern of hair service, her third son, Samuel, may have been instrumental in her decision to open a hair goods emporium in 1874 at 19 N. Main in Ann Arbor. Mrs. Maggie Berry (also spelled Berrie) was Shewcraft's competition. Berry, yet another African-American woman, entered the hair care trade circa 1874. She arrived from

New York that same year as Shewcraft proclaiming that she had apprenticed with the "famed Miss Jennie Robinson." Mrs. Berry established her shop at 43 S. Main, but in the early 1890's, just before her retirement, she moved it to Fourth Avenue near Ann Street.

Meanwhile, women in the hair care business catering exclusively to women were emerging throughout the county. Ypsilanti could boast of having several. Miss Norah Casey's surprisingly modern sounding advertisements offered back combing or teasing as a service. Miss M. E. Williams, an African-American woman, also provided services exclusively for women as did Mrs. G. N. Noyes, who announced to the ladies of the community in March of 1878 that she had moved her shop to above VanTuyl's drug store. Not to be excluded in this burgeoning service industry, Lillie Jones and Mrs. Lizzie Freme began Jones and Freme Hair Goods on Main Street in Chelsea. And Saline also offered among its Main Street merchants "a hairdresser with window displays of wigs and switches." [10] That description undoubtedly refers to the shop of Lottie Eaton, a Caucasian. Miss Eaton was still in business two decades later; however, she had moved to Ypsilanti which, in the 1880's offered no fewer than two hair dressers (one of whom was African-American) and four shops for hair goods (two of which were operated by African-Americans: Mrs. Anna McCoy and Miss Lulu Thompson). Of these women, Lottie Eaton remained in business the longest.

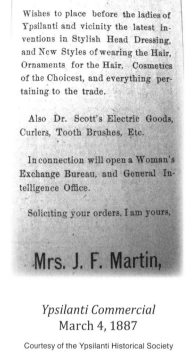

Ypsilanti Commercial
March 4, 1887

Courtesy of the Ypsilanti Historical Society

A few women in Ann Arbor combined hair care with other enterprises. Sara (Mrs. L. M.) Graham arrived from England via Pennsylvania, Ohio and Canada. Sara was twenty-eight when she married Levi Graham with whom she had three daughters. By the time she began providing hair care in late 1870's, she probably had been widowed. Mrs. Graham started her business at #4 N. State Street, Ann Arbor, with only hair care but soon expanded to include selling fancy goods. In 1878 she advertised worsted goods. In addition, Mrs. Hannah Graves, previously discussed as a dressmaker, reversed that order. She decided to capitalize on the growing hair care industry to balance the declining demand for custom dressmaking. She did this by offering hair care at her shop on Main Street circa 1892.

Caucasian women who entered the early hair care business also may have done so as a result of marrying barbers though this pattern is not as pronounced as it is for African-American women. Minnie (also called Minna) Trojanowski offers perhaps the best example of a Caucasian woman in the beauty trade. Minnie married Julian R. Trojanowski. He had a barber shop located first at 30 E. Washington, then at 332 S. State Street and finally at 1110 S. University. All three shops were in Ann Arbor. When he married, his wife began offering services to ladies in the rooms above his shop. In the early 1890's she advertised her "Ladies' Bathroom and Hair Dressing Parlors." With each move of the barber shop, she also moved, each time transforming her business. As bathrooms began appearing in homes, she discarded the bathing option in favor of simply providing hair care.

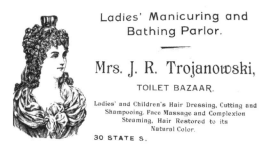

Ladies' Manicuring and Bathing Parlor.

Mrs. J. R. Trojanowski,

TOILET BAZAAR.

Ladies' and Children's Hair Dressing, Cutting and Shampooing. Face Massage and Complexion Steaming, Hair Restored to its Natural Color.

30 STATE S.

According to the booklet, *Ann Arbor Today*, published in 1905, "The modern barbershop has its parallel in the hairdressing parlors of today, many of which are palaces of luxury and convenience." The author of that statement surely must have visited a shop such as Minnie Trojanowski's. As indulgent as that comment makes such parlors sound, they became even better. By 1921 Minnie had expanded her offerings to include not only "fashionable hairdressing" done with "rainwater shampoos" but also hair goods and manicures. She even highlighted the fact that "Facial massage [was] a specialty." [11] The Trojanowskis were a successful part of the Ann Arbor scene for three decades, meeting the needs of residents and changing with the times.

Trojanowski was not alone in her expansion into services previously not offered. Emily Faithfull in her *Three Visits to America* commented, "The manicure is as well known in the States as the chiropodist, and earns an excellent living by the novel employment of beautifying nails." [12] In addition to manicuring, chiropody, which means performing pedicures, emerged as a popular service. One of the earliest women to advertise as a chiropodist was Miss Elizabeth J. Foley. Miss Foley had been a dressmaker, but about 1910 she switched careers. As her 1913 advertisement says, she then was offering manicures, facials and "scalp treatments" at her shop located 921 Huron Street in Ann Arbor. By 1920 Miss Foley was no longer listed as a resident. That left the field wide open for Bertha E. Schad and Edna F. Goodrich. Their shop which provided hair goods, hairdressing, manicuring, chiropody and facial massage opened in 1911 at 1921 Washington Street in Ypsilanti.

Just as people were becoming accustomed to the idea of female photographers and hair care providers, an advertisement in the *Ann Arbor Courier* on November 24, 1876 introduced yet another new and different service for the people of Washtenaw County. Some local readers may have even skipped over Miss Culver's advertisement since they would not have recognized the title word, "Kindergarten." Miss Culver was promoting a totally new opportunity for both herself and children of Washtenaw County.

The concept of a "children's garden" or in German a "Kindergarten" began in the early nineteenth century in Europe but came into its own under the tutelage of Friedrick Froebel who first used the term in 1837. Margarethe Meyer-Schurz and her sister, Berthe, met Froebel in 1849. Two years later Berthe and her husband opened a kindergarten in England. Margarethe taught there before immigrating to the United States. Once settled in Watertown, Wisconsin, she opened in 1856 the first kindergarten in the United States based on Froebel's ideas of social cooperation and creative play. Elizabeth Peabody of Boston heard about Schurz' school and went to visit.

I would announce to the people of the city that I have organized a school on the "kindergarten" plan and am prepared to educate children between the ages of three and seven years in the principles set forth in the same and will gladly receive the patronage of those having little ones of said ages. For terms inquire at 31 William Street, corner of Division Street, Ann Arbor, Michigan

Miss Peabody already possessed a formidable reputation. She was a charter member of the Transcendalist Club and handled the business side for the Transcendentalist newspaper, *The Dial*. She also opened a bookstore where she and Margaret Fuller held discussions concerning issues relevant to women. After visiting Schurz, Peabody opened the first English language kindergarten (Schurz' was in German). Peabody also published *Kindergarten Culture* in 1870 and edited the *Kindergarten Messenger* between 1873 and 1877. It was Elizabeth Peabody who, when Mrs. Schurz died in 1876 picked up the baton as spokeswoman for early childhood education in America. She continued her efforts until her own death in 1894.

Despite successes such as those of Mrs. Schurz, Miss Peabody and Miss Culver, the idea of early education or kindergarten did not become a household word in Washtenaw County for several more decades. Its ultimate success must be attributed, at least in part, to Miss Edith Adams of Saline, Michigan. After studying at the Michigan State Normal School for three years, Edith did post-graduate training in Chicago and Boston. It certainly must have been in Elizabeth Peabody's Boston that Adams became a devotee of the kindergarten system. Returning to Ypsilanti circa 1903 she became instrumental in developing the concept of early education as a regular part of the public school curriculum. Adams not only taught at the Normal School but became the director of the Woodruff Model School where future teachers trained. Soon she was made supervisor of all kindergartens in Ypsilanti. She continued in that capacity until she retired in 1939.

Edith Adams

Courtesy of Eastern Michigan University

Few today have ever heard of Miss Edith Adams. Only two significant legacies to her survive. One is the 1833 Baptist parsonage where she and her family lived. Henry Ford saved it from inevitable destruction in 1937 when he moved it to Greenfield Village, Henry Ford's Museum of American life in Dearborn, Michigan. Hundreds of thousands of visitors each year come to Greenfield Village and see her former home. And the vast majority of those visitors, whether they recognize the fact or not, are the living embodiments of her second legacy because they undoubtedly attended kindergarten as part of their public school educations.

Just as the term kindergarten was new to people of the nineteenth century, so modern readers are unfamiliar with the occupation of canvassing. This is the only emerging opportunity for nineteenth century women discussed in this volume that did not expand into the twentieth century. But in 1878 when two Washtenaw women, Miss Elie Marey of Manchester and Mrs. E. Henry of Dexter, worked as "canvassers," it was a fairly common way to earn a living. Since there are no other references to these particular women, history is forced to speculate as to their actual jobs. The term "canvasser" could refer to several things. It could have been a person who sought, took or counted votes in an election. That seems unlikely for women of this time. More probably a woman might have solicited payment or subscriptions for a newspaper or magazine or they might have sold advertising. The *Ypsilanti Commercial* ran ads in November 1872 stating: "Canvassers Wanted. We want some wide-awake persons, male or female, young or old, to thoroughly canvass this county, and secure subscribers for the *Commercial*. We will pay good wages." So it is highly possible that Miss Marey and Mrs. Henry did something like that.

However, there also existed a third possibility: that of selling book orders. Before the Civil War, Sarah Emma Edmonds obviously felt no one would hire her to sell even religious books, so she did what other women did, she changed her identity. In 1856 she cut her hair and donned men's clothing to become a canvasser/salesman. By the time the Civil War began, Sarah was living in Flint, Michigan, under the alias of Frank Thompson. Small wonder then that Sarah abandoned her book job and joined the army when the call came for enlistments. She served as a Union soldier and spy until she contracted malaria and fearing Frank "Flint" Thompson's real identity would be discovered, she left her regiment to check herself into a hospital dressed as Sarah. Upon recovery, she discovered Frank Thompson had been listed as a deserter. She continued dressing in female attire and became a nurse for the duration of the war.

By the 1870's, however, when Sarah Emma Edmonds was married and the mother of two sons, canvassing as an opportunity for women became more common. Howard House of Detroit advertised in the *Ann Arbor Courier Weekly* in 1877 for local canvassers to sell a book which Howard House described as "a good book for Lady Canvassers." [13] This was clearly an occupation for women of some education and refinement because respectable women such as Dr. Kinne's wife in Ypsilanti was the agent in 1889 for a book entitled, *Physical Life of Woman* by Dr. George Napheys. It does not appear that Mrs. Kinne did any traveling in order to market the book, yet some respectable women did. The June 1872 issues of the *Ypsilanti Commercial* announced that a Mrs. French would be in town as canvassing agent for several novels, one bound in Moroccan leather with gilt trimmings. The ad also stated that Mrs. French was the wife of the former superintendent of the woolen mill. She probably was widowed by that time. According to *What Can a Woman Do?* published in 1885, selling subscription books paid very well especially if the book were popular. Some women, said the author, earned as much as $2,000 per year as canvassers. Two thousand dollars was an enormous amount in 1885. It would approximately equal the income of a full professor at the University of Michigan and be more than triple a public school teacher's salary at that time, yet Emily Faithfull in her *Three Visits to America* published the year before Rayne's book, claims to have heard from a source at Houghton Mifflin that an ex-school teacher was earning $5,000 for only eight or nine months work selling encyclopedias. According to Faithfull, that woman was considered by her employers to be "one of the best" canvassers in the country. Obviously canvassing was a tremendously lucrative opportunity for women.

Another opportunity regarding books emerged in the latter part of the nineteenth century. This involved not selling copies of books but organizing and operating libraries which were only then becoming available to the public. Before that time, libraries were private affairs owned by individuals. There seems to be some contention about where the first *public* library opened its doors. Boston? Philadelphia? New York? It might even have been Franklin, Massachusetts, where in exchange for naming the town after him, Benjamin Franklin donated books for the use of the local residents. The town fathers had requested a church bell, but Deistic Franklin preferred secular learning to religious worship. Other early libraries tended to be club sponsored or subscription libraries which date back to the eighteenth century. They often specialized in certain types of books: medical, legal, historical etc. It was not until the 1880's that libraries open to the general public began to appear.

In Ann Arbor, Michigan, the public library began very humbly. It was the product of both the local high school and the Ladies Library Association, which was established in 1866. No

Abbie Mize

Courtesy of the Bentley Historical Library,
University of Michigan

sooner had Ann Arbor's Union School opened its doors in 1856 than one of its first teachers began lobbying for a library. That teacher was Miss Abbie Mize, who was born in New York in 1832. Years later in 1880, the school hired Lucinda Goodrich to supervise its collection. Her salary of $52 for the entire year sounds indecently low unless one realizes that she was only allowed to work during school vacations. Many years later in 1909, Miss Goodrich initiated children's story telling first at the library and then at the schools.

Until 1884 the Ann Arbor Schools stored its library, consisting of 2,000 volumes, in the Superintendent's office. At that time it was moved to its own room on the second floor of what was by then the high school building at the corner of Huron and State Streets. The school district hired Nellie Loving to supervise the new facility. She was expected to work regular school hours, so her salary was raised to $200 a year. It was much better than Miss Goodrich's but only a fraction of what her teaching colleagues earned. Granted she had no particular training for the job, nor did the Board of Education think she would have much to do even though the library at that time was technically open to the public. Her employers even urged her to bring needlework to the library to keep her self busy, but they made it clear that she should be prepared to function as a substitute teacher if needed.

The fact that Miss Loving had no formal training was not in the least unusual. Library Science was in its infancy in the nineteenth century. Not until 1876 did Melvil Dewey publicize his system which catalogued books according to their subjects. Before that time, books had been arranged by the date on which they had been acquired. The year 1876 was also the birth date of the American Library Association. Both Dewey's system and the American Library Association advanced librarianship as a profession. Miss Loving proved she was not one to sit back and do needlework. She took a sabbatical in 1892/93 to obtain a degree in Library Science from the University of Wisconsin. Her substitute for that year was glad to see Loving return because in her opinion there was too much work and too little income for the job she had been doing. Perhaps the School Board began realizing that running a library was not so easy after all because in 1899 they hired Miss Helen A. Smith as an assistant for Miss Loving.

Meanwhile, industrialist Andrew Carnegie had begun endowing public libraries. The first Carnegie library appeared in 1889. By 1904 just as the Ladies' Library Association and the Ann Arbor Schools were initiating talks to join forces and apply for a Carnegie grant, Ann Arbor's High School burned. Fire threatened to consume the collection of books Miss Loving had "lovingly" increased to four times the number of volumes there had been in 1884 when she was hired. But the community quickly galvanized and rescued more than 8,000 books from the fire. The books were stored in the Methodist Church across the street until a new school building could be erected. When the new building, a beautiful beaux arts construction, opened, it began a symbiotic relationship with a brand new Carnegie library built adjacent to it. Both the public and students utilized the same library.

When the buildings ruined by fire were rebuilt, Miss Loving initiated classes to teach the high school students how to use the library. She believed in the power of knowledge and

Thought to be the only public school/ Carnegie library combination in the United States, the Ann Arbor High School and the Library buildings were razed in 2007 to make way for the University of Michigan's North Quad. Local preservation efforts succeeded in saving only the old library façade (right) and some decorative pieces from the school building.

the fact that books were the key to that knowledge. She had dreams of making that philosophy part of every resident's life. "I don't care what you read; but read," she would tell students. Later Miss Loving requested that the School Board establish branch libraries to relieve the crowding. She initiated children's rooms. When the city refused in 1911 to help with a downtown branch, she rented a room for $45 per month and paid a woman $10 a month to keep it clean. That was a significant amount of money considering how little she earned. Loving even took books to the YMCA and to the fire station so that the men might read during their leisure moments. To encourage all citizens to read, she listed new books in the newspaper. Not until 1922 did she step down from her role as head librarian. Even then she assisted at the library which by then owned 20,000 volumes, ten times more than it had when she began.

Nellie Loving lived alone and died in relative obscurity long before the Ann Arbor District Library decided to name a branch on Packard Road in her honor. Sadly, that branch of the library has since been closed and replaced by the Mallett's Creek branch. That newer building does have a room named after Miss Loving, but there is no indication of who Nellie Loving was or why a reading room would be named for her. Fortunately, an Ann Arbor Historic Street Exhibit panel on the Huron Street side of North Quad, provides both the photograph to the right and a brief statement concerning Miss Loving's contributions to the development of the Ann Arbor Library.

Nellie Loving
Courtesy of the Ann Arbor District Library

It was not just public schools which developed libraries. Colleges and universities developed extensive collections though it was not until later in the century that women were hired to supervise and expand those collections. Michigan State Normal School hired a woman as librarian in 1892. When Miss Genevieve Walton began her career, she, like Nellie Loving, had no particular background in library science. Walton went to a six-week summer institute in Amherst, Massachusetts, where Dewey had first developed his cataloguing system, to learn something of the field. Later she received a master's degree from St. Mary's in South Bend, Indiana. Just as Miss Loving had increased Ann Arbor's collection, Miss Walton's original 11,000 volume collection grew to exceed 70,000 volumes by the time she retired. Unlike Nellie Loving, Miss Walton,

Genevieve Walton

Courtesy of Eastern Michigan University

though she was obviously knowledgeable about the Dewey Decimal System, chose to make some changes she considered logical. For example: she lumped together travel and history because she felt they really were talking about the same thing. Despite that idiosyncrasy, Miss Walton became the co-founder the Michigan Library Association, serving as its first president.

Library work was not Miss Walton's first choice for her life's work. She originally wanted to be a painter and even studied art in Italy, but trouble with her eyesight curtailed that ambition. Once she decided to become a librarian, however, she put her entire heart and soul into that endeavor. Walton began recruiting student assistants at the library. Her two-hour, training sessions were held on Saturday mornings. They evolved into an eight-week, non-credit course required of anyone wishing to work in the library. Her successor, Miss Elsie Andres, paid Miss Walton the highest compliment she could when she said that those Saturday training sessions put Miss Andres way ahead of her peers when she started her formal library training. Miss Walton did not limit herself to providing only books. She was famous for arriving on cold snowy mornings with a huge pot of hot coffee for whoever was in the library. She also was known to take students home for lunch. One of those students recalled that it was her art books that inspired him to begin his own collection. Miss Walton, who resided in Ypsilanti her entire seventy-five years, survived long enough to see Michigan State Normal School evolved into Eastern Michigan University which built a separate library facility in 1930 (now Ford Hall). Walton personally donated the circulation desk.

Librarianship was a natural fit for some women who desired to work. It was an occupation requiring a high level of education, so it is not surprising that the vast majority of librarians were upper middle or upper class women. It was considered a clean and dignified occupation; therefore, highly respected within the community. An added advantage for women was that, with libraries popping up across the country, there was an abundance of jobs needing to be filled so male librarians did not feel threatened by the women. Lurking underneath all those positive attributes, however, was a less agreeable reason for why, by 1910, seventy-nine percent of librarians were women. This was not something that evolved over the years but clearly was an attitude that existed from the very beginning. Frederick Perkins, author of an 1876 article entitled "How to make Town Libraries Successful," recommended hiring females as librarians not because he was a proponent of equal opportunities for women but because women

Circulation Desk

Courtesy of Eastern Michigan University

could be hired for significantly less money than men.

The American Library Association was another by-product of the 1876 Centennial Exposition. This fair was one of the most significant public events in the country's history. The planning began a decade earlier just as the Civil War was ending. Its advocates saw the exposition as a way to unify the country and instill pride in the war-torn nation. Its goal was to let the world know that the United States, one hundred years after its Declaration of Independence, had arrived as a world class power. To emphasize that end, the exposition was supposed to open on the anniversary of the battle of Lexington; however, delays postponed it until May. Thirty thousand exhibits filled two hundred buildings across 285 acres of land. Despite the early summer being the hottest in memory, ten million people, one fifth of all Americans and hoards of foreigners, traveled to Philadelphia to see the wonders of the age. Dr. Lister was there trying to get fellow physicians to recognize germ theory. He was not very successful, but Machine Hall was an unqualified achievement. A Corliss steam engine appearing enormous enough to drive the entire industrial age dominated the building's fourteen acres. Less immense exhibits equally astounded visitors. Names, then unknown but which soon would change the world, were there: Bell, Edison, Westinghouse, Eastman and Remington. The United States, indeed the entire world, was on the edge of unprecedented change.

Nowhere were changes more evident than in the world of American business. Industrialization required not just factories but clerical support. As a result, offices and office work experienced a revolution in the years after the Civil War. In fact, the changes began during the war itself. As with most wars, male labor during the Civil War was scarce, so the federal government began hiring women to clerk in offices such as the Treasury. Robert McClelland, Secretary of the Interior, declared that it was improper for women to do clerical work. He swore he would stop it. Fortunately his view did not prevail. In contrast, Treasurer General Spinner declared that his female employees did "more and better work" [14] than their male counterparts who were paid twice as much as women. Female clerks simultaneously infiltrated the Patent office and its offshoot, the Department of Agriculture, where Lois Bryan Adams, daughter of Washtenaw County pioneers John and Sarah Bryan, was one of its first clerks in 1862.

> In early 1807, Secretary of Treasury Albert Gallatin asked President Jefferson to appoint some women to federal office. In a letter dated January 13, 1807 Jefferson replied, "The appointment of a woman to office is an innovation for which the public is not prepared; nor am I." [15]

War time gains might have been lost had not technological innovations revolutionized the entire nature of office work. Before the Civil War, penmanship had been a critical skill for clerical workers, be they male or female. Several women, cross-dressing in order to become soldiers in the Civil War, ultimately became clerks to the officer in charge. The most incredible story concerns a woman calling herself Charles Martin. Jefferson Davis, it is said, offered her a commission in the Confederate army if she would change sides. And Davis knew she was a woman. Another woman, Mary Jane G. from Trenton, Michigan, (name withheld by the Detroit newspaper because her parents were members of society) clerked for a general.

Then in 1872 Densmore and Sholes began mass-producing typing machines in America. Within three years of the machines hitting the market, Remington, which had taken over production, advertised salaries of $10-20 per week for anyone who could master the skill of typewriting. That sounds splendid except typing was not as easy as one might think. Mark Twain purchased one of the first machines and quickly abandoned it as too frustrating. Writing to the Remington Company in March of 1875, Twain refused to write an endorsement for the machine. "Please do not even divulge that I own a machine...[I] don't want people to know that I own this curiosity breeding little joker." [16] Women, however, became skilled "typewriters," for it was the typist not the machine that was so named. Women soon demonstrated that they could type so quickly that the keys jammed on the machines. The solution to this problem resulted in the odd configuration found on today's keyboards. This revised keyboard layout was specifically created to slow the process in order to prevent jamming as the letters struck the paper.

Typing and other office work such as stenography and accounting were attractive to women for a wide variety of reasons. Since these occupations had not existed in the same form before, they did not have gender stereotypes attached to them which would have hindered women's entry into the field. In addition, office work, like teaching, was considered a clean, respectable, middle-class occupation yet, unlike teaching, office work paid more and did not curtail a young woman's social life. Finally, women were particularly qualified because clerical work required a high school education which far more females than males obtained. Photographs of graduating classes, such as the one to the left illustrate that 75% of students were female. The Ypsilanti class of 1900 was overwhelmingly female with only seven males in a class of twenty-nine. These local statistics coincide with national norms of that time. Working class boys were leaving school early to begin earning money. Males who stayed in high school until graduation went on to university and no longer were content to do office work. Opportunities abounded for them elsewhere.

Ypsilanti High School class of 1883

Courtesy of the Ypsilanti Historical Society

In fact, many teachers left the schoolroom to work in offices where the pay was better though still far less than that earned by a man. Typists averaged $6-10 per week year round while a stenographer was paid $12-16. That might not sound like much, but such a salary would average about $600-700 per year in an era when an unskilled male made $200 and a semi-skilled man earned $400-500. Office work was, however, a dead-end job. Women realized they could not expect any advancement or significant increase in salary.

Public high schools responded to the demand for office workers by establishing commercial curricula. Although it had offered a class in book-keeping as early as 1856, Ann Arbor High School began a one year commercial course in 1872, a two year program in 1887 and a three year commercial program in 1882 including stenography, typewriting, letter writing, business forms etc. Although the school eventually referred to a girl who understood stenography by the elevated title of "stenographic amanuensis," there was a certain stigma attached to students in those classes. "... the high school faculties look upon the commercial department as a somewhat inferior department...[with] oft-expressed regret on the part of some member of the faculty that ...an ambitious boy or girl ...[who]has been obliged to give up the literary course and take instead the commercial course."[17]

Ann Arbor High School Business Room

Courtesy of the Washtenaw County Historical Society

It seems highly probable that such a stigma was attached to the practical training of the commercial department, yet that did not preclude daughters of Ann Arbor's oldest families from preparing themselves for office jobs. One of the most famous of those daughters was Lucy E. Chapin, who was named for her maternal grandmother, Lucy Ann Clark (Kingsley). Lucy Ann Clark came to Ann Arbor with her mother, importing to the tiny nascent village in 1827 its first piano. One of Ann Arbor's favorite legends is that, when she played, Potowatami warriors would dance outside her home. Lucy Chapin inherited that piano and later donated it to the Washtenaw County Historical Society. It is not surprising, considering her family's background, that local history became Miss Chapin's avocation. But she did not just sit in her parlor assembling scrapbooks. For forty-two years she worked as the assistant to the secretary of the University of Michigan, who was called the Steward at the time of her hiring in 1881.

Born in 1856, Miss Chapin graduated from Ann Arbor High School in 1876 and served for forty-three years as its alumni association secretary. Among her other accomplishments, she was "instrumental" in raising the Perry Scholarship Fund. So well known was she that her obituary made the front page of the *Ann Arbor News* in 1940, right next to stories about the war in Europe and FDR's calls for unity. Miss Chapin died at her home at 803 E. Kingsley, a street named for her grandfather, James Kingsley.

Such public high school courses certainly were not the first of their kind in the county. Decades earlier there were several local schools that would prepare men and women for work in the business world. The earliest one was a "School of Bookkeeping" begun by John Branigan in the basement of St Andrew's church in Ann Arbor. According to Ann Arbor educator, Anna Clinton, Mr. Branigan's school was not successful because there was "no demand for bookkeeping, as businesses were small and each merchant was his own accountant." [18] Her analysis is very credible since it was only 1842 when Branigan's school opened and clerical office work had not yet reached the tipping point. Another early school, which accepted both men and women, was that of Mr. A. R. Danton and his "Lady" who advertised themselves in 1860 as "professors of penmanship." Despite their inflated title and the universally valued skill of penmanship, their school did not survive. Neither did another one begun in December 1865 above Bach's store in Ann Arbor. Twenty-five years later in the 1890's, the Stenographic Institute of Ann Arbor also advertised its curriculum; however, none of these Ann Arbor schools were anything but temporary. It was Ypsilanti that became home to the most enduring business school. That school is, in fact, still operating today which makes Cleary College (now called Cleary University) 130 years old and still going strong.

P. Roger Cleary opened his school in 1883. It was not the impressive edifice of 1886. pictured to the right. It was just a few rooms above the Sherwood's Shoe Store in the Warden Block, and it began primarily as a penmanship school. Cleary, however, managed to attract as his first students the two daughters of Florence and Judge Babbitt. The Babbitt family's reputation would have been helpful in assuring the success of Cleary's school, but it was Cleary's innovative ideas that ultimately made his school such an enduring part of the community. The Cleary program was popular because it was flexible, allowing students to stop and resume without penalty. Cleary later offered shorthand, typewriting, and English at $30 per term. He even provided room and board.

Cleary College circa 1893

Courtesy of the Ypsilanti Historical Society

Not only did Mr. Cleary educate his students, he took charge of placement for his graduates. At first, his efforts met with curt replies if anyone replied at all. Of the eighty businesses which he contacted in those early years, none were interested in employing his graduates. Mr. Cleary often told the story of his first student to finish shorthand and typewriting: Miss Mabel Parmalee. An architecture office in Detroit "hired her paying her half the salary of the man who had been doing the same job and said she would turn out twice as much work." [19] Miss Parmalee was only the sixth woman to be hired in this capacity in the city of Detroit. The office, unfortunately, was a smoke-filled, coarse environment little used to the presence of women. Cleary felt gratified when he returned to find her working in a spotless office devoid of tobacco smell.

Cleary Faculty in 1888, with three women in the faculty, one of whom was Elizabeth Hatten.

Courtesy of the Ypsilanti Historical Society

She even had placed flowers on her desk. In this way she was testimony to the refining influence of women. By 1891 requests for graduates exceeded the school's capacity even though its student body had grown to three hundred with fifteen teachers, some of whom were women. In Elizabeth "Libby" Hatten's shorthand class, women outnumbered men two to one. Mrs. Hatten taught at Cleary College for at least twenty years.

Cleary College offered training irrespective of race. Carrie M. Hayes (Mrs. Egbert Bow) of Ypsilanti was the first African-American woman to graduate from that institution. She completed her training in 1903 and secured a job with Dr. Samuel Goldberg of Detroit as a stenographer and bookkeeper. Her career there was cut short after three years when, as has happened to so many women then and now, her father's illness required her to return home to Ypsilanti. Carrie Hayes put her family responsibilities before her own career.

It is unfortunate that Cleary's first graduate, Mabel Parmalee, did not leave a record of what it was like to be a working girl in the late 1880's. How did she handle living and working in Detroit where she must have boarded somewhere and lived primarily, if not entirely, off her own earnings? Lacking any diary which preserved such information, we must rely again on Mrs. M. L. Rayne's 1885 book, *What Can a Woman Do?* in which she included an account by a young lady without any other means of support who was working in Cleveland, Ohio. This twenty-year-old orphan, who described her job as "principally writing letters and helping to keep the books of my employer, who does a business of upwards of seventy-five thousand dollars a year," earned a meager $7 a week She carefully calculated her annual income of $364. Then she deducted the cost of room, board, church, car fare and clothing as well as a possible week's wages lost due to illness, she found her budget left only $19 for any unforeseen expenses for the entire year. That was a frugal existence indeed, yet the girl claimed many young women she knew were trying to survive on only $4 per week. Mrs. Rayne labeled her "a good manager" which she surely was. A salary of at least $10 per week was what it apparently took for a working girl living on her own to avoid falling into destitution.

Falling into destitution was not something Ann Arbor's Marie Rominger feared. She lived her entire life in her family's home on Fifth Avenue (now a parking lot). Nor is it likely that she took business classes at Cleary College since it did not open until 1883. It is, however, highly possible she learned book-keeping at Ann Arbor High School before becoming in 1880 the first woman in the city to be hired by Allmendinger & Schneider Flour Mill as a book-keeper. She had just turned seventeen. Naturally there was some criticism. One man said to her father, "A girl in a place filled with men – why it's – it's just not proper." [20] Lela Duff in *Ann Arbor Yesterdays* comments that Miss Rominger dressed in a very masculine way in order to cope in a man's world. Duff continued by saying that in her later years, Miss Rominger abandoned her "assumed masculinity" of bobbed hair and tailored suits. [20] It is reasonable to assume that Marie eventually did affect such a masculine style due to her occupation; however, family photos circa 1885 show two very feminine young Rominger sisters who are indistinguishable

Proper or not, Rominger continued as a book-keeper until the early twentieth century when she forsook office work in order to pursue other interests such as art and writing. One of Rominger's art works was a series of wooden panels etched with wood burning tools. Miss Rominger also authored a history of the citizens of Ann Arbor who had emigrated from Germany. She even wrote the book in German.

Within three years of Miss Rominger's hiring, she was no longer the lone woman in her field. She was joined by others such as Minnie Gregg who became the book-keeper for Hangsterfer and Co. Within nine more years, Ann Arbor's pool of female book-keepers had risen to eight

Marie Rominger and her siblings.

in addition to seven female stenographers.

For Mattie Palmer of Dexter, office work was just an extension of her family duties. Mattie was the only surviving daughter of Martha and Luther Palmer. Her father came to Washtenaw County in 1869 and bought 162 acres of farmland. By 1891 he was a major fruit producer in the area, selling 125,000 baskets of berries a season. Not only did Mattie take care of her widowed father's house, she served as his secretary and book-keeper. Miss Palmer was, in addition, a talented vocalist who also gave music lessons.

Marie Rominger and Mattie Palmer were typical of national trends. So popular was office work that women quickly became the majority of office employees. By 1910 83% of the typists and stenographers in the United States were women while 29% of book-keepers, accountants and cashiers also were female. These statistics are in stark contrast to those of 1870 when only 2.5% of all clerical workers were women.

The world of the nineteenth century experienced radical changes, and the activities of women were a reflection of those changes. Urbanization created both the need and the potential clientele for a growing number of specialized schools and personal services. Technology always brings change. Today change has come with the form of the computer and the internet. A century and a half ago it was the photograph and the typewriter. Women were alert to these new opportunities and quickly took advantage of them to earn purses of their own.

---

[1] Before photography, artists would spend the winter painting assorted combinations of bodies. Then they would travel around painting heads for the bodies. Their system was efficient, but the heads and bodies didn't always suit each other. Emily Kickinson's parents bought such a painting of their children.

[2] Phototree.com

[3] Mrs. L.A. Catey, "History of Saline," *Impressions* (Ann Arbor: Washtenaw County Historical Society, 1945, #5), 1-2.

[4] *Ann Arbor City Directory* (1886), 69.

[5] M. L. Rayne, *What Can a Woman Do?* (Detroit: R. B. Dickerson and Co., 1885), 127.

[6] Rayne, 128.

[7] Annette Gordon-Reed, *Hemingses of Montecello* (New York: W.W.Norton and Co.,2008), 155.

[8] *Dexter Leader* May 29, 1874.

[9] Mary Steinbeck, "Memories of Dexter," *Impressions* (December 1953), 3.

[10] Bessie Collins, "History of Saline" *Impressions* (July1956), 6.

[11] *Ann Arbor City Directory* (1921), 535.

[12] Emily Faithfull, *Three Visits to America* (Edinburgh: David Douglas, 1885), 304.

[13] *Ann Arbor Courier*, May 18, 1877

[14] Margery W Davies, *Woman's Place is at the Typewriter* (Philadelphia: Temple University Press, 1982), 51.

[15] R.B. Bernstein, *Thomas Jefferson* (New York: Oxford University Press, 2003), 137-8.

[16] Frank Masi, *Typewriter Legend* (Secaucus, NU: Matshushita Electric Company of America, 1985), 24.

[17] Davis, 36.

[18] Anna Clinton, "Ann Arbor Schools," *Impressions* (June 1951), 3.

[19] Nancy L. Snyder, *One Hundred Years of Business* (1983), 19.

[20] Lela Duff, *Ann Arbor Yesterdays* (Ann Arbor, Friends of the Ann Arbor Library, 1962), 151.

CHAPTER EIGHT: WOMEN AND HIGHER EDUCATION

Finally after years of debate, it happened. The year was 1870. "The die is cast," wrote University of Michigan student E. Evans to Anna E. Dickinson on February 4 of that year, "we have a lady student in the University." [1] Ironically this tradition breaking event happened the very same spring as the first recorded, organized game of football[2] at the University of Michigan. Football, the University student newspaper reported, "bids fair to be popular." [3] The same certainly was not being said about higher education for women, yet what began that spring with one lone woman on campus quickly became a tsunami. Despite the fact that interim University President Henry Frieze expressed his delight at the decision, the admittance of women to the University of Michigan acquired the label, "A Dangerous Experiment."

The decision was "dangerous" as far as the Regents were concerned for several reasons. First was the very concept of co-education. Victorian conservatives claimed that a university education took women out of their legitimate social sphere and placed young women in dangerous proximity to young men who were generally acknowledged to be rowdy and unruly without proper supervision. That certainly was the message sent to the public; however rhetoric is not reality. Those who scratch the surface will detect a far more credible rationale – male egoism. A report from the Michigan State Legislature in 1859 asserted, "Women as a class have in no instance been found inferior in intellect...nor have they lost any of that delicacy of sentiment

136 years later, the University of Michigan commemorated the admission of women to the University with a plaque which is located in the foyer of Angell Hall. [4]

or refinement" in co-educational schools, BUT (and here they reveal the true crux of the matter) the University of Michigan as "the highest institution of learning in the state" can only have students who are "the most accomplished masters" without "a loss of dignity." [5] It was the diminishment of their "dignity," not social chaos, that they feared would result if women were admitted to the University of Michigan.

Significantly, nowhere in the Regents' Proceedings is a concern for women's health mentioned, yet as demands for improved education of women grew in the nineteenth century, the public simultaneously began being bombarded with assertions that education would destroy women's health. Such concerns, dubious though they were, had been floating around for decades. Dr. Charles Meigs in his famous 1847 lecture, "Distinctive Characteristics of the Female," claimed that a woman "has a head almost too small for intellect but just big enough for love."[6] William Potter, another doctor, told a New York audience, "A sterile wife or invalid mother was the result of inappropriate educations." [7] Women's health issues caused much concern and debate in the nineteenth century. Men portrayed women as delicate creatures who must be protected so that they could fulfill their God-given role as mothers. One male physician went so far as to describe the female of the species as being a uterus around which God had built a woman. All of these "learned" men agreed that a woman's vital force needed to be directed towards her reproductive capacity rather than being thwarted or diluted by wasting her energies on learning.

To be perfectly fair, it was not only men who supported such ludicrous theories. Conservative female voices such as that of Mary Terhune, wife of a Presbyterian minister and mother of six, contributed widely to the debate. Using the pseudonym of Marion Harland, Mrs. Terhune became a popular and prolific writer of novels and books filled with domestic advice. She also lectured and gained a national reputation as a "domestic advisor" which evolved into a syndicated newspaper column. In her autobiography, Mrs. Terhune praised newspaper writing as "influence of the best kind," because it provided a platform from which she could promote conservative public attitudes. In 1882 Terhune published *Eve's Daughters* in which she maintained ideas such as, "The mother should keep her daughter with her, and near her, until the turning point between childhood and girlhood is safely passed and regularity of habits [menstruation] is established." [8] This should be an "absolute rule" in every home. Female voices such as Mrs. Terhune's reproduced Meigs' message in their popular parenting books and articles.

Dr. Edward Clarke of Harvard became the most widely read "expert" on this subject. He believed that, if a young woman's energies were directed towards her brain, it would retard the development of her sexual organs and thus hinder her from reproducing. And his ideas were very well received by much of the public. Today it sounds ridiculous, but his book, *Sex in Education* published in 1873, was a best seller which went through seventeen printings in just thirteen years. In Ann Arbor, where women only recently had been admitted to the University of Michigan, shops could not obtain sufficient copies of Clarke's book. One local bookseller bragged that he had sold two hundred copies in a single day and chuckled, "The book bids fair to nip coeducation in the bud." [9] It did nothing of the sort. Neither did Clarke's second book, *Building a Brain*, in which he asserted that, if women's health continued to decline in America, the country would have to send to Europe for women to bear the next generation.

Naturally not everyone agreed with Dr. Clarke. Julia Ward Howe was one who made her opposition public. Ironically, Clarke's book was an outgrowth of a talk he had been asked to give to the New England Women's Club in Boston. He was invited by Julia Ward Howe because once he had berated male medical students who had driven female students from a classroom. Everyone expected him to deliver a lecture supporting women. Waffling, Clarke told the Women's Club that women might have the "right" to train as doctors, but he did not believe they were physically capable of the rigors of advanced study. Appalled at Clarke's change of heart, Howe edited a collection of rebuttals in 1874. One of the contributors to that work was Professor Fairchild of Oberlin College. Oberlin had been a co-educational college for almost four decades.

Fairchild's specific statistics provided tangible evidence refuting Clarke's purely speculative conclusions. "A breaking down in health does not appear to be more frequent with women than with men. Out of 84 [women] who have graduated since 1841, seven have died, a proportion of one in twelve. Of three hundred and sixty-eight young men who have graduated in the same time, thirty-four are dead, or a little more than one in eleven. Six fell in the war; and leaving out those, the proportion of deaths remains one in thirteen." [10] Thus, according to Professor Fairchild, the death rates between men and women were quite similar. The facts simply did not support Dr. Clarke's assumptions. Mrs. Howe, herself concluded that, if there were a health problem, its source lay not in education but in just the opposite. "Girls", she wrote, "have the dispiriting prospect of a secondary and derivative existence, with only so much room allowed them as may not cramp the full sweep of the other sex." [11]

Mrs. Howe's words echoed another author who contradicted Dr. Clarke's opinions even before he had written them. Miss Harriett Martineau minced no words in her own book, *Society in America*, published forty years before Clarke's book hit the presses. Having traveled throughout the United States circa 1835, she described what she saw as the appalling state of American womanhood. This era especially in the East and South marked the beginning of the cult of leisure as both a status symbol and a trap. Women, Martineau said, filled their time with charities and going to "preachings." They read, but "thinkers are rare." The American woman, according to Martineau, had her "intellect confined...her health ruined, her weakness encouraged, and her strength punished..." [12] Miss Martineau went so far as to claim that women were so bored and full of despair that they were consuming alcohol in secret. This dreadful state of affairs, Martineau suggested, could be easily remedied by letting women make their lives meaningful.

Small wonder then that Miss Martineau's book created a barrage of criticism when it was published in 1836. It is worthy of note, however, that Martineau's impression of the State of Michigan at that time was that it was one of three regions where women's health was "vigorous." That should not be too surprising since Michigan in Miss Martineau's day was the western frontier settled only a decade prior to her visit and not yet a state. She found the people, including women, in this western area "the freest people I saw in America." [13] Had she revisited Michigan in 1870 she would have had to revise her opinion. Instead she would have agreed with Mary Walsh, author of *Doctors Wanted: No Women Need Apply*, who believes, "It was more than coincidence that the medical campaign to define women by their reproductive organs came at a time when they [women] were seeking to define themselves in other ways."[14]

For all the sound and fury the public heard about women's health, few in the medical profession correlated illness with the changes in lifestyle imposed on teen-age American girls. Some American girls when young were "much in the house;" [15] however, the majority enjoyed the freedom to be tomboys until adolescence. Dr. Anna S. MacLeod, a professor at University of Maryland, after an extensive study of diaries, has concluded that "Any image of prim and proper little girls who imbibed with their mother's milk a deep concern for the state of their clothing dissolves before the autobiographical accounts." [16] And, according to MacLeod, their tomboyish behavior was sanctioned by their mothers. One example she sites is that of a girl in Cincinnati who fell and hurt herself. Her mother's response was not that she shouldn't be climbing so high but that she needed to learn to climb better. MacLeod's study also concluded that boys and girls shared the same chores which were not gender based and that girls played with boys other than their brothers.

It was the abrupt cessation of that very freedom that often caused problems. The freedom and fun of childhood usually ended with the onset of menses which occurred in the nineteenth century at approximately at the age of sixteen. Doctors and articles which advocated women's delicacy frequently cited a disease called chlorosis as an typical example of young women's fragility. One male doctor described the effects of chlorosis as "like some delicate plant deprived of the beneficient rays of the sun, she [the sufferer] is a flower which withers and drops away even before its blooming." [17] Her decline was interpreted as her being too pure and good for this ugly world. They also suggested that it was a problem of epidemic proportions. Modern evaluations refute claims of both the nature and extent of the illness. Dr. Nancy Theriot, professor and chair of gender studies at the University of Louisville, noticed that chlorosis, which was particularly prevalent in the 1870's and 1880's, affected only a small number of middle class, adolescent girls. She also recognized strong similarities between it and anorexia: puberty, depression and appetite disturbance. Despite the frequent contemporary mentions of girls whose skin turned a sickly green color, Theriot states that amenorrhoea, a cessation of menstruation, was the major symptom of chlorosis. She believes, based on the evidence, that girls who suffered from this psychosomatic illness were rejecting the narrow adult female role society demanded. Their excessive weight loss not only prevented the onset or continuation of menstruation, it was a visible rejection of the mature female body. Moodiness, depression, and a withdrawal from social interaction were side effects. Chlorosis resulted in their becoming objects of care and concern in stark contrast to the idealized adult feminine role of self-sacrificing caregiver. Such girls were psychosomatically rejecting the physical corseting of adult women and the metaphorical corseting of their lifestyles.

Diary entries and autobiographies tell us time and time again how empty young women's lives were and how desperately they sought intellectual stimulation and purpose in their lives. Ellen Richards, before beginning a nationally recognized career as a chemist, despaired of life until she read of the opening of Vassar. She immediately matriculated and continued her education until she gained a second degree at MIT. Likewise, Jane Addams experienced seven years if debilitating depression until she found her life's work at Hull House in Chicago. And Charlotte Perkins Gilman, before decamping to California to begin her career as an author, was the victim of Dr. Meigs' celebrated "rest cure." This popular response to women's expression of dissatisfaction and frustration was a long period of solitary confinement with absolute sensory deprivation. Gilman describes such an experience in her Kafkaesque short story, "The Yellow Wallpaper." The only way out of that room, that is the only possible "cure," was total capitulation. Only when a woman was completely docile and compliant would she be released unless, of course, she went totally insane first. Harriet Hunt, one of the country's earliest female physician, diagnosed the source of so many women's "medical" problems correctly. When "the mind had been uncultivated- intelligence smothered- aspirations quenched. The result was physical suffering." [18]

Women's attire was another reason for their supposed delicacy. The Victorian stereotype is that every room had to have a "fainting couch" so that when a woman swooned, she could recover on the couch. Women might swoon, of course, if they were so tightly-laced in a corset that they could no longer breathe adequately. Indeed, tight lacing could cause internal damage that could complicate pregnancy thus increasing the mortality rate of women in childbirth. Corsets could constrict the waist by 2.5-6 inches exerting 21-88 pounds of pressure, according to an 1887 study. This was not new information. More than a decade earlier Ypsilanti physician, Ruth Gerry, bewailing the dictates of fashion, had warned, "How nice it would look on her tombstone... 'she died early but... [she had] the smallest waist that was ever known.'" [19]

Nor was it just corsets that confined women. Fashionable outfits restricted and hindered movement in other ways. Neither the bell skirt popular in the mid-nineteenth century, which served as both a germ magnet and a fire hazard, nor the hobble (just consider the term itself) skirt of the 1880's and early 1900's made movement easy. The former was like wearing a hula-hoop around one's legs with cold air swirling all the way to the waist. The latter forced women to walk in little shuffling steps like a Japanese geisha. Neither did the design of sleeves which prevented women from raising their arms nor the weight of a complete ensemble promote movement. An entire fashionable outfit might weigh 15-20 pounds exerting particular pressure on the hips. Dr. Mary Walker argued that traditional women's fashion, "shackled and enfeebled" its wearers. [20] "A woman in the ordinary Dress [sic] expends more vitality in wearing such a Dress, than a horse does wearing his harness." [21] In addition, women's shoes were very confining, thus limiting women's ability to walk distances. Dr. Walker was a woman who lived what she believed. First she adopted the bloomer style of clothing. She soon rejected that in favor of male attire which she wore for the rest of her life. Like so many modern women, she was more comfortable and could function more easily in pants. When criticized for her unorthodox appearance, she asserted, "It is the times that are behind me." [22] Despite the limitations fashion made upon women, Michigan coeds did not follow Dr. Walker's choice - at least in public. Neither did they accept the idea that they were too fragile to pursue an education. Pursue it they did, and their health did not suffer from the experience.

> Dr. Dio Lewis, a proponent of nineteenth century dress reform, believed that "A woman with contracted feet, contracted waist and contracted size may fret a man with her nervousness, but she can never seriously challenge his authority." [23]

The first woman officially to attend the University of Michigan was Madelon Stockwell. She was an appropriate choice for this distinction since she came from a family of educators. Her maternal grandfather was one of the first pioneers in Albion, Michigan, where he opened the Wesleyan Seminary (now Albion College). Her father moved there from Connecticut to teach in 1843. A year later, he married Louisa Peabody. A year after that Madelon Louisa Stockwell was born. She was still a little girl when her father died on the way to the gold fields of California. Madelon's mother home schooled her until she was twelve. At that time she entered Wesleyan Seminary from which she graduated in 1862. She continued her studies in Kalamazoo where Lucy Stone urged her to apply to the University of Michigan.

Stockwell was twenty-five in February of 1870 when she first matriculated at the University of Michigan to study Greek. Mr. Evans in the letter he wrote to Anna Dickinson also noted that Miss Stockwell was "good looking and intelligent...I have no doubt [she] will hold her own with any member of her class." [24] I am sure Miss Stockwell would have been gratified had she heard such words. According to Lucy Stone, Madelon was given a more severe entrance exam than men were given. Despite that, the University admitted her as a sophomore – not a freshman – which testifies to the level of her accomplishments. She graduated in 1872 and married a classmate named Charles Turner. Dr. Crocker, who taught Greek at the University, attended their wedding in April 1873. He bemoaned the marriage, claiming it demonstrated the "disastrous effect of co-education." We can only speculate as to what he meant. Was he unhappy that she married at all? That seems unlikely considering the times. Did he think all the effort put into her studies was wasted if she were a wife? Did he find Mr. Turner in some way unacceptable? Why would he have come to the wedding if he disapproved of it? Is it not possible that Crocker, in the midst of the wedding festivities perhaps with a glass of wine in his hand, was speaking facetiously? History leaves no statement of the tone of his voice thus we can only hypothesize as to his motivation.

Madelon Stockwell

Courtesy of Albion College
Archives and Special Collections

We know for certain today that a dormitory was named in her honor; however, few realize that, though Stockwell Hall might be named for her, she did not endow it. Despite an honorary degree by the University of Michigan in 1912, she left virtually her entire estate of $330,000 (over four million in today's dollars) to Albion College when she died at age seventy-nine in 1924. (Education doesn't seem to have ruined her health.) It is true that she had family ties to Albion, but one cannot help but wonder if her cold reception at Michigan was not part of her decision. Lucy Stone went on record saying that Stockwell had "unpleasant experiences" [25] at the University. Perhaps Madelon was in the class where the professor insisted on addressing everyone, including females, as "Gentlemen" thus effectively ignoring any woman's presence in the room. No doubt she also read the student newspaper, *The Chronicle*, which recorded how one professor responded to a dog's wandering into his classroom. When students tried to remove the dog, the professor told them to stop. "That dog," he said, "is a resident of Michigan. Don't you know we now recognize the right of every resident of the state to enjoy the privileges afforded by the University?" [26] Such hostility did not succeed in frightening Stockwell or others away. In the fall, she was joined by thirty-four more women: eleven in the Literary Department, three in Pharmacy, eighteen in Medicine and two in Law. Within six years that number had jumped to 117. By 1887 it rose to 284. In the Literary Department (now called L S and A for literature, science and arts)) 68% of the women graduated in comparison to 66% of the men. The University soon had to admit that these women "held their own in study and also in health." [27]

But it was not easy for any of the women who first broke the gender barrier. Olive San Louis Anderson, one of the first female graduates of the University of Michigan, railed against the attitudes of her day in a novel she wrote in 1878. *An American Girl and her Four Years at a Boy's College* is a thinly veiled account of her experiences as a coed. Anderson, who came from Mansfield, Ohio, and graduated from the University of Michigan in 1875, named her protagonist Wilhelmina. Then she shortened it to the rather masculine nickname of Willie to symbolize how women were perceived as infringing on a masculine domain. Willie's mother is scandalized that her daughter wants to go to the university. She cites all the standard reasons why this would not be a good idea. Willie's health would suffer. She would be conspicuous in a male environment, and such education would destroy religious faith. But Willie boards a

Olive San Louis Anderson

Courtesy of the Bentley Historical Library,
University of Michigan

train and goes to "Ortonville" anyway. Once there, she is finds that none of the boarding houses will accept her. Ultimately the university steward takes her to his cousin who gives her a room. Willie says, "A freshman year in college is full of trials for a boy; but for a girl, who enters an institution where boys have held undisputed sway for generations, every day brings persecutions which he never feels." [28] Yet Willie persists despite the problems and realizes that by her sophomore year, both the boarding house owners and the professors have discovered that women do actually make excellent students. Anderson's book is a novel; therefore, it is fiction though based on her own personal experiences. It is so autobiographical that a surviving copy has marginal notes with the names of the real people upon whom the characters are based. After graduation, Anderson moved to California where she drowned on June 5, 1886 while swimming in a river.

The experiences of other students in the last quarter of the nineteenth century were mixed. In 1878, the year Anderson's book was published, ten percent of the students at the University of Michigan were female. They were, for the most part, neither accepted nor acceptable. Another of the first female students said that she had rented a pew in a local church, but the only "Christian" to speak to her there was the man who collected the fee for the pew. By 1880 when Elizabeth Farrand was writing her *History of the University of Michigan*, she commented that most female students were treated with "indifferent courtesy" and were "welcomed by a small minority." [29] Attendance at the university certainly could not have been easy for these early co-eds who, as a group, were so outstanding. It was a case of natural selection. Only the very strong and very motivated would have entered the fray. Of those only the best would have endured. Being a woman in a male dominated university was not an experience for weaklings or quitters.

Despite the negatives, women arrived each semester in ever growing numbers, and they had no intention of going away. By the end of the century, they had become part of the university scene. This was especially true for women in the literature and arts program. No one seemed to have a problem with their studying the humanities. It was in the professional schools that women found their reception somewhat cooler. In fact, statistics circa 1895 indicate a disturbing trend. Surveying the three preceding

1889 graduates of the
University of Michigan.

Courtesy of the Bentley Historical Library,
University of Michigan

years, the total number of coeds had risen to 576, but the number entering professional schools had dropped steadily from 8% to 7% and finally to 6% in only those three years. And women who remained at the University to teach were always cognizant of their inferior status.

Lucinda Stone wrote a letter to the *Detroit Tribune* which published it on July 26, 1891. In that letter, she criticized the University for allowing women to enter as students but not hiring them to teach. Stone maintained that "It is not really co-education until it is co-educating. Until men and women both and together form the teaching force and influence the institution." It wasn't until five years after Stone's letter that the University of Michigan conferred the rank of full professor on a woman. Before that time they were allowed to teach at the University but only as instructors or assistants or demonstrators with lower salaries commensurate with their lesser positions.

Louise Reed Stowell

Courtesy of the Bentley Historical Library,
University of Michigan

This distinction had special import for Louise Marie Reed. She was not the first woman to earn both undergraduate and graduate degrees, but she was the first woman to teach at University of Michigan. Born in 1850 in Grand Blanc, Michigan, she graduated from the University of Michigan in 1876 and 1877 respectively. After graduation she declined an offer of $2500 per year as President of the Imperial College of Japan for Women. That offer was significantly more generous than any professor's salary at the University of Michigan. Instead she chose to remain at Michigan as an assistant in microscopic botany earning only $750 a year. As so many women have done throughout history, her decision definitely seems to have been influenced by her relationship with Charles H. Stowell. They married soon after, and he became a professor of histology and microscopy. During the time she taught at the University, Mrs. Stowell remained sensitive to the problems female students faced. Something as simple as a safe place to rest or study was absent from the campus facilities. The student union continued to be off limits to women at that time. So Mrs. Stowell took it upon herself to establish a lounge for female students in a room on the east wing of University Hall. She furnished it herself with items from her own home, and it was still being used in the 1930's when it was replaced by the Michigan League, a building constructed specifically for female students.

In 1889 both Louise and her husband accepted positions in Washington D.C. where she worked for the Department of Agriculture. President Benjamin Harrison appointed her as a trustee of the Washington D. C. Girls' Reformatory. She chaired the Committee on Sanitation (a remnant of the Sanitation Commission established by President Lincoln at the beginning of the Civil War); she was the first woman on that city's school board. In addition, Mrs. Stowell published not only a textbook in her field but more than a hundred articles. She edited a monthly professional journal for seven years. And she was the first -- and for a long time, the only -- female member of the Royal Society in London. Despite all those accomplishments, she is not listed in the University of Michigan's *Catalog of Graduates, Non-graduates and Members of the Faculty 1837-1921* which presumably lists all faculty during that time period. Mr. Stowell, wrote to the University of Michigan in 1911 asking the Board of Regents to have his wife officially listed as part of the faculty. He was ignored. Marna Osband of Ypsilanti wrote with the same request twenty years after Mr. Stowell letter. Nothing happened. That slight to Mrs. Stowell has yet to be corrected properly, which is why her accomplishments remain unrecognized. Fortunately Edwin B. Mains saw fit to include a summary of her work in the *University of Michigan, an Encyclopedic Survey* published in 1951. He concluded, "Her title [assistant] did not do justice to her responsibilities and attainments." [30] It certainly didn't.

The women who taught at the University of Michigan slightly later than Mrs. Stowell fared no better in financial compensation but were somewhat more recognized publicly. A few of them are listed in the *Alumni Catalogue* as part of the faculty and were pictured in the *1896 Ann Arbor Headlight*. Among these is Alice Louise Hunt who was, for twenty years, an assistant in drawing at the University. She supplemented her $350-$750 annual salary there by serving as the superintendent of drawing for the Ann Arbor Public Schools between 1885 and 1893. Miss Hunt graduated from the Cooper Institute in New York.

Dr. Jeanne C. Solis

Courtesy of the Bentley Historical Library,
University of Michigan

The *Headlight* also featured Dr. Jeanne C. Solis, a native of St. Clair, Michigan. Dr. Solis graduated from the University of Michigan School of Medicine in 1892. She specialized in mental and nervous diseases. For a salary of $500, she taught as a demonstrator in the electro-therapeutics department until 1897. Then she entered private practice in Ann Arbor. She also established and maintained a private hospital where Doctor Solis treated patients for more than fifty years.

Marion Nute is the third woman whose photograph appears in the *Headlight*. She came from Boston to train as a doctor, graduating in 1897 at the age of twenty-four. She later returned to the Boston Area where she practiced medicine until 1939. Not only was Dr. Nute on the staff at the New England Hospital for Women and Children, she also was a member of the faculty of the Boston School of Physical Education.

Dr. Marion Nute

Courtesy of the Bentley Historical Library,
University of Michigan

Miss Fanny E. Langdon is not pictured In the *Headlight* because she began teaching in 1897 as an instructor in botany and zoology (annual salary, $900) only to have her promising career cut short when she died of a ruptured appendix in 1899. Records of the Regents' Proceedings mention several dozen other women. Few stayed for any length of time since none of these exceptional women were given the recognition and income they would have received had they been men. They understood that the possibility of their becoming full professors at the University of Michigan was simply out of the question at that time. Better opportunities existed elsewhere.

Women at Michigan State Normal School in Ypsilanti seem to have been held in higher esteem. The faculty in 1868-9 consisted of eleven educators, four of whom were women, and many were Michigan residents. The most well known was Julia Ann King who served

A nervous diseases class at the University of Michigan

Courtesy of the Bentley Historical Library,
University of Michigan

as preceptress of the school. King was born in Milan, Michigan, which in 1838, the year of Julia's birth, was part of Monroe not Washtenaw County. Once when she was a young child, her mother woke her in the middle of the night. Her baby sibling was ill, and her father had broken his leg. Someone needed to go for help and clearly her mother could not leave, so she gave Julia a lantern and sent her out into the dark to walk through the forest of frontier Michigan. One can only shudder imagining what that must have been like for such a small child, but she accomplished the task. It certainly shows something about her fortitude.

Julia attended a nearby log school but claimed her first botany and zoology lessons were found in the swamp near her home. She attended Adrian High School and Michigan State Normal School. She not only graduated from the Normal School in 1858 but did a year of post graduate work. After working in Lansing, Kalamazoo and Charlotte, Michigan, in top level administrative positions, she returned to the Normal School as the Preceptress. Every Friday at four in the afternoon, Miss King held what she called her "conversations" which students and many Ypsilanti residents both attended.

Julia Ann King

Courtesy of Eastern Michigan University

Bertha Goodison

Courtesy of Eastern Michigan University

Miss King was chair of the history department. She held the rank of full professor earning the same salary as the top seven male professors, an achievement that would not all of her department's members except one were female. Female faculty members not only existed in every department at Michigan State Normal School; by 1910, women formed the majority of every department except natural science in which two of the five members were female. And many of those faculty members were long time Michigan residents.

Bertha Goodison, who taught at the Michigan State Normal School, not only grew up in Ypsilanti, her father also taught at Normal School. The two Goodisons led the art department for more than fifty years. Bertha also graduated from the Normal

School in 1894 at the age of twenty-six. She began teaching there in 1900 and continued teaching until the day of her death in October, 1937, nine days after her sixty-ninth birthday. During the summers and on sabbaticals Miss Goodison continued her studies at Harvard and Columbia Universities and in Paris and Florence. Her obituary said she had "a brilliant intellect" as well as artistic talent. In her will, she left all her paintings, mostly oils, to the school. Two portraits of faculty members painted by Miss Goodison hung for many years in the library.

Goodison's colleague, Mary A Rice was a Michigan native, too. Since she was born in 1825, her parents were among the very first to settle the area. Rice recalled her childhood surroundings as wild and her rural education as "desultory." As with so many women who later in their careers taught in colleges, Miss Rice began her teaching career in rural schools. She also taught in Saginaw, Michigan, before receiving her degree from Michigan State Normal School in 1861. In a memoir, she illustrated her philosophy of class management with an example. Controlling an unruly student was simple, she said. All a teacher, then or now, has to do is to convert him to a new life by proving to him that, "he was indispensable to my happiness in supplying us with wood and water." Once she understood that she "learned to select the worst or most unfortunate pupil as a helper." [31] Rice taught English language and literature at Michigan State Normal School for fourteen

Mary Rice Fairbanks
Courtesy of the Ypsilanti Historical Society

years. She organized the first literary club at the school which was called, in her honor, the "Riceonian." After fourteen years of teaching there, she spent the summer of 1884 traveling abroad. Upon her return, she married Dr. Fairbanks and retired from teaching. Mrs. Fairbanks passed away in Petoskey, Michigan. She was eighty-two.

Yet another Normal School teacher from Michigan with a long career was Ada A. Norton. Daughter of Roswell and Lucy Norton, she earned her BA from Albion College in 1877 and then her MA in 1894. She was an excellent mathematician which brought her first to the high school in Northville, Michigan, and then to Quincy, Michigan, as both preceptress and instructor in mathematics. Finally in 1891 she came to Ypsilanti where she taught at Ypsilanti High School. By 1901 her reputation was impressive enough that Michigan State Normal School hired her. She remained on the faculty there for thirty years, passing away in Ypsilanti in 1939.

Lucy Osband
Courtesy of Eastern Michigan University

Unlike King, Goodison and Rice-Fairbanks and Norton, Lucy A. Osband was not born in Washtenaw County or even in Michigan. She, like so many Michiganders, came from New York. Educated at home until age sixteen, she then entered Newark Union School. She was the only girl in her class. She began teaching at the age of nineteen but succumbed to ill health which her daughter later said was "incipient TB." Lucy spent two years teaching in Virginia regaining her health before she returned to New York. There she attended Genesee College, which is now

Syracuse University. Originally Genesee Seminary, like Oberlin in Ohio, was from its establishment in 1832 a co-educational institution. Osband graduated valedictorian in 1864. It was she who refused the honor of being recognized because her future husband was in the same class and she did not want to outshine him on graduation day.

Later, after she and her husband moved to Michigan they both taught at Olivet and Albion Colleges. In 1882 the couple moved to Ypsilanti where she joined the faculty of the Normal School. Mrs. Osband taught everything from literature to calculus, but her specialty was botany. Within two years she became head of the Physical Science Department where she remained until 1895. In addition to her regular duties, Mrs. Osband also guided classes in "Swedish Work" which was a form of calisthenics. She was not paid for these classes, and there was no appropriate venue for them, so she held them in the chapel until a room in a basement was provided. By 1888, however, the Normal School offered a class on the theory and practice of Physical Culture. Osband then started campaigning for a gym which was finally built in 1894, the same year as the establishment of the Physical Culture Department.

Mrs. Osband clearly was not the stereotypical Victorian school teacher as the following story clearly demonstrates. One day she heard that an interurban trolley had killed a horse near Belleville, just east of Ypsilanti. She gathered up her class, hopped onto the next trolley and went to see the unfortunate horse. Then she paid a farmer to deliver its body to the school where she kept its skeleton in her classroom in Sherzer Hall. Later it was moved – ever so carefully – to Room 331 in the new Jefferson Building. Unfortunately, the skeleton now appears to be lost.

Mrs. Osband's physical culture class.
Courtesy of Eastern Michigan University

Ruth Hoppin was yet another woman who did not fit the stereotype. Her career touched both Ann Arbor and Ypsilanti as well as Three Rivers, Michigan. Though born in 1833 in New York, her family came to Michigan in 1837, the same year Michigan attained statehood. Her memories of that frontier existence were that it was very wild with deer and wolves as well as Indians as her nearest neighbors. She began her teaching career in a little school in Park Township. Records indicate that in 1849 that school had children from twelve families during a summer term for which the teacher received a total salary of $6.75, the equivalent of $196 today.

Ruth returned to New York to study before entering Oberlin College. She must have been an impressive student because she was invited to teach preparatory classes there at the same time she was a student herself. In this way she worked her way through college. Her career then took her to Jonesville, Illinois, for two years before working in Three Rivers, Michigan, for five years. Then she moved to Ann Arbor. Hoppin was very active in supporting soldiers leaving for the Civil War. Her great regret was that she was not a boy; therefore, she could not join them. She did, however, wage her own small battles at home to acquire sufficient equipment both for Michigan's soldiers and her students. Miss Hoppin disapproved of rote memorization which was used by most of her contemporaries as a teaching method. One day, for example, she was explaining the solar system to her small charges. In order to do so, she put a boy with fiery red hair revolving in the center of the room. He was the sun. She then added children of varying sizes running around him to represent the planets. Such methods were progressive indeed.

Ruth Hoppin

Courtesy of Eastern Michigan University

Miss Hoppin was both the Preceptress and a teacher at Ann Arbor High School for three years before returning briefly to Three Rivers, Michigan, in 1865. Finally in 1867 she became the Preceptress of the Michigan State Normal School in Ypsilanti, a post she filled for fourteen years. In addition to her duties as Preceptress, she taught history and botany, spending her summers at Harvard studying eastern flora. She left Washtenaw County in 1881 to accept a professorship of botany and biology at Smith College. Her resignation at the Normal School was accepted with "unfeigned regret" at their loss of a woman who "has brought accurate scholarship, rare tact and unusual executive ability..."[32] She remained at Smith College until health problems forced her to move to a milder climate.

Feeling better after five years in the south, Miss Hoppin returned to Ann Arbor to attend the University of Michigan where she earned her Masters in 1891. She was fifty-three years old at the time. The University offered her an honorary degree, but she declined, saying that she preferred to write her thesis and take her degree in "the regular way." She taught only briefly after that because of recurring health issues. Though eventually blind, she continued teaching privately in Three Rivers, Michigan, until her death in 1903.

Another woman whose career wove back and forth between Ypsilanti and Ann Arbor was Mary Goddard. Born in Illinois in 1870, she began by teaching rural school in Illinois and then taught for a year at Ann Arbor High School. In 1900 she graduated from the University of Michigan and began her thirty-eight year career as a botany professor at Michigan State Normal School. In 1908 she spent a year studying abroad, and in 1924 she received her Master's from the University of Chicago. Miss Goddard obviously loved everything she did. The *Normal College News* commented at her retirement that there were many "touching memories of hurried breakfasts and early morning jaunts afield in search of everything from snakes to locusts."[33] One of her publications was a plea to save the vanishing native shrubs of Michigan. In a totally different vein, she also wrote a history of the Underground Railroad in Ypsilanti. Upon retiring at age sixty-seven, Miss Goddard returned to Ann Arbor to live with her brother who was a professor at the

Mary Goddard

Courtesy of Eastern Michigan University

University of Michigan. She died eighteen months later. Michigan State Normal School named one residence hall for Julia Ann King; the sister hall was dedicated to Mary Goddard.

Abigail Pearce also graduated from the University of Michigan. She earned a Bachelor's degree in 1895 and a master's in 1914. Those educational credentials served her in good stead during her long teaching career with Michigan State Normal School. Born in Ingersoll, Ontario, her parents, Joseph and Janet Pearce moved to Grand Haven, Michigan, in 1860. Abigail graduated from Grand Haven High School and taught there for four years. In 1878 she graduated from Michigan State Normal School majoring in languages. After a few years teaching in St. Clair and Durand, Michigan, she returned to Ypsilanti to begin teaching at the Normal School. The decision to come back to Ypsilanti turned into a forty-one year career actively teaching and five more years as Professor Emeritus. Miss Pearce organized the Shakespeare Club in 1897 and the Laonian Dramatic Circle in 1915. In 1927 she published a small book entitled *Scriptures in the Making*. After a long and fruitful life spanning seventy-five years, Miss Pearce passed away in December of 1935.

Women such as Madelon Stockwell Turner, Louise Reed Stowell and Abigail Pearce were living proof that education, instead of harming women, actually provided them with longer lives despite the inevitable obstacles put in their way. In November, 1881, seventeen recent college graduates met at the home of Marion Talbot in Boston, Massachusetts. They recognized the need for a group which would support female graduates, seek equity and help graduates find jobs. Within two months the Association of Collegiate Alumnae (the name originally given to the American Association of University Women) could boast sixty-five members from eight colleges and universities including Wellesley, Vassar and University of Michigan. Within a few years the group had over a thousand members. One of the ACA's first projects was to put to rest, once and for all, the concept that education would hurt a woman's health. It sent 1,290 surveys to its members. Over 700 were answered and returned. The Massachusetts Department of Labor in 1885 published the results of their survey which showed that 78% of the members were in excellent health while only 5% replied indicating fair health. The study concluded, "College [educated] women appear to enjoy better health than the national average." [34] These women were healthier both physically and mentally because education had enriched their lives.

The availability of better education opened innumerable doors for the women of the nineteenth century. The majority of women still married and raised families. Married or single, women were able use their talents and educations to develop a meaningful life's work of their own. For the first time in history large numbers of women could teach in something other than rural, one-room schools. They could join the faculties of colleges and universities. With a wider forum, their educations reverberated through their students to the society at large. Their way was not easy, but better educations resulted in better lives – better for both the individual and the society.

[1] Letter from E. Evans to Anna E. Dickinson, Albion College Archives and Special Collections.

[2] Albeit "Football" in the European usage.

[3] Wilfred B. Shaw, *The University of Michigan* (New York: Harcourt, Brace and Howe, 1920), 129.

[4] The first tax supported state university to admit women was the University of Iowa. In 1856, 83 men and 41 women matriculated there.

[5] Justin Kestenbaum, ed., *A Pioneer Anthology: the Making of Michigan* (Detroit: Wayne State University Press, 1999), 289.

[6] Walsh, Mary Roth. *Doctors Wanted No Women Need Apply* (New Haven: Yale University Press, 1977), 111.

[7] Martha Verbrugge, *Able-Bodied Womanhood* (New York: Oxford University Press, 1988), 121.

[8] Marion Harland, *Eve's Daughters* (New York, Scribner, 1885), 87.

> The very title of this book tells us a great deal about the attitude of the author. For centuries women had been blamed for the sin of Eve. After all, without Eve, we would still be in the Garden of Eden.

[9] Olive San Louis Anderson, *An American Girl and her Four Years at a Boys' College* (New York: D. Appleton and Co., 1878), 98.

[10] Julia Ward Howe, ed. *Sex and Education: A Reply* (New York: Arno Press, 1972), 202-3.

[11] Howe, 28.

[12] Harriet Martineau, *Society in America Vol III* (London: Saunders and Otley, 1837), 106.

[13] Martineau, 21.

[14] Walsh, 141.

[15] Howe 27.

[16] MacLeod, Anne Scott. "The Caddie Woodlawn Syndrome, "In *The Girl's History and Culture Reader*, edited by. Miriam Forman-Brunell, and Leslie Paris (Urbana: University of Illinois Press, 2011), 203.

[17] Barbara Welter, *Dimity Convictions: The American Woman in the Nineteenth Century* (Athens, OH: Ohio University Press, 1976), 63.

[18] Welter, 60.

> Dr. Harriet Hunt began her career by 1835. She learned about medicine by apprenticing to another doctor.

[19] *Ypsilanti Commercial*, January 6, 1872

[20] Glenda Riley, *Inventing the American Woman, An Inclusive History, 2nd ed.* (Wheeling, IL: Harlan Davidson Inc., 1995), 72.

[21] Dale Walker, *Mary Edwards Walker* (New York: Tom Doherty Associates, 2005), 59.

> Dr. Walker worked in Civil War hospitals and even did a bit of spying for the Union. She was awarded the Congressional Medal of Honor. She was an outspoken dress reformer. At first she wore a bloomer outfit but after the war she began wearing male attire which she did for the rest of her life. While not a resident of Washtenaw County or even Michigan, she was honored when the Walker Army Reserve Center near Grand Rapids, Michigan, a training center for the 334th medical group was dedicated to her. Its commanding officer said, "We named this center for her because she was a great citizen soldier." The center is now in California.

[22] Walker, 1.

[23] Dio Lewis, *Dio Lewis Treasury* (New York:, Canfield, 1887), 687.

[24] Evans.

[25] Lucy Stone, *Detroit Tribune*, July 26, 1891.

[26] McGuigan, 33.

> The Michigan State Superintendent of Public Instruction declared that "all persons resident of the State" had a right to be educated at the University. I cannot help but wonder if he was doing a political slight of hand because the use of the word "person" was a legal loophole. Were women "persons?" According to Blackstone's *Commentaries on the Laws of England*, written in the eighteenth century, but also a fundamental legal work in America, women were not persons. The professor, who called all students "gentlemen," was referring to the Regents' resolution of January 5, 1870, which was stated a bit differently. It said that "every resident "of Michigan had the right to attend the University.

> The *Michigan Daily* did not begin until 1890. Before then *University Chronicle*, begun in 1867, was the eight page bi-weekly newspaper.

[27] Elizabeth Farrand, *History of the University of Michigan* (Ann Arbor: Register Publishing House, 1885), 273.

[28] Anderson, 55.

[29] Farrand, 203.

[30] Edwin B. Mains, "Botany," in *The University of Michigan: An Encyclopedic Survey, Vol 2,* ed. Wilfred Shaw (Ann Arbor, University of Michigan Press, 1951), 498.

[31] Mary Rice Fairbanks, "A Sketch of the Life of Mary Rice Fairbanks" in "Fairbanks Collection" at Ypsilanti Historical Archives, 10.

[32] Daniel Putnam, *The History of Michigan State Normal School* (Ypsilanti, MI: Scharf Tag, Label and Box Co., 1899), 167.

[33] Annie G Howes et al, *Health Statistic of Women College Graduates* (Boston: Wright and Potter Printing Co., 1885), 9.

CHAPTER NINE: WOMEN JOIN THE PROFESSIONS

To professionalize or not to professionalize; that was the question both men and women in the nineteenth century faced. Some chose to reject the idea of becoming paid professionals while others, indeed most, welcomed the exclusiveness that professionalization conferred. Amateurism prevailed in 1894 when the first modern Olympic Games began. Participants then were primarily collegiate males from middle and upper class homes who preferred to reserve the games for their own socio-economic group, thus effectively eliminating working class athletes who obviously needed to be compensated for wages lost from their jobs. By determining that only amateur athletes could participate, the first modern Olympics became an experience limited to an elite group.

In contrast, but for much the same reasons, occupations requiring extensive education chose to professionalize. The field of medicine was the earliest to do so. Professionalization began by organizing first state associations and then in 1847 the American Medical Association. As a national organization, members then determined the appropriate qualifications for membership thus creating what is known as "occupational closure." The first group of "amateurs" the AMA decided to suppress was midwives. It made sure that the licensing examinations contained information only available in medical schools which did not accept women. Such a decision also removed apprenticeship as acceptable training to become a doctor. In so doing, it eliminated competition and enhanced its members' prestige. Because the medical field required extensive and specialized training within a university setting, it followed that doctors expected to be well paid for their services.

Before 1870 when the University of Michigan opened its medical school's doors to female students, opportunities for women who were interested in becoming educated in the medical field were almost non-existent. Elizabeth Blackwell managed to be admitted to Geneva Medical College in New York. Apparently the school thought it was a joke when she applied and were shocked when she actually arrived. Geneva hastily graduated Blackwell after only one year of instruction and then closed its doors to women. Dr. Blackwell, however, pioneered training female doctors in the United States. After the Civil War she opened the Women's Medical College. Once it was established, she returned to England and did the same there.

The fact that established medical schools before the Civil War would not accept women certainly did not stop them from practicing. Women were welcomed at a wide array of alternative medical schools which evolved in the first half of the century to combat the harmful practices of what was labeled "heroic" medicine. Professional doctors of the time, perhaps in an effort to earn the incomes they felt they deserved, were providing extreme measures to demonstrate their expertise. Bloodletting, emetics and laxatives were widely prescribed. Side effects of popular drugs like calomel and mercury harmed patients more than they helped which is why many Americans turned to alternative methods for relief.

Ypsilanti doctor, Helen McAndrew is a perfect example of an early female doctor who received her training at an alternative medical school. Mrs. McAndrew came to Ypsilanti with her husband, William, circa 1850. After her son was born, she left him in another's care and went to New York to study. Despite some criticism, the fact that she did so did not seem to bother her son who later commented, "She had a talent for nursing. She could hire her own housework done." [1] McAndrew studied at the Russell Trall's Hydropathic and Hygienic Institute supporting herself as a bookbinder, a skill she had learned before she married. When Dr. McAndrew returned to Ypsilanti, she discovered that only women and African-Americans would utilize her services, a fact that did not dismay her. Then her luck changed. One of Ypsilanti's prominent citizens, Mrs. Samuel Post, was critically ill. None of the regular doctors were able to help. Her husband was desperate, so when his gardener recommended Dr. McAndrew, Mr. Post summoned her. Within a few weeks Mrs. Post was well, and Dr. McAndrew's reputation secure.

Dr. Helen McAndrew and Family
Courtesy of the Ypsilanti Historical Society

What miracle did Dr. McAndrew provide? The answer might appear, by today's standards, to be just good common sense. She tossed out all the harsh chemical medicines other doctors had prescribed and fed Mrs. Post tasty food and lots of fluids. She moved her bed to the window and every day told Mrs. Post how much better she was. Many of these "irregular" medical practices, like hydropathy, were based primarily on good hygiene, diet and exercise. Alternative medicine has again become popular since the late twentieth century because it is less invasive. Believers in alternative medicine now, as then, are convinced of its superiority to "regular" medicine. Laura Haviland of Adrian, Michigan, literally staked her life on hydropathy. When in 1845 an epidemic of inflammatory erysipelas swept the area around her home killing her parents and her husband, she decided "to trust myself with water treatment ... This was done and every bath brought relief to respiration, and my lungs became entirely clear though my neck and throat were still badly swollen and inflamed. Cold applications frequently applied soon overcame that difficulty and in three days the disease seemed entirely conquered." [2] Mrs. Haviland's regimen gently relieved her symptoms while allowing her body to heal naturally.

So successful was such an approach that Dr. McAndrew opened her Water Cure Sanitarium in an octagon house built by her husband at 105 S. Huron. Octagon houses became popular midcentury due to O. S. Fowler. Mr. Fowler was a popular public speaker. [3] In 1850, he gave lectures in Ann Arbor and in 1853 published a book recommending octagon construction.

The McAndrews' octagon house.

He extolled the virtues of that design because it allowed for more light and air circulation. Harriet M. Irwin of Charlotte, North Carolina, patented a hexagonal house plan in 1869. Her patent, #94116, was the first architectural patent ever granted to a woman. A few houses in her area were built according to her design, but it never gained widespread interest like octagonal houses. No doubt this was due in part to the fact that Fowler lectured and wrote thus disseminating the idea to a wider audience. Only two octagonal houses remain in Washtenaw County. Neither is the McAndrew house. One, however, is in Ypsilanti. It has been moved to River Street. The other one is the Nathan B. Devereaux house in Northfield Township. According to Marilyn Devereaux Harrington, her great-grandfather heard O. S. Fower speak in Ann Arbor and decided then and there that he would have such a house despite the complaints of the men he hired to build it. Mrs. Harrington was raised in that octagon house and her mother continued living there until her death in 2010.

The very fact that the McAndrews chose to build such a unconventional home demonstrates their commitment to a less invasive and more all encompassing view of health and medicine. When Mrs. McAndrew went to New York to study, there were twenty-one well known water cure establishments in the east. By the time she opened her own, there were twenty-seven more in "rural" i.e. western areas such as Ypsilanti. Dr. McAndrew encouraged "guests" to swim in the Huron River. She even piped in mineral water which was discovered in Ypsilanti when the Ypsilanti Paper Company drilled for water to supply its plant. One anonymous fan composed a jingle about the benefits of the local mineral water: "If you are sick, just try our cure/ Drink Ypsilanti's water pure." [4]

Despite the demands of her practice, Dr. McAndrew was a committed social activist. She and her husband, before coming to Ypsilanti, had been forced to leave Baltimore after teaching African-Americans to read. The couple continued their efforts by assisting in the Underground Railroad which was very active in southeast Michigan. Mrs. McAndrew was also a conspicuous advocate of temperance as well as women's suffrage. Finally in 1871 she and Dr. Ruth Gerry formed a circle of women called the Band of Hope whose purpose was to encourage the University of Michigan to accept women into its medical school.

Dr. Ruth Gerry, also of Ypsilanti, trained at the Medical College of Pennsylvania (now Drexel University) in Philadelphia. She wrote her thesis on malaria which was such a problem to early settlers of Michigan although they called it "ague." Graduating in 1865, she began her practice in Ypsilanti eventually enlarging her home at 57 Pearl Street to house the Ypsilanti Free Hospital. This facility "befriended, nursed and restored to health" anyone in need.[5] Though its mission was to assist women, Dr. Gerry's hospital also treated many students at Michigan State Normal School especially those not from the area. Despite these positive contributions, the Washtenaw County Medical Association rejected her as a member in 1871. One of its members complained to the press that he did not know why women wanted to go where they knew they were not wanted. Amazingly just a year later she and two other women from outside Washtenaw County were accepted as members of the Michigan State Medical Society. The cause of this abrupt change of heart on the part of the medical community could have been the fact that in 1872 Amanda Sanford became the first woman to graduate from the University of Michigan's School of Medicine, an event that surely indicated the changing times, thus putting pressure on the medical community to accept women.

Sadly, Dr. Gerry died a few years later of consumption, which was the name given then to tuberculosis. Consumption was the scourge of the nineteenth century. More women in Washtenaw County died from consumption than from any other cause. Dr. Gerry was only forty-eight when she passed away on Dec. 8, 1876. She was buried in Highland Cemetery in Ypsilanti. Her work, however, was continued by other female doctors in Ypsilanti.

Dr. Ruth Gerry's
tombstone.

Ypsilanti experienced no shortage of women practicing medicine though the roster varied as doctors came and went. Dr. Ruth French is probably the most extreme example. She opened her office in 1877 to fill the vacancy left by Dr. Gerry. By 1882, however, French was coming and going with some regularity. First she was in Topeka, then she opened an office in Detroit with Saturday hours in Ypsilanti. In 1883 she settled in Knoxville returning to Ypsilanti in 1884 before returning to Kansas in 1886. Dr. French travels finally ended in Petaluna, California, where she died in 1905 after a horse kicked her in the head.

Dr. Belle Warner, another University of Michigan School of Medicine graduate, began her practice when Dr. French left in 1882. There was some local speculation that Dr. Warner believed she had purchased Dr. French's practice only to find French back in town in 1884. Dr. Warner then left thus making a space for Dr. Flora Hubbard Ruch. Originally from Adrian, Michigan, Dr. Ruch was in 1882 yet one more University of Michigan School of Medicine graduate. She treated patients in Ypsilanti between 1884 and 1888. Dr. Ruch practiced medicine in other Michigan cities for more than fifty years. Dr. Ruch's daughter continued the family tradition by also attending medical school.

Even though the University of Michigan School of Medicine began accepting women, there was considerable resentment and opposition. Amanda Stanford, the first woman to graduate from the Medical School was "hooted and showered with abusive notes at graduation."[6] At first the women were taught in separate classes except for inorganic chemistry which the professors must have considered a safe enough topic to teach both sexes simultaneously. The University even paid professors $500 extra, in other words, approximately 20-25% of their salaries to teach women. Dr. Alonzo B. Palmer was a professor in the School of Medicine. In the beginning, he was an especially outspoken opponent of women's admittance. "I cannot see how right minded women can wish to study medicine,"[7] he said. It is gratifying to note that just a few years after women were admitted, alumna Mrs. H. "Hattie" J. Hilton, MD, whose office was at #88 Ann Street, had received enough positive feedback from the same Dr. Palmer to offer his name as a reference when announcing the opening of her practice.

The stone hitching post still stands outside Dr. Hilton's home and office.

There was particular opposition, and not just at the University of Michigan, to women's studying obstetrics and gynecology. Male physicians claimed that women did not have the courage and firmness necessary in emergencies that can occur during childbirth. Such a claim is amazing since women had been functioning as midwives for millenia. Certainly Mrs. George T. Smith of Denton, Michigan (just east of Willow Run), would have been shocked to hear such a claim. For more than two generations she, as midwife, attended at least a thousand births. Her patients obviously were happy with her courage and firmness during childbirth. All ten grandchildren of Aurilla and Jothan Goodell as well as some of their great-grandchildren were safely delivered by Mrs. Smith. An equally ridiculous concern was suggested by another professor. He worried lest women, in their desire to remain active in the profession, might use their knowledge to kill their children so they were not burdened in their professional life. I am confident he meant to abort rather than to murder a child already born. Such fears were, in truth, expressions of the male physicians' own need to maintain control of that particularly lucrative field of medicine. Male doctors certainly must have realized that women would prefer female doctors over themselves which would be detrimental to their practices for two reasons.

First and foremost was the fact that illnesses of women comprised many physicians' primary source of income. If women specialized in OB-GYN, male doctors' financial security would be in jeopardy. A second reason might have been to regain some measure of social control. Limit a woman's knowledge of reproduction, and you limit her choices outside of motherhood. One of the most prevailing misconceptions (no pun intended) about the era is the idea that most people in the nineteenth century, especially women, were ignorant concerning the reproductive process. This is simply not true. Earlier in the century it had been a common practice to send birth control literature to young women about to be married. At least a dozen sex manuals were readily available often illustrated with anatomical drawings and each supporting its preferred contraceptive method. Virtually every current method except the pill was available in the nineteenth century.

A woman also could end an undesired pregnancy surgically or by ingesting an abortifacient drug. During the middle of the century, women could end a pregnancy at one of the many "resorts" that were available. Madame Restell in New York City is the most famous – or infamous – depending on one's perspective. Restell was so well known that the eponymous label "Restellism" became a euphemism for abortion. Madame Restell derived so much money from her services that she was able to build one of the first mansions on Fifth Avenue across from Central Park. When she died in 1878, she left an estate valued today at $11-13 million dollars. Abortion at that time clearly was being utilized as a form of contraception.

The very year that Restell died, a report by the Michigan Board of Health stated that fully one in three pregnancies in Michigan ended in abortion. In considering that statistic, one needs to recognize that the term "abortion" until the mid- twentieth century included spontaneous abortions which today we would call miscarriages. The report continued by saying that 75% of those "abortions" involved "respectable married ladies." That comment suggests what other sources confirm. Married women were trying to limit the size of their families, and very often they were doing so with the knowledge and approval of their husbands. As the century progressed with more and more people living in urban areas, a large family increasingly became a financial liability. Ironically these efforts at family planning were occurring at the very same time that laws were being passed to curtail information and products about contraception.

In 1873 Congress passed the Comstock law, which prohibited distribution of contraceptive information and devices through the U.S. mail. As indirect evidence of the popularity of contraception at that time, one only has to consider how much of this interstate communication it would take to convince the United States Congress actually to pass such a bill. The answer is a lot. Lots and lots and lots. Contraception in all its forms was big business. And despite the fact that it was acquiring a social stigma it had not possessed before, women found ways around it. For example, many over the counter medicines such as Dr. Cheeseman's Pills[8] cautioned buyers not to take it if they might be pregnant as it *would* cause a miscarriage. It did not take women long to realize that if they wanted a miscarriage, all they had to do was take the drug. Further evidence supporting widespread knowledge about and use of contraception is found in one of the first sex studies, done by Dr. Clelia Mosher (Eliza Mosher's cousin). Her admittedly limited study found that 84% of the women interviewed practiced some form of contraception. That statistic would include the practice of abstinence which was advocated by the well publicized Voluntary Motherhood campaign supported by such leading figures as Elizabeth Cady Stanton, herself a mother of seven. It should not be surprising that all this discussion and debate concerning birth control coincided with the emergence of women in the public arena and would contribute to the inevitable backlash.

In spite of such hostility and controversy, female doctors did enter the specialty of women's medicine. In fact, the first woman to head a major university's department of medicine specialized in that very field. Dr. Bertha Van Hoosen, herself a University of Michigan graduate, was chief of obstetrics and gynecology for Loyola University. Van Hoosen graduated from the University of Michigan Literary Department in 1884 and the Medical School in 1888. She then moved to Chicago where she began her long career. She also co-founded and was first president of the American Medical Women's Association founded in 1915. She retired to Romeo, Michigan, where she died in 1952.

Dr. Bertha Van Hoosen at the beginning of her career, left, and at the end, right.

Courtesy of the Bentley Historical Library, University of Michigan

Somehow during her busy lifetime, Dr. Van Hoosen found time to write her autobiography, *Petticoat Surgeon*, which was published five years before her death. In it she provides a mixed impression of what it was like for women at the University of Michigan in those early days. Though her undergraduate work was a "foregone conclusion," her choice of medicine did not receive parental support. Her father explained to her, "Your mother cries whenever your studying medicine is mentioned, and I cannot furnish money for you to do something that hurts her so much. Why not teach school, or better still, come home and stay with us." [9] Despite the lack of financial support, Bertha was determined. Neither the paltry salary she earned her second year as an assistant demonstrator in anatomy, nor the chilly reception women faced in the Medical School daunted her. She later recalled that male students in a medical class made clicking noises and threw paper wads and kisses when a female student in a lovely hat entered. "The anathemas against 'hen-medics' [especially] came from the students in the literary department, both men and women." [10] But she persevered, praising the courses in anatomy while calling the surgery department archaic. Her professor, to her dismay, did not accept the controversial germ theory then being advocated by Dr. Ignaz Semmelweis. Yet she declared the professors to be fair to women though she criticized the school for not offering its students more females in the faculty. Responding to an alumni survey in the 1920's, Dr. Van Hoosen said, "When such women as Alice Freeman [Palmer] came into their own, it was never with the aid and encouragement of the Alma Mater. As far as giving women a chance in the teaching faculty, the University of Michigan is our Pseudo Mater not our Alma Mater." [11] Alice Freeman had become the president of Wellesley College at age twenty-six.

Of the early female graduates of University of Michigan's School of Medicine, many distinguished themselves in a variety of ways. Most, like Van Hoosen, of course, moved elsewhere to practice, but some remained in the county. Without a doubt, the most famous locally is Eliza Mosher. Even as a young girl at the Friends' Academy in Union Springs, New York, Mosher dreamed of becoming a doctor. Her mother, like Van Hoosen's, was somewhat less than enthusiastic. In fact, Mosher recalled her mother stating categorically, "I would rather pay your expenses in a lunatic asylum...than send you to medical school." [12] Even so Eliza began her studies at New England Hospital for Women and Children. When the University of Michigan announced its willingness to accept women, Mosher and four friends literally jumped for joy and promptly applied. Mosher, however, had to postpone her matriculation for a year so that she could care for her mother during her final illness. Once Eliza became a student at the University of Michigan, however, she quickly distinguished herself. Despite the antagonism towards female students, it was Mosher who was chosen by Dr. Palmer to demonstrate a difficult operation for the men's clinic.

After graduation, Dr. Mosher established a thriving practice in Poughkeepsie, New York, only to abandon it two years later to become the resident physician for the Massachusetts State Reformatory for Women which was the first institution of its kind in the United States to be operated by and for women. By the time Mosher left, she had established a nursing school at the prison. She then studied in London and Paris before returning to Brooklyn, New York, to reopen her practice. She once told an interviewer that the landlords of Brooklyn not only raised their rents when a woman inquired, some refused to let female doctors hang signs to advertise their professions. In addition to her regular practice, Dr. Mosher taught for several semesters at both Wellesley and

Dr. Eliza Mosher

Courtesy of the Bentley Historical Library, University of Michigan

Smith. After that, she spent a decade as a professor at Vassar. These colleges for women were staunch advocates of proper diet and exercise as well as intellectual training for their students. The accomplishments Dr. Mosher made during this period of her life are even more amazing when one realizes that she lived in continual pain due to a knee injury. After seven years of suffering, which required crutches and often bed rest, she devised a surgical procedure to alleviate her symptoms. No sooner had she solved that problem than she was diagnosed with breast cancer. In 1891 she underwent surgery for that condition. With health restored, she resumed her career.

Five years later, in 1896, that University of Michigan's President Angell wrote to Dr. Mosher offering her a job as the first dean of women for the 647 female students at the University of Michigan. She turned him down. He sweetened the offer with a full professorship in the school of Literature, Science and Arts. She declined. She insisted on being in the medical school, but the faculty there refused to include a female. Finally Angell played his trump card. He told her about the Barbour Gymnasium for women that had just been funded and was in the process of being built.

In early 1890's Joshua Watermann of Detroit donated $40,000 to build a gym for males and females, but in the end only men were allowed to use it. Regent Levi L. Barbour, a champion of women students, gave $20,000 and Regent Charles gave $10,000 with provision that women raise the remaining $15,000. Women throughout the state of Michigan responded. Amy Collier (Montague) who attended the University 1895-1897 remembered her first experience in "organization on a large scale" when she and others planned a "Leap Year ball at the Waterman Gymnasium to raise a fund for the new Woman's Gymnasium." [13] A thousand couples attended. In addition, Lucy Stone, president of State Federation of Women's Clubs, urged members to contribute. Small donations of less than

The Barbour Gymnasium

Courtesy of the Bentley Historical Library, University of Michigan

$10 poured in from average women who would never see the building they helped to fund.

A gymnasium might not seem like much of an incentive to a modern reader, but the nascent women's physical education movement led by none other than Wellesley College was a pet project of Eliza Mosher's. Though disappointed not to be in the School of Medicine, she accepted Angell's offer. It was a pivotal moment. Dr. Emma Pearson Randall, class of 1899, commented, "The completion and opening of the Women's Gymnasium… and the appointment of Dr. Eliza Mosher as the Dean of Women" were two of the most important events that she experienced at the University. [14]

During Mosher's tenure, every female student was given a thorough physical examination as well as a smallpox inoculation. Each female student was required to take physical education and was encouraged to abandon wearing corsets. Dr. Mosher, probably much to the dismay of Crescent Works, a corset manufacturer located at 306-7 S. Main Street in Ann Arbor, patented an alternative undergarment that would cause less physical damage. And female students were also expected to take Dr. Mosher's hygiene/physiology class, which she felt was critical if they were to understand the importance of lifestyle on their health. Dr. Mosher even designed an "appropriate exercise costume" made of no less than twelve yards of black serge. For all this she was paid the same $2500 salary ($2000 if she chose to continue in private practice) as any full professor who was male. Mosher was the first female to become a full professor at the University of Michigan. Her salary apparently caused some complaint from faculty wives who disagreed with the idea of equal pay for equal work believing married men should make more than an unmarried woman.

Eliza Mosher might have remained permanently in Ann Arbor and not returned to her practice in New York if one small event had turned out differently. In 1898 Elizabeth Bates, another New York physician, who was neither a University of Michigan graduate nor a person who had any connection to the state of Michigan, left her entire estate of $130,000, a considerable sum, to the University of Michigan. Dr. Bates wanted her generous gift to be used to endow a chair in the Medical School for diseases of women and children. According to the University, the only stipulation included in the Bates gift was that the University continue to admit women. Mosher was ideal for the Bates Professorship, but the Regents in their meeting of June 1898 never considered her. They immediately set out to find "the proper man" [15] to fill the post. Eliza Mosher was never allowed to teach in the Medical School. Instead Dr. Mosher's contributions to the University were commemorated in other ways. One of the most permanent was naming a new dormitory for female students after her. Dr. Mosher, however, probably would have been more moved to know that a fund was established in her name to loan tuition money to female students.

> In 1891 some alumnae tried to provide funds to cover the salaries of female professors they wanted the University to hire. Their offer was refused. Eight years later Catharine Kellogg and a Detroit group of women tried to endow a chair for a female professor in what would today be called women's studies. The Regents tabled their offer – indefinitely.

During the twenty-seven years after Dr. Mosher left the University of Michigan, she continued practicing medicine in New York. She was senior editor of the *Medical Woman's Journal*. She authored a book about health for girls. She founded the American Posture League as well as the Cleaner Brooklyn Committee. For most people that would be enough, but Dr. Mosher also

Dr. Alice Snyder

developed posture supporting chairs for kindergarten children and for rapid transit as well as personal apparati for posture enhancement. Despite a second radical surgery for breast cancer in 1906, Dr. Mosher lived to the age of eighty-two. In 1927, the year before her death, she was the oldest female practicing medicine in the entire United States.

Joining Dr. Mosher in her enthusiasm and support of women's health was Dr. Alice G. Snyder. Snyder graduated from the New Haven Normal School of Gymnastics in 1893 and had previous experience in her field as Director of the Gymnasium at Nashville College for Young Ladies. Then she was hired as an instructor at the University of Michigan in 1896. For several years

Snyder juggled her responsibilities as an instructor with studying medicine.

Then in 1898 Snyder was allowed to hire a substitute at her own expense so that she could concentrate on her medical studies. Two years later she finally graduated from the medical school; however, her university salary even after receiving her medical license was only $900 per year. Dr. Snyder continued to serve as director of the Barbour Gymnasium until being demoted to assistant director in 1904. The new director was a man. Needless to say, in such a climate, Dr. Snyder chose to leave the University of Michigan and move elsewhere. She eventually married another physician named Hugh Thompson. They had a son who continued his mother's interest in young people's health by becoming a pediatrician. Dr. Alice Snyder Thompson died of cancer in 1940.

The young woman Dr. Snyder hired as her substitute was Miss Helen H. Bender. After subbing for Snyder for the 1898-99 academic year, Bender continued at the women's gymnasium as assistant to Dr. Snyder. She also became Ann Arbor High School's first "physical culture" teacher in the fall of 1899. The school had provided a voluntary class as early as 1876. They were held at Hangsterfer Hall on Main Street. Hangsterfer Hall had a large third floor space that was used by the community for performances, dances etc. It also was the venue for the 1863 Sanitation Fair

Women's Field Hockey 1905 at the University of Michigan.

Courtesy of the Bentley Historical Library, University of Michigan

to raise money to support the Union effort in the Civil War. So it would be a logical place for such a class. Not until 1896 did Ann Arbor High School required physical education. Miss Edith Steffener circa 1997 stated in an unpublished history of the Ann Arbor schools that such classes met "behind closed doors." Though completely covered, the exercise costume was still "considered shocking." So concerned were educators about the possible prurient motives of observers that the University of Michigan at that time censored who could enter to watch women's athletic games. As for Miss Bender, she left Ann Arbor and moved to Columbia, Missouri.

Fannie Cheever-Burton

Courtesy of Eastern Michigan University

Michigan State Normal School's equivalent to Dr. Snyder was Fannie Cheever Burton, the daughter of William E. and Mary Hewitt Cheever. Fannie was born in Ypsilanti in 1864. She graduated from Ypsilanti High School and then the Michigan State Normal School in 1883. After her marriage, she and her husband moved to Chicago. Those five years in Chicago were the only ones she spent away from Ypsilanti. They were, however, very significant years for Mrs. Burton. Her earlier training was in modern languages. It was at the University of Chicago that she was introduced to physical education for women. It was also in Chicago that her husband died.

Mrs. Burton returned to Ypsilanti to accept the position

as head of the brand new Physical Education Department at Michigan State Normal School. She served in that capacity for the twenty-eight years between 1894 and 1922. During that time, she not only improved the physical education of students but brought the same message to women of the community for whom she organized a ladies' physical culture class quoting to them that their bodies were temples which they should glorify. This class would have been much like Lucy Osband's which stressed weights and slow movements to stretch and enhance the muscles. "The interesting condition of the body known as being *delicate* is no longer in vogue," asserted Burton. [16] Proper food, ventilation and exercise, she told her students, was what all women need. She encouraged them to play tennis – and even baseball. Mrs. Burton was assisted in her efforts by the construction of a fully equipped gymnasium at Michigan State Normal School. It is true that men and women used the same gymnasium building, but it was completely divided down the middle by floor to ceiling walls so each gender's activities were isolated. In 1922 Mrs. Burton became the social assistant to the Dean of Women. She continued in that capacity until shortly before her death on October 31, 1935.

A variation to the standard calisthenics and movement taught in Washtenaw County schools was Mrs. Annie Ward Foster's Delsarte Physical Culture and Dance School where she served as director in 1894. The Delsarte Method was brought to the United States by Steele MacKaye who opened his own school in New York City in 1872 incorporating elements of gymnastics into the Delsarte method of recomposition, alignment and opposition to train actors. The method urged practitioners to project inner feelings through a softening and relaxing of the body. Isadora Duncan, the famous dancer, was strongly influenced by the Delsarte method. Mrs. Foster's school, located at 46 S. State Street, which also served as her residence, doesn't appear to have caught on in Washtenaw County. Perhaps it was too avant-garde. Or she may have discovered a better opportunity elsewhere. She was gone two years later.

As a result of the opportunity to attend the University of Michigan, several women remained Ann Arbor to have long careers in medicine. One of the earliest was Sophia Hartley. Dr. Hartley was born in Germany in 1835. She came to Michigan via Fort Wayne, Indiana. Her first husband, Dr. Meindermann of Adrian, passed away in 1870. Sophia enrolled in the medical school in the same class as Eliza Mosher. During her training, Sophia met and married Dr. John Hartley. They opened a joint practice after graduation.

Dr. Sophia Hartley

Courtesy of the Bentley Historical Library,
University of Michigan

An advertisement from 1878 for both Doctors Hartley reads: "J. D. Hartley MD and Mrs. Hartley MD/ German and English/ Physicians and Surgeons/ Mrs. Dr. Hartley will limit her practice to the treatment of diseases peculiar to Ladies and children." After 1882 her home and office was located at 608 E. Williams Street. It was sold in 1914 to the University Musical Society and was then called Pilgrim Hall. It has since been demolished and replaced by the Douglas Memorial Chapel. Sophia Hartley did not retire until around the turn of the century and in 1917 passed away in Milwaukee.

Two years after Dr. Hartley graduated, another Sophia finished her medical instruction and began her practice which lasted until her death twenty years later. She, too, was married but, unlike Dr. Hartley, had children. This Sophia was Sophia Dean who was born circa 1829. She married Jacob Volland and had two daughters: Cora born circa 1859 and Lillie born circa 1870. These dates indicate that when Sophia began medical school, her younger daughter, Lillie, was only four or five; therefore, Dr. Volland, like so many modern women, juggled first obtaining a university education and then maintaining her career with her family responsibilities. She died suddenly in July 1897.

There is a serendipitous connection between Dr. Mosher and Dr. Volland which transcends the fact that they were both students at the School of Medicine at the same time. Dr. Mosher's house, when she was Dean of Women, was located at 1215 Volland Street. Named for the Volland brothers, one of whom was Sophia's husband, it connected East Washington Street to Geddes Road. The street is gone now having been gobbled up by campus expansion. However, that led to a second coincidental connection between these two women. The location of the former Volland Street is the site of Mosher Hall, the dormitory named for Sophia Volland's contemporary, Eliza Mosher.

Mary Augusta Wood-Allen is a third woman who graduated in the same class as Mosher and Hartley. She, like Dr. Volland, was married with children thus balancing family with a very busy career, and ultimately incorporating other family members in her business. She practiced medicine for a few years before using her medical background in other ways. She became a lecturer and author. Her lectures for the Women's Christian Temperance Union addressed many of the same topics as her writing. The titles clearly reveal their content: *Almost a Man, Almost a Woman, What a young Woman Ought to Know, Marvels of our Bodily Dwelling* etc. The purpose of her volumes were very similar to that of Eliza Mosher's book. Both women believed that the average American, particularly the average American female, should be better educated concerning hygiene, reproduction and general health. Embedded within Wood-Allen's message about the body was the encouragement girls needed to fulfill their potential. For example, *Almost a Woman* begins with a girl named Helen talking to her father about whether are not boys are better than girls. The father says they are not, just different. "Tell me what great things a woman can do," asks Helen "She might be a chemist," replies her father. [17] In order to reach even more people with her message, Dr. Wood-Allen began a monthly magazine called *The American Mother* (later titled *American Motherhood*) for which she remained chief editor until her death in 1908. She, her husband and her daughter, Rose, resided at 1317 Washtenaw Avenue in Ann Arbor where the entire family participated in Mary's life's work. M.C. Wood-Allen managed Wood-Allen Publishing while Rose helped with *American Mother*. When Dr. Wood-Allen died, the family was living in Washington D.C. Her body was cremated – a very avant-garde and controversial choice in 1908 – and her ashes returned to Ann Arbor for interment.

From just these few examples, it is obvious that medicine, in as much as it welcomed women at all, was one of the few professions that included a significant number of married women. At a time when only 5% of married women worked outside the home, 35% of all females practicing medicine were married. Like Ann Arbor's Dr. Hartley, Christine Anderson married while in medical school. Originally from Iowa, Anderson earned her BS from Knox College in Galesburg, Illinois. She then taught for two years before coming to the University of Michigan's School of Medicine. There she met and married Clarence Taylor who supervised the engineering lab. After graduating in 1888, Dr. Anderson-Taylor opened her office at in Ypsilanti. [18] Also like Dr. Hartley, Anderson specialized in treating women and children. She served two years as vice president of the Washtenaw Medical Society. She died in August of 1904 at the age of forty-two and is buried in Highland Cemetery in Ypsilanti. Her obituary states, "She had a large practice [and] stands high in her profession and is considered ...one of the best physicians and surgeons without regard to sex." [19]

Doctors Hartley, Volland, Wood-Allen and Anderson were allopathic doctors. That means they practiced "regular" medicine. Their contemporary, Charlotte Fitzgerald, chose the University of Michigan's other school of medicine: homeopathy. Homeopathy was part of the wider movement for alternative health care in the nineteenth century. "By mid-century Homeopathy had become a significant part of American medicine." [20] It was wildly popular which is why traditional doctors became very defensive about this choice of treatment. The issue was so sensitive that it contributed to the delay in appointing H. P. Tappan as president of the University of Michigan. Apparently, Regent Dr. Zina Pitcher was adamantly opposed to homeopathy. He actually wrote in June of 1852 to Tappan's physician, Dr. Vanderburgh, in New York, inquiring as to his opinion of homeopathy. Dr. Vanderburgh's sympathetic reply "resulted in Tappan's temporary defeat." [21] Chapman's *History of Washtenaw County, Michigan* states, "One of the most embarrassing questions in the history of the University has been the subject of homeopathic medicine. The legislature of the state early required the Regents to appoint at least one professor of homeopathy in the medical department. But the Regents declined to comply." [22] As with the question of women at the University, the Regents believed acceptance of homeopathy would lessen the reputation of the school. Years later in 1875 when they could no longer refuse, the Regents solved the problem by offering two distinct schools of medicine: the allopathic and the homeopathic. Even that did not completely solve the problem since faculty remained divided on the issue. At times it got so out of hand that on one occasion an allopathic professor of surgery and a professor of homeopathy actually came to blows right in the middle of campus.

It was during this difficult time, a few years after the technical "resolution" of the controversy, that Charlotte Fitzgerald graduated from the School of Homeopathy in 1879. She practiced in Ann Arbor until the turn of the century when she retired and passed away in 1906 in Plymouth, Michigan. Nurse Emily Hollister's diary is filled with complimentary statements about Dr. Fitzgerald who was the attending physician for many of Hollister's patients For example, on November 17, 1891, Hollister says "the good skill of Dr. Fitchgerald [sic] carried her [the patient] through." [23] Again In January of 1894 she credits Fitzgerald with saving the life of Bessie Toop for the second time. Dr. Fitzgerald died in Plymouth, Michigan, in 1906,

Several Washtenaw County medical women gained national prominence. One was Eliza Mosher; the other was Lydia Adams DeWitt. Both of these women were listed in the first edition of *Notable American Women*. Lydia Adams was born in 1859 in Flint, Michigan. After graduating from high school, she began teaching. At age nineteen, she married Alton D. DeWitt, another Flint native who also was a teacher. Mrs. DeWitt con-

Dr. Lydia DeWitt

Courtesy of the Bentley Historical Library
University of Michigan

tinued teaching in Port Hope and Athens, Michigan despite bearing two children during that time. Obviously those communities were sufficiently in need of teachers that they did not, like Washtenaw County, prohibit married women from teaching. After her graduation from Michigan State Normal School circa 1890, Lydia and her husband moved to South Haven, Michigan, where she held the position of preceptress until returning to Ann Arbor in order to attend the University of Michigan. She received her medical degree in 1893 when she was thirty-four years old. Years later when the Alumni Association asked her how she would characterize the influence of the University of Michigan on her life, Dr. DeWitt replied enthusiastically, "It made me what I am." [24]

Clearly her advanced education changed the direction of her life, but it also must have put great strain on it. Dr. DeWitt began teaching at the University of Michigan where she remained for twelve years. While on the faculty, she was rejected by the all male Faculty Research Club, so she organized the Women's Research Club and served as its president. During that time though, certainly by 1904, she and her husband separated. Then in 1910 she moved to St Louis where she served as assistant city bacteriologist and instructor in pathology at Washington University. Finally two years later, she was invited to the Sprague Institute at the University of Chicago where she did research and taught pathology. Her obituary listed her many accomplishments in the field of the anatomy of the pancreas, but it is her work focusing on the chemistry and chemotherapy of tuberculosis that seems to be the basis of her fame and rightly so since tuberculosis was the scourge of the nineteenth century, especially for women. It was quite unusual for a woman of her era to receive any recognition for her professional accomplishments; [25] however, Dr. DeWitt's alma mater did acknowledge her merit. In 1914, she was given an honorary doctorate by the University of Michigan. She would probably be even more pleased to know that today the University of Michigan annually bestows the Lydia Adams DeWitt Awards which help finance scientific research by female faculty members. Dr. DeWitt passed away in 1928, the same year Dr. Mosher died.

Dr. Katherine Crawford

Courtesy of the Bentley Historical Library,
University of Michigan

Five years after Dr. DeWitt graduated, so did Katherine Crawford. Despite the fact that both were women, Crawford's experiences differed radically both because of her slightly later graduation date and because she was an African-American. Her family resided for many years at 1116 Fuller Street in Ann Arbor. She taught briefly in St. Louis before beginning her studies at the University of Michigan. When asked how her education at the University affected her life, Crawford wrote: "It recreated me by developing innumerable latent qualities or possibilities, by giving me a much broader life of usefulness..." Yet despite her many accomplishments, Dr. Crawford's life appears to have been a difficult one. Of her studies at the University, she also recalled that "Some experiences were exceedingly bitter ...[unclear writing] immensely so, as I view them after more than a quarter of a century, but they taught me my capacity for endurance." She began her practice of medicine in Toledo, Ohio. Writing in a 1904 letter to the University Alumni Association, she said: "I am meeting with fair success in treating women and children. Two years ago I was called home on account of my mother's impaired health. Professional work occupies not a first place (sic) by any means, yet I now have quite a neat little practice which I expect to see enlarged when I can devote more time to it." [26]

In 1911 Crawford left Ann Arbor to spend six years teaching and practicing medicine in San Francisco. After that she worked in Florida at a missionary school. Her report to the Alumni Association in 1928, however, is one of despair. "Greetings and sincere hope that your health, wealth and prosperity far exceeds mine." She returned to Ann Arbor soon after that too ill to resume her practice. Dr. Crawford died without near relatives and on public assistance in Detroit in 1943. She is buried in Ann Arbor's Fairview Cemetery. It would appear from her comments that she felt much of her life was "full of work" but "negative so far as visible results." [27] She may not have become wealthy, but she hopefully took pride in the fact that she was one of only 155 licensed African-American female physicians practicing in the United States in the 1890's. That accomplishment alone qualifies hers as a success story.

Some of Dr. Crawford's difficulties were caused not just by her gender and race but by her time in history. Between 1871 and 1900, four hundred women graduated from the University of Michigan's School of Medicine. Enrollment that had begun modestly with eighteen females in 1871 had risen to seventy by 1894. After that women's participation in the University of Michigan's School of Medicine declined. National statistics concerning female physicians illustrate a similar pattern. The year 1915 was the apex of the participation of women in medicine until later in the century when the number of women physicians began to rise. [28] In 1915 there were 9,015 female doctors in the United States, yet even that impressive number equates

> Everyone in the Ann Arbor area is familiar with the Galen Society through its holiday collections to support the children's hospital. Today the Society includes many women, but it was not always so. The Society's 1914 constitution, Article III, Section 2 specifically stated," NO women shall be members." [29]

to only six percent of the total.

That decline can be attributed to a conservative backlash, not just in medicine but in society at large. It began in the final two decades of the nineteenth century as a direct result of women's very success in rapidly broadening their fields of endeavor. By 1891 though there were 4,557 licensed women physicians in the United States, only 115 of those women had been admitted to male-dominated medical societies. Men, nervous about the inroads made by women, could only have been even more disturbed by the 1897 report by the Commissioner of Education which stated that female students in the nation were receiving honors in greater proportion to their numbers than were the male students. Since Crawford graduated in 1898, she was just beginning her career when the tipping point came whereas her predecessors such as Mosher, Hartley and Volland had begun their careers almost twenty years earlier.

Therefore, it is not surprising that by 1910 the number of women doctors in both the nation and in Washtenaw County had declined. In Washtenaw County in 1910, Ann Arbor still could claim six female physicians including Hartley, DeWitt (but she was about to leave), and Crawford, but there were none in any of the villages and only one in Ypsilanti: Ellen B. Murray. Dr. Murray was born and raised on a farm in Superior Township just north of Ypsilanti. She received her early education at rural schools before graduating from the Michigan State Normal School in 1885. After a few years teaching, she attended the University of Michigan School of

Ellen Murray 1885

Courtesy of the Ypsilanti Historical Society

Medicine graduating in 1895 when she was twenty-eight. Four years later despite the tide beginning to turn against women in the profession, Dr. Murry's reputation was such that she was elected vice-president of the Washtenaw County Medical Society, the very same society that was so reluctant to admit Dr. Gerry in 1871. Dr. Murray married and moved to Massachusetts.

The decline of women in the Medical School coincided with establishment of a nursing school. The very same male doctors who did not want women in medicine welcomed them as nurses. It was, according to Mary Roth Walsh, author of *Doctors Wanted, No Women Need Apply*, it was a "question of power...Women as nurses...posed no threat to the male physician." [30] In fact, several women who graduated from the University of Michigan's School of Medicine found themselves working as over-qualified nurses for the first few years after graduation. One such woman was Adella "Della" Pierce. Della was born in Granby Center, New York in 1854. She earned both a bachelor's and a master's from Albion College. Upon graduating from the Michigan's School of Medicine in 1890, she accepted the position of ward mistress of the University Hospital. She did not remain long. Better things awaited her elsewhere. She moved to Kalamazoo where she became one of three females practicing medicine. Before she died in 1935, not only had her practice lasted forty-two years, but she had served as Vice President of the Kalamazoo Academy of Medicine as well as Vice President of the Michigan State Medical Society.

Dr. Adella Pierce

Courtesy of the Bentley Historical Library, University of Michigan

Nursing for most of the twentieth century was the domain of women; however, they did not enter the professional world until after the Civil War. That cataclysmic event acted as the catalyst for so many changes in women's lives. Readers may be surprised to discover that the most famous nurse of all, Clara Barton, had no training or experience when the war began. Her only nursing had been her care of an invalid brother. Then came the Civil War with its hundreds of thousands of wounded. The government and army were absolutely unprepared for the magnitude of the devastation. Women even went to the front lines to care for and transport the wounded to hastily constructed hospitals a safe distance from the fighting. In 1861 President Lincoln established the U.S. Sanitation Commission. As members of that group, women collected and distributed supplies, inspected and nursed in hospitals throughout the Union and former Confederacy. Their efforts were received with overt hostility by both male nurses and surgeons. At the beginning of the war, army nurses were males without any training. During the first year of the war, convalescing soldiers performed nursing duties. But it soon became transparently obvious that keeping fighting men from the battlefields was counter-productive thus opening the doors to women.

Some women who became nurses during the war were no more trained than Barton. Frequently they traveled to Washington D.C. or another big city to care for a relative who had been injured. Many remained once they saw the need for more caregivers. Such was the experience of Julia Wheelock Freeman. She and her sister-in-law left Michigan for Washington as soon as they received word that her brother, Orville, had been wounded. But they were not quick enough. He died three days before their arrival. Julia's sister-in-law returned immediately to care for her children; however, Julia stayed. Though she had no special training, she remained for three more years nursing the wounded and dying. In 1870 she published her memoirs of that experience in a book entitled, *Boys in White*. The white referred to the sheets in which she helped wrap the dead.

A tiny contingent of Civil War nurses had received professional training from Dr. Elizabeth Blackwell who began a program for that specific purpose in 1861 in New York. More opportunities for female nurses training began to appear. Within seven years of war's end, the New England Hospital for Women and Children opened the nation's first official school of nursing followed the next year, 1873, by Bellevue Nursing School in New York. In Ann Arbor, it took a bit longer.

Though the University of Michigan Hospital was established in 1869, there was no mention of nurses at that time. Instead "a janitor or steward was in charge with his wife serving as matron." [31] In 1876 the hospital was enlarged and two nurses, one male and one female were recommended. The *University of Michigan: An Encyclopedic Survey* claims that nursing was "so menial" [32] that there isn't even a mention of them in the Regents' Proceedings until 1881 when two young male doctors and Mrs. Margaret Allerdice were hired as nurses for $300 per year. Even the assistant librarian at the University made twice that amount. Then a Mrs. MacManus was hired as matron. There is no record of whether or not she had training for that position. I suspect not. She may have been the only person willing to take a job with such a daunting description of duties. Her job was "to take care of the hospital, furnish and cook the food, do all the work usually required of a matron, collect the board bills of the patients, do the laundry and board such nurses as necessary." [33] One wonders how any woman – or man – could keep up with all of that.

Emily Green Hollister

All in all, nursing in the later third of the nineteenth century was neither a profession nor was it yet considered a respectable occupation. There were even some rather disreputable types who claimed to be nurses when the care of patients was the last thing on their minds. They ignored their charges and often stole from them. That certainly was not the case with one Washtenaw County woman named Emily Green Hollister, who entered the field in 1887. She and her youngest child, Martha, personify the changes that occurred in the nursing profession during the final decades of the twentieth century.

Emily Green was born in 1839 in Ann Arbor. She attended local schools before marrying Edward Hollister who had an eighty acre farm just north of Whitmore Lake. Emily was only sixteen when she married in 1856 and moved to the farm. In that tiny farm house, she gave birth to eleven children, ten of whom survived to adulthood. That alone would recommend Mrs. Hollister as a caregiver. Child mortality rates were so high at that time that women, when asked how many children they had, would reply they had so many children living. A popular children's book published in 1847 was entitled *Physiology for Children*. Mrs. Jane Taylor, the author, instructed her young readers concerning the sobering statistics of child mortality. According to Taylor, 50% of all (Caucasian) children died before age eight. One in three lived to age fourteen, and one in four survived to age twenty-one. David S. Reynolds in *Waking Giant* gives modern credence to Mrs. Taylor's statistic saying that one of three Caucasian children and fully one of every two African-American children died in the nineteenth century.

The Hollisters were not unfamiliar with the struggles in life. Eventually; hard times threatened to take the family farm, so Mrs. Hollister moved to Ann Arbor and began her nursing career. She wrote in her journal: "It was November of the year 1887 that we were visited by sickness and death and misfortune. I was compelled to leave my dear family to go out into the world to seek employment to keep my home." [34] Mrs. Hollister found a great many of her patients through the recommendations of prominent Ann Arbor physicians such as Doctors Beakey, Darling and Vaughan. Her first case in Ann Arbor concerned the six Kuster children who were ill with typhoid. All of them survived. Mrs. Hollister, though lacking any professional training, approached her job with dedicated professionalism. Photographs such as the one on the previous page show her looking very capable in her spotless nursing attire. Her youngest child, Martha, was only eight years old when Mrs. Hollister was forced to seek employment that paid only $10 per week and took her away from her own family for extended periods of time.

Hollister traveled to Toledo, Detroit and Lansing as well as all over Washtenaw County to care for her patients. Each entry in her diary begins, "I am come to nurse..." In January 1899 Mrs. Hollister journeyed all the way to New York with a baby whose mother had died in childbirth. She wrote in her journal that she had "delivered her precious charge into the arms of Grandma Lowry." [35] Her journal is filled with such stories. She clearly was a kind and generous person. In 1888 just when her own family was having financial trouble and she was just beginning her work, she dropped everything and hurried to Tecumseh, Michigan, where her sister had just died. She returned with her sister's three youngest children until their father could re-establish himself. In 1911, twenty-four years after beginning her nursing career, she retired with her husband to Hamburg, Michigan. They are buried in the cemetery of St. Stephen's Episcopal Church where her father-in-law had been pastor.

Mrs. Hollister's youngest child, Martha, followed in her mother's admirable footsteps. Martha, however, was able to "improve" on her role model because, by the time she was ready to begin her career, the University of Michigan had opened its School of Nursing. It began slowly. In 1891 only seven or eight students enrolled for the two year course. They were required to be between twenty and thirty years of age. According to Professor Linda Strodtman, historian of Michigan's School of Nursing, "education was not the primary goal of...nursing schools..." Most early schools were established by hospitals, principally to provide student nurses as staff for caring for patients with education of the nurse taking a secondary role. The U-M was no different." [36] Anna R. Harrison, a graduate of that first class described her day as so full of work on the ward that "we could not have the instruction we really needed for lack of time." There were "splendid lectures given" in the evening if one had the time and energy to attend. [37] Jane Pettigrew, a trained nurse then studying to become a doctor, developed the original program of study for the first class of students; however, the class experienced several

Martha Hollister

Courtesy of
Marian Hollister Dieckman

supervisors before they finished their training. Other than Mrs. Alice Padfield, a widow trained in Detroit, who was head of nursing 1893-96, all others in charge of the Nursing School during its first decade remained only a year each. Life was not any easier after graduation. According to Martha Hollister's niece, Marion Hollister Diekmann, Martha was unable to find employment after she graduated because most hospitals still preferred male nurses. She traveled west to work on a reservation. After that she moved to Portland, Oregon, where she married and remained for the rest of her life.

In addition to the University's School of Nursing, private schools evolved at this time in conjunction with private hospitals. Dr. Reuben Petersen, head of the Ob-Gyn Department at the University of Michigan, opened his own hospital at 620 Forest Street in Ann Arbor because of overcrowding at the University Hospital. He began his school of nursing in 1907. Elba Morse, whose career spanned fifty years, graduated from Petersen's in 1909, six years after Martha Hollister graduated from Michigan. Morse taught both at Petersen's and the University until WWI when she joined the Red Cross. After the war, she was one of the first rural public health nurses in the thumb region of Michigan. She is said to have driven more than 300,000 miles and used up nineteen vehicles in her efforts. Morse established a health camp in Big Bay, Michigan, and was superintendent of the Upper Peninsula Clinic for twenty years until retiring in 1965 at the age of eighty.

It wasn't just people in the Upper Peninsula that needed home nursing. Residents of Washtenaw County also needed help. To answer that need, a volunteer group emerged in Ann Arbor. At first they called themselves the Circle of Kings' Daughters, but the group was later referred to as the Visiting Nurses Association of Huron Valley. This group began by paying hospital bills for indigent patients. In 1909, however, it began hiring trained nursing personnel for home nursing care. The city of Ann Arbor, in conjunction with the association, hired twenty-nine year old, Miss Addie I. Amaden, a trained nurse, at a salary of $60 per month. She certainly earned her money as she personally cared for 200-300 patients each month. Miss Amaden, worked in this capacity until 1913. She came from Defiance County, Ohio, where she had been born and raised, and she returned to the family home. Her parents were elderly by 1913 which very probably motivated her move, but she continued nursing in a hospital in Ohio.

Ypsilanti appears to have responded to the need in a more timely manner than Ann Arbor. It hired its own city nurse, Mary Hoover, several years before Miss Amaden's service began. Born in Ontario, Miss Hoover came to Michigan in 1880. She first attended the Michigan State Normal School but then graduated from Harper Hospital in Detroit. Harper was another by-product of the Civil War. Residents of Michigan wanted the United States government to establish a hospital for Union soldiers in Detroit. Harper Hospital benefited from a gift of over $30,000 from Mr. Walter Harper and a $15,000 gift from his housekeeper, Nancy Martin, as well as governmental support. After the Civil War the government turned the hospital over to its Board of Directors with the proviso that veterans would be accept there. Harper Hospital provided one of the earliest schools of nursing in the country.

Miss Hoover, having received training at Harper Hospital continued her studies at the University of Michigan. Only then did she began her career as a private nurse. Very quickly in 1906 the town of Ypsilanti hired her to provide medical assistance to those who could not afford a physician. She also worked in schools not only treating illnesses but also educating the children in preventative care. Her nursing services were so valued by the community that when the city could no longer budget for the project, the members of the Ypsilanti American Legion Post unanimously voted to pay Miss Hoover's salary.

Mary Hoover

Courtesy of the Ypsilanti Historical Society

In the first years of the twentieth century, there was a real demand for skilled home nursing. Unlike Morse, Amaden and Hoover, who worked under the auspices of the civic or a private sector support group, Ida Mae Thumm worked independently – but not alone. Described as "a charming, courageous and dependable side-saddle nurse who traveled each day to her patients on horse-back,"[38] she and her family lived on a farm in Superior Township which her brother Charles had operated since their father's passing in the 1870's. It appears that none of the Thumm siblings ever married. Younger brother, William, had been listed as a farmer, too, but by the 1910 census he was labled "incompetent." So it would appear that sister Hannah/Anna took care of the home for all four while Ida Mae traveled to patients' homes. One of her patients was Mabel Hiscock who was born in 1882 and married her husband, Walter in 1901. Mabel was diagnosed with tuberculosis, which was the bane of the nineteenth and early twentieth century. The doctor put her on a regimen of complete bed rest. Thumm also cared for Margaret and Nellie Nanry, daughters of John William Nanry. Miss Thumm would stop by each day with medication prescribed by the doctor. As Ida traveled the countryside, she often collected patients. Some of those patients she took with her to the family home which she and her siblings converted into a hospital. Then doctors would stop by each afternoon at about 5:00 to check on the patients staying there.

Dentistry was another profession that Washtenaw County women did not enter until the end of the nineteenth century. As a specialized field, dentistry, as we know it, did not develop until the eighteenth century. Before then, the only remedy for tooth pain was extraction. People who provided this service were called "tooth drawers." That label accurately describes Washtenaw County's first female "dentist," Sovengire/Susannah Kimmel. Mrs. Kimmel and her family were prominent pioneer settlers in Superior Township. In fact, her husband, Henry, is credited with giving the township its name. Chapman states that in 1825 Mr. and Mrs. Kimmel and their seven children traveled thirty-nine days from Pennsylvania; however, Mrs. Kimmel's obituary in the August 8, 1871 issue of the *Ypsilanti Commercial* provides what is probably more correct information. It confirms the 1825 date but says that they came from Illinois "cutting their road through the forests of Indiana and Michigan." Mrs. Kimmel, died at the age of eighty-four. She was described as "a tall, commanding figure with gentle blue eyes."[39] She proved to be "one of the most useful women of pioneer times" because she developed a skill for extracting teeth while still running a household of forty. There is no record of who all those folks were or how many teeth she pulled. Such details, like so much information, did not seem sufficiently important at the time to be preserved.

Considering the dental problems of the era, Mrs. Kimmel was probably kept busy. In addition to the problems normally causing tooth decay, the nineteenth century created its own dental problems through the liberal consumption of a medicine called Calomel. Calomel was none other than mercurous chloride. It was used for a wide variety of illness ranging from syphilis to constipation. Dr. Benjamin Rush advocated its use and promoted his own "bilious pills" as a panacea for whatever ails you. Lewis and Clark packed Rush's pills for their 1804 expedition. The problem was that its use weakened gums so much that teeth loosened or fell out. It damaged the bones of the upper and lower jaw, the palate and tongue. It also made a person's hair fall out. In light of those side effects, the metallic halitosis it caused appears singularly unimportant.

The August 29, 1855 *Ann Arbor Journal* addressed other dental hygiene concerns. It warned its readers not to try to take care of their own teeth. Particularly it cautioned them against using acid to brighten their teeth. The article urged people "to have this [dental cleaning] done properly." To do so "it is necessary to obtain the aid of a practiced hand, with appropriate instruments...It is best to obtain the assistance of the dentist." It repeated the word "professional" three times just to be sure readers got the point. Even when it does not use the word "professional," it says the same thing. The article advised its readers that "no one but an educated [ie. professional] dentist" should work on their teeth. A young woman named Jennie in Ypsilanti did exactly that: she contacted a professional dentist. In her journal for the summer of 1862, she wrote that she had gone to the dentist and had seventeen of her teeth extracted *in one sitting*. The dentist gave her brandy and chloroform, but she claimed she "almost died" from the discomfort but planned to return soon for impressions so that dentures could be made. In contrast to Mrs. Charles Fisher of Lansing, Michigan, Jennie was pretty lucky. Mrs. Fisher went a dentist named R. H. Clark assisted by a Dr. Thoms. Dr. Clark, "extracted fourteen teeth when the patient began to sink..." [40] Mrs. Fisher, age twenty-seven, died.

As had occurred in the medical field, dentistry became professionalized in the nineteenth century though a decade or so later than medicine. Women also joined the field of dentistry but a bit later than they had medicine. In 1860, the U.S. Census records indicate that no women were practicing dentistry. This statistic, however, is misleading, for there was at least one woman who was actively practicing. That woman was Emeline Roberts Jones of Connecticut. In 1854 at the rather tender age of seventeen, Miss Roberts married Daniel Jones who was a dentist. She became interested in his profession and began using discarded teeth that he had extracted to practice filling cavities. When he realized how good she had become, her husband allowed her to share his practice. By 1859 she had became his partner. This training stood her in good stead, for her husband died just five years later leaving her with two small children. She moved to New Haven, Connecticut, and opened her own practice which she maintained until 1915 when she finally retired at age seventy-eight. Emeline Roberts Jones was the first American woman known to have opened her own dental office

Like early professionals in medicine, Mrs. Jones did not graduate from any established school of dentistry. She learned via the old fashioned method of working under the supervision of a practicing dentist who in her case was her husband. Before the professionalization of medicine, dentistry and law, practitioners apprenticed to earn the necessary skills. As national organizations and licensing evolved, so did institutional learning. Pennsylvania led the way in the training of women dentists as early as 1866. The University of Michigan, which ranked third in the number of women graduated before 1893, entered the arena significantly later since its dental school did not have its first female student until 1880. By then five Michigan women had graduated from the Pennsylvania schools, and a total of sixty-one women were practicing dentists in the United States.

The first women to attend the University of Michigan's School of Dentistry were foreigners such as Vida A. Latham who came from England but remained in the United States the rest of her life. She went on to get a medical degree from Northwestern University and remained in Chicago where she founded the American Association of Women Dentists. Every one of her ninety-one years of life was filled with activities of which she was immensely proud. She was far too busy and satisfied to marry. When asked by the University of Michigan Alumni Association to take a survey, she scratched out the line for information about a husband in order to include more of her own accomplishments.

The first School of Dentistry building

Courtesy of the Sindecuse Museum of Dentistry, University of Michigan

In contrast, Ida Gray, class of 1890, who also settled in Chicago, was married twice. Miss Gray (Mrs. Nelson Rollins) was the first African-American woman to graduate from Michigan's School of Dentistry. It was Dean Jonathan Taft himself who served as her preceptor. Taft, though dean, maintained a dental practice in Cincinnati. It was there that Gray performed the required practicum before she could enter the Dental School. Dr. Taft apparently was a great supporter of women entering the field. In an article in the *Dental Register,* November 1887, Taft is quoted by Jennie Kollock Hilton, a University of Michigan School of Dentistry alumna, saying "There have been fifteen ladies graduated in our dental college, and I am proud of all of them."

1885 Dental Clinic at the University of Michigan

Courtesy of the Sindecuse Museum of Dentistry, University of Michigan

One of those fifteen women was Elsie Adelaide Hallock. She graduated from the School of Dentistry in 1885 and remained there as an assistant to a professor of clinical dentistry until she married John T. Martin, another dentist, in 1888. They moved first to Muscatine, Iowa, where they raised their three children before moving in 1934 to California.

A few years later Caroline "Carrie" Marsden Stewart became the first university trained, female dentist to establish a private practice in Washtenaw County. Born in Macon City, Missouri, the daughter of Dr. I.N. and Nellie Stewart, Carrie began studying at the

Carrie Marsden Stewart

Courtesy of
the Sindecuse Museum of Dentistry,
University of Michigan

University of Michigan, School of Dentistry in 1889. Her admittance was unusual for two reasons: she was only eighteen, and she was admitted by examination rather than having obtained preliminary experience through a practicum with an established dentist. Miss Stewart received her DDS, Doctor of Dental Surgery degree in 1892. Then she began post graduate studies though there was no post graduate degree at that time. In 1893 after presenting a paper entitled "Pathogenic Micro-organisms Found in the Mouth" to the Dental Society, she went to Fort Worth, Texas. She returned the next year. I suspect she left because there was no advanced degree available and returned as soon as the University of Michigan established a post graduate degree, a Doctor of Dental Science (DDSc). Michigan became the first university in the United States to offer such a degree. Stewart completed her graduate studies in 1894 becoming the first woman to earn a DDSc. Armed with these impressive credentials, she opened her dental office in Ypsilanti at 37 N. Huron Street. A report given by Dr. John A. Watling, an alumnus of the University of Michigan School of Dentistry, claimed that she soon left Michigan seeking a better climate for her health in Fort Worth. She married Joseph Gibson, a teacher, in 1901. They settled in Wichita Falls, Texas, where she continued to practice dentistry. She wrote to a friend in 1914, responding to an inquiry, saying that she could recommend a good dentist but she no longer accepted male patients. She did not provide any reason for limiting her practice to women and children. Dr. Stewart was widowed in 1921. Twenty six years later she died at the age seventy-six. Clearly the Texas climate must have agreed with her.

The only other University educated female dentist to practice in Washtenaw County before World War I opened her office at 109 W. Liberty in Ann Arbor in 1906. Anna Dieterle, unlike Dr. Stewart, was raised in Ann Arbor. She was youngest of seven children born to John and Christina Dieterle. Anna graduated from Ann Arbor High School before working as a bookkeeper circa 1889-99. Then she decided to attend the University of Michigan School of Dentistry where she became the 32nd woman to graduate, but she was the only woman in her 1904 graduating class. The school had been averaging three to four female students each year, however, but there were none in 1906-7 perhaps because Dean Taft had died and not yet been replaced. Eight years after opening her private practice, Anna not only continued that practice but became the Dental Inspector for the public schools of Ann Arbor. Within two years she was providing that service for all Washtenaw County schools. Her program was one of the first, if not the first, public dental inspection programs in the United States. Dr. Dieterle passed away in 1930 at the age of fifty-five.

Mrs. Rayne's 1885 book published in Detroit asserted that every dentist's office has a "lady attendant," whose duty it is to "hand water for rinsing the mouth, hold napkins, or replace instruments, steady a nervous lady's head, soothe a frightened child," [41] No such woman has left a record of such a job in Washtenaw County. That does not mean, however, that there were no female dental assistants.

The University of Michigan also offered potential students a degree in Pharmacy. Several Washtenaw County women graduated with a degree in pharmacy, but none of its graduates appear to have utilized their training locally. Catherine Watson, who graduated in 1876, may have planned just such a career in Ann Arbor, but she died suddenly the following year. Ypsilanti, however, did have two females who identified themselves as "druggists" but both apparently learned by apprenticing. One was Harriet Gillett Dimick and the other her daughter, Emma Lynn Dimick.

Harriet's husband, Stowell Dimick, began in Ypsilanti as a general merchant circa 1850. Twenty years later he was clerking in a drug store. Within three more years he partnered with store owner D.W. Shipman. Five more years passed, and Mr. Dimick was sole proprietor of the store listing himself as a "druggist." He would have been about fifty-six at that time. It was then that his daughter, Emma Lynn, age twenty-five, also was listed was a druggist. Emma appears to have learned her skills from her father who may have obtained his information from his years with Mr. Shipman. The Dimick's drug store underwent a radical change by 1883. Emma by then was out of the business. She had married Alva J. Worden. Mr. Dimick was still acting as manager of the store with none other than Mrs. Dimick as the druggist. She, like Emma, must have learned her skills from her husband. Mrs. Dimick's career as a druggist lasted less than a decade because she passed away just before Christmas 1888. At that point Mr. Dimick appears to have retired.

Despite the trials and tribulations of early women doctors and dentists, the medical fields appear to have been a much easier domain to enter than law. While medicine could list over 4500 women in that profession by the turn of the century, only 200 women had been admitted to the United States bar. The first was Arabella Mansfield in 1869 in Iowa, but she had apprenticed rather than attended law school. Myra Bradwell is the most famous of these early female lawyers who apprenticed. When in 1870 the Illinois Supreme Court rejected Myra Bradwell's application for a law license, despite her high score on the bar exam, she took her protest all the way to the U. S. Supreme Court. Hers was the first case to use the fourteenth amendment as part of her argument before the Court, but in 1873 the Court declined to over-turn the Illinois decision to refuse her a license thus creating the precedent that allowed each state to decide for itself whether or not it would permit women to practice law. This was a tremendous setback for women everywhere in the United States.

Although Mrs. Bradwell was a resident of Illinois, her experiences reflect the male establishment's attitude toward all women aspiring to become attorneys. Advocates for women in the legal profession seeking equity through the state and federal courts were hindered for decades by similar rationalizations against women practicing law. In Mrs. Bradwell's case, her rejection was at first based primarily on the fact that she was a married woman. A married woman in most states had no legal right to own property or enter into any contract. This being so, how could a woman practice law? While this was technically the rule, Bradwell pointed out an inconsistency. The state of Illinois had indeed made a contract with her when it agreed to publish the decisions of the Illinois Supreme Court in the *Chicago Legal News*, a professional journal which she owned. At that point the Court changed its rationale to the most popular argument which was that, as a woman, law was beyond her appropriate sphere.

U.S. Supreme Court Justice Joseph Bradley's response to Bradwell vs State of Illinois is a clear statement of this justification. He maintained that her claim to "the privileges and immunities of women as citizens to engage in any and every profession, occupation or employment in civil life [could not be affirmed because]...the natural and proper timidity and delicacy which belongs to the female sex evidently unfits it for many of the occupations of civil life. The constitution of the family organization which is founded in the *divine* ordinance, as well as the nature of things, indicates the domestic sphere as that which properly belongs to the domain and functions of womanhood. The harmony, not to say identity, of interests and views which belong or should belong to the family institution is repugnant to the idea of a woman adopting a distinct and independent career from that of her husband. ... The paramount destiny and mission of woman is to fulfill the noble and benign offices of wife and mother. This is the law of the Creator." [42] In other words, she was out of her appropriate social sphere.

Though mostly unspoken, the final reason the legal establishment gave for denying women licenses was really just a reflection of men's concerns about maintaining their control of political power. Many feared that allowing women to practice law would open the floodgates to their participating in the government. If that were not sufficient, there was the pesky issue of women's suffrage. How could a disenfranchised woman argue the law in court? If the male establishment began accepting women as attorneys, the whole question of women's suffrage would rise to the surface. Such unintended consequences, they felt, must be avoided at all costs. Just a few years later in 1879, however, the U. S. Supreme Court waffled on the issue by ruling that women indeed could present cases to the Court which presumes, I guess, that they come from a state that has given them licenses.

Myra Bradwell did not apply for a license again though she finally received her license in 1890 based upon her original application. Meanwhile, she did as so many women did when their expertise was rejected by the male establishment. She used her knowledge of the law to develop a related field of endeavor. She expanded her influence as editor of the *Chicago Legal News* which she had begun in 1868. It was a publication upon which attorneys relied to provide current and accurate information concerning laws and legal precedents. In fact, its content was considered so reliable that one trial lawyer quoted it in court. When the Judge questioned it, the lawyer offered the Judge the latest issue of the *News* in which the recently passed law was summarized. The judge accepted it. Bradwell also used her paper as a forum for advocating for equity for women.

Myra Bradwell died in 1894. Her daughter experienced a very different scenario than her mother. By the time she wanted to study law, there were quite a few universities that would accept women. Many of these schools were in the Midwest. Miss Bradwell graduated at the top of her law class at Northwestern in 1882. Unlike her mother, she did receive a license and was allowed to practice law in Illinois. But her more positive experience in the 1880's was not by any means the first. Karen Morello, author of *The Invisible Bar* observed, "The farther away women were from the restrictions of northeastern society, the better able they were to strike out in areas of their own." [43] Thus it should not be surprising that the nation's first college educated woman admitted to the bar was in the "western" state of Missouri.

The first school to open its law school doors was the University of Iowa in 1868. Washington University and Northwestern quickly followed suit. The University of Michigan was fourth, yet according to Drachman's *Sisters in Law*, "Admission of women to University of Michigan was significant because it was the premier law school in the Midwest and the largest law school in the country." [44] Thus Ann Arbor can claim credit for educating a great many women who became attorneys. And perhaps that is the reason that twenty-seven year old Sarah Killgore, Michigan's first female to graduate immediately transferred there from Northwestern University School of Law when it became a option.

Elizabeth Cady Stanton and Susan B. Anthony were guests of Mr. and Mrs. Israel Hall in Ann Arbor when Anthony wrote on March 5, 1871 to Isabella Beecher Hooker that they had met Miss Killgore who was attending the University of Michigan School of Law. "...she is a bright earnest spirit of good physique - & promises well. She is but one girl - among 300 of her Law Class - only think 1100 Students in this University - & thirty girls only - but they are coming & soon will equal in number the boys - " [45]

Sarah Killgore

Courtesy of the Bentley Historical Library
University of Michigan

Stanton's prediction that women would come was correct, but they never came to the Law School in numbers equal to the boys. I am sure, however, that Mrs. Stanton and Miss Anthony were gratified later to hear that Miss Killgore (Wertman) went on to become the first woman admitted to the bar in Michigan. She and her husband moved to Indiana in 1878. Indiana, however, would not give any woman a license, so Sarah worked in her husband's office and raised a son and a daughter. Later they moved again. In Ohio, she once again was admitted to the bar. The final years of her ninety-two year life span were spent in Seattle.

Like so many graduates, Killgore did not stay in Washtenaw County to practice. Mary E. Foster, the fourteenth woman to be admitted to the bar in the entire United States, did. Foster not only stayed, she and her family exemplify the incredible changes that had occurred in Michigan during the nineteenth century. Mary was born June 2, 1825 and came to the Michigan Territory with her parents, Mr. and Mrs. John Lowry, when she was barely one year old. They settled in Lodi Township just south of Ann Arbor. There they experienced all the hardships of pioneer life: the isolation, the continuous labor to clear and plant the land, and the illness that was so prevalent in the early years. According to a report Mrs. Foster gave to the Michigan Pioneer Society, her father was so continuously stricken with ague (malaria) that he

Mary Foster

once told his wife he wanted to quit and go back east. Mary's mother replied firmly "No, I cannot do that. We came to secure a home for ourselves and our children." [46] Mrs. Lowry had no intention of going back. She assured him she would do the field work herself until he felt better.

Nothing in Mary Foster's early life suggested that she would do something as daring as becoming an attorney. She attended rural schools except for two years at a select school in Ann Arbor. It really was not until her marriage to William G. Foster, an Ann Arbor attorney, that the law entered her life. Mr. Foster was her third husband. She had been widowed twice prior to that. After a decade of marriage, he, too, died. It was then that Mary entered the University of Michigan School of

Law graduating with high honors in 1876.

She opened her law office that fall. Mary Foster was fifty-two years old. At fifty-two, most people are starting to make retirement plans. Not so Mary Foster. She was just beginning her career which is now commemorated by the Women Lawyers' Association with the annual "Mary E. Foster Award." Despite that ultimate recognition, Mrs. Foster experienced a great deal of prejudice. As the first woman to graduate from the University of Michigan who chose to remain in the area to practice, she sent shockwaves through the male community who capitalized on some financial difficulties she had to defame her in the press. Had she been a man, it is doubtful any of her private affairs would have been noticed, but since she was on the cutting edge for the advancement of women, her troubles became the focus of a series of newspaper articles. Ultimately she resolved her financial difficulties and won a libel suit against the *Detroit Post and Tribune* though the all male jury demonstrated its disdain by only awarding her six cents in damages. None of this slowed her down.

Mrs. Foster, by then in her sixties, maintained her practice, was an active member of the Pioneer Society of Michigan, and participated in the WCTU, the Women's Christian Temperance Union A friend of Foster's using only the initials OBT wrote of Foster, "She has practiced in the courts with much success, her expectations have been more than realized; she has overcome much prejudice by her calm decided opinions and prompt action that has put to shame the unmanly ignorant and selfish that ever assume to know just what use women should make of the talents given, or experience gained." [47]

Oratory is an integral part of the legal profession, yet for women, speaking in public was highly controversial in the nineteenth century even at a progressive school such as Oberlin College. When Lucy Stone graduated as valedictorian of her class in 1847, she was prohibited from giving her own valedictory address. She could write it, but a male would read it. Stone declined to write the address. Frances Wright's Fourth of July oration in 1828 is considered the first significant public address by a woman; however, the abolition and suffrage movements drew women such as Anna Dickinson into public speaking both on and off the lecture circuit. In Washtenaw County, at the first Pioneer and Historical Society meeting in 1874, local women such as Roccena Norris and Elizabeth Farrand wrote papers for presentation, but they were read to the audience by men. Five years later, however, Mary Foster read her own paper.

Eleven years after Foster graduated, Mary Collins Whiting of York and Pittsfield Townships also finished law school at the age of fifty-two and became "widely recognized as one of the most capable lawyers at the bar of this state." One of six surviving children of George and Phebe Collins of York Township, Mary graduated first from the Michigan State Normal School. She taught English and music until her marriage to Ralph Whiting at age nineteen. In contrast to Mary Foster's marital tragedies, Mary Whiting's marriage lasted more than fifty years. She and her husband lived in Ann Arbor. Among her varied interests besides law and the management of a hundred acre farm were extensive real estate brokerage and insurance businesses. "She has thoroughly informed herself concerning the value of properties in this section of Michigan and has a large real-estate clientage." [48] Yet when asked of what she was most proud, Mrs. Whiting's reply included none of those professional achievements. She was most proud, she said, of a hospital and school in Korea which she established in 1893. Beakes characterizes her as a woman who "has demonstrated the right to rank with the men of ability, possessing an intellectual force and determination that makes for success..." [49] Clearly she was just that, a success. Mrs. Whiting died in 1912 and is buried in Ann Arbor's Forest Hill Cemetery.

Mary Collins Whiting

It took almost a century after Mary Foster began her practice in Ann Arbor for Ypsilanti to obtain its first "Lady Lawyer," Sharon Philbrook, in 1974. And there were no female lawyers in any of the smaller towns or villages. Women in the law experienced the same backlash that happened to the "hen-medics." One need only compare the comments of two University of Michigan presidents to see the change in attitude between 1870, the year women first were accepted as students at the University of Michigan and the end of the century.

Interim President Henry Frieze reported in 1871 that there were "two [female students] in the Law Department... one has already graduated. The Law Department encountered no difficulty in the admission of women to the course of lectures already organized for men. No separate lecture course is found necessary or desirable..." [50] His view was that women were highly capable and an asset to both the University and their chosen profession. In contrast, President James B. Angell's report to Regents in 1900, when only forty-one women had earned law degrees at Michigan, stated, "The number of women in the Law School is always small. Of those who graduate only a few engage much in practice in court. Some study the profession for the express purpose of assisting their fathers in office work. A few have taken the course in whole or in part with a belief that a knowledge of law would enable them to be more efficient teachers. It seems improbable that any considerable number of women will find it congenial or remunerative to follow the profession of law." [51]

What makes this statement by Angell so intriguing is that it would seem to contradict his earlier behavior. Dorothy McGuighan in her book *Dangerous Experiment* consistently maintains that Angell was a firm advocate of co-education. He had been so supportive of women such as Alice Freeman (Palmer) when she was a student in the 1870's. He allowed her to enter the University even though she had not passed her entrance examination. And when she needed to drop out to earn money, he found her an excellent position as a school principal in Ottowa, Illinois, where she made $700 for only five months work. Angell also recommended her for a professorship at Wellesley College. And all of that is true. McGuighan, however, did not include in her book any information about Freeman's experience at the 1887 celebrations for the University of Michigan's fiftieth year in Ann Arbor. The program listed all the dignitaries attending. It carefully labeled each with his official title: governor, senator, colonel etc. Heads of universities were consistently listed as "President," but Alice Freeman, President of Wellesley College, was just called "Miss." True, she was about to resign as president, but no one knew that yet. She did not submit her resignation until the following month. So we must ask ourselves which assessment is the more honest. The answer is neither. It wasn't that President Angell viewed women as inferior or unsuitable for higher education. He apparently had no problem with women in the Literary Department where 66% of the graduates entered the teaching profession. He just appears to have felt that women were inappropriate in the School of Law and incapable of maintaining independent careers as attorneys. Angell was dead wrong concerning his assessment of women's potential in the law, but he was certainly right about women not finding the law "congenial."

Even while outwardly appearing supportive and kind, some professors were also very patronizing, if not downright condescending, to the women students. Thomas Cooley, who was impeccably polite to the female students in public, wrote in private "...for the most part [the female students are] of the unlovely class, some of them afford the boys some amusement." [51] As for "the boys" they may have had much the same ambivalence towards the arrival of women in the law school. Their ambivalence has left historians with a mixed message. To their credit, they invited women to join the Webster Club as early as 1874 and allowed a woman to read an essay at the club's public exercises in 1875. And female students served first as secretaries of the club beginning in 1875. A decade later a woman was secretary of the class; however one cannot help but notice that the women were only allowed to be the secretaries, the tedious recorders of others' actions. By the turn of the century, Michigan's School of Law "once a haven for women seeking legal education" [52] had succumbed to the same backlash as had the medical school. Women were still allowed, but the climate was decidedly less open. Between 1870 and 1920, 26,761 men had graduated from the University of Michigan's School of Law while for women the number was only 162.

Perhaps that is why Grace Carleton did not practice law per se despite her 1898 degree from the University of Michigan's School of Law. After graduation she served as the deputy treasurer of Chippewa County, Michigan. She was well suited for that job because, before she attended law school, she had been the deputy collector of customs for the port of Sault Ste. Marie, Michigan. For most of her career, however, she worked in the law office of Moore and Goffin in Detroit as chief mortgage clerk. Finally, about the time of the death of Mary Collins Whiting, Miss Carleton returned to Ann Arbor where she was a founder of the Sarah Caswell Angell (named for the wife of University President Angell) DAR chapter and served as one of the first presidents of the Ann Arbor Women's Club. In 1916 she bought a home on Olivia Avenue, where Ann Arbor historian, Wystan Stevens, as a boy, did odd jobs for her in the 1950's.

In the final decades of the nineteenth century, many occupations, that had been accessible through apprenticeship with an experienced practitioner, became closed to all but those with university training. This trend solidified with the passage of time. That did not, however, hinder the trend towards professionalization, especially once universities began admitting women. While the population of the United States between 1890 and 1920 grew by 68%, the number of professionals increased even more. The number of professional males during that same thirty-year period increased by 78%. Impressive as that statistic may seem, it pales in comparison to the 226% gain for the number of women entering the same professions. By 1920, 8,882 women in the United States were practicing medicine, and 1,829 had become licensed dentists. Even the profession of jurisprudence which was so unwelcoming to women had expanded from 208 female attorneys in 1890 to 1,738 in 1920.

[1] "McAndrew Collection" at Ypsilanti Historical Archives, Ypsilanti, MI.

[2] Laura Smith Haviland, *A Woman's Life Work* (Grand Rapids, MI: S .B. Shaw, 1881), 42-3.

[3] Fowler charged 12.5 cents for a man and the bargain price of 25 cents for a man and two women.

[4] *Ypsilanti Commercial*, January 19, 1884.

[5] "Gerry File" at Ypsilanti Historical Archives, Ypsilanti, Michigan.

[6] McGuighan 38

[7] Janet Tarolli, "First Ladies in Medicine at Michigan," *Medicine at Michigan* (Ann Arbor, University of Michigan School of Medicine, Vol. 2 (2000). Available at ww.MedicineatMichigan.org/magazine/fall/women/default.asp

[8] Dr. Cheeseman's pills were widely advertised in newspapers such as Ann Arbor's *Local News and Advertiser* 11/23/1858.

[9] Bertha Van Hoosen, *Petticoat Surgeon* (Chicago: Pellegrini and Cudahy, 1947), 52-3.

[10] Van Hoosen, 62.

[11] Doris Attaway and Marjorie Rabe Barritt, ed., *Women's Voices: Early Years at University of Michigan* (Ann Arbor, Bentley Historical Library, 2000), 20.

[12] Eliza Mosher, "Fifty Years as a Woman Doctor," as told to Esther A. Coster at Bentley Historical Library at University of Michigan, 5.

[13] Attaway, 156.

[14] Attaway, 54.

[15] "Regents' Proceedings, June, 1898" at Bentley Historical Library, University of Michigan.

[16] *Ypsilanti Commercial*, September 15, 1893.

[17] Mary Wood-Allen, *Almost a Woman* (Cooperstown, NY: Arthur H. Crist Co., 1911), 26.

[18] Dr. Anderson was assisted by Dr. Emily Benn, a Michigan graduate from Guelph, Ontario.Dr, Dr. Benn died in 1902.

[19] Olive San Louis Anderson, *An American Girl and her Four Years at a Boys' College* (New York: D. Appleton and Co., 1878),5.

[20] William Rothstein, *American Physicians in the Nineteenth Century* (Baltimore: Johns Hopkins University Press, 1972), 158.

[21] *The University of Michigan: An Encyclopedic Survey, Vol 3, ed.* Wilfred Shaw (Ann Arbor: University of Michigan Press, 1951), 1004.

[22] *History of Washtenaw County, Michigan* (Chicago: Charles C. Chapman Co., 1881), 314.

[23] Emily Hollister, "Emily Hollister Diary," in "Richard Teall Hollister Collection" at Bentley Historical Library, University of Michigan, 11.

[24] "Alumnae Questionaire" in "Alumni Association Records," Bentley Historical Library, University of Michigan.

[25] In 1891, though there were 4,557 women who were licensed physicians, only 115 or 2.5% of them had been admitted to male dominated medical societies.

[26] "Alumnae."

[27] "Katherine Crawford," in "Necrology Files," at Bentley Historical Library, University of Michigan.

[28] It was not until the 1960's that the number of women in the University of Michigan's School of Medicine was the same as it was in 1894. Of course, by then that number represented a far smaller percentage of the students enrolled. For the entire United States, in 1970 only eight percent of all medical students were women. That number increased every year until 2011 when 48.3% of the graduates of medical schools were women.

[29] Gender bias remains in the Michigan Alumnus, the magazine representing the Alumni Association which was formed in 1897. Despite the fact that women are represented within the covers of the magazine, the title remains "Alumnus" which is a male graduate. Even "alumni" is the word for male graduates.

[30] Mary Roth Walsh, *Doctors Wanted No women Need Apply* (New Haven: Yale University Press, 1977), 142.

[31] "Early U-M Student Nurses," *Impressions* (Ann Arbor: Washtenaw County Historical Society, October-November 1984), 3.

[32] Shaw, 498.

[33] "Early,"3.

[34] Hollister, 3.

[35] Hollister, 5,

[36] "Early," 2.

[37] "Early," 2

[38] Gertrude Hiscock Nanry, *Lest it be Forgotten* (1987), 77.

[39] *History of Washtenaw County, Michigan* (Chicago: Charles C. Chapman Co., 1881), 1067.

.

[40] *Ypsilanti Commercial*, June 16, 1893.

[41] M. L. Rayne, *What Can a Woman Do?* (Detroit: R. B. Dickerson and Co., 1885), 109.

[42] Jane Friedman, "Myra Bradwell: On Defying the Creator and Becoming a Lawyer." *Valparaiso University Law Review* 8 (1994): 1298-99.

[43] Virginia Drachman, *Sisters–in-Law* (Cambridge, MA: Harvard University Press, 1998), 11.

[44] Drachman, 46

[45] Stanton, Elizabeth Cady and Susan B. Anthony, *Selected papers of Elizabeth Cady Stanton and Susan B Anthony, 1866-1873*, ed. Ann D. Gordon (New Brunswick, NJ: Rutgers University Press, 2000), 419.

[46] "Echoes of the Past," *Pioneer and Historical Collection, Vol 2* (Detroit: Wm Graham's Press, 1880), 543.

[47] "Ellen Martin Papers," at Bentley Historical Library, University of Michigan.

[48] Samuel Beakes, *Past and Present Washtenaw County, Michigan* (Chicago: St. Clarke Publishing Co., 1906), 162.

[49] Morello, 52.

[50] Morello, 54.

[51] Drachman, 57.

[52] Drachman, 133.

CHAPTER TEN: Women in Business

Women in the nineteenth century were involved in a wide variety of business ventures. If we were to give a prize for the most exotic way a woman earned a living, it surely would go to Sarah Ann Raub and Ann Johnson. Raub had a "thriving business" in Ann Arbor on Northfield Road in the mid 1800's while Johnson, an African-American widow, plied her trade circa 1883 at her home near Oak and 12th streets in Ypsilanti. Both of these women supported themselves as fortune tellers. Apparently Raub used handbills to advertise her services to "inquire into the mysteries of the future." She charged fifty cents for men, but only twenty-five cents for women. Raub also stated categorically that she did not work on Sunday. [1] Such an occupation should not really surprise us since the nineteenth century was prone to believe in the occult. Séances and clairvoyant medicine were especially popular in the Midwest.

Most women, however, supported themselves in much more conventional ways such as taking in lodgers. Unfortunately, history has chosen not to note much about such women. Yet there certainly were women who took in boarders as soon as the county was settled. It was such a necessary service, and one perfectly suited to a woman's training. The earliest public reference to a woman who took in lodgers was on January 16, 1832. On that date a legal notice in the *Western Emigrant* newspaper announced that the goods of Orville Foster, an "absconding debtor," had been given to Abigail Willcoxson. While it does not say explicitly that she was his landlady, it certainly suggests that. According to Wendy Gamber in *The Boarding House*, "Boarders...frequently departed without paying what they owed" [2] Since such people were sneaking away they could not walk out with their belongings. Because Foster disappeared without paying his bill, the court allowed Mrs. Willcoxson to recoup at least part of what he owed her by acquiring or selling his belongings.

Mrs. Willcoxson at that time was the forty-seven year old widow of Gideon Willcoxson, a prominent lawyer, who died in 1830. Born Abigail Graves, Mrs. Willcoxson came from New York to Ann Arbor with her husband in 1827. They had two sons and a daughter between the ages of ten and twenty at the time of Mr. Willcoxin's death. It is highly probable that Mrs. Willcoxson began taking in boarders to help support herself and her children after her husband passed away. The fact that she filed with the court for compensation suggests she had a good understanding of law which she may have acquired from her husband. She later married another lawyer, George W. Jewett. Mrs. Willcoxson died at the home of her daughter, Mrs. John Maynard, in 1877, exactly fifty years after she arrived in Ann Arbor,

In the early days when the Willcoxsons arrived, dozens of inns or taverns catered to settlers and later to stagecoach passengers. Joseph Arnold married his wife Margaret in New York in 1822. They then came to Dexter where they built a two-story frame house which was "used as a favorite inn by the weary westward-bound emigrant." [3] Years later, A.D.P. Van Buren reported to the Michigan Pioneer and Historical Society his experiences coming to the Michigan Territory in 1836. He said there was a common saying that "every mile was an inn." That may have been a bit of an exaggeration, but there were a great many taverns or inns along the roads. No one questions that fact. The problem is that women's participation in the operation of those establishments has not been recorded. Who took care of Mr. Arnold's two-story house that functioned as an inn? One seriously doubts it was Joseph who washed the linens and cooked the food.

Van Buren further noted that his family's first night west of Detroit was spent in something less grand than Mr. Arnold's inn. It was just a one room cabin with a loft. "It was the smallest compass to which an inn might be reduced. The host and his wife... availed themselves of this way of making money." [4] The charge for lodging, Van Buren notes, was only twenty-five cents while food for either humans or oxen was fifty cents. For that fifty cents, however, the humans were given a satisfying dinner of bread, butter, boiled potatoes, fried pork, pickles and tea. At their next stop, Van Buren recalled a pretty girl waiting table for them. Mr. Van Buren's mention of the wife and the serving girl indicate an active presence of women that no doubt existed in most inns.

Likewise, Laura Ripley Wallace, the widow Daniel D. Wallace, was eighty-two years old in 1890 when the *Saline Observer* interviewed her about her experiences in the early days of Washtenaw County. She and her husband were very typical of early settlers. She was born in New York where she married Wallace, who had come to New York from Vermont. The Wallaces emigrated in 1831. She was twenty-three at that time, and the mother of an infant son, Edwin. Laura stayed in Ann Arbor (presumably at a boarding house such as Mrs. Willcoxon's) while her husband explored the area. He soon bought property in Saline. By 1833 the Wallaces had built their own tavern which they called the "Half-way House." It is important to note that the word tavern at that time did not indicate a saloon; very often they were just inns. According to Mrs. Wallace, "*they*," i.e. she and her husband, ran it until 1848 "and many a weary traveler sought its hospitality, as the travel toward Chicago was great at that time, and nearly all went via the Chicago turnpike, through this place." [5] Though Mrs. Wallace does not refer specifically to her duties at the Half-way House, she clearly was an active participant in its operation. Her husband had many other business obligations that demanded his energies. During those fifteen years, Mr. Wallace built the Presbyterian Church, the Baptist Church, Dell School and the Mooreville Hotel. In addition, he operated a lumber yard and a mill. It certainly would appear that a good deal, if not all, of the management of the Half-way House fell on Mrs. Wallace's shoulders despite her being mother to five children in those years.

The Census of 1850, the first to list occupations, indicates a half dozen or so male inn-keepers such as Mr. Anson or Aaron (the writing is unclear) Goodrich in Saline and Charles Brush in Bridgewater. There is no indication in the census that Julia Goodrich or Hannah Brush were employed at all, yet common sense suggests that they, like Laura Wallace, probably played a very active role in maintaining the inns despite having children to tend. Mrs. Goodrich was a mother of ten, and Mrs. Brush, five. Likewise Mrs. Silas Brown of Ypsilanti quite probably helped Mr. Brown in "his" inn. Lucy Brown was twenty-six in 1850 and cared for the five children from her husband's previous marriage in addition to whatever duties she performed at the inn. In Ann Arbor, there were several similar cases. N. H. Egleston, E. Sprague, John Pettibone and Edward Campbell, each maintained inns. The census indicates no participation from Ema Egleston, Lorelia Sprague, Julia Pettibone, or Ann Campbell. Mrs. Egleston was only twenty-four and had a newborn in 1850. Mrs. Sprague had a son, age eleven. Pettibone, age twenty, did not have any children yet, but Ann Campbell, age twenty-six, had two, ages eight and six. Between their own domestic chores and the extra work generated by the inns, these women were undoubtedly very busy.

In much the same manner, although secondary sources agree that boarding houses were the domain of women, owners were generally identified as a male. As Gamber states in her 2005 book concerning this service, "Boarding house keeping was women's work. Even when husbands and fathers styled themselves proprietors, wives and daughters, sometimes assisted by female servants, performed the labor that keeping boarders entailed." [6] The 1850 Census includes the names of several men who listed their occupation as "boarding house." Tate Dickerson (spelling unclear), for example, was a thirty-one year old male with a wife named Mary, age twenty-nine. They had two children, ages seven and three. His occupation was owning and operating a boarding house in Ypsilanti worth $1300. It may have been the husband who claimed ownership, yet Mary certainly performed the labor.

It was not just transients who required rooms in boarding houses, inns or hotels. Statistics indicate that fully one third to one half of all urbanites in the nineteenth century either took in or were themselves boarders. In addition to high school and university students, many young married couples preferred to live in such establishments until they had sufficient funds to establish their own homes. Emily Faithful noted in her book, *Three Visits to America*, that "Young married couples generally begin their career in hotels where they can obtain all they require on moderate terms..." She continued by saying, "when a growing family or increasing banking balance suggests the establishment of a home," couples move on. There was another important reason why couples moved into their own homes that Miss Faithfull seems to have missed. The concept of "home" as an idyllic private retreat from the bustling world grew in popularity as the century and urbanization evolved. As Gamber put it, "But only with the rise of home as a cultural icon did numerous Americans begin to perceive boarding as a social problem."

> On December 14, 1845 Lucy Ann Smith wrote to her mother in Vermont announcing the arrival of her daughter, Edwina Jane.
>
> *"We have now been keeping house about 8 weeks have been obliged to keep a girl all the time am in hopes soon to be able to do my work with the help of a little girl who is going to board with us and go to school."* [9]

Almost any crisis could send a family from its home to a boarding house. During the Civil War, thousands of wives were left alone at home when their husbands went to fight. Often they moved to a relative's home. Sarah Norton, however, chose to live in a boarding house in Ypsilanti. She wrote in her diary on March 30, 1864, "Ma could have boarded me for three dollars a week, but I thought I could board myself cheaper." [10] And so she did just that. A boarding house allowed her some independence and companionship during the time her husband was away at war.

Men also found lodging answered their immediate needs. Apparently Marianne Buchoz was unhappy in her marriage to Louis R. Buchoz. She must have made her own New Year's resolution to start a new life because on January 1, 1850, Mr. Buchoz published the standard announcement required of all deserted husbands: "Notice: Is hereby given, that my wife Marianne Buchoz, formerly of Whitmore Lake, has left my bed and board without just cause, and this is to caution all persons against trusting her on my account, as from this date, I will not pay debts of her contracting except such as I will previously agree to pay." Only a week later Mr. Buchoz ran another item in the *Argus*: "NOTICE: BOARDING wanted for five persons in a genteel and respectable family in the Upper Town of Ann Arbor. My family is composed of myself, one daughter 17 years old, one do.[daughter] 11, one boy 13 years of age, one do.[son] 7. I would prefer a boarding place near some of the best schools. One large room and two bed rooms, or two rooms and one bed room, with or without furniture. Any letter sent to the subscriber on the subject, will be promptly tended to." Whatever the reason Mrs. Buchoz deserted her husband and four children, she left her spouse with more responsibilities than he could handle, so he chose to abandon housekeeping in favor of a boarding house. Mr. Buchoz eventually solved his domestic problem by marrying again. His second wife's name was Caroline. They had a daughter named Isabella who died in 1863 at age two and a half.

An incredible number of people seem to have lived in boarding houses as their health was failing. Though sometimes portrayed negatively in journalism and literature, Wendy Gamber assures readers that boarding houses "served as venues for courtship, schools for the upwardly mobile, old age homes and even hospitals." [11] Nurse Hollister filled her journal with entries concerning patients who resided in boarding houses in Ann Arbor. In addition to Ellen Morse's where Hollister said she was treated very generously, she called Mrs. Motley's on Jefferson "a noted boarding house." [12] Hollister's work also brought her to Mrs. Depue's on Division Street no less than three times. And Mrs. Gray, Hollister noted with a certain amount of empathy, was a mother of eight children while also keeping a boarding house on North University Street which she ran with her mother, Mrs. Spade. Some sick boarders recovered, and some did not. Fifty-one year old Patrick Boyle of Northfield, for example, passed away at Walker House on May 26, 1876 due to "congestion of the lungs." He may have chosen Walker House because of a personal connection. The Walkers had lived in Northfield before moving to Ann Arbor.

Walker House was also initially "operated" by a man. William Walker identified himself in the 1860 Census as a "hotel keeper" but in the *1868 City Directory* his is listed as a carpenter and boarding house owner. Mr. Walker, originally from New York, was a farmer before he, his wife and six children moved to Ann Arbor's Third Ward. Mrs. Walker is one of the many women who did the work but did not get much credit for it until after her husband's death in March of 1872. At that time she began to list herself as the proprietor of the boarding house on the southwest corner of Catherine and First Streets. Keeping track of Mrs. Walker is tricky because her name is one of the most inconsistently spelled even for the nineteenth century. She is Saline, Cyllana, Selina, and even Selma. Selina, however, appears to have been the preferred spelling for Mrs. Walker who was born in 1810 in New Jersey to a family named Taylor.

What makes Walker House noteworthy is that it was still around fifty years later. Selina Walker maintained the boarding house at 17 N. First Street until 1889. Then in 1890 Esther A. Walker, widow of Selina's son, John J. Walker, took over. Her house at 15 W. Catherine was located around the corner from the original boarding house. By the twentieth century Walker

House had moved yet again. This time it moved just around another corner to 303 W. Miller. But it was still run by a Walker. For a second generation, the boarding business supported a Walker widow. No other boarding house in Washtenaw County remained in business within one extended family for so long.

Operating a boarding house was a preferred choice for many women who found themselves alone but with families to support. Much as mothers today are finding jobs that allow them to work at home using telephones and computers, a boarding house allowed women to earn an income while still at home where they could supervise their children. John Morrison boarded at the Bicknells on Pearl Street in Ypsilanti while he was working nearby. Mrs. Bicknell was married to a Baptist preacher in Lenawee County. The income from Mr. Bicknell's ministry, no doubt, was insufficient to meet the needs of his family. In addition to his wife's efforts, both of his daughters worked in local factories. Morrison was surprised and gratified that they would accept him as a boarder since he was a Catholic and they obviously were not.

The vast majority of female boarding house owners were married women, very often widows like Mrs. Vogel. Mary Weimann Vogel (1858-1931), was the widow of Ann Arbor butcher, Martin P. Vogel. She supported herself and their four children by purchasing a house at 217 W. Huron after her husband's death (circa 1907) and operating it as a boarding house. Despite the preponderance of married women in the boarding house trade, there were a few single women. Anne Gillett, the sister of photographer, Lucretia Gillett, used their home in Saline as a boarding house between 1870 and 1890. Likewise in Ann Arbor, Clara C. Kingsley managed C. Kingsley Millinery on Washington Street before starting to receive boarders at 13 S. Thayer.

Mary Weinmann Vogel

Courtesy of the
Washtenaw County Historical Society

One of the biggest problems for researchers is that most boarding houses did not advertise. They obtained boarders by word of mouth which makes it difficult to locate all the establishments. Frequently the owner of a full house would refer potential boarders to other women of her acquaintance. This lack of public advertisements makes research especially challenging when seeking African-American boarding houses, yet it seems obvious that such women must have existed even if they are not in the city directories, newspapers, or even the censuses. One known example was Mrs. Isa Stewart, a widow in Ypsilanti, who operated a boarding house in the 1870's and 1880's at the southwest corner of Buff and Adams. Mrs. Stewart was born in Kentucky circa 1824. Her two daughters were born in 1852 and 1854. Both of her daughters were born in Canada. This leads me to believe she, like so many African-Americans prior to end of the Civil War, fled to Canada only to return to the United States when times were safer for people of their race. It is possible she was a free woman in Kentucky; however, the more likely scenario is that she was born enslaved and escaped. By 1870 she was a widow caring not only for her two teenage daughters but two children whose last name was Mcquan. What their relationship to her was remains a mystery. Both Mcquan children were born in Michigan in 1859 and 1860. Mrs. Stewart continued her service until her death in 1884.

Electra Knight, left, and Harriet Knight, right.
Courtesy of the Washtenaw County Historical Society

Some women never intended to start a boarding house. They slipped into that role gradually. The Knight sisters would be a prime example. Harriet and Electra Knight were actually half sisters, both daughters of Rufus Knight. They moved into Ann Arbor from the family farm on Scio Church Road in 1892 when Harriet was sixty-three. They purchased 311 E. Ann Street from a Mrs. Rhoda Royce whose husband, James, had built the house in 1866 for $900. Nine years after moving in, Electra was severely injured when a horse kicked her. Harriet cared for her younger sister until her own death in 1910.

They began taking as boarders children of relatives who wanted to attend Ann Arbor High School. Their great niece, Edith Knight (Behringer), roomed with them for eight years. Later they accepted adults outside of the family. Many were doctors and nurses who chose to board with the Knights because of their proximity to the University Hospital.

Boarding houses existed everywhere offering shelter to travelers and working folk. Even families who did not technically operate boarding houses often took in people outside the family. Frequently these were their own employees. Miss A. M. Rogers boarded with her employer, Olive Coe, in Ypsilanti. Miss Coe's millinery competitor Mrs. S. M. Vincent provided rooms for two of her employees, C. Turner and Georgiana Young. Even Dr. Helen McAndrew and her husband accepted one of his employees as a boarder. In Ann Arbor, Frederick Batties, an African-American barber, simply stated in the *1860 City Directory* "bds. [boards] With the boss." Unfortunately he does not say who that was. In the same way, George Schetlerly, a cooper who lived near Miller and Main, provided housing for Jacob and John Schiltz, also coopers. Finally, the future home of Dr. Daniel Kellogg in Lower Town, Ann Arbor, provides a variation on this pattern. That residence in the late 1830's was a boarding house for the employees of the nearby Jones and Foley's paper mill. Boarding employees not only minimized salary costs but also increased an employer's ability to find and retain adequate help.

The existence of both the Normal School in Ypsilanti and the University of Michigan in Ann Arbor made housing in each of those towns especially significant. In Ann Arbor, when the University began, the students were housed in dormitory rooms on campus. That ended fifteen years later when University President Henry Tappan announced that it was a waste of the University's space and energy to provide housing. The University, he claimed in his 1853 inaugural address should not be interested in providing "a night's sleep" but "libraries and laboratories for the day's work." [13] Thus he initiated his plan to end student housing. He challenged the citizens of Ann Arbor to provide sufficient local housing for students. In this way, "The housing and feeding of them [the students] became the primary source of income for dozens of citizens and a secondary source for hundreds more." [14] In the *1860 Ann Arbor City Directory*, three male students identified Mrs. C. Dorman as their landlady. Mrs. Dorman's home was located on Washington near Michigan Avenue in Ypsilanti. Mrs. Bauer also operated a popular boarding house at 623 Huron Street in Ann Arbor. Mrs. Bauer, a widow, took motherly care of the young men who boarded with her. She mended their clothes, fed them, and cared for them when they were ill.

Students also found lodging in homes that were not boarding houses per se but took in an extra person to provide extra income. George Pray boarded with Earl and Francis Gardiner circa 1842. It was at the Gardiners that Pray met his future wife's younger sister. She was also boarding there while attending the Clark School for Young Ladies. Why the Gardiners took boarders is unclear. Mr. Gardiner appears to have been a successful businessman since he was the editor of the *Argus* newspaper. Obviously they had the space and welcomed the supplementary income. In a similar manner, Professor Ten Brook and his first wife boarded a student named Thomas Palmer. The Ten Brooks resided in one of the four pro-

A boarding house at
526 Jefferson Street in Ann Arbor.

Courtesy of the Bentley Historical Library,
University of Michigan

fessors' houses on the University of Michigan campus. Palmer told his mother in a letter dated January 9, 1846, "I went to Mrs. Welsh's to board, but I did not like it as well as I expected for they had their meals very irregular... I am now at Professor Ten Brook's whom I like very well, also Mrs. Ten Brook." [15] He went on to say that the Ten Brooks were charging him the same amount (12 shillings per week) that he had paid at Mrs. Welsh's. Such arrangements existed throughout Washenaw County. Dr. S.A. Babbitt, a dentist in Ypsilanti, had O. Strade, a student, boarding in his home in 1860. Likewise in Lodi Township, many students at the renowned Nutting Academy roomed with nearby farm families. This may have included a considerable number since in 1851 Nutting had 142 students.

Such arrangements, it was hoped, bestowed not only a little extra income on the families but a certain civilizing constraint on youthful and sometimes overly exuberant tenants. According to historian, Wendy Gamber, "middle class and even wealthy families took boarders into their homes... in order to keep 'a close check' on the single men of the town." [16] Reports are mixed as to whether this theory actually worked. To refute such a theory, one only need mention how in 1898 during a holiday recess, a group of students gathered in a back room of a boarding house and began drinking. By two in the morning their carousing brought their landlady to the room asking them to be quiet. They did not comply, leaving the woman no alternative but to summon the police who made sure the party ended. Unfortunately for the landlady, her boarders chose to avenge themselves the very next day by seeking rooms elsewhere, leaving her without income. In contrast to that sad account of human behavior, Miss Jessie Beal agreed that landladies could have a powerful effect on the behavior of boarders. "The best influence at Ann Arbor was the atmosphere of refinement which characterized Mrs. Motley's boarding house and the gentle dignity of the little lady whom all who were as fortunate as to eat under her roof came to honor and admire." [17]

Miss Beal represents yet another adaptation communities were forced to make when female students began attending local schools. The impact was particularly felt in Ann Arbor when the University of Michigan, Miss Beal's alma mater, began to admit women in 1870. Female students, too, needed housing. Olive San Louis Anderson, one of the first women at Michigan, described in her autobiographical novel that boarding houses would not accept her protagonist. Only through the intercession of the University Steward was she given a room in the house of his cousin. The second year, her character had less trouble as house owners came to realize the benefits of having female tenants. Elizabeth Farrand confirms Anderson's description. According to Farrand, "There was at first in Ann Arbor a decided prejudice against lady students. Many boarding places were not open to them and several years passed before the oddity [of female students] ceased to affect people." [18]

University of Michigan coeds studying in their boarding house room.

Courtesy of the Bentley Historical Library, University of Michigan

Lucy Maynard Salmon and Louise Hall, two of the first female students, searched for three days before finding a boarding house that would accept them." The impression left by Alice Freeman (Palmer), however, was quite the opposite viewpoint. She maintained that she easily found "nicely furnished [rooms] with everything one could want" on State Street right across from Campus Square. [19] The house to which she refers was probably that of Mrs. Catherine McManus. In addition to Mrs. McManus, Mrs. Motley and Mrs. Popkins also accepted female students. Fortunately for us, Alice Freeman preserved some of the details of her life as a boarder in 1872. Like most college students away from home for the first time, Freeman gloried in her independence taking pride in finding her own place to live, arranging for her laundry to be done and purchasing sufficient fuel for winter. Her wood bill during her senior year was $12. Room and board varied from $3-5 a week.

A few young women resided in local homes that did not usually accept boarders. Alice Hamilton, class of 1893, roomed with Dr. and Mrs. Albert Prescott. Alice came from a very protective, upper middle class environment. She preferred the security of a private home owned by a deacon of the Presbyterian Church. Why the Prescott's accept Alice is not clear, but Alice wrote to her cousin Agnes, "I fancy they have not very much money and they never took a 'roomer' but once before." Whatever their reason for accepting Alice, she soon became one of the family and was introduced around town as "Mrs. Prescott's Miss Hamilton" [20] It is interesting to note that, though Alice roomed at the Prescott's, she ate at a boarding house operated by Mrs. Emily Hertel. There she dined with three other young women and six men. Her only complaint about Mrs. Hertel was that her tea was not "real." [21]

Women, whether they were students or not, usually boarded in houses that rented to men as well as women. The intimacy of such arrangements came under increasingly strident criticism as Victorian social standards gained ascendancy. The public imagined all sorts of debaucheries taking place when unrelated males and females resided together, yet none of the female university students remembered anything awful happening. Louise Willebrands recalled using a room at Miss Dowdegan's on William Street as a sitting room where she and her roommates would entertain male friends after dinner. [22] Genevieve O'Neill stated, "Boys and girls were put upon their honor who roomed in the same dwelling, and I never saw a girl 'fall' or knew a boy to demean himself by attempting to a lead a college girl astray." [23] Ethel Winifred Chase concurred with Genevieve's opinion. "Never in three years was I ever subjected to any personal annoyance or insult in the houses where I resided." [24]

Despite such supporting testimonies, University policy changed to accommodate public opinion. The freedom enjoyed by female students who had remained fairly unsupervised by the University came to an abrupt halt in 1902 with the arrival of Myra Jordon as the second dean of women. She instituted a program of allowing female students to live only in recognized and approved houses such as one on Madison run by Mrs. Popkins. Mixed gender housing was eliminated. Genevieve O'Neill, a student who had experienced coed housing, believed this was counterproductive. According to O'Neill, "The intermingling of boys and girls in the same home brought about a democratic and broadminded outlook upon life as well as a mutual understanding between the sexes." [25]

It is, therefore, symbolic that the first University sponsored dormitory for women was named for Eliza Mosher and Myra Jordon, the first two deans of women. It was during their tenures, particularly during Jordon's, that the University became more and more concerned about women's housing. The building of Mosher-Jordan Hall in the 1920's was not only a reversal of the University's earlier hands-off housing policy, but even more important, it signaled a trend towards closer supervision of female students. The announcement of the impending construction of Mosher-Jordan Hall was met with outrage by students as well as the community. Seven thousand local citizens signed a petition which was sent to the governor urging his help. Development of University operated housing, they believed, would jeopardize the business interests of Ann Arbor where boarding houses relied on students for their livelihood. The University of Michigan, however, went ahead with its plans and built more dorms. Boarding houses, already in decline nationally, responded by quickly transforming themselves into rental apartments creating what Milo Ryan described as a "rabbit warren" [26] of rooming houses which filled the side streets near campus – just as they do today.

In Ypsilanti Bethiah Hiscock Wilbur owned two houses located at 317 and 319 Pearl Street. These structures illustrate the gradual trend away from boarding houses and towards rooming houses. The difference is simple but significant. Boarding houses provided meals; rooming houses did not. Bethiah's husband, Ward Wilbur was twenty years older than she and died two months before their daughter, Lena, was born in 1856. Bethiah at the time was only twenty-one. Mrs. Wilbur's first idea for supporting herself and her daughter was to convert her summer kitchen into a room where she instructed girls in the skill of sewing suits and coats. She placed a peddle foot sewing machines under each of the six windows. Mrs. Wilbur was very forward looking since sewing machines were a relatively new technology at that time. She also rented apartments in the two houses. For the next fifty years, Mr. and Mrs. Wells rented the first floor of #317. When Bethiah died in 1892, her daughter, Lena Marie Wilbur, inherited the buildings which remained much the same until Mrs. Wells died in 1913. At that time Lena had Mr. Wells convert the one upstairs apartment into three smaller rentals each with a kitchenette. Then Mr. Wells moved upstairs and began subdividing the first floor in order to maximize Lena's income from the property.

Hattie Crippen

In many cases taking in lodgers was the only means a woman had of retaining a large family home on a marginal income, and it was, according to *Harper's* in 1882, one of the few ways to earn money and "not lose social class." It is easy to see how Hattie Crippen became the owner of a rooming house. Miss Crippen's family was solidly middle class. Hattie taught for a while. Her father, John W. Crippen, had been minister of the First Methodist Episcopal Church. And Mrs. Crippen frequently brought home girls who needed a room. Hattie recalled the first girl who stayed with them. She was "despondent because she could not get work and planned to kill herself."[27] Luckily, Mrs. Crippen found her a job with a seamstress. Her actions, however, were charity not business.

Hattie and her mother were instrumental in organizing the first local YWCA (originally called Young Women's Christian Association) and became charter members in 1906. Hattie herself served for five years as the organization's first president. Later she served as secretary. She was paid only an honorarium for these offices. The YWCA's primary goal was to teach basic education classes, provide Sunday afternoon worship (perhaps timed to accommodate the schedules of most domestic servants) and offer respectable social opportunities. One of its early flyers advertised "a women's rest room" which was free to all women. This would be much more than a bathroom. It would be a lounge with tables, chairs and couches such as one still finds in larger department stores. In addition, the YWCA was able to provide inexpensive housing for women first above the First National Bank and later above the Ann Arbor Post Office between 1895 and 1904.

After Hattie's parents died, she remained in the family home at 507 E. Ann Street which she turned into a rooming house by inviting her friends to rent from her. Having once been a teacher, Hattie's house was a natural for other female educators and members of the YWCA. Nellie Loving, who served as secretary of the YWCA in 1894-5, and Alice Porter, who served in 1895-96, each lived at Miss Crippens. Miss Crippen died in 1955 at age ninety-two. She was buried beside her parents at Forest Hill Cemetery.

Rooming houses, such as Miss Crippen's, became very popular at the end of the century. From the renter's perspective, they offered more privacy since they did not provide communal meals or parlors. From the owner's vantage point, they were far easier to operate because they did not involve serving food which could become a complicated process since some boarding house owners actually served individual meats and charged each boarder accordingly. Instead a rooming house owner need only rent pleasantly furnished rooms to a genteel clientele such as Ann Arbor English teacher and local historian, Lela Duff, who also lived at Miss Crippen's. Over the years, Lela developed a sincere fondness for her landlady; however, such an affectionate relationship was unusual because roomers did not often interact with their landlords.

Since there was far less interaction between a building's owner and renters in rooming houses, there are even fewer anecdotal recollections passed down for future historians to find. In boarding houses, daily interaction between owner and boarder who shared meals and parlors occasionally resulted in splendid memories. There is a charming tale, circa 1848, about Randolph Rogers and the lady who operated his boarding house. Unfortunately because Rogers is the one who later became a famous sculptor, he is the focus of the story rather than his landlady who remains anonymous. Apparently Rogers, then age twenty-six, arrived at the house long after supper had been served and the dishes washed. His kind landlady had saved his dinner. When she cleared the table, he had already left for his room, but she found a surprise on his plate. Rogers had fashioned a perfectly formed little figure of a baby out of his bread. That, no doubt, was his way of thanking her for her forbearance. One wonders if his landlady tossed it into the garbage laughing at his silliness or, and I think this more likely because she apparently was a supporter of his efforts, she kept the little bread baby as a memento.

It was only a step up from running a boarding house or an inn to operating a hotel or a restaurant. What exactly distinguishes a boarding house or inn from a hotel remains obscure. Perhaps it was simply size. In the *1878 City Directory*, Mrs. E. H. Jackson of Ypsilanti called her establishment at #4 Huron Street in Ypsilanti "Hotel de Jackson." Despite its rather pretentious name, it was essentially a boarding house that rented rooms by the day or week and served "warm meals at all hours." In fairness to Mrs. Jackson, she might have been using "hotel" in the French manner meaning "house." She did not remain long in business so perhaps the grandiose name backfired.

> HOTEL De JACKSON,
> MRS. E. H. JACKSON,   PROPRIETOR.
> Board by the Day and Week.   Warm meals at all Hours.
> No. 4 South Huron street,   .   .   YPSILANTI, MICHIGAN.

Mr. and Mrs. Henry Stebbins operated a hotel and restaurant business in Dexter. Mrs. Stebbins's parents, whose name was Wilsey, emigrated with their baby daughter when Michigan was just a territory, so Edna grew up there. Henry Stebbins, however, only arrived in 1859, a year before their marriage. The groom was twenty-eight; the bride, twenty-four. Soon after their marriage, they established a hotel and restaurant business, which was later continued by their only child, Charles William Stebbins, born in 1861. By 1870 they had eleven residents. Seven years later, they bought an old grocery building and raised the roof to add more rooms. They named this establishment the Eureka House. Edna cooked for the hotel which had twenty-three rooms. They charged $2 per day which included three meals. Twenty-three or more mouths to feed and twenty-three rooms to clean surely kept Mrs. Stebbins busy especially after her husband passed away in 1884. Three years later their son, Charles, leased the hotel

Downtown Dexter, Stebbins House on the left.
Courtesy of the Bentley Historical Library, University of Michigan

from his mother and changed its name to Stebbins House. He and his wife, Clara, continued the family tradition. The proceeds of Stebbins House provided a living not only for Charles and Clara and their six children; the lease also supported Edna who died in 1921 at the age eighty-six.

A bit farther west in Chelsea, Michigan, a similar situation evolved. Mr. and Mrs. Boyd established their hotel circa 1887. Eight years later Mrs. Boyd became the only women mentioned in the *Chelsea Headlight*. On page nine, it states that both Mr. and Mrs. Boyd were working together as proprietors. "He [Mr. Boyd] is ably assisted in caring for the comfort of his guests by his very pleasant wife..."

Mrs. Ella Josephine Stark's hotel was larger. It had a capacity of fifty rooms. She began her business career with her husband, Lyman C. Stark. They opened a restaurant at 808 Detroit Street in Ann Arbor circa 1899. Mrs. Stark was fifty-four. They soon moved closer to downtown when they purchased the property at 210 N. Fourth Ave. There they operated a hotel. Within two years, however, Mr. Stark was gone, and Mrs. Stark was the sole proprietor. The hotel, as described in *Ann Arbor Today* published in 1905, was "The best medium priced house in the city." It provided a dining room, steam heat and electric bell service. A room in 1905 cost $1.50 per day. The article continued by describing Mrs. Stark. "[She] is a business woman of unusual ability, knows the demands of the public and meets them successfully." In 1908 Mrs. Stark began a brief partnership with Charles H. Dawes. While Dawes oversaw the Ann Arbor business, she turned her attention to opening a restaurant in Whitmore Lake. Her partnership with Dawes lasted less than three years; the restaurant, only four. Her next business endeavor in Washtenaw County was again as proprietor of a hotel. This time it was the Clifton House in Whitmore Lake. By 1912, however, she was back in Ann Arbor operating yet another restaurant at 204 N. Main.

The final decades of the nineteenth century witnessed the steady development of public restaurants, like those owned by Mrs. Stark. Before that time, food would have been served primarily in hotels, taverns and boarding houses. The 1874 directory for Ann Arbor lists saloons and restaurants together as a single category in its business section. This illustrates the fact that people at that time saw saloons and restaurants as similar entities. It would be unlikely that a young female would patronize one of those establishments. Instead they (and males, too) became "day residents" at boarding house where they could take their meals.

Mrs. Gauntlett, on the right, in front of her home with meal sign over the door.

In the mid-eighties, University of Michigan student, Mae Beadle (Frink) and a friend ate at a different boarding house than where they lived because the food was cheaper ($2.25 vs $3) and much better quality. Thirty years later, Mrs. Sarah E. Gauntlett prominently displayed a sign over the door of her boarding house in Milan proclaiming "MEALS." Mrs. Gauntlett was well known locally as "an outstanding cook" [28] so she probably had quite a few "day residents." Mrs. Gauntlett was born in New York circa 1870. She had worked as a dressmaker in the 1890's before turning her talents to food and lodging. Her husband, Archie M. Gauntlett, was thirteen years her senior. He apparently relied on his wife's income for support and never had a full time job.

The emergence of small restaurants and lunch counters resulted not only from boarding houses transitioning into rooming houses but also the burgeoning development of office workers seeking noon meals but not requiring or desiring the slow and elaborate meals served in hotels. There were only a few such establishments in the 1880's. One was operated by Ellen Wasser at 33 S. State in Ann Arbor. The real growth in this business came in the 1890's. Mrs. Caspary had begun as a baker, but by 1892, she recognized the potential provided by new consumers and opened a restaurant as well. She was not alone. Mrs. Emilie G. Backhaus began her restaurant in the same building as her home at #5 E. Ann. Mrs. Louisa A. Burchfield was part owner with Richard Jolly of R.E. Jolly and Co., of a restaurant located at 26 S. State. Mrs. Burchfield's husband was the proprietor of a tailor shop where her older son also worked, and her younger son and daughters were students when she became a restaurateur. In addition, Miss Caroline Schiller had a restaurant just a bit farther south on State at #48. Two years later, Mrs. Mary J. Ashton opened her restaurant at 26 E. Huron. Mrs. Ashton, who lived on Ashley Street, is worthy of note because she appears to be the only African-American restauranteur advertizing at that time. These women indicate that Ann Arbor led in this entrepreneurial effort since no female operated establishments were advertised in Ypsilanti or any of the villages until after 1892. It was not until 1908, the year Mrs. Stark began her Whitmore Lake restaurant, that restaurants unconnected to boarding houses, inns or hotels started to appear in other areas of Washtenaw County. That was the year Mrs. M. E. Cook opened a restaurant in Milan. She was soon followed by Mrs. Lilian Ross who opened a cafe also in Milan in 1910.

Women not only owned restaurants, they worked in restaurants as waitresses and cooks. This was not a new field. Women had been employed in hotels for years. The development of small cafes and restaurants simply widened women's employment options. It certainly came in handy for Cora Grossman (Jenter), pictured at the right, who found a job working for Charlie Seckinger circa 1909. According to Cora's descendent, Karen Jenter, the job did have one drawback. Seckinger's restaurant served homemade ice cream. One of Cora's duties was to clean the ice cream pails on Saturday evenings so they would be ready for the next week. By the time she finished washing the pails, the ice cream had melted and soured. Cora worked for Seckinger until she married in 1916. Though she had four children and eight grandchildren, neither she nor they ate much ice cream.

Cora Grossman

Courtesy of Karen Jenter

Providing lodging and food were not the only businesses women had in the latter decades of the nineteenth century. A few shrewd women combined real estate speculation with operating a boarding or rooming house. In Ann Arbor the most well-known woman of this sort was Ellen Morse, grand-daughter of Leonard Morse, one of the first pioneers in 1824. Ellen's brother died at thirteen, but Ellen and her mother Hannah (also called Hanorah) lived in Ann Arbor all their lives. Chapman's *History of Washenaw County* says that Ellen was married to someone named Slater; however, by the time she appeared in the directory of 1873, she was using her maiden name as she continued to do for the rest of her life. It would appear that the marriage was not successful because if Slater had died, she probably would have continued to use his name.

307 N. State Street, Ann Arbor, MI

In addition to expanding one's business into restaurants, Morse increased her wealth by operating more than one rooming house at a time. In 1873, Ellen Morse was living in her mother's home. Twenty years later the roles had switched with Hannah boarding with Ellen. Between the two of them, they owned seven properties. Some of those Ellen built, and several she renovated. All were on North State Street. Ellen herself lived in several of her houses. Morse charged $1.75 per week if a tenant provided his or her own wood. And she did her own housekeeping thus becoming a familiar figure on State Street as she carried pail and mop from house to house. Regardless of the image that conjures, Ellen had a reputation of being a shrewd business woman whom builders could not overcharge. The *Ann Arbor Courier* of March 1879 quoted a local merchant who said, "She is as sharp and close a purchaser as I have to deal with, being perfectly conversant with price, style and quality of goods."[29]

Ellen Morse's houses had a profound effect on the community even after she retired. She sold the house at 307 N. State in 1915 to Alexander and Lena Wallace. Their daughter Minnie continued using it as a rooming house. Today it is one of Ann Arbor's historic buildings which remains in use as a co-operative house filled with students. The house that belonged to Ellen's mother at 403 N. State became an Old Ladies' Home before that facility transitioned into the Anna Botsford Bach Home which then moved to Liberty Street. Even more significant is the fact that Morse donated 419 N. State (her most permanent residence at the corner of Kingsley) to the Sisters of Mercy. It was in that house that the Sisters began the first St. Joseph's Mercy Hospital. Within a few years though, they found it had become too small for their needs, so they built a brick building at Glen and Catherine Streets. Today St. Joseph Hospital is a huge complex in Ypsilanti.

When one thinks of ways people invested their money in the nineteenth century, manufacturing and transportation come to mind as the source of great fortunes. Often we don't think about real estate, yet it was a particularly profitable investment during the speculative years before 1860. But real estate has offered a solid investment throughout most of American history. People just don't imagine women as part of that investment, but they were. When Grace Carleton (Chapter Nine) retired and returned to Ann Arbor in 1916, she purchased a home in a relatively new neighborhood on a street named Olivia. Before 1891 that area stretching from Hill Street to Wells, and Baldwin to White, was undeveloped land. Then Mrs. Olivia Bigelow Hall, a widow, purchased it. She knew the area well because she and her husband, Israel,[30] had lived for many years on the corner of Washtenaw and Volland after coming to Ann Arbor from Toledo.

Olivia Hall

Courtesy of the Bentley Historical Library, University of Michigan

Mrs. Hall was a huge supporter of both education and women's suffrage. Between 1877 and 1890, she gave four receptions for suffrage leader, Susan B. Anthony. She even deeded some land to Miss Anthony who was in financial need since she never earned a salary for her efforts. Miss Anthony wrote to thank Mrs. Hall on October 5, 1877, saying, "Tears came to my eyes... may I prove myself worthy."[31] Thanks to Hall, Miss Anthony at last had "a purse of her own" which was something she believed every woman should have.

After Mr. Hall's death, Olivia followed in his footsteps as a real estate investor. She bought the area including the old fairgrounds and had it subdivided and platted as the Olivia B. Hall subdivision #1 in 1891 (pictured below) and #2 in 1896. The first document states,"Know all men by these presents, that I, Olivia B. Hall, ... as proprietor, have caused the land ... to be surveyed, laid out and platted to be known as the Olivia B. Hall Subdivision." That was the legal language required of such a document, but one can sense the pride Mrs. Hall must have felt at her accomplishment. One of the innovations upon which Mrs. Hall insisted was that the houses in her subdivision be constructed a full sixty feet from the street. Until that time houses were built quite close to the street. By setting the houses farther back on the lots, Mrs. Hall gave the neighborhood an elegant appearance which is still highly valued today. Originally Mrs. Hall named a street not only for herself but one for her husband. She called his Israel Avenue. It has been renamed since as Cambridge Avenue, but Olivia Street remains as a reminder of a woman with great vision and investment savvy.

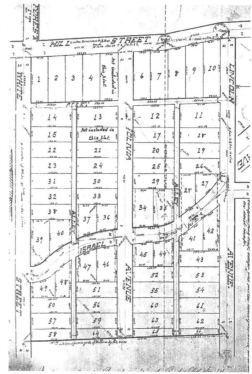

Mrs. Hall's contributions to local real estate development dispel another historical myth. Women were often quite wealthy members of the community in which they lived. In 1887 twenty percent of the tax payers in Ann Arbor who paid more than $50 in taxes, which was considerable at that time, were women. These affluent women had money in their own names and often used it to buy and sell property. One of those properties is an Ann Arbor landmark, the Hoban Block. Situated between Main Street and Fourth Avenue on Ann Street, the Hoban block was built not by Mr. Patrick Hoban but by Mrs. Hoban. Mr. and Mrs. Hoban married in 1842. They had five children. Mr. Hoban at first was a farmer. After that he had a store in Ann Arbor. When he died in 1861, his wife was left to devise some investment that would support her and her family. So she built the "substantial brick business house...at the cost of several thousand dollars." [32] She then became the landlord to whom rents were paid.

Women throughout Washtenaw County earned money as landlords. Mrs. F. L Cooper, a resident of Ann Arbor since the 1830's made her living as a dress and cloak maker, but she also invested wisely in real estate. According Chapman, Mrs. Cooper was "remarkably successful

Hoban Block

as a land speculator." [33] In addition, there was Mary Collins Whiting, previously discussed in connection with her role as an attorney. She, too, supervised her own real estate business. In Chelsea, a doctor's wife, Mrs. Ida May Palmer, "was very active in local real estate....She bought and sold large amounts of farm land as well as commercial properties and house lots." [34] In Dexter Elizabeth Hallen Dancer (Mrs. John Dancer) purchased the Gates Block from Dr. W. F. Gates nine years after the doctor had it built in 1900. Meanwhile in Milan, Susan M. Gay built what the *Milan Leader* called a "humongous" two story building. Completed in 1893, it became the home of the Gay's general store and the Freemason Lodge occupied the ground floor while the second floor functioned as an auditorium. The store boasted a working fireplace which no other business in Milan except the hotel could offer. William H. Gay managed the general store while Edward Gay supervised the Gay Opera House. Investments such as these made profits for the women involved even if they did not actually run the businesses located in their buildings. The profits supported their lifestyles thus would be another form of work in which women were actively involved.

In Ypsilanti a slightly different scenario emerged concerning the Opera House. Beakes describes the domed Opera House as "one of the prettiest for its size" in the state. Designed by Mortimer L. Smith of Detroit, it was built at a cost of $20,000 circa 1880 and had a 28' wide stage. Medallion portraits of famous people such as Professor Pease of the Normal School surrounded the stage. Simeon Draper managed the Opera House, but his mother, Emma Draper, owned it. Sadly that edifice fell victim to the 1893 tornado that ripped through downtown Ypsilanti. Nothing was left of the building except a few partial walls. In fact, a serving

The Ypsilanti Opera House after the 1893 tornado.

Courtesy of the Ypsilanti Historical Society

girl was buried under the debris. Fortunately, she was rescued without serious injury, but the Opera House was ruined. It fell to new investors, not the Drapers, to rebuild it.

Virginia Penny in her 1862 book, *How Women Can Make Money, Married or Single*, asserted that "the rearing of flowers has ever been a charming pastime to many of our sex. When pleasure can be combined with profit," she said, "it is well." [35] Several Washtenaw County women obviously agreed with her. Just a bit northwest of Olivia Hall's subdivisions, where the University of Michigan's School of Social Work is located today on South University Avenue, there was a large home with sprawling greenhouses. This was the site of Cousins and Hall Florists, owned and operated by Eliza Hall Cousins and her brother. Eliza's first husband, William Cousins, worked there as well before his death in 1890. Her daughter, Lillian, later joined in the business.

After five years of widowhood, Eliza married Thomas P. Brogan. For a long time I wondered how these two met. Thomas did not live in Washtenaw County. He hailed from Medina, Michigan, in Lenewee County. So how, I asked myself, did he meet the widowed Eliza Cousins? It would appear that he was introduced to her by his older brother, James, who just happened to be Cousins and Hall's delivery man. After their marriage, Thomas worked with her at the florist shop for a few years but soon established a confectionery business on Main Street. Cousins and Hall Florists, however, continued well into the twentieth century.

Eliza Hall Cousins Brogan

Chelsea, Michigan, has its own tale of a lady florist. The Clark family had lived in Chelsea for many years when their daughter Elvira was born in 1880. Elvira graduated from Chelsea High School and taught for four years. After that she was ready for something new, so in 1901, she opened a greenhouse adjacent to the family home at 7010 Lingane Road. The house is still there, but a new barn had to be built on the greenhouse foundation when the original building was destroyed by fire.

Cousins and Hall delivery truck.
Courtesy of the Bentley Historical Library, University of Michigan

Chelsea Flower Shop

By the time Elvira married Christian Visel (pronounced Vee-zul) in 1910, her business was more successful than she had ever dared hope. Mrs. Visel never had children; she poured all of her energies into her business. Soon clients in Ann Arbor were urging her to open a store there. In 1931, a few years after her husband passed away, she did just that, and the Chelsea Flower Shop at 203 Liberty Street was born. She continued to operate personally that shop until 1951.

Many women, like Mrs. Visal, owned their own shops and stores. A shop, which once designated a place to buy merchandise, ceased to be used that way in the early 1800's. After that time, a shop indicated a place where something made or done as in a millinery shop or flower shop. Merchandise was sold in stores. Nor should we accept the stereotypic description of the gullible female store owner. In J. P. Johnston's autobiography *Twenty years of Hus'ling*, he describes his life in Ann Arbor peddling furniture polish. He remembered talking both a male grocer and male butcher into paying a dollar each for one of his bottles of polish. When he got to a bakery (he doesn't say which one) operated by a woman, he immediately changed his price. "Realizing that her intuitive quickness and shrewdness surpassed that of my two gentlemen patrons," he confessed that he cut his price in half. [36]

Bertha Muehlig with other store employees.

Courtesy of the Bentley Historical Library, University of Michigan

One of those shrewd women began her career as a book-keeper in 1891 but went on to become Ann Arbor's most well known business woman. Her name was Bertha Muehlig. Bertha's grandfather, Florian, came from Swabia, as did many Ann Arborites of German descent. Bertha, however, was born in Ann Arbor, the daughter of John and Amelia Muehlig. After she graduated from Ann Arbor High School in 1891, Bach and Roath hired her as book-keeper for their store. She continued working at the store after Bruno St. James took proprietorship in 1895. Muehlig was still working for him in 1911 when he died. At that time she assumed ownership of the St. James store. Thirteen years later, Muehlig purchased the building itself. She continued selling dry goods which included both materials for home sewing as well as ready-made clothing and linens. She kept a careful watch on her salespeople. She had a spring-operated cash carrier at the store which delighted both children and adults. The saleslady would insert the receipt and money in the brass tube which then would whiz from the counter through tubes to the mezzanine where Muehlig herself acted as cashier.

Her shrewdness in business did not mitigate her generosity. Having never married, she shared her prosperity with many local groups such as Donovan School and the Anna Botsford Bach Home. The store and Miss Muehlig are both gone now, but the building still stands on the northwest corner of Washington and Main Streets in Ann Arbor.

Bertha Muehlig is widely recognized because of her long history in Ann Arbor and the fact that people are still alive today who remember her and her store. Well-known though she is, she was not, by any means, the first woman in to open her own store. As early as 1874, Mrs. Ernestina Roehm had an emporium at #4 Washington Street in Ann Arbor. She appears to have been a widow with a son named George who lived with her at this time. Roehm handled almost as wide a variety of goods as did Muehlig. She offered worsted fancy goods, hosiery, corsets, patterns, Germantown wool, embroidery, slipper patterns, canvas, gold and silver paper, hair goods etc.

Brass parts of Muehlig's cash carrier

Courtesy of the
Washtenaw County Historical Society

It is a good thing that Mrs. Louisa Richards, who opened her store that same year, was located in Dexter. She might have provided serious competition for Roehm had she been in Ann Arbor. Mrs. Richards, also a widow, was apparently a very resilient woman. In 1870 she was part owner in a shop for ladies that carried millinery, fancy goods, lace, jewelry and hoop skirts. This store burned not just once but twice. Undaunted, Louisa continued her efforts so that within a few years she had expanded her stock sufficiently to be able to refer to her store as "the Best 5 and 10" not just in the village or the county but in the entire country. Her claim was undoubtedly an exaggeration; however, from the list of goods itemized in her advertisement in the 1883 Directory, she was justifiably proud. She carried handkerchiefs, hosiery, Brownware, tinware and miscellaneous household items. Mrs. Richards' business career spanned two decades.

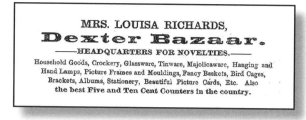

Two women in Ypsilanti also established a notions store which stayed in business for over twenty years. The partnership of Jennie Moore and Eliza Stewart began circa 1885. Jennie's father, Tunis Moore, was a merchant, but Eliza's father, Allen Stewart, was a doctor. Despite their different backgrounds, they formed a partnership that lasted until 1908. Their store located at 29 North Huron was sometimes referred to as Moore and Stewart, Stewart and Moore or the Bazarette. It was a "notions" store. In other words, it carried just small items of clothing, arts and crafts as well as knitting or sewing supplies. As such, it was a store frequented primarily by women. Like so many enterprises, it probably took a while to become profitable which is why Eliza also worked in the post office. By 1905 they moved their store to 106 Congress/Michigan Avenue. At that time, it was Jennie who branched out. While still maintaining the business partnership, she began selling insurance. The two women even lived together in a house purchased by Eliza.

When the partnership between Stewart and Moore ended, Mrs. Emily Keavy became the proprietor of the Bazarette. Her

Interior of the Bazarette.
Courtesy of the Ypsilanti Historical Society

The Bazarette is the building with the peaked cornice.
Courtesy of the Ypsilanti Historical Society

residence was listed at the same address, so she lived above the store. Frances K. Higley also lived there. Higley may or may not have clerked in the store.

The years 1908-1917 were full of change for Eliza Stewart. Jennie Moore dropped out of the picture, and Eliza's sister, Frances, died in 1908. Eliza's other sister, Sarah, who had been living with Frances, moved into Eliza's home at 117 North Huron. Since the Bazarette was no longer an option for Eliza, she opened another store in her home. That seems odd to modern audiences, but it was quite common then. Within another five years, the sisters were aging. Eliza gave up the shop circa 1914. Sarah Stewart, age sixty-five, passed away the following year, and Eliza Stewart, age seventy-one, died in 1917.

Anna Spathelf

Anna Marie Spathelf, a contemporary of the Stewart sisters, began her career clerking at Lodholz' grocery store located at 1000 Broadway in Ann Arbor. The Lodholzes were not strangers to Anna. Her father, George, had lived with the senior Lodholzes when he first arrived from Germany. George Spathelf and Henrica Spathelf Lodholz may have been brother and sister. So it is not surprising that Anna would seek employment in their store, which by then was operated by their son, William Lodholz. Nor is it surprising that neither George Spathelf Jr. nor Anna Spathelf chose to follow in their father's footsteps as a carpet weaver. The day for that had passed. (Chapter 2) George opened a meat store in 1890 in the Huron Block on Broadway. Circa 1907 when she was twenty-seven, Anna took over the Lodholz' business where she continued to sell provisions, notions, staple and fancy goods. Meanwhile, the Spathelf siblings experienced several tragedies. First their father passed away in 1903. Then less than a year later both Anna's nephew and her sister-in-law, Ida, died. As a result, the family recombined into one household which was beneficial not only to her widowed mother but to her two young nieces, Ida and Rena. Anna never married; she continued to living with her brother, George, for the rest of her life. George eventually abandoned the meat market in favor of real estate, but Anna continued to operate her store. George died in January 1931. Only three weeks later, Anna was hit by a car while walking home from church. She also died. Thus a store that had been been managed by three generations of women in the same family: Henrica Spathelf Lodholz, Mary Moses Lodholz and Anna Spathelf, closed.

Most of the women who owned and operated stores, like Anna Spathelf, came from working class backgrounds. That was definitely not true of Almira F. Lovell who began her own retail establishment at 332 S. State Street in 1895. Her middle initial made it easy to find her in census records. The irony is that she apparently had no middle name. She used an "F" to distinguish herself from the aunt after whom she was named. She claimed the "F" meant nothing. I find that hard to believe. With twenty-five other letters from which to choose, something must have led her to selecting that particular letter. I suspect she may have chosen it because she came from Flint, Michigan. Almira was the daughter of Henry R. and Mary Lovell. Mr. Lovell was a judge for the Probate Court in his county. After earning her bachelor's degree from the University of Michigan, Almira worked for seven years as a clerk for the Probate Court in Flint.

She and her sisters were dynamic, curious and active women. Her sister, Hellen/Helen graduated from the University of Michigan in 1887. She became a professor of Greek at Hardin College in Missouri and established a translation bureau in Kansas City, Missouri. Helen was the only one of the sisters who married. Almira's other sister, Harriet, also attended the University of Michigan. After graduation, she taught physics for a year, and then went to Turkey as a teacher and missionary. She died in Turkey in 1894. Almira's path through life was equally diverse and productive.

When she purchased the store on State Street, she focused at first on dressmaker's materials and fancy goods because that is what the previous owner, Miss Walton, sold. Then she began to diversify. In 1904 she added a tea room. The next year her entrepreneurship expanded again when she became an agent for Peters Dry Cleaning. Her most unique and successful effort, however, occurred when she took advantage of her location so near the university to begin designing and selling college souvenirs. Beginning with twelve designs, Miss Lovell quickly increased to a hundred dif-

Postcard view of State Street in Ann Arbor.
Courtesy of the Bentley Historical Library, University of Michigan

ferent items. One of her first was a calendar with various views around the campus. As a sideline, she even offered china-painting lessons. Despite the success of these endeavors, circa 1910 Miss Lovell closed her various enterprises and moved to the east coast where she put to use her practical business skills versus her knowledge of classical languages and literature to teach at a business school in New London, Connecticut. By 1932 she was dean of that school.

These women and many others owned and operated their own stores. They were at the door or behind the counter receiving customers on a daily basis. The county also had a few women who owned stores but did not manage them. Mrs. Hannah Higgins, nee Costello (pronounced Cos' tello), went into business but far afield of the traditional fancy goods or dry goods so popular with other lady retailers. Her company not only provided furniture, boots and groceries (fish was a specialty) but also offered undertaking services. By the end of the century, advertisements offered an iron bed for $3.25; a solid oak table, $1.50; overalls, 35 cents, and sardines in oil for five cents. Hannah, no doubt, bought this store because it had been previously owned by her paternal uncle, John Costello. In fact, a descendant suggested in his account of the family that her parents also may have been involved in the original company which began circa 1869. It is plausible that by 1879, the Costellos had run into financial trouble, and Mrs. Higgins had the financial resources to continue the business. A notice in the July 4, 1879, *Dexter Leader* clearly states that she had "bought out the stock of furniture and undertaking goods" of "the late firm of Costello and Co." It continues by saying that she will continue the store in the same place on the south side of Main Street with her uncle, John Costello, there to "act as my agent in managing the business." The year following her purchase of the store, Mrs. Higgins added the Dexter Flour Mill to her growing list of businesses. It, too, had once been partially owned by John Costello. Descendant Sheldon Higgins claims that a "new flour processing [procedure] from Minnesota ultimately ruined business." He also remembered Mrs. Higgins owning a rental house. Clearly she was an astute woman who found productive ways to invest her money. Hannah passed away in Dexter in February, 1910, at the age of sixty-three. Her son, George, a trained undertaker, who had been operating the business, closed it and moved to Lansing in July, 1910, presumably due to health issues.

In similar fashion, Helen L. Dodge and her son, Fred, bought a store on Main Street in Whitmore Lake from Alvin and Harriet Stiles in 1888. Here, too, it would appear Mrs. Dodge left the day-to-day details to her son who managed the store for three years until he and his wife moved to Fergus, Michigan, to open their own store. At that time, shortly after their marriage, Henry and Almira Pray Dodge took over management of the Whitmore Lake store (Chapter Four). Henry was Helen Dodge's twenty-one year old younger son who had just graduated from Cleary Business College. His bride, Almira, had attended Ann Arbor High School where she may have studied business. Both Henry and Almira were actively involved in the store. As the years went by, however, it was Almira became the primary retailer. The couple continued operating the store until shortly after her death in 1903.

Not everyone could open their own stores; however, it obvious to anyone scanning the local directories or censuses that clerking in retail establishments was a very popular way for a young woman to earn a living even though being a saleswoman in a store did not make the "top ten" list of occupations in the national census until 1910. Even then it came in last place. But women were involved as clerks in stores throughout the century.

One of the earliest notations of a woman clerk in a store in Washtenaw County is Miss Mary E. Parker. Miss Parker, was one of six children. She no doubt took this job to help her family pay its bills. Her widowed mother operated a boarding house. Miss Parker began clerking for Yost, Tisdale and Co. in Ypsilanti in 1860. She was twenty-five. The store where Mary worked sold dry goods and millinery. It also offered "made to order clothing." In the early 1870's many women, like Mary Parker, began to seek employment in "appropriate" retail businesses. One might wonder what constituted an "appropriate" business. Some worked for other women who had proven themselves successful in owning and operating retail stores. Usually these stores provided "lady-like" goods and were patronized primarily by a feminine clientele. Other young women worked in family-owned businesses. In Ann Arbor, Emily Schairer clerked at Daniel Schairer's dry goods store on Main Street in 1883 while Fannie Stimson was working at J.D. Stimson's groceries and crockery. Josephine Higgins clerked in her mother's store in Dexter as did her sister Johanna while Allie Bortle did the same in Saline for J. H. Bortle. Working within a family-run business provided not only spending money but excellent training.

Ethan E. Trim came to Ypsilanti in 1890 and established his boot and shoe store at 204 Congress. He is pictured here outside his new store with his sister, Nellie. She continued to work at Trim and Co. for at least a decade.

Courtesy of the Ypsilanti Historical Society

Even if a young woman worked outside the family and for a male proprietor, some stores were considered more "appropriate" than others. This judgment clearly was based in part on how the business dealt with female employees. The higher the standards, the more appropriate the employment. Many retail stores had very high expectations for employees. They wanted their employees to be refined. Before she married, Milo Ryan's mother, Sue Pulcipher, worked at Schairer and Millen in Ann Arbor as a clerk under head clerk, Lizzie Diehl. Miss Pulchipher had attended Ann Arbor High School for two years and worked in several offices before finding her niche at Schairer and Millen. There Mr. Millen treated each female clerk like a member of the family "provided she behaved herself and in public maintained the poise of a young lady of quality" [37] As honorary members of the family, former clerks such as Milo Ryan's mother were not only granted a lifetime discount at the store but greater respect while they were employed.

A few women ranged farther afield. They found jobs as clerks in offices rather than retail establishments. In 1883, Miss Emma Hawkins was working as deputy registrar of deeds in Ann Arbor. Carrrie Daw clerked at the *Saline Observer* office in 1892. Jessie Graham in 1894 was an agent for the American Pacific Express. But it was Maude Carpenter who turned her clerking job into a lifetime career. Maude was born in Northfield in 1854. She began her career as a substitute postal clerk in Ypsilanti under H. D. Wells; however, when the post office was moved to its Michigan Avenue location (now a branch of the Ypsilanti Public Library), she became the full time money order clerk. Money orders were an important financial service provided at that time by the U. S. Post Office. When she began, she issued an average of twelve per day. By the time she retired she had several assistants and was issuing hundreds of money orders per day. As Miss Carpenter headed towards retirement, the Ypsilanti Post Office declared that it had issued a million money orders in its history, and she had handled most of them. Maude Carpenter died in 1904.

These outgoing and often successful business women of the last quarter of the nineteenth century give the impression that the powerful Cult of True Womanhood had diminished by that time. Nothing could be further from the truth. The term "working woman" was still an oxymoron to many people. It not only was a contradiction of terms, but it prohibited any working woman from being considered "a lady." Yet the vicissitudes of fortune often left destitute women who previously had been wealthy ladies. They found themselves trapped by the Cult of Womanhood. They could not go out to work; therefore, they could not earn money to support themselves. To the rescue came a concept that emerged in Philadelphia in the 1830's. A group of wealthy women, empathizing with their downfallen peers, organized the first Woman's Exchange, then called the Depository, where consignors could bring fancy goods they made to be sold. The creator of that fancy work could, in this way, remain anonymous. In fact, the heavily veiled consignors often arrived at night at the back door. Even the group's records have not preserved their names. In this way the genteel poor could become somewhat self reliant yet never lose face by joining the working class.

The Depository remained in business for decades without much expansion. It was the 1876 Philadelphia Centennial Exhibition that provided the tipping point. Candace Wheeler and Mary Choate, inspired by what they saw there, established the New York Woman's Exchange which became an overnight success story imitated in cities throughout the United States. Despite jokes in the press about dimwitted husbands hoping to exchange their wives for better women, soon 16,000 consignors were bringing goods to various Exchanges for sale. This new version of the Depository concept expanded its vision to include just about anything a woman could make or grow. Certainly the decorative arts remained its primary focus. This was a real moneymaker since the Victorian style became a baroque abundance of decoration. Simultaneously hand-made goods gained value in a time of increasing production of ready-made products by factories. By 1891 there were sixty-six Exchanges in the country earning $400,000 for their consignees. One woman made a thousand dollars a year making pies. One thousand dollars at that time was slightly less than the salary of an assistant-professor at the University of Michigan. A woman who painted screens earned $1300 which would have exceeded the hypothetical professor's salary. This was not charity; this was an inspired compromise between individual needs and social constraints.

Not only did the Exchanges provide opportunities for consignees, but they also expanded the experiences of the affluent women who formed their philanthropic backbone. These women managed the financial details of operation. They bought buildings and put into use all the marketing tricks found in the exclusive emporiums where they, themselves, shopped. The original Philadelphia group set the tone by placing the first exchange in the middle of the most fashionable shopping area and just a few blocks from the offices of *Godey's Lady's Book*, which, of course, dictated the styles sold in the surrounding stores. They wanted to emphasize that this was a classy business – not charity. This was not like today's thrift stores. It was more like an elegant import shop or art gallery. There was, however, one job these socially conservative women would not do and that was to actually be seen working in the store itself. That would dispel, in their minds, the fragile balance between philanthropic work, which they considered appropriate for ladies, and wage-earning work. Instead they hired women who had no such compunctions, and they paid them well. One record indicates that a female Exchange agent was earning $234 per year at a time when a male working in a retail establishment would average $250. Neither salary was princely; however, it does demonstrate that Exchange salaries were on par with the marketplace.

In 1889 a Woman's Exchange opened in Detroit. That may seem pretty far from Washtenaw County, but it really was not. With the availability of trains and the interurban trolleys, the journey took less than two hours each way. That might make it difficult for local women to transport large quantities of goods, but it would still be available for fancy work. A woman also might be able to arrange transportation for her goods through a male relative. The very nature of the Woman's Exchange maintained, above all, these women's privacy, so we are left with only speculation, but it was a possibility which serves to remind us that, even as the worlds of business and the professions appeared to be opening their doors to women, there remained a prevalent attitude among conservatives that "real" ladies did not work outside the home. Such conservatives were undoubtedly scandalized when newly widowed, Elizabeth "Libbie" Custer, wife of George Armstrong Custer and a native of Monroe, Michigan, exclaimed at an organizational meeting for the New York Woman's Exchange, "Why, we are all working women, not a lady among us." [38]

In Dexter, Mrs. Flora Smith and Mrs. Minnie Snyder opened their own version of a Woman's Exchange in 1910. They included this exchange in their Entertainment and Favor Shop in the Rehm Building. Theirs was not part of the national group of exchanges, like the one in Detroit though it handled similar products on consignment: needlework, art, paper dolls, and dressed dolls. Mrs. Smith and Mrs. Snyder advertised that they would accept "anything salable." That included baked goods, but those were considered only on Wednesdays and Saturdays. What made their exchange quite different from those in the national group was that Mrs. Smith and Mrs. Snyder actually operated theirs themselves, thus making them wage-earning women, not philanthropic ladies.

Mrs. Snyder, nee Wheeler, was married to a farmer named Gardner. She had one daughter. Little else is known about her except that she died in 1913 at the age of fifty-five. Flora Bostwick Smith, however, became quite well-known in Dexter. The Exchange and Shop were just a starting point. Mrs. Smith's husband, James, whom she married in 1901, operated a grist mill with his father. They had two sons. Her local fame comes from the fact that she not only served as the Dexter Village librarian, the Village notary, and the Village treasurer but as the unofficial Village historian. Her weekly column in the *Dexter Leader* called "Then and Now" continued for years. Apparently her descendants still have more than a hundred scrapbooks in which she collected local historical information before her death in 1945. She spent all but one of her sixty-seven years in Dexter.

In addition to retail sales, any quick survey of the city directories of the post Civil War period will indicate clearly that one of the most prominent industries of the time was insurance. Insurance, especially in case of fire, was extremely popular as urban areas expanded. Since most buildings were made of wood, any fire would spread quickly to surrounding buildings. Life insurance was also popular to protect women against the very need which drove some widows to Women's Exchanges. Insurance opened opportunities for women as well as men. Frances Willard in her 1897 book, *Occupations for Women*, stated that "Nearly all the prominent life insurance companies now have a woman's department." [39] She also encouraged women to consider insurance sales by telling her readers about two Vassar College graduates who sold insurance and had recently been listed in a periodical as the top female wage earners.

Ypsilanti Commercial October 23, 1888

Courtesy of the Ypsilanti Historical Society

In Ypsilanti Mrs. Julia Edwards Sherman sold insurance. Her father, David Edwards, had come to Ypsilanti from Vermont via Massachusetts in 1840 and was elected mayor twice. Julia was born in Ypsilanti in 1845. She and her husband, George, as so many did, began their married life at Follett Hotel. They had one son also named George. He was born 1866. She operated her insurance sales office from her private residence at 316 Cross Street approximately ten years before her husband's death circa 1894 and ended the working portion of her life circa 1900.

Mrs. Sherman's slightly younger contemporary, Mary L. Hamilton also sold insurance. Born in 1854, Mary was one of the eight children of Warren and Anna Hamilton. Mr. Hamilton originally farmed in Salem Township, but in 1868 the family moved to Ann Arbor where he became an agent for the Mutual Fire Insurance Company. Mary was educated in Salem Township schools and then at Ann Arbor High School. She may have worked briefly as a domestic circa

1883; however by 1886, nine years after her father's death, she was employed as a book-keeper for her older brother, Alexander W. Hamilton, whose law office also handled insurance, real estate and loans. Just to confuse matters, he married a woman also named Mary. The 1880 census enumerator noted Mrs. Mary E. Hamilton as "boarding." More accurately, they took in boarders.

Within a few years, Alexander's sister, Miss Mary L. Hamilton was so thoroughly apprenticed in the trade that in 1895, at the age of forty-one, she began her own business in the Henning Block in Ann Arbor (201-211 E Huron) representing various fire and life insurance companies whose policies covered "many thousands of dollars." Miss Hamilton also "negotiated many important realty transfers" and demonstrated a "wide knowledge of property values."[40] She never married and always lived in the large family home at 219 Thayer Street. After her mother's death in 1897, Mary became head of the household and appears to have taken in lodgers. Many years later she and her brother were living out their last years together in that house. In 1930 he was eighty-two, and she was seventy-five.

The second half of the nineteenth century sent mixed messages to and about women. On the one hand, more and more women were taking advantage of opportunities to work outside the home and obtain, as Susan B Anthony, called it, "a purse of their own." Traditional sources of income such as operating boarding houses expanded to include hotels and restaurants. Women ran their own stores and clerked in ones owned by others. Though most women concentrated their efforts in stores selling items preferred by women, their clientele was not exclusively female. Insurance sales and university souvenirs would have been products appropriate for both genders. Conservative social elements continued to preach about the proper female sphere and the cults of True Womanhood and Leisure, but they were ignored by thousands of women who were active in the world of business.

[1] O. W. Stephenson, *Ann Arbor: The First Hundred Years* (Ann Arbor: Ann Arbor Chamber of Commerce, 1927), 202.

[2] Wendy Gamber, *The Boardinghouse in Nineteenth Century America* (Baltimore: Johns Hopkins University Press), 2007, 47.

[3] *History of Washtenaw County, Michigan* (Chicago: Charles C. Chapman Co., 1881), 726-7.

[4] A.D.P. Van Buren "Pioneer Annals" in *Michigan Pioneer and Historical Collection*, Vol 5 (Lansing, MI: W.S. George and Co., State Printers and Binders, 1884), 241.

[5] *Saline Observer*, September 18, 1890

[6] Gamber, 7.

[7] Emily Faithfull, *Three Visits to America* (Edinburgh: David Douglas, 1884), 323.

[8] Gamber, 3.

[9] "Lucy Ann Smith Papers," at Bentley Historical Library, University of Michigan.

Lucy Ann is Mrs. Morton Smith and her daughter, called Jennie, married into the Keal family.

[10] "Sara Jane Norton Diary," March 30, 1864 in "Austin Norton Collection," at Ypsilanti Archives, Ypsilanti, MI.

[11] Gamber, 32.

[12] Emily Hollister, *Emily Hollister Diary* in "Edward Teall Hollister Collection" at Bentley Historical Library, (University of Michigan), 5.

[13] "Regents' Proceedings," 1853, at Bentley Historical Library, University of Michigan, 12.

[14] "Regents," 1857, 646.

[15] Russell Bidlack, "Andrew Ten Brook, Forgotten Figure in Ann Arbor History," *Impressions* (Ann Arbor: Washtenaw County Historical Society, November/December 1981), 4.

[16] Susan Strasser, *Never Done: A History of American Housework* (New York: Pantheon, 1982), 148.

[17] Attaway and Barritt ed., *Women's Voices: Early Years at University of Michigan* (Ann Arbor, Bentley Historical Library, 2000), 91.

[18] Elizabeth Farrand, *History of the University of Michigan* (Ann Arbor: Register Publishing House, 1885), 202-3.

[19] Ruth Bordin, *Alice Freeman Palmer: Evolution of a New Woman* (Ann Arbor: University of Michigan Press, 1993), 42.

[20] Barbara Sicherman, *Alice Hamilton: A Life in Letters* (Cambridge MA: Harvard University Press, 1984), 37.

[21] Laurence Goldstein, ed., *Writing Ann Arbor* (Ann Arbor: University of Michigan Press, 2005), 54.

[22] Attaway, 91.

[23] Attaway, 92

[24] Attaway, 92.

[25] Attaway, 92

[26] Milo Ryan, *View of a Universe* (Ann Arbor, MI: McNaughton and Gunn, 1985), 180.

[27] "Newspaper Clippings File" at Washtenaw County Historical Society.

[28] *Milan Area Leader*, June 17, 1984.

[29] "County News," *Ann Arbor Courier*, April 25, 1879

[30] Mrs. Hall named a street after her husband; however, it was changed to Cambridge.

[31] Susan B Anthony's October 5, 1877 letter to Olivia B. Hall in "Olivia B Hall Papers" at Bentley Historical Library, University of Michigan.

[32] *History*, 1007.

[33] *History*, 977.

[34] Cynthia Reynolds, *Our Hometown* (Chelsea MI: Sleeping Bear Press, 2001), 51.

[35] Penny, Virginia, *The Employment of Women* (Boston: Walker, Wise and Co.), 1863. 140.

[36] J. P. Johnston, *Twenty Years of Hus'ling* (Chicago: Thompson and Thomas, 1887), 53.

[37] Ryan, 37.

[38] Kathleen W. Sander, *The Business of Charity: The Woman's Exchange Movement 1832-1900* (Urbana, IL: University of Illinois Press, 1998), 1.

[39] Willard, Frances E., *Occupations for Women* (New York: The Success Co., 1897), 165.

[40] Beakes, 367

CHAPTER ELEVEN: COMMUNICATION AND POLITICS

The nineteenth century, especially the late nineteenth century, witnessed an explosion in communication technology comparable in its impact to that of the internet on the late twentieth century. When the nineteeth century began, a letter might take weeks to arrive with news. Newspapers existed but were not as ubiquitous as they would become in the Jacksonian era and later. Books and pamphlets were printed in the United States, but books were especially costly. The concept of immediate contact with another person would have seemed, in the early nineteenth century, as impossible as landing a man on the moon. Technology such as the telegraph let alone the telephone, were the stuff of science fiction. Only some fanciful person like Jules Verne could imagine such things. But as the United States continued its spread from the Atlantic to the Pacific evolving into a wealthy industrial nation, it needed and acquired improved methods of communication.

The introduction of first the telegraph and later the telephone opened entirely new sectors of employment opportunities for women. Visitors to the United States commented admiringly on these advances. "The girls employed as 'telegraphists and telephonists [sic]," wrote Miss Emily Faithful in *Three Visits to America*, "have plenty to do in America" [1] Samuel Morse began this communication revolution in 1844 by stringing a telegraph wire from Washington D.C. to Baltimore, a distance of thirty-four miles. Soon, telegraph lines spread throughout the United States. The supply of skilled operators, however, lagged behind. The nation's first female telegraph operator, Sarah Bagley, slipped into the field almost serendipitously. She learned the skill from the previous operator who happened to board with her family. Miss Bagley's career began in 1846 in Lowell, Massachusetts. But the industry could neither wait for nor depend upon such impromptu training to occur, so schools such as the Cooper Institute in New York began to appear. And, since telegraphy was intricately involved in railroad efficiency, railroad companies, such as the Baltimore and Ohio, started their own training centers. There was particular demand for operators during the Civil War when battles could be won or lost depending upon efficient communication. Telegraph operators were vital at the very time the army was siphoning off males to fight in the war. A few women even served in the Military Telegraph Corps. Whether employed by the private sector or the military, the decades preceding and including the Civil War offered opportunities for female employment as telegraphers.

As so often happens after a war, Civil War veterans wished to displace the female workers. Male workers formed the National Telegraphic Union in 1863 excluding females as members. That sparked a heated debate over women's role in the telegraph office. There were the usual petty insults and allegations concerning women's incompetence and unprofessionalism. One man, who signed his name T.A., probably hit the nail on the head when he wrote to the trade's magazine, *The Telegrapher*, admitting that the real crux of the problem was that the men felt they needed the jobs more than the women did. Despite male resentment, by 1870, 355 women were employed in telegraphy throughout the United States. But those 355 comprised only 5% of a total number, 7961, and only forty-five of those 355 women worked in the Midwest.

Female telegraphers of that era dealt with danger as well as resentment. The danger did not come from the men but from the hazards of the job itself. Long, sedentary hours in poorly ventilated rooms weakened their health. They were especially vulnerable to tuberculosis. At least one woman incurred serious burns when lightning hit the wires, traveled to the "key" and connected with her metal corset stays. While such an occurrence appears rare, operators both male and female definitely developed what they called "glass arm." Today's computer users experience the same problem. We know it as carpal tunnel syndrome. Arm braces to protect operators began to appear in trade magazines just as arm rests and supports are familiar at modern keyboards.

The final problem women experienced was in the nature of compensation. As with office workers, the job was better than some, but it still paid wages lower than those given to males. Reduced remuneration for female workers was common from the very beginning of the industry. As early as 1849, John Speed who built the Erie and Michigan Telegraph line wrote to Ezra Cornell, one of Samuel Morse's early associates, saying that he was hiring women who were "abundantly qualified to do the business better than any boy or man that we can afford to pay in those places." Despite the lower pay scale, telegraph offices continued to attract women. Phoebe Atwood, an operator in Albion, Michigan, was sufficiently pleased with her salary to become upset with any woman who would choose the drudgery of sewing when she could earn more as a telegraph operator. By the time telegraph communications peaked at the turn of the century, thousands of women earned their living in the field. According to the 1890 Census, 8,411 Caucasian and sixty-three African-American women were telegraph operators. Virtually all of those were native born Americans. Despite this trend and the availability of local training opportunities, the job did not seem to attract women in Washtenaw County, though there was at least one: Miss Sarah A. Weir who worked at the American Telegraph Office in Ypsilanti in the late 1870's.

It was the telephone that spelled the end of the telegraph era. Even though it paid approximately twenty percent less than the wages paid a skilled telegrapher, significant numbers of women entered the field. Ann Arbor was on the cutting edge. Not only was it the first location in Washtenaw County to acquire telephone service, but it was less than three years behind the very first service in the nation, which began in Boston in 1878. True, Boston could command subscriptions from sixty individuals or businesses while the Ann Arbor system began more humbly in January of 1881 with only twenty-five subscribers. It utilized the third floor of Reinhardt's store at #42 S. Main Street for a switching station despite the building owner's worries about it being a possible fire hazard. In those formative years, telephones often linked only two locations. For example it might provide communication between a business and the owner's home as it did for Mr. Cornwell. It was not until the number of phones in a community increased that the job of exchange operator developed. Even then in the beginning, there were so few subscribers that no numbers were necessary; one simply gave the operator a name. She, by plugging an electrical cord into the familiar switchboard, connected the caller to the recipient. By 1883, however, ninety-six homes and businesses in Ann Arbor had subscribed. The fee per year for such modern communications was $36 for a residences and $48 for businesses. Photographer Jefferson Gibson obviously felt it was well worth the money. His advertisement in the 1883 City Directory specifically notified potential customers that he had "Telephone Service."

Ypsilanti's telephone service followed in the summer of 1881. Service there was so novel an idea that in order to stimulate subscriptions, the *Ypsilanti Commercial* in its May twelfth issue actually listed the potential uses for a telephone: call a doctor, check arrival times of a trains, order groceries, be awakened in the morning and, of course, converse with friends. Such efforts must have worked because Ypsilanti's first office, located in the Ypsilanti Paper Company's building, served sixty subscribers.

> Dozens of companies offered telephone service in the nineteenth century. Michigan Telephone Company, located in Ann Arbor was one of the most successful of those companies. In an 1898 advertisement, the company boasted that it had 16,000 subscribers and serviced 600 cities in Michigan as well as 10,000 cities nationwide with a total of 60,000 subscribers.

Virtually all telephone operators were women. At first, companies hired men such as Harry Neat of Ypsilanti (1881) as operators, but according to Caroline Bird in *Born Female*, "They [the men] did not do well and were soon replaced by girls," like Mr. Neat's co-worker Nellie Parlor. "Confined, disciplined personal services did not attract American men..." [2] Not only were virtually all operators women, ninety percent were single women under the age of twenty. That description fit quite a few Washtenaw County girls. The use of the word, "girl," is not a derogatory label but an indication of just how young some of the early operators were.

Eva Case

Courtesy of Karen L. Jenter

One of the earliest examples of such a girl is Eva May Case. She was born in Manchester and attended school there; however, in the spring of 1883 at age fourteen, she left high school to become the operator for the Manchester Telephone Exchange. At that time, the exchange was located in the *Manchester Enterprise* office. Though Eva looks quite mature in this photograph, she was only sixteen when it was taken. Soon after, she and her family moved to Jackson, Michigan. There she became the society reporter for the *Jackson Citizen Patriot* until February of 1892 when she became ill at work. She was taken to the home of Dr. W.F. Mills where she died. She was twenty-three years old.

The year Eva Case died, Maggie Sharpe was working at the Ypsilanti Telephone Office. She probably also operated telegraph lines since she consistently listed herself as a telegraph and telephone operator. Soon after the picture to the right was taken in 1892, she moved to Ann Arbor. There, a slightly more experienced and sophisticated Maggie used her full name, Margaret E. Sharpe, but continued as an operator for several more years.

About a decade after Maggie Sharpe, Adena Lehman (Holmes) became a telephone operator in Manchester. Adena, or Deanie as she liked to be called, was the oldest child of Frederick and Frederika Lehman. Her father died in 1894. She was only six, and her mother was pregnant with her sister. There is no record of how Mrs. Lehman managed to support her family after she was wid-

Margaret "Maggie" Sharpe
Courtesy of the Ypsilanti Historical Society

owed. Despite the family's hardships, Deanie received eight years of schooling in Manchester followed by two years at the local German School. Circa 1904, she began her job with the Manchester Telephone Exchange. She would have been about sixteen at the time. Similar to Eva Case, Deanie and her family obviously needed the income she could earn. Deanie appears to have continued working at the telephone exchange until she married in 1914. The marriage ended in divorce in the early 1930's. At that time Deanie did not return as a telephone operator. She worked for Mary Kern who owned a tavern in Manchester.

Adena "Deanie" Lehman
Courtesy of Karen Jenter

Slightly northeast of Manchester lies Dexter, Michigan. It was home to Miss Minnie Daley who probably deserves recognition for three reasons. First is because she was significantly older that the girls previously discussed which made her unusual. Born in 1876, Miss Daley lived her entire life in the family home on Forest Street often with several of her siblings. In 1906 she succeeded Viola Stockford as manager of the Michigan Bell telephone exchange. The second thing that makes Daley significant is that she occupied her position for such a long time. She continued in that capacity for thirty-four years. It truly was a lifelong career. The final importance associated with Miss Daley's career is that it marked the end of opportunities in her field. Not only her job but those of thousands of women became obsolete with the innovation of electronic dialing.

Telegraph and telephone, however, are not the only methods of communication. Dozens of women in the Washtenaw County worked in the printing business. The existence of female printers dates back at least to the early eighteenth century. In fact, Benjamin Franklin learned the printer's craft from his older brother's widow, Ann Smith Franklin. When she died in 1735, he repaid the favor by training her son, James. Similarly Elizabeth Timothy of Charleston was a well known publisher and editor. It was Benjamin Franklin who sponsored her and her husband when they began their printing business in South Carolina. Unlike so many married men who worked with their wives, Mr. Timothy always acknowledged his wife as a full partner. After the American Revolution and by then widowed, she became the "state printer" for South Carolina for seventeen years. Despite having large families needing care, both Ana Franklin and Elizabeth Timothy clearly had worked in the business long before losing their husbands.

In addition bookbinding, a subset of the printer's craft, had been a job available to women throughout the nineteenth century. It was one of the few occupations cited by Harriet Martineau in her 1836 *Society in America* as being open to American women. According to Martineau, "Women are employed in printing offices as compositors as well as folders and stitchers." [3] Until automation hit the industry, occupations such as paper folder were recognized trades. Books were printed on large sheets of paper which were then carefully folded into pages which the stitcher would then sew together. For a long time those pages were not cut so the reader had to have a tool, like a letter opener, to cut apart the pages. This left a slightly ragged edge rather that the clean cut edges of modern books. Some facet of the bookbinding process was the way Dr. Helen McAndrew of Ypsilanti earned her living both before her marriage and during her medical training in the 1850's. In Ann Arbor bookbinding became an occupation that appealed to quite a few women. As early as 1860 Margaret McMahon, a nineteen-year-old immigrant from Ireland, worked as a paper folder. Miss Julia Stocking was a book folder in Ann Arbor in 1872. Miss Stocking lived with her mother who probably was a widow. Another Julia, though this time with the last name Traver, worked as a book folder two years later while Lucy Steiner listed herself generically as a book binder in 1878. By the 1880's and '90's there were several publishing companies in the county: Sid W. Millard and David Fisher plus two newspapers: the *Ann Arbor Register* and the *Ann Arbor Courier*. All were hiring women as not only bookbinders but as printers and press feeders.

Even newspapers that did not expand into book publishing provided job opportunities for women. Newspapers have been an important part of Washtenaw County since the early days of settlement. Harriet Martineau related that, when she traveled from Detroit to Chicago in 1835, she bought an Ann Arbor newspaper. She commented, "It could happen nowhere out of America that so raw a settlement as that at Ann Arbor, where there is difficulty in procuring decent accommodations, should have a newspaper" even one as "badly printed" as the one she purchased. Her brutally honest comments were, in a way, a backhanded compliment. That there should even be a newspaper is a testament to the spirit of the pioneers and the need for communication. One wonders if Miss Martineau realized that Washtenaw County's first newspaper, *The Western Emigrant*, had begun only six years after the very first settlers arrived in the county. At the time she was reading the paper she described, she could have been reading the *Argus* or the *State Journal*, which had replaced the *Emigrant*. By the latter part of the century, every community had its own newspaper, and those papers were hiring women. *The Chelsea Standard*, *The Chelsea Herald*, *The Saline Standard* and *The Ypsilanti Sentinel* hired Nettie Hoover, Maude Freer, Carrie Davenport and Grace Quackenbush, respectively, as printers. The word, "printer," however, does not convey exactly what it was that these women did. Other women of the time such as Mattie Barnum at the *Ypsilanti Commercial* referred to herself as a compositor while Nina Davison said she was a typograph operator. All of these women probably worked as typesetters. Others such as Sara Giles at the *Courier* were press feeders as was Emily Hayley

The experience of Margaret Blosser in Manchester is a perfect example of women such as these. Margaret's father, Mat Blosser, bought *The Manchester Enterprise* circa 1867. Not only did the whole family help by folding the papers on publication day, Margaret learned to set type when she was only twelve. At that time, type was set by hand. Each letter had to be added individually. It was painstaking work despite the amazing swiftness of skilled typesetters. The invention in 1884 of the linotype machine, a keyboard-operated mechanism, made the process more efficient and suitable for young women with typewriting skills. Whether Margaret ever used such a machine when she joined the *Enterprise* staff after graduating from high school, isn't known. Margaret worked as a compositor for the paper until she married B. Fred Burtless in 1900. They moved out of the county, but later in her life, Margaret returned to finish her life in Manchester.

Margaret Blosser and her father.

Courtesy of the Bentley Historical Library, University of Michigan

Lucille Johnson (DeRyke) of Milan also assisted her father, LeRoy Johnson at the *Milan Leader* which she later edited herself. They utilized a linotype machine which an uncited newspaper article at the Dexter museum described as a "gawky-looking machine about the size of a baby grand piano that sounds like some 19th century slot machine as it shudders, clinks clanks and carts words into molten metal one line at a time." These bulky machines dominated the newspaper industry until the 1960's when it transitioned to a photo chemical process.

Lucille Johnson with her father.

Courtesy of the Milan Historical Library

Women's efforts were not limited to menial tasks such as typesetting; women also wrote, edited and even owned newspapers and magazines. Journalism, however, was a tough field for women to enter because of the need for reporters to go anyplace at anytime for a story. Such a lifestyle was considered inappropriate and even dangerous for a woman. As journalist Kate Field said, "In [daily] journalism a woman's sex is her misfortune, and nothing but undaunted pluck can obtain for her what is within easy reach of less able men..." [5] Field continued, however, saying that women could succeed more easily as correspondents. Marna Osband, daughter of William and Lucy Osband, was a correspondent covering the 1893 Chicago World Fair for her father's paper.

There appears to have been a fine line between the more acceptable role as a "correspondent" and the job of a reporter. Unlike a reporter, a female correspondent seems to have chosen where and when, but the line between the two is blurry. Kate Field, herself, was a correspondent as was Elizabeth Jane Cochran. Miss Cochran is better known by her pseudonym, Nellie Bly (1864-1922). Miss Cochran achieved her fame (some would say notoriety) primarily due to two feats. One was the result of Jules Verne's book, *Around the World in Eighty Days*. Could it really be done? The answer was an unqualified, "yes." Cochran actually made it in only seventy-two days. Her second and more serious adventure occurred when she pretended to be insane in order to write an expose of mental institutions. She was "committed" to the Women's Lunatic Asylum on Blackwell's Island which turned out to be worse than she ever expectated, but it was fodder for her famous *Ten Days in a Mad-House*. Next to that, Marna's accounts of the fair in Chicago seem mild indeed, but they were doing basically the same job.

Two years later, Marna graduated at age twenty-five from the University of Michigan with a degree in literature. She then did a year of graduate work. But she had been working as the assistant editor at her father's newspaper, the *Ypsilantian*, since he purchased it in 1888. In the 1890's the *Ypsilantian* was an eight-page weekly, costing $1.50 per year. An advertisement in the city directory asserted, "The *Ypsilantian* discusses fearlessly all live questions, has the best local correspondents, gives all local news, the best writers contribute to its columns and it is the best advertising medium." Mr. Osband clearly believed his paper was "the best," and he was not hesitant to employ women. In addition to his own daughter, Jean McNicol gathered news for his paper. Marna continued her career as a professional journalist for more than half a century.

Miss Field also extolled the opportunities for women as editors. Lois Bryan Adams would be just such a woman. While her marriage and career pulled her away from Washtenaw County, her family was one of the very first to settle near Ypsilanti, and her mother, Sarah, was one of the few women who, despite her myriad labors, kept a diary of that experience. So writing came as a natural outlet for Lois who began circa 1851 by contributing articles to the *Michigan Farmer*. She then became editor of its household department and collection agent for overdue subscriptions. That quickly evolved into her role as a partner and finally the owner. The onset of the Civil War forced her to sell her magazine, but she continued to send the *Detroit News and Advertiser* detailed articles concerning war-related news from Washington, D.C. where she had moved to work in the U.S. Department of Agriculture. Her published opinion of the woman question was, "...if women were earlier taught that they could work with other tools than the needle, the spelling book or the utensils of the kitchen, there would not be half so many helpless ones in the world." [7] That obviously wasn't how Mrs. Adams had been raised in Washtenaw County.

Many times in this book, readers have encountered the name of Mrs. Martha Louise Rayne as author of the best-selling book, *What Can a Woman Do?* Despite being mother of ten children (though only two survived to adulthood), she authored five novels and one other non-fiction work as well as owning and editing a magazine. Mrs. Rayne joined the staff of the *Detroit*

Free Press in the 1870's. These activities alone would have given her a place in history, but she was not content until she opened a school of journalism in 1886. This school, according to the 1910 *Who's Who* was not only the first journalism school in the United States but the first in the world. Mrs. Rayne then opened a second school in Chicago. As a charter member of the Michigan Women's Press Association and the Michigan Women's Press Club, Mrs. Rayne consistently advocated for women in the field of journalism. Her contributions were formally recognized in 1998 when she was inducted into the Michigan Journalism Hall of Fame in East Lansing which awards annually the Martha Rayne Award for outstanding media research. She is also one of a select group to be honored by the Michigan Women's Hall of Fame.

Martha Louise Rayne

It is doubtful that Emma Helber ever studied journalism let alone planned for a future in the newspaper business. She was daughter of Saline's Dr. Helber. She was born in Michigan in 1859 and graduated from Michigan State Normal School in 1878 with a degree in modern languages. She, no doubt, met her future husband, Louis Liesemer, in Saline where he edited the *Saline Standard*. The year after her graduation, 1879, was a very busy one. They married and moved to Ann Arbor where for six months Louis was associated with the *Democrat*. Then the Liesemer's began a paper of their own. Their newspaper, however, was quite different from the other local newspapers because their paper was written in German. This was a shrewd move on their part. At that time nearly half of Ann Arbor's population was of German descent, and one of every nine citizens was German-born. And that was just Ann Arbor. Other newcomers from Germany lived throughout the county. Emma's own father and mother were immigrants. That meant a lot of potential subscribers who would like to read the news in their native language. In this way, the newly married Emma Liesemer started her married life and her professional life at the same time.

Emma's husband possessed practical experience, but his education never went beyond elementary school. She was, according to the 1891 *Portrait and Biographical Album* "a talented and noted writer for various journals, and assisted her husband materially..." [8] Beakes was even more complimentary. He stated that the paper was "a success from the start and was ably edited by Mr. Liesemer's wife, a very talented woman." [9] Even the Chapman publication, usually so reticent concerning women and their accomplishments, gave her much of the credit for the paper's success, referring to Emma as a writer "of more than ordinary ability," [10] Unfortunately

Mrs. Liesemer passed away in 1888. Very probably she died of complications due to childbirth because there is a stone inscribed "Our Baby" next to hers in Forest Hill Cemetery in Ann Arbor. Her husband carried on for awhile, but the paper went through almost annual changes in partnerships after her death.

Emma Bower

In the same year as Emma Liesemer's death, 1888, another Emma assumed leadership of the *Ann Arbor Democrat* following the death of her brother. Emma Bower, Ann Arbor's most well-known newspaper woman, served as owner/editor until 1893, proving, according to Beakes, that "a woman could run a local newspaper as successfully as a man could." [11] Miss Bower was a woman of great energy and ability who influenced both local and state affairs. Her public working life fell into three separate stages. First, she graduated from the University of Michigan's Homeopathic School of Medicine in 1883. She practiced medicine locally for a few years until she forsook that career in order to replace her deceased brother at the *Ann Arbor Democrat.* That comprised her second career. Her third and final occupation was as the Great Record Keeper of the Ladies of the Modern Maccabees, a fraternal and benevolent society organized in 1878. Its primary purpose was to obtain life insurance policies for its members. This was no small undertaking as the group had 86,000 members of which almost one-third lived in Michigan. Miss Bower supervised thirty assistants in her office. She also published the *Lady Maccabee*, which historian Samuel Beakes claimed had "one of the largest circulations of any paper in the state." [12] In her spare time Bower served as president of the Woman's Press Association and Vice President of the International Council of Women. Between 1906 and 1926 her office moved away from Ann Arbor, first to Port Huron and then Detroit. Upon retirement, however, Miss Bower returned to Ann Arbor where she died in 1934. She, too, was buried at Forest Hills Cemetery.

Before she moved to Port Huron, however, Miss Bower organized the Political Equality Club of Ann Arbor. The 1850 Michigan Constitution gave women a legal right to property but not the vote. As a result many residents of Michigan were wealthy women. For example, Mary Grant of Ypsilanti was the widow of Elijah Grant. In the 1860 Census she listed her occupation as keeping house; however, she also indicated to the census enumerator that she had $60,000 in real estate and $30,000 in personal property. An estate of $90,000 in 1860 is the equivalent of almost three million dollars today, yet Mrs. Grant and other wealthy women had no say in the political arena. Bower's group sued the local school system because female property owners were denied their rights as taxpayers to vote in local elections. The Michigan Supreme Court settled the case in 1881 upholding the women's rights. That decision established a statewide precedent which provided a crack in the political system through which women began to gain leverage.

The question of women's political rights had been fermenting throughout the century. Exactly ten years prior to the Michigan Supreme Court's decision, which allowed women to vote in local school elections, Nanette Ellingwood Gardner made Michigan history when she presented herself at the Detroit polls in April of 1871 stating that she was a taxpayer and, citing the Fourteenth Amendment, demanded her right to vote. Mrs. Gardner was a widow with substantial business interests which she personally had managed since the death of her husband. State election officials acquiesced and allowed her to vote. On June 30, 1871, Gardner wrote a letter to Sojourner Truth describing what Gardner claimed was the first ballot. cast by a woman. She did not know that some women actually voted in the eighteenth century. Lydia Taft in

Uxbridge, Massachusetts voted in 1756. And women living in New Jersey between 1776 and 1807 could vote if their property was worth fifty pounds or more. Finally, some cross-dressing women serving as soldiers in the Civil War voted in the 1864 election of Abraham Lincoln. Gardner's ballot does, however, predate that of Susan B. Anthony. Anthony's famous arrest and trial for voting in a national election did not happen until 1872-3. In any case, Nanette Gardner could lay claim to being the first woman in Michigan who voted. In 1881 she moved to Ann Arbor where she lived the remaining nine years of her life.

Mrs. Gardner's move placed her in Ann Arbor when Sara Bishop became the first woman elected to the Ann Arbor School Board in 1883. The following year, Emma Bower and Anna Botsford Bach [13] also joined the Board. Bach became the first female to serve as president while Bower became first treasurer and later, in 1899, president. Miss Bower remained on the Board for nine years until her professional life caused her to move to Port Huron. Similar events happened in Ypsilanti where Jennie Bristol Kinne, wife of Dr. Amasa Kinne, became a Trustee of School District #4 between 1892 and 1908. Originally from Jonesville, Michigan, Jennie married Dr. Kinne in 1862. Serving on a school board, however gratifying for these women, was not a true vocation; rather it was a public service. According to Ellen Bach, Anna's daughter, her mother believed the men on the School Board resented her as a woman serving as president. It surely must not have been easy for any of these pioneering elected officials. Nor was it any easier for women who were appointed to paid political positions.

Anna Botsford Bach

The job of postmaster was a Presidential appointment. The President had the final say, however, men in various political roles especially the Postmaster General lobbied for or against candidates. For example, in 1847 Postmaster General Cave Johnson did not want women filling such an important job. Citizens of Columbus, Ohio, had written to him requesting that a widow assume the position her husband had held. Mr. Johnson replied saying, "...[It]has not been the practice of the Department to appoint females...the duties required of them are many and important and often of a character that ladies could not be expected to perform..." [14] Did Mr. Johnson not realize that Mrs. Ann Gentry had been postmaster in Columbia, Missouri, since 1838 (and would continue until 1876)?

Quite a few women in Washtenaw County also served as postmasters. Local records refer to them as "postmistresses." That apparently isn't the correct term. They were female postmasters. The first was Ruth B. Foster who was appointed in July 1854. She was one of 128 female postmasters throughout the United States at that time. Ruth was the widow of a miller in Scio Village and served until 1860. Virtually all of the early appointees were widows of former postmasters. Their husbands had been chosen because they usually operated a business considered to be a central location convenient to all. In Scio Village they were millers. Similar to Mrs. Foster, Mrs. Julia A. Owen served as postmasters at Whitmore Lake for five years beginning in 1862. The tradition continued when Rachel Thomas Low of nearby Webster Township gained her position as postmaster circa 1880 when her husband, William, died. She served until 1900 when the Webster post office was discontinued and rural free delivery (RFD) mail began. Harriet Wheeler Bowers of Mooreville also served as postmaster. Her "qualifications" were that her husband, the local doctor cum postmaster, passed away. In nearby Milan, however, something new was happening. The Milan postmaster was an unmarried woman named Nettie Palmer. A few years later, Ella Marsh became postmaster in Saline at a time when the Post Office was located at Uphaus Electric.

Making sure the mail got through was no easy task especially in the early days. John Thompson told how he carried the first mail between Ann Arbor and Jackson along Indian trails. He put the letters in his hat. As transportation improved, so did the mail service between towns. Getting the mail to each individual however, was often more problematic. Lists of unclaimed letters were regularly published in local papers. The *Argus* of July 7, 1836, dedicated two columns to a list of names on unclaimed letters in Pitt (the original name of Pittsfield Township), Scio, Saline, Dexter and Ann Arbor. Though unsaid, the reader can sense the frustration of local postmasters. "Please come get your letter; we are tired of storing it." Or maybe they really wanted to say, "A letter takes weeks to travel from the east coast. The least you could do is to pick it up in that same amount of time." In Saline the Post Office tried to solve the problem of uncollected mail by opening on Sundays so that farmers could pick up their mail when they came to town for church. The idea was practical but highly controversial. It was critical that people claim letters because most early mail was sent COD. Thus the cost of unclaimed letters had to be absorbed. Prepaid stamps solved this glitch in the system, but they were not issued until 1847 and for the next eight years they were optional. After 1855, stamps were required.

Emma Maxfield served as Mrs. Marsh's assistant in Saline while Cora Warren was assistant postmaster in Dexter and May Bodine the assistant in Manchester. I suspect the title of "assistant postmaster" was just a nicer way of saying "clerk." The amount of mail in Washtenaw County steadily increased in the last decade of the century requiring the hiring of clerks, many of whom were women. The earliest female postal clerk appears to have been Amelia Noble who worked in Ann Arbor in 1873. By 1883 all the postal clerks, but one, were women. Two of the female clerks were married; the other two were single. By 1892, however, only Mary Sullivan worked as a sorting clerk at Ann Arbor's post office, which then was located at the corner of Main and Ann Streets. In a similar fashion, Ypsilanti employed two female postal clerks in 1883, but only one in 1892. All of those clerks were single as were the women who worked for village post offices. Lucile Ward of Milan and Flora Helfer of Chelsea worked in their respective post offices circa 1894. Miss Grace Collins served as a full-time assistant in Saline while Miss Myrtie Bordin clerked temporarily during the rush season. Miss Collins was still in the employ of the Post Office in 1905 when the photograph to the left was taken.

Grace Collins

Courtesy of the Saline Historical Society

Frances L. Stewart's career with the postal system is the best documented among the women so employed. Frances was born to a prominent family in Ypsilanti in 1841. Her father was Dr. Allen Stewart. She graduated from Michigan State Normal School in 1861 and taught for a few years since it was required of all Normal School graduates. As with so many women of her era, teaching must not have suited her, for in 1863 she returned from Coldwater to become assistant to the postmaster of Ypsilanti. Miss Stewart continued in that position for twenty years. When the Ypsilanti postmaster, a man named Spencer, resigned in 1883, citizens circulated a petition to have Miss Stewart appointed as his replacement. Twelve leading citizens of the town presented more than 1,200 signatures to U.S. Senator Palmer. The result of that petition was that Stewart was duly appointed by President Arthur.

Frances had two sisters: Eliza and Sarah. None of them ever married. They spent their entire lives in close proximity to each other. For a long time they all lived together in a house at 314 Cross Street which was owned by Frances. Sarah was a painter, but Eliza even worked for Frances during her tenure as Postmaster though Eliza was involved at the same time in a notions store (Chapter 10).

Despite Frances' flawless reputation, her leadership only lasted five years. According to a letter written by her sister, Sarah P. Stewart, "Some of our politicians went and told her frankly that, although they were more than satisfied with her service, they could not afford to give such an office to a woman who could not help [them] in a political way." She was replaced by a Mr. Cremer and demoted to being a clerk, a job from which she quickly resigned.

Frances Stewart

Courtesy of the Ypsilanti Historical Society

Frances Stewart died in 1908, so she (but not her sisters[15]) was spared reading the 1913 *Daily Ypsilantian's* "Special Chautauqua Edition" which denigrated her reputation by saying, "The game of politics was played in a lively fashion in the Eighties...[when] after the politicians had been bluffed by a monster petition [Miss Stewart had been appointed]." The article said nothing of the fine work she had done for so many years during her time at the post office. Her efforts were so exemplary that a postal inspector, who had spent a week in Ypsilanti during her tenure, upon seeing that she had passed away, wrote her sister. He told her how, even decades later, he had a clear recollection of Miss Stewart because of the admirable way she ran her office. She must have made quite an impression to elicit such praise from a virtual stranger after so many years. The Ypsilanti post office's loss was Michigan State Normal School's gain because Miss Stewart became the secretary of the Normal School. At first she was sole manager of the office and keeper of all the records and accounts. Later she acquired assistants. She continued in that capacity until her death and was recognized as "a kind and wise Counselor much loved and always remembered with grateful affections." [16]

Emma Amelia Hall, whose brother and sister lived in Ypsilanti, may have heard about the political machinations Frances Stewart experienced. If she did, she surely sympathized with Miss Stewart. Her own experiences were equally disillusioning. Miss Hall was not a postmaster. She became the first woman in Michigan to receive an appointment as superintendent of a state institution. In that capacity, she discovered, as did Frances Stewart, just how difficult it could be for a woman to enter the political sphere. Born in 1837 to Reuben and Abby Hall in Lenewee County, Michigan, Miss Hall graduated from the Michigan State Normal School in the same graduating class as Frances Stewart. She taught for a little while in Ypsilanti and then at a Professor Sill's Seminary for Young Ladies in Detroit before finding her true calling at the Detroit House of Correction, which had just then begun a program to educate inmates.

Miss Hall's career illustrates the dramatic changes in nineteenth century society's perception of "fallen women" i.e. prostitutes and felons as well as affirming the goal of the State of Michigan in providing correctional facilities that were truly reformatories rather than just prisons. Not only was Michigan the first state to eliminate the death penalty as part of its 1837 constitution, it led the way in specialized treatment of minors and women. An 1861 a Michigan law discriminated between adult male felons and both youthful males ages sixteen to twenty-one and women. Unless either of those were convicted of murder or treason, he or she was sent, not to Jackson Prison, but to the Detroit House of Correction. This brand new facility could not fill its three hundred cells just from Wayne County, so it accepted women and youths from thirty-six counties in Michigan on a contract basis after 1862. It also received individuals convicted in Federal court.

Women comprised almost one-third of the total inmate population at Detroit but were housed separately within the House of Correction and supervised exclusively by women. Even the institution's chapel had a seven-foot wall separating the women from the men. This represented a real breakthrough in correctional thinking. As early as 1828 reformers in New York were demanding, but not getting, separate housing for female prisoners. But Detroit went one step further by initiating in 1865 a "grading" system within the women's section to encourage behavioral change. Lower graded prisoners, either new or defiant, lived in individual cells when not at work. Matrons maintained silence to promote reflection as promoted by the Auburn system. Inmates were given adequate food but no tea or coffee. When an inmate qualified for a higher level, she slept and worked with others. Though supervised by a matron, the women could chat while they worked or ate. Their clothing, diets and reading material were better than lower level inmates' thus giving new inmates a motivation for cooperation and reform.

Detroit also instituted educational programs for inmates. According to Superintendent Zebulon Brockway, who hired Professor H.S. Tarbell and Emma Hall to teach at the prison, the program was unbelievably successful. Almost all prisoners attended the evening classes. Their progress after only 210 hours of instruction surpassed that of children in the public schools after 975 hours. Results were "so astonishing," said Brockway, "as to be scarcely credible."[17] Prisoners also attended a multitude of lectures given on subjects ranging from the writings of Charles Dickens to monetary and banking practices.

Emma Amelia Hall

Courtesy of the Ypsilanti Historical Society

Meanwhile Detroit had done something really ahead of its time. It had established the Detroit House of Shelter for Women. Governor Bagley told the State Legislature in February 1872 that by doing so Detroit had achieved his "ideal of what all prisons might be." [18] This distinctly non-prisonlike house welcomed former inmates who lived there as a half-way house. Residents also included women who had been granted what today would be called parole due to good behavior, and the house accepted any destitute woman who was in danger of falling into prostitution and/or crime. After a brief hiatus for remodeling in 1870, it was this institution for which Miss Hall became Superintendent. The women in her care did all their own domestic chores as well as manufacturing braided chair seats. They made chair seats because the Detroit House of Correction had chosen chair manufacturing as its work program. Shelter women had their own bedrooms intended not as an isolating punishment but as a normal social kindness. They learned to sew and read and write. Religious devotion was stressed. This was the fertile ground in which Emma Hall developed her ideas and skills.

When the Shelter closed in 1874 due to a need for office space and housing for guards not because of any fault of the facility itself, Miss Hall became matron at the State Public School in Coldwater, Michigan, which was a facility for destitute or orphaned children. Once that program had been launched, she moved on to the State School for the Deaf and Dumb in Flint. Again she served as superintendent, this time for six years. Finally in 1881 Hall was appointed by the Governor as Superintendent of the new Reform School for Girls. Each of these moves marked a step up the ladder of reputation and responsibility.

The State of Michigan established a boys' reformatory in 1856, but another quarter of a century passed before it saw fit to do likewise for "wayward" girls. The town of Adrian's 1880 offer was deemed best by the State, for it donated forty acres of choice farmland just a half mile north of the city. There was a house, two barns and other out-buildings on the land. Adrian also donated $3,000 to help establish

Industrial School for Girls

Courtesy of the Bentley Historical Library, University of Michigan

the facility which was planned around the cottage model. The girls lived in small cottages to establish a more homelike atmosphere such as that achieved by Detroit's House of Shelter. Eighty-five girls lived there in the first fourteen months from the fall of 1881 through 1882. Of those eighty-five, many were ill from a prolonged lack of shelter and food. Thirteen could not read at all and only two could read Appleton's fifth reader. Forty-three could not write; seventy-seven either knew no arithmetic or only very basic addition. Once there, like the women in the Detroit House of Shelter, the girls did their own domestic chores as well as gardening and learning to make butter and to sew.

Zebulon Brockway, one of Michigan's leaders in penal reform, called Hall, a "pioneer in women's reformatory work." [19] It certainly seems that she earned her $1,000 a year salary, but she also discovered to her dismay just how limited her power was. Though her innovations such as the cottage system and moral conversations similar to those of Julia King at Michigan

State Normal School were successful, ultimately she was discharged. Brockway, who admired Hall tremendously, warned her of the inevitability of the Board's opposition to what it called "frills." One such "frill" mentioned in Hall's diary was the expenditure of $5.50 per pair for glasses for girls with vision difficulties. Hall saw girls who could not read because they could not see. The Board of Control only saw expenditures of $123 in today's purchasing power for each girl. Also the Board demanded a larger "cottage" housing sixty girls versus the expense of houses half that size. Such a change proved more economical but lacked the homelike intimacy which made the small cottages so successful.

The Board of Control, which was composed of five members, one of whom was Mrs. Mary Cooley of Ann Arbor, asserted in a newspaper account that Hall's dismissal was due to ill health and/or faulty business management. Miss Hall retorted with a clear public statement of denial. She denied ill health and stated that she had submitted her reports in a timely manner. Those reports demonstrated that the school spent only nine cents per person per day for food. The Board contended that the school cost twice as much as did the Boys' Reformatory and had yet to help pay for itself as did the boys' facility. What the Board was overlooking was the fact that the boys' facility had been in operation for twenty-eight years. Any organization or business costs more and has less profits when it is being established. The boys' reformatory had had almost three decades to establish itself and develop its commercial enterprise.

Miss Hall accused the Board of sabotaging her leadership, a charge taken up by an editorial published by fifty prominent supporters in Adrian. That editorial claimed that her authority as superintendent had been diminished to such a point that very little was left. That statement appears to be accurate since the Board during Miss Hall's final year barred her from attending its sessions. Her sister, Fannie, however, believed that she was "bounced" due to religious views and use of the Bible as a required reading for inmates. That would seem odd since chapel and devotional time were an integral part of all reform literature and had been implemented in Detroit's innovative correctional plan.

Some evidence does support the idea that Miss Hall was ill-treated by the Board. The most credible is Mr. Brockway's statement in his autobiography. There he states "[a] want of sympathy on the part of some women members of the institution board induced her [Hall] to resign." [20] Other supporting evidence is more circumstantial. First, many of the girls burst into tears when she announced she was leaving. They clearly saw her efforts as beneficial. Second, other employees also tendered their resignations in support. This seems to be particularly powerful evidence that Miss Hall was a popular and effective leader. On the other hand, her death in December 1885, less than two years after leaving Albion may suggest that there may have been health issues though her brother, Dr. William Hall attributed her heart failure to the emotional strain caused by the conflict with the Board of Control. There can be no definitive conclusion as to what actually transpired. What is important is that, despite her difficulties in Adrian, Emma Amelia Hall was one of the two female members of the National Prison Association Board in 1884, and she was the first woman

Emma Amelia Hall

Courtesy of the Bentley Historical Library,
University of Michigan

in Michigan to receive a state appointment. While her vocation moved her all around Michigan and finally to New Mexico, she always claimed Ypsilanti, where her unmarried older brother, Dr. William Hall, and her sister lived, as home.

No other Washtenaw County woman was successful in entering and staying in the political arena until Estelle Downing was elected to the Ypsilanti City Council in 1919. In that same year Marna Osband became "the first Washtenaw woman to enter county politics." [21] She served on the Republican State Central Committee from 1919 to 1926. By then World War I was over, and the world was rapidly becoming a very different place from what it had been just a few decades before.

---

[1] Emily Faithfull, *Three Visits to America* (Edinburgh: David Douglas, 1884), 303.

[2] Caroline Bird, *Enterprising Women* (New York: W. W. Norton and Co., 1976), 33-4.

[3] Harriet Martineau, *Society in America, Vol 3* (London: Saunders and Otley, 1837), 149.

[4] Martineau, Vol 1, 313.

[5] Faithfull, 74.

[7] Evelyn M. Leasher, "Lois Bryan Adams and the Household Department of the Michigan Farmer," *Michigan Historical Review,* Vol. 21 (1995), 110.

[8] *Portrait and Biographical Album of Washtenaw County* (Chicago: Biographical Publishing Co., 189),413.

[9] Samuel Beakes, *Past and Present Washtenaw County, Michigan* (Chicago: St. Clarke Publishing Co., 1906), 622.

[10] *History of Washtenaw County, Michigan* (Chicago: Charles C. Chapman Co., 1881), 570.[1]

[11] Beakes, 621-2.

[12] Beakes, 249.

[13] Anna Botsford Bach was one of the daughters of Elnathan Botsford.

[14] Andrew Balfour, www.The Post Office Papers/WomenPostmasters.htm

[15] Sarah died in 1915 at age sixty-five. Eliza was sixty-three when she died in 1917.

[16] "Frances Stewart Collection" at Ypsilanti Archives, Ypsilanti, MI.

[17] Zebulon Brockway, *Fifty Years in Prison Service* (New York: Charities Publication Committee, 1912), 74.

[18] Brockway, 104.

[19] Brockway, 409.

[20] Brockway, 415.

[21] *Ypsilanti Daily Press*, May 7, 1947.

CONCLUSION

Emily Faithfull traveled three times from England to America during the 1870's. Her objective was to investigate "how America is trying to solve the most delicate and difficult problem presented by modern civilization." [1] What could that problem have been? Urbanization? Transportation? Communication? None of the above. That most delicate and difficult problem was called in the mid-nineteenth century "the woman question." By the end of the century it acquired a slightly different label: "the new woman." This "new woman" was at first simply a woman who strove for economic independence – a purse of her own. By the early twentieth century, the term connoted far more radical social freedom.

Young women began shocking society. They bobbed both their hair and their skirts. They abandoned the outfits considered stylish in the nineteenth century. They joyfully discarded clothing, which could use up to one hundred yards of fabric and weigh twenty pounds, in favor of dresses requiring no more than three yards of fabric and no corset. By doing so, they were also rejecting the Rubenesque figures of their mothers. Instead of taking pride in showing off their corset enhanced décolletage, they bound their breasts to minimize them. With more of their bodies revealed and no longer cinched in by corsets, women began striving for weight loss and sun tans. The word "diet," which until then had been used only as a noun, began being used as a verb. No longer did "diet" refer to what one ate but to the act of reducing ones food consumption for the purpose of lessening one's size and weight. The result was an androgynous appearance which scandalized the older generation because it blurred traditional lines of demarcation for gender.

In Michigan, pioneers had long ago stopped speaking in hushed tones about the ubiquitous threatening presence of wolves. Thanks to street lights, residents no longer sought the shelter of their homes when darkness fell. With improved transportation, inhabitants, especially women, were not limited to the area which they could traverse by foot or, if wealthy, by carriage. The mobility afforded by public trains and trolleys allowed young women in particular to become increasingly more independent and less supervised. Girls left home to attend colleges and universities where they trained and boarded with young men. Then they found employment which often was in proximity of men.

Add to this heady mix of social change, two popular new trends. First, the bicycle. Bicycles or "wheels" were not in and of themselves new, but their wide-spread popularity was. In the 1890's bicycles became the rage. Jonathan Marwil in his *History of Ann Arbor* states that there were seventeen bicycle shops in Ann Arbor alone. And "wheels" were not limited only to the young. Francis Willard, longtime president of the Women's Christian Temperance Union, one of the most popular progressive groups, published a little book in 1895 called *How I Learned to Ride the Bicycle.* Willard was no teenager. She wasn't even a young woman. She was fifty-three years old. Her spirited message to America's females was much the same as Emma Willard's had been earlier. Go forth and do likewise. And they did. When a bike path from Ann Arbor to Whitmore Lake was constructed, Florence Babbitt's daughters actually rode their bicycles all the way from Ypsilanti to Whitmore Lake and back

Alice and Nan Babbitt

Courtesy of the Bentley Historical Library, University of Michigan

again along that new path. That would be a trip of approximately twenty-two miles. "Wheeling" said Susan B, Anthony, "has done more to emancipate women than anything else." [2]

Bicycles began a trend that found fruition in the automobile. Gertrude E. Woodard, daughter of Charles and Elizabeth Woodard of Ypsilanti, led the way. Miss Woodard graduated first from Ypsilanti High School and then in 1892 from Michigan State Normal School. Upon graduation, she became the assistant librarian to Genevieve Walton at her alma mater before going to Chicago where she was a research librarian. When she returned to Ypsilanti, she was hired by the University of Michigan as the assistant librarian for the School of Law. [3] In 1901 she decided she needed a vehicle to transport her to and from the Ann Arbor campus. Eschewing public transportation, she decided to purchase a car.

Gertrude Woodard

Courtesy of the Ypsilanti Historical Society

That may not seem radical today, but it certainly was in 1900. At that time the United States had a population of seventy-six million but virtually no paved roads. 1900 was the year that William McKinley became the first United States president to be seen riding in a car. It was also the first year that automobile advertisements began to appear in American magazines such as the *Saturday Evening Post* resulting in forty-eight thousand people attending the first national automobile show in New York. Both the Ford Motor Company and the Firestone Tire and Rubber were established in 1900. The times they were a-changing, and Gertrude Woodard, by not just purchasing but driving her own automobile, was a living harbinger of radical alterations in American society.

When Miss Woodard informed Dean Hutchins of her plan to buy a car in order to drive to work, he, "brought his hand down emphatically on the arm of his chair, exclaiming 'What in the world do you want with an automobile!" [4] Woodard was undeterred by his response. She decided to purchase a Covert Motorette which was produced by Bryon V. Covert, a former bicycle manufacturer. She even traveled to the factory in New York to spend four days learning to drive and care for her new vehicle.

Miss Woodard's vehicle was primitive by today's standards. It only went eighteen miles per hour and had no reverse gear. When she cranked her car to begin her journey home, it made so much noise professors had to pause their instruction until she was on her way. The good news was that it required only a pint of gasoline for her daily journey. She always carried spare gasoline, an extra battery and a sheet of burlap for extricating her car from muddy roads. So informed was Miss Woodard that she could tell the difference in grades of gasoline. Ten years later she paid $3.50 for her license and driver's card. By then there were 1,239 other cars licensed in Michigan. Gertrude never married and never had an accident. She lived most of her ninety-six years with her sister, Ada, in Ypsilanti. She died 1966.

These "new" women were not just abandoning the constrictions of their corsets, driving automobiles and working; they were striving to abandon all the narrow confines of Victorian society. Just as girls today are influenced by celebrities regarding behavior and style, so the young women of Washtenaw County imitated the celebrities of their day. One of those celebrities was Alice Roosevelt who was the living embodiment of the new American woman. Alice was the daughter of President Theodore Roosevelt by his first wife who died a few days after Alice's birth. She traveled, spoke in public, danced, played golf and tennis, and swam. She even smoked in public. Her physically active life became a model for many women of the early twentieth century. By 1902 the "new woman," based on the Alice Roosevelt model, was being incorporated into popular fiction. The character of Florence in "The Making of a Man" in Karl E. Harriman's *Ann Arbor Tales*, plays both golf and tennis and smokes. Young women, like the Milan girls pictured below were organizing themselves into athletic clubs.

Milan Girls' Athletic Club circa 1906

By 1913, the Ypsilanti Garment Company claimed that its largest special line of apparel was for athletic girls to whom they sold "gymnasium outfits" and suits for swimming.[5] This suggests a massive change in behavior and resulting attitudes since in 1901 when the University of Michigan's Dean of Women, Dr. Eliza Mosher, required invitations for men to watch the University of Michigan girls' basketball team. "Only students of good moral character," said Mosher, "will be permitted to see the co-eds in their gym suits..." [6]

Society appeared to be bowing low before this "new woman;" however, just as when a diver reaches the apex of his dive and is suspended for a fraction of second in nothing but thin air, he or she knows the plummet downward is about to begin, so women in early twentieth century felt the male-dominated society renewing its efforts to restrict their options. Alice's father, President Theodore Roosevelt, was one of the most popular and consequently influen-

The University of Michigan's girls' basketball team in 1908.

Courtesy of the Bentley Historical Library, University of Michigan

tial, political figures of the early twentieth century. Theodore Roosevelt, when young, was, in many ways, fairly liberal for his time. He wrote his undergraduate thesis at Harvard on the topic of equal rights for women. He also supported equal pay for women. By 1905, however, he apparently had modified his attitudes considerably. The speech he delivered before the National Congress of Mothers on March 13 of that year was a concise reflection of the fears of Roosevelt's generation.

For decades women had been attending the nation's colleges and universities. They had entered all the professions. By 1900 there were over seven thousand female physicians and over eight hundred female dentists. In the United States 1,010 women were licensed attorneys. True, the largest number, 327,614, were teachers, but the nation also included 1,041 female architects, 3,373 female members of the clergy, and 2,194 female journalists. And, after more than a half a century of advocacy, women were approaching the very portals of political power. Meanwhile, the birthrate among the established WASP (White Anglo-Saxon Protestant) society had fallen dramatically from seven children per family to three. Among some groups of college graduates, the rate was less than one. It was common knowledge that educated women married less often. An 1895 study showed that only 55% of college educated women married compared with 90% of less educated women. A study at the University of Michigan in 1908 indicated that only 52% of that institution's female graduates were marrying. If the field were narrowed to women receiving doctorate degrees, the number would slip to 25%. In fact, the last four decades of the nineteenth century witnessed the highest rate of unmarried women in the history of the United States. Not only did fewer educated women marry, they almost always married later, often in their mid-thirties, which severely limited their child-bearing potential. Yet Roosevelt was savvy enough to realize (and probably believed it sincerely) that women had the right be educated and did contribute within their professional lives to the country as a whole.

The compromise on which he settled formed the essence of his 1905 speech. The future of the entire country, he declared, rested on the choices women made. Women's behavior was far more important to the future than whatever their husbands were doing, for it was up to the women to bear and raise the next generation. Any woman who did not conform to that ideal, according to Roosevelt, "merits contempt." And "the existence of women of this type [ones who did not marry and reproduce] forms one of the most unpleasant and unwholesome features of modern life." [7] Roosevelt continued by denouncing divorce, rates of which he considered "fairly appalling." Birth control was a sin. He conceded that women had the right to careers but only after they had fulfilled their primary function in society as mothers. His ideas still resonate with many throughout the United States.

511 Elizabeth Street may be the very house in which Mrs. Wells had her day care business.

Perhaps the most telling sign of changing times in Washtenaw County and an event that undoubtedly would have upset Roosevelt was the arrival of day nurseries. These were child care centers for working mothers. This infant industry reflected the increase in the number of working women – especially married women – who needed income from whatever employment they found. Milo Ryan described a Mrs. Sarah Ames who lived near him when he was a boy and ran a day nursery. His memory of the nursery is valid, but he probably was not referring to either of the two women named Mrs. Sarah Ames who lived in Ann Arbor at that time. The name that escaped him was Mrs. Ethel Wells. In 1911 Mrs. Wells opened her nursery at 217 N. First Street in Ann Arbor. Later Wells moved the child care center across the street from St. Thomas Catholic Church which placed it in Ryan's neighborhood. Mrs. Wells, a widow, appears to have had an earlier career as a laundress and ironer. Later her remarriage to a Mr. Bradford curtailed her entrepreneurial efforts though, if Ryan's memory is correct, her acceptance of an African-American child in the nursery with subsequent complaints by neighbors, may also have contributed to her closing her facility.

Athletics, declining birth rates and emerging child care facilities indicate changes in the fabric of society. As Joshua Zeitz pointed out in his book, *Flapper*, the 1920's signaled a radical departure in almost all facets of society. For example, the traditional mode of courtship was collapsing. No longer did men known to the family sit on the front porch or in the parlor, carefully chaperoned, as they had just a decade or two earlier. Young women were meeting men at work and at public entertainments such as dance halls, parks and restaurants. Even if girls did live at home, the streetcar and automobile allowed them to leave the home for a "date." The very term, "date," did not exist in that context until the twentieth century when suddenly it became the man's prerogative to ask the woman out, and he was expected to pay for food or entertainment. Zeitz, as well as others, suggests that this was because most working girls made so little money that they could not afford to pay while men, who earned more generous salaries, could. Not only did this system of "treating" include the unspoken expectation of sexual exchange, it also signaled a subtle but profound shift in relationship that reflected the changing attitudes of society. In an earlier time, the woman and her family decided whom she would allow into her home to court her. She – not he – did the inviting.

That shift in prerogative appears rather ironic. Women, by the very act of exercising their freedom to "go out" were, in actuality, losing their autonomy. This change in courtship patterns was indicative of a general social backlash women experienced in the first seventy years of the twentieth century. Women had won the battle but lost the war. While they continued to work in greater numbers than ever, the optimism of earlier days vanished, as did many of their occupational choices. Beakes proclaimed euphorically in his 1906 history, "Almost every avenue of business activity is open to women," [8] yet by 1920 women were finding it more and more difficult to gain acceptance and promotion even within occupations designated as appropriate for them. Females who strayed into fields deemed appropriate only for males experienced an increasingly cool reception. Even if a woman managed to teach at a major university such as the University of Michigan, her work was not honored. Florence Hazzard preserved the comments of an assistant professor of chemistry. Hazzard did not name this woman (no doubt to protect her source) but said that she was single and, at the time of the discussion, retired. Though she had a pension from the University, Hazzard found her "almost bitter." The former female professor said, "I had all the responsibilities but never the standing of men one rank higher. I had to fight every step of the way. When my rank was raised, I would be given the lowest salary at that grade, and slowly raised. Men who were my juniors in age and experience were advanced more rapidly, routinely. No woman was again appointed to our department faculty. But I stayed on. There was a depression, you know, and I was lucky." [9] Needless to say this professor's name was not mentioned in the University's *Encyclopedic Survey*'s chapter regarding the history of the Chemistry Department.

Nor was it just males in society, then or now, who clamored for women to remain near hearth and home. Ida Tarbell who personified the word "success" for her own generation advocated much the same. Tarbell was born in 1857. She was the only woman in her graduating class at Allegheny College in 1880. She studied three years at the Sorbonne in Paris and had an internationally recognized career in journalism, yet this same Ida Tarbell, celebrated in the *New York Times* 1922 list as one of the most admired women of the time, paradoxically did not support her female contemporaries in their battle for civil and social freedoms. Tarbell refused to endorse women's right to vote and was, according to Paula Treckel, a specialist concerning Tarbell, "the same woman who asserted that women's place was in the home and that they were incapable of greatness in a man's world because of their nature." [10] This! From a woman who remained an unmarried career woman! It boggles the mind.

Society has always been ambivalent about how to treat intelligent females who do not fit the mold society has prescribed for them. On one hand, such women might be admired for their uniqueness, their skills and even their daring. On the other, they were denigrated for their nonconformity. To evoke such contradictory emotions, women need not necessarily have worked. Nor was it only men who found such women a challenge. A clear example of this paradox is a young woman who lived in Washtenaw County during its earliest days. Her name was Frances Trask. She was the cousin of Mrs. Dix, wife of the founder of Dixboro, Michigan. Mrs. Dix, immediately after her marriage in March 1825, was transported to the wilds of the Michigan Territory where her husband had purchased land the previous year. Dixboro in 1826 had a population of only seventy-five. Frances agreed to accompany her cousin on what to most women would have been a rather intimidating experience. I suspect Miss Trask considered it an adventure and anticipated the experience with much enthusiasm since it would have freed her from the stifling society of the east coast. Mrs. Dix, in turn, no doubt desired her cousin's company in part because Trask did not quite fit the mold. Perhaps she found strength in her less conventional cousin.

Elizabeth Ellet in *Pioneer Women of the West* characterizes Trask as "somewhat on the Amazon order." Being called Amazonian was neither a compliment in 1825 when Trask was young nor in 1852 when Ellet's book was published. It suggested an appearance and behavior that was ill-suited for a woman and certainly not lady-like. Trask, it is said, had an energy and a confidence that made her stand out among her peers. "In cases of sickness she could do more than any one [sic] else, and would watch for many nights together, bearing fatigue under which an ordinary constitution must have sunk." In addition to physical endurance, Miss Trask was known for her "rapier sharp wit." These characteristics created a reputation that endured long after she moved with Mr. and Mrs. Dix to Texas in 1833. The interesting part of the story of Frances Trask is that, when she finally returned to Dixboro years later, people who had not met her but only heard of her, waited expectantly to meet this unusual, if not slightly infamous, woman. They were quite surprised to find that in the interim, Miss Trask "had grown absolutely quiet and dignified." No longer was she "the dashing, sprightly creature she had been represented" to be in local lore. The ultimate irony is that instead of appreciating this "improvement," they felt disappointed – even cheated.

Miss Trask was born almost two hundred years ago, yet the mixed message girls received in her time are still the messages girls hear today. Modern girls are told they can do anything – be anything. Simultaneously, they are weaned on Disney fairy tales in which the handsome prince always rescues the fair maiden and rides off into the sunset with his blushing bride. When girls are a bit older, pop culture molds them into little more than sexual objects. Even that most dominant symbol of women's subjugation, the corset, is re-emerging in stores. And the fact that there is so little women's history taught in public schools or realistically portrayed in fiction and film exacerbates the problem for maturing girls. Without providing an authentic background, how can society expect its young women to come to some reasonable understanding as to what their role within that society should be? Without a clear understanding of the past, how is anyone supposed to shape the future?

One author wrote, "Little does the girl of today coming to meet life, with all its changed conditions, know what it has cost in real heartbreak to bring this condition about. She cannot realize the social ostracism, the coarse ridicule, the scorn and contempt which was heaped on the heads of the first women who ventured to ask for a broader outlook, a better chance for women." Without knowing the source of that comment, one would assume it was intended for twenty-first century girls and refers to the women's movement of the 1970's. It does not. Indeed it was written over a century ago by Frances Willard in her 1897 book, *Occupations for Women*. [11] "La plus change, la plus la meme chose." [12]

Courtesy of the University of Michigan

Because of ignorance about women of the past, what they endured and what they achieved, modern girls have difficulty understanding the present. A friend of mine recently sat with her ten-year-old niece, Anya, at a University of Michigan honors convocation for graduates. As they waited for the festivities to begin, Anya was quite interested in the seal of the University which decorated the program. The seal presents the lamp of knowledge resting on a large book. Below is the motto: "Artes, Scientia, Veritas." Under that, boldly inscribed, is the year 1817. Anya inquired about the symbols, the Latin words and the significance of the date. Then Anya's attention was stolen by the arrival of the dignitaries on stage. In a few moments, Mary Sue Coleman was introduced with the caveat that she was the first woman to become president of the University of Michigan. Anya turned to her aunt in incredulous amazement and exclaimed, "But that is almost two hundred years!" How, Anya wondered, could only one woman ever have had that job when it had been such a long time? Anya may not know much about "Artes" or "Scientia," but out of her innocent mouth came "Veritas." How indeed could such a thing happen? The answer was beyond Anya's experience. It simply did not coincide with her perception of the role of women in her society.

Knowing the past enriches the present and directs the future. Florence Babbitt understood that truism. That is why, a little over a century ago, she stood for two days on a wintry street corner distributing gifts to the children of Ypsilanti. Florence offered the children toys in the hope it would stimulate their interest in the past. I have no toys; I can only offer words. But words will resonate long after a person abandons an interest in toys. After all, it has been through words – or the lack thereof – that women have become history's ghosts. Their presence in our historical narrative is spectral and vague; their accomplishments hidden like unpleasant skeletons in dusty attics. Thus it is appropriate that words, which have for so long been utilized to erase women from history, should now be used to re-evaluate the past in order to promote a more balanced view of women's contributions outside of the home.

---

[1] Emily Faithfull, *Three Visits to America* (Edinburgh: David Douglas, 1884), vii.

[2] Gail Collins, *America's Women* (New York: Harper Collins Publishers, Inc., 2003), 280.

[3] Miss Woodard was one of the founders of the American Association of Law Librarians.

[4] *Ypsilanti Daily Press*, October 30, 1954.

[5] "Chatauqua Edition," *Daily Ypsilantian*," 1913.

[6] Lela Duff, *Ann Arbor Yesterdays* (Ann Arbor, Friends of the Ann Arbor Library, 1962), 121.

[7] Theodore Roosevelt. "On Motherhood," www. nationalcenter.org/TheodoreRoosevelt Motherhood. Html

[8] Samuel Beakes, *Past and Present Washtenaw County, Michigan* (Chicago: St. Clarke Publishing Co.,1906), 163.

[9] "On the side of the Persons" in Florence Hazzard Papers at Bentley Historical Library, University of Michigan, 16.

[10] www.tarbell.allegheny.edu/tarbell.html

[11] Frances E. Willard, *Occupations for Women* (New York: The Success Co., 1897), 446.

Bibliography of Published Sources

Achenbaum, Andrew. *Old Age in the New Land*. Baltimore: Johns Hopkins University Press, 1978.

Adams, Lois Bryan. *Letter from Washington 1863-1865*. Edited by Evelyn Leasher. Detroit: Wayne State University Press, 1999.

Albanese, Catherine. *Nature Religion in America*. Chicago: University of Chicago Press, 1990.

Alcott, Louisa May. *Hospital Sketches*. Boston: James Redpath, , 1863.

– *Work: A Story of Experience*. Boston: Roberts Brothers, 1873.

Alden, Cynthia W. *The Ways of Earning Money: A Book for Women*. New York: Sully and Kleinteich, 1904.

Anderson, Margo. "History of Women and the History of Statistics," *Journal of Women's History,* Vol 4, Spring 1992, 14-36.

Anderson, Olive. *An American Girl and her Four Years at a Boys' College*. New York: D. Appleton and Co., 1878.

Ann Arbor Business Men's Association. *City of Ann Arbor: Its Resources and Advantages*. Ann Arbor: Courier, Book and Job Printing, 1887.

Ann Arbor Historic District Commission. *Old Fourth Ward*. 1982.

Aron, Cindy. *Working at Play*. New York: Oxford University Press, 1999.

Attaway and Barritt ed. *Women's Voices: Early Years at University of Michigan*. Ann Arbor: Bentley Historical Library, 2000.

Bacon, Margaret. *Mothers of Feminism*. New York: Harper Collins, 1989.

Barker-Benfield, G.J. *The Horrors of the Half-Known Life: Male Attitudes toward Women and Sexuality in Nineteenth Century America*. New York: Routledge, 2000.

Baym, Nina, ed. *Women's Fiction: A Guide to Novels by and about Women in America 1820-1870*. 2nd ed. Urbana: University of Illinois Press, 1993.

Baxter, William E. *America and the Americans*. London: G. Routledge and Co., 1855.

Beakes, Samuel. *Past and Present Washtenaw County, Michigan*. Chicago: St. Clarke Publishing Co., 1906.

Berg, Barbara J. *The Remembered Gate: Origins of American Feminism*. New York: Oxford University Press, 1978.

Bernstein, R.B. *Thomas Jefferson*. New York: Oxford University Press, 2003.

Bird, Caroline *Enterprising Women*. New York: W. W. Norton and Co., 1976.

Bird, Caroline with Sara Briller. *Born Female: The High Cost of Keeping Women Down.* New York: David McKay Co., 1968.

Blanton, De Anne and Lauren M. Cook. *They Fought like Demons.* Baton Rouge: Louisiana State University, 2002.

Bordin, Ruth. *Alice Freeman Palmer: Evolution of a New Woman.* Ann Arbor: University of Michigan Press, 1993.

–*University of Michigan, A Pictorial History.* Ann Arbor: University of Michigan Press, 1967.

–*Women at Michigan.* Ann Arbor: University of Michigan Press, 1999.

Bremer, Fredericka. *Homes of the New World.* London: Arthur Hall, Virtue and Co., 1853.

Brodie, Janet Farrell. *Contraception and Abortion in Nineteenth Century America.* Ithaca, NY: Cornell University Press, 1994.

Broughton, Catherine. *Suggestions for Dressmakers.* New York: Morse-Broughton Co. 1896.

Brumgardt, John, ed. *Civil War Nurse: Dairy and Letters of Hanna Ropes.* Knoxville: University of Tennessee Press, 1980.

Buley, R. Carlyle. *The Old Northwest Pioneer Period 1815-1840.* Bloomington, IN: Unversity Press, 1983.

Burgess, Lauren Cook. *An Uncommon Soldier: The Civil War Letters of Sarah Rosetta Wakeman.* New York: Oxford University Press,1995.

Cassedy, James. *Medicine and the American Growth 1800-1860.* Madison: University of Wisconsin Press, 1986.

Church, Ella Rodman. *Money Making for Ladies.* New York: Harper and Bros., 1882.

Clavers, Mary, aka Caroline Kirkland. *A New Home – Who'll Follow?* 5th ed. New York: C.S. Franses and Co., 1855.

Cocks, James. *A Pictorial History of Ann Arbor 1823-1974.* Ann Arbor, MI: Bentley Historical Library, 1974.

Colburn, Harvey. *History of Ypsilanti.* Ypsilanti,MI: Ypsilanti Centennial Committee on History. 1923.

Collins, Gail. *America's Women.* New York: Harper Collins Publishers, Inc., 2003.

Comfort, George. *Woman's Education and Woman's Health.* New York: T.W. Durston, Syracuse, 1874.

Committee of the Association of Collegiate Alumnae. *Health Statistics of Women College Graduates.* Boston: Wright and Potter Printing Co., 1885.

Coontz, Stephanie. *The Way We Never Were.* New York: Basic Books, 1992.

Cooper, Patricia. *Once a Cigar Maker.* Urbana: University of Illinois Press, 1987.

Corselius, Cornelia. *Financie.* Ann Arbor: Register Publishing Co., 1885.

Cott, Nancy et al. *Root of Bitterness: Documents of the Social History of American Women.* Boston: Northeastern University Press, 1966.

Creighton, Margaret. *The Colors of Courage: Gettysburg's Forgotten History.* New York: Basic Books, 2005.

Dary, David. *Frontier Medicine.* New York: Alfred A Knopf, 2008.

Davies, Margery W. *Woman's Place is at the Typewriter.* Philadelphia: Temple University Press, 1982.

Davis Lecture Committee, ed. *Essays in the History of Medicine.* Urbana: University of Illinois Press, 1965.

Deckard, Barbara S. *The Women's Movement.* 2nd ed. New York: Harper and Row, 1979.

Degler, Carl. *Age of the Economic Revolution 1876-1900 2nd ed.* , Glenview, IL, Scott Foresman, 1977.

    –At Odds: Women and Family. New York: Oxford University Press, 1980.

    –"Is there a History of Women?" Oxford: Clarendon Press, 1975.

    –"What ought to Be and What Was: Women's Sexuality in the Nineteenth Century." *American Historical Review*, December 1994, 1467-1490.

DeBare, Ilana. *Where Girls Come First.* New York; Penguin Books, 2004.

D'Emilio, John and Estelle Freedman, *Intimate Matters: A History of Sexuality in American.* New York: Harper & Row, 1988.

Dexter, Elisabeth. *Colonial Women of Affairs. 2nd ed.* Clifton, NJ: Augustus M Kelley, 1972.

Donnelly, Walter ed. *The University of Michigan: An Encyclopedic Survey.* Ann Arbor: University of Michigan Press, 1958.

Drachman, Virginia. *Enterprising Women.* Cambridge, MA: Published by President and Fellows of Harvard College, 2002.

    –*Sisters–in–Law.* Cambridge, MA: Harvard University Press, 1998.

    –*Women Lawyers and the Origins of Professional Identity in America.* Ann Arbor: University of Michigan Press, 1993.

Duff, Lela. *Ann Arbor Yesterdays.* Ann Arbor, Friends of the Ann Arbor Library, 1962.

    –*Pioneer School.* Ann Arbor: Ann Arbor Board of Education, 1958.

Dunbar, Willis. *Michigan.* Grand Rapids, MI: W B. Erdmans Publishing, 1995.

    –*Michigan Through the Centuries.* NewYork: Lewis Historical Publishing Co., 1955.

Earnest, Ernest. *The American Eve in Fact and Fiction 1775-1914.* Urbana, University of Illinois Press, 1974.

Edmonds, S. Emma. *Nurse and Spy in the Union Army.* Hartford, CT: W.S. Williams, 1865.

Eggleston, Larry. *Women in the Civil War.* Jefferson, NC: McFarland and Co., 2003.

Ehrenreich, Barbara and Deirdre English. *For her Own Good: Two Centuries of the Experts' Advice to Women. 2nd ed.* New York: Random House, 2005.

    –*Witches, Midwives and Nurses.* Old Westbury, NY: Feminist Press, 1973.

Ellet, Elizabeth. *Pioneer Women of the West.* Philadelphia: Porter and Coates, 1875.

Ewing, Elizabeth. *Dress and Undress: A History of Women's Underwear.* New York: Drama Book Specialists,1978.

Fahs, Alice *The Imagined Civil War.* Chapel Hill: University of North Carolina Press, 2001.

Farrand, Elizabeth. *History of the University of Michigan.* Ann Arbor: Register Publishing House, 1885.

Faithfull, Emily. *Three Visits to America.* Edinburgh: David Douglas, 1884.

Fisher, Paul. *House of Wits: An Intimate Portrait of the James Family.* New York: Henry Holt and Co., 2009.

Fleming, Thomas. *Intimate Lives of the Founding Fathers.* New York: Harper Collins, 2009.

Foote Edward. *Plain Home Talk about the Human System.* New York: Wells and Co., 1871.

Foster, Gustavus. *The Past of Ypsilanti.* Detroit: Fleming and Davis, 1857.

Freeman, Carol W. *Of Dixboro.* 1979.

Freedman, Estelle B. *Their Sisters' Keepers: Women's Prison Reform in America 1830-1930.* Ann Arbor: University of Michigan, 1981.

Friedman, Jane. *Myra Bradwell.* Buffalo, NY: Prometheus Books, 1993.

–"On Defying the Creator and Becoming a Lawyer." *Valparaiso University Law Review* 28 (1994): 1287-1304.

Friedman, Lawrence. *Crime and Punishment.* New York: Basic Books, 1993.

Fuller, George. *Economic and Social Beginnings of Michigan 1805-1837.* Lansing, MI: Wynkoop Hallenbeck and Crawford Co., 1916.

–*Historic Michigan.* Dayton, OH: National Historical Association, 1928.

Fuller, Margaret. *Women in the Nineteenth Century.* New York: Norton and Co., 1971.

Gallman, J. Matthew. *America's Joan of Arc: The Life of Anna Elizabeth Dickinson.* New York: Oxford University Press, 2006.

Gamber, Wendy. *The Female Economy: Millinery and Dressmaking Trades 1860-1930.* Champaign, IL: University of Illinois Press. 1997.

–*The Boardinghouse in Nineteenth Century America.* Baltimore: Johns Hopkins University Press, 2007.

Garrison, Dee. "Tender Technicians: the Feminization of Public Librarianship 1876-1905" *Journal of Social History,* Winter 1972-73, 131.

–*Apostles of Culture: The Public Librarian and American Society, 1876-1920.* New York: The Free Press, 1979.

George, Carol, ed. *Remember the Ladies.* New York: Syracuse University Press, 1975.

Gibson, A.H. *Artists of Early Michigan.* Detroit: Wayne State University Press,1975.

Giles, Daphne. *East and West.* Ann Arbor: Davis and Cole, 1856.

Goldstein, Laurence, ed.. *Writing Ann Arbor.* Ann Arbor: University of Michigan Press, 2005.

Gordon, Linda. *Woman's Body, Woman's Rights.* New York: Grossman Publishers, 1976.

Gordon, Lyndall. *Lives like Loaded Guns: Emily Dickinson and her Family's Feuds.* New York: Viking Press, 2010.

    Vindication: A Life of Mary Wollstonecraft. New York: Harper Collins, 2006.

Gordon-Reed, Annette. *The Hemingses of Montecello.* New York: W. W. Norton and Co., 2008.

Graves, Mrs. A.J. *Woman in America.* New York: Harper and Brothers, 1843.

Green, Nancy. "Female Education and School Competition 1820-50." *History of Education Quarterly* 18 (1978): 129-142.

Groomes, Katherine Steeb. "Memories of an Ann Arbor Girlhood," Ann Arbor: Sesquicentennial Journal (1974): 7.

Grimm, Joe. *Michigan Voices.* Detroit: Wayne State University Press, 1987.

Hale, Sarah J. *Sketches of the American Character.* Boston: Putnam and Hunt, 1830.

Hall, Richard. *Patriots in Disguise.* New York: Paragon House, 1993.

Halttunen Karen. *Confidence Men and Painted Women: A Study of Middle Class Culture in America 1830-1870.* New Haven: Yale University Press, 1982.

Harriman, Karl E. *Ann Arbor Tales.* Freeport, NY: Books for Libraries Press, 2002.

Hartman, Mary and Lois Banner ed. *Clio's Consciousness Raised: New Perspectives on the History of Women.* New York: Harper Row, 1974.

Hartmann, Susan. "Paradox of Women's Progress 1820-1920." *The Forum Series,* St Louis, MO: Forum Press, 1975.

Haviland, Laura Smith *A Woman's Life Work.* Grand Rapids, MI: S .B. Shaw, 1881.

Hennings, Thomas P. *Looking Back.* Whitmore Lake, MI: Northfield Township Historical Society, 1985.

History of Washtenaw County, Michigan. Chicago: Charles C. Chapman Co., 1881.

Hill, Joseph. "Women in Gainful Occupations 1870-1920." *Census Monograph* IX, 1929.

Hoffer, Peter C. *Past Imperfect.* New York: Public Affairs, 2004.

Hoffman, Charles Fenno. *A Winter in the West: by a New Yorker.* Vol. 1, New York: Harper and Brothers, 1835.

Hogeland, Ronald, ed. *Women and Womanhood in America.* Lexington, MA: D.C. Heath and Co., 1973.

Hollister, Emily. *The Diary of Emily Jane Green Hollister: Her Nursing Experiences 1888-1911.* Edited by Deborah D. Smith. Ann Arbor : Historical Center for the Health Sciences, University of Michigan, 1991

Hollick, Frederick: *Marriage Guide or Natural History of Generation: A Private Instructor for Married Persons and Those about to Marry both Male and Female.* New York: T. W. Strong, 1850.

Holton, Woody. *Abigail Adams.* New York: Free Press, 2009.

Hooks, Janet. *Women's Occupations Through Seven Decades. U.S. Department of Labor Bull #218.* Washington, DC: U.S. Government Printing Office. 1947

Horowitz, Helen L. *Rereading Sex.* New York: Alfred A Knopf, 2002.

Howe, Julia Ward, ed. *Sex and Education: A Reply.* New York: Arno Press, 1972.

Howes, Annie et al. "Health Statistics of Women College Graduates." Boston: Wright and Potter Printing, 1885.

Hunt, Linda L. *Bold Spirit.* New York: Anchor Books 2003.

Isabel, Egbert R. *A History of Eastern Michigan University.* Ypsilanti, MI: Eastern Michigan University Press, 1971.

Jepsen, Thomas. *My Sisters Telegraphic: Women in the Telegraph office 1846-1950.* Athens, Ohio University Press, 2000.

Johnston, J. P. *Twenty Years of Hus'ling.* Chicago: Thompson and Thomas, 1887.

Katzman, David. *Seven Days a Week.* New York: Oxford University Press, 1978.

Keays, Hersilia. *Road to Damascus.* Boston: Maynard and Co., 1907.

Kelley, Mary ed. *Woman's Being, Woman's Place.* Boston: Hall Publishing 1979.

Kessler-Harris, Alice. *Out to Work.* New York: Oxford University Press, 1982.

Kestenbaum, Justin, ed. *A Pioneer Anthology: the Making of Michigan.* Detroit: Wayne State University Press, 1999.

Kitch, Carolyn. *Girl on the Magazine Cover.* Chapel Hill: University of North Carolina Press, 200l.

Kleinberg, S. J. *Women in United States 1830-1945.* Brunswick, NJ: Rutgers University Press, 1999.

Knowlton,Charles. *Fruits of Philosophy or A Private Companion of Young Married People.* 1st ed, New York: Peter Pauper Press, 1937.

Larkin, Jack. *Reshaping of Every Day Life.* New York: Harper and Row, 1988.

Leasher, Evelyn M. "Lois Bryan Adams and the Household Department of the Michigan Farmer." *Michigan Historical Review, Vol. 21 (1995): 100-119.*

Leavitt, Judith, ed. *Women and Health in America.* Madison, WI: University of Wisconsin Press, 1999.

Lee, Anna S. "Maternal Mortality in the United States," Phylon, 3rd quarter 1977, 259-266.

Leonard, Elizabeth. *Yankee Women: Gender Battles in the Civil War.* NewYork: Norton and Co. 1994.

Lerner, Gerda. *Creation of Feminist Consciousness.* New York: Oxford University Press, 1993.

–*Female Experience.* Indianapolis, IN: Bobbs-Merrill Educational Publishing Co., 1977.

–*The Majority Finds its Past.* New York: Oxford University Press, 1975.

–*The Woman in American History.* Menlo Park, CA: Addison Wesley, 1971.

Livermore, Mary. *My Story of the War.* Hartford, CT: A.D. Worthington and Co., 1890.

    –*What Shall We Do with our Daughters?* Boston: Lee and Shephard, 1883.

Lewis, Kenneth E. *West to Far Michigan.* E. Lansing, MI, Michigan State University Press, 2002.

Logan, Mary. *Part Taken by Women in American History.* New York: Arno Press, 1972.

MacLeod, Anne Scott. "The Caddie Woodlawn Syndrome" In *The Girl's History and Culture Reader*, edited by Miriam Forman-Brunell, and Leslie Paris, 199-221. Urbana: University of Illinois Press, 2011.

Mahun, Arwen P. *Steam Laundries.* Baltimore: Johns Hopkins University Press, 1999.

Mann, James. *Ypsilanti: A History in Pictures.* Chicago: Arcadia Press, 2002.

Marryat, Frederick. *Diary in America.* London: Longman, Orme, Brown, Green and Longmans 1839.

Marsh, Nicholas. *Remembering Delhi Mills.* Ann Arbor: Braun-Brumfield Inc., 1984.

    –*Scio Village: Ghost Town with a Past.* Mansfield, OH:Book Masters Inc. 1995.

Marshall, Albert. *Unconquered Souls.* Ypsilanti, MI: Marlan Publishers, 1993.

Martineau, Harriet *Society in America.* London: Saunders and Otley, 1837.

Marwil, Jonathan. *History of Ann Arbor.* Ann Arbor: Ann Arbor Observer Co., 1987.

Masi, Frank. *Typewriter Legend.* Syracuse, NJ: Matsushita Electric Corporation of America, 1985.

Massie, Larry B. *Potawatomi Tears and Petticoat Pioneers.* Allegen, MI:, Priscilla Press, 1992.

Mays, Dorothy *Women in Early America.* Santa Barbara, CA: ABC Clio, 2004.

McCullough, David. *The Greater Journey.* New York: Simon and Schuster, 2011.

McCutcheon, Marc. *Writer's Guide to Everyday Life in the 1800's.* Cincinnati: Writer's Digest Books, 1993.

McGuigan, Dorothy. *Dangerous Experiment.* Ann Arbor: Center for the Continuing Education of Women, 1970.

McLaughlin, Andrew C. *History of Higher Education in Michigan.* Washington, DC, Government Printing Office, 1891.

McLaughlin, Marilyn. *Ann Arbor – A Pictorial History.* St. Louis. MO: G Bradley Publishers Inc, 1995.

McLeod, Anne Scott. "The Caddie Woodlawn Syndrome" in *The Girl's History and Culture Reader*, edited by Miriam Forman-Brunell, and Leslie Paris, 199-221. Urbana: University of Illinois Press, 2011.

Merk, Frederick. *History of the Westward Movement.* New York: Alfred A Knopf, 1976.

Mesick, Jane. *The English Traveler in America.* New York: Columbia University Press, 1922.

Michigan Civil War Centennial Observance Committee. *Michigan Women in the Civil War.* Lansing, MI: 1963.

Mohr, James. *Abortion in America: Origins and Evolution of National Policy.* New York: Oxford University Press, 1978.

Mohun, Arwen P. *Steam Laundries.* Baltimore: Johns Hopkins Press, 1999.

Morello, Karen Berger. *The Invisible Bar: The Woman Lawyer in America 1638 - the Present.* New York: Random House, 1986.

Mott, Frank L. *History of American Magazines 1741-1850.* Cambridge, MA: Harvard University Press, 1930.

Nanry, Gertrude Hiscock. *Lest it be Forgotten.* 1987.

Nuland, Sherwin. *The Doctor's Plague.* New York: W.W. Norton, 2003.

Norris, David A. *Life During the Civil War.* Niagara Falls, NY: Moorshead Magazine, 2009.

Okrent, Daniel. *Last Call: The Rise and Fall of Prohibition.* New York: Scribner, 2010.

Owen, Robert Dale. *Moral Physiology.* London: E. Truelove, 1870.

Parker, Gail. *Oven Birds: American Women on Womanhood 1820-1920.* Garden City, NY: Anchor, 1972.

Peckham, Howard. *The Making of the University of Michigan.* Ann Arbor: University of Michigan Press, 1967.

Pedersen, Erik. "The Forgotten Lady." *Ypsilanti Gleanings*; *(Winter 2005):3-6., 16.*

Penny, Virginia. *The Employment of Women.* Boston: Walker, Wise and Co., 1863.

Phelps,Elizabeth Stuart. *Chapters from a Life.* New York: Arno Press, 1980 (originally 1896)

Phillips, Kevin. *Wealth and Democracy.* New York: Broadway Books, 2002.

Pierson, George Wilson. *Tocqueville in America.* Baltimore: Johns Hopkins University Press, 1938.

Pivar, David J. *Purity Crusade Sexual Morality and Social Control 1868-1900.* Westport, CT: Greenwood Press, Inc., 1973.

Portrait and Biographical Album of Washtenaw County. Chicago: Biographical Publishing Co., 1891.

Putnam, Daniel. *History of Michigan State Normal School.* Ypsilanti, MI: Scharf Tag, Label and Box Co.,1899.

Quaife, Milo. *The Bark Covered House.* edited by William Nowlin. Dearborn, MI:Historic Commission, 1992.

Rayne, M.L. *What Can a Woman Do?* Detroit: R. B. Dickerson and Co., 1885.

Reade, Margory and Susan Wineberg. *Historic Buildings of Ann Arbor, Michigan.* Ann Arbor: Ann Arbor Historical Foundation and Ann Arbor Historic District Commission, 1998.

Reynolds, Cynthia. *Our Hometown.* Chelsea, MI: Sleeping Bear Press, 2001.

Reynolds, David S. *Waking Giant.* New York: Harper Collins, 2008.

–*Walt Whitman's America.* New York: Alfred A Knopf, 1995.

Riley, Glenda. *Inventing the American Woman, An Inclusive History.* 2nd ed. Wheeling, IL: Harlan Davidson Inc., 1995.

–*Divorce: An American Tradition.* New York, Oxford University Press, 1991.

Robins, Natalie. *Copeland's Cure. Homeopathy and the War between Conventional and Alternative Medicine.* New York: Knopf, 2005.

Rosen, Ruth. *The Lost Sisterhood: Prostitution in America, 1900-1918.* Baltimore: Johns Hopkins University Press, 1982.

Rosenberg, Carroll and Charles. "Female Animal: Medical and Biological Views of Woman and her Role in 19th Century America." *In Women and Health in America*, edited by Judith Leavitt, 111-130. Madison: University of Wisconsin. Press, 1999

Ross, Isabel. *Silhouette in Diamonds.* New York: Harper and Brothers, 1960.

Rothman, Sheila. *A Woman's Proper Place.* New York: Basic Books, 1978.

Rothstein, William. *American Physicians in the Nineteenth Century.* Baltimore: Johns Hopkins University Press, 1972.

Ryan, Milo. *View of a Universe.* Ann Arbor, MI: McNaughton and Gunn, 1985.

Sander, Kathleen W. *The Business of Charity: The Woman's Exchange Movement 1832-1900.* Urbana: University of Illinois Press, 1998.

Sapinsley, Barbara. *Private War of Mrs. Packard.* New York: Paragon House, 1991.

Scharff, Virginia. *Taking the Wheel.* NewYork: Free Press, 1991.

Schwartz, Hillel. *Never Satisfied A Cultural History of Diets, Fantasies and Fat.* New York: Free Press, 1986.

Schultz, Jane. *Women at the Front.* Chapel Hill: University of North Carolina Press, 2004.

Scott, Anne Firor. *The American Woman: Who Was She?* Englewood Cliffs, NJ: Prentice Hall, 1971.

   –Making the Invisible Woman Visible. Urbana, IL: University of Illinois Press. 1984.

Shackman, Grace. *Ann Arbor Observed: Selections from Then and Now.* Ann Arbor: University of Michigan Press, 2006.

   –Nineteenth Century Ann Arbor A Photographic History. Chicago: Arcadia Press, 2001.

   –Webster. Webster Township Historical Society and Webster United Church of Christ, 2007.

Shaw, Anna Howard. *The Story of a Pioneer.* New York: Harper and Brothers. 1915.

Shaw, Wilfred B . The University of Michigan. New York: Harcourt, Brace and Howe, 1920.

Shaw, Wilfred B. ed. *The University of Michigan: An Encylopedic Survey.* Ann Arbor: University of Michigan Press, 1942

Sherr, Lynn. *Failure is Impossible: Susan B. Anthony in her Own Words.* New York: Times Books, 1995.

Sicherman, Barbara. *Alice Hamilton: A Life in Letters.* Cambridge MA: Harvard University Press, 1984.

Silber, Gina. *Daughters of the Union: Northern Women fight the Civil War.* Cambridge,MA: Harvard University Press, 2005.

   –Gender and Sectional Conflict. Chapel Hill: University of North Carolina Press, 2008.

Silk, Julia. *The Campaign of Julia Silk*. Ann Arbor: Courier, 1892.

Sillman, Sue Imogene. "Miss Ruth Hoppin, Educator." *Michigan History Magazine X*; *(1926):552-568*.

Silvey, Anita. I'll Pass for your Comrade. New York: Clarion Books, 2008.
Simmons, Christina. *Making Marriage Modern*. New York: Oxford University Press, 2009.

Smith, Catherine and Cynthia Greig. *Women in Pants*. New York: Harry N. Abrams, 2003.

Smith-Rosenberg, Carroll. "Female World of Love and Ritual." In *The Girl's History and Culture Reader*, edited by Miriam Forman-Brunell, and Leslie Paris, 149-178. Urbana: University of Illinois Press, 2011.

Snyder, Nancy L. *One Hundred Years of Business*, 1983.

Snyder, Thomas, ed. *120 Years of Americal Education: A Statistical Portrait*. U.S. Department of Education, 1993.

Solomon, Barbara. *In the Company of Educated Women*. New Haven: Yale University Press, 1985.

Stansell, Christine. "Women on the Town: Sexual Exchange and Prostitution." In *The Girl's History and Culture Reader*, edited by. Miriam Forman-Brunell, and Leslie Paris, 80-103. Urbana: University of Illinois Press, 2011.

Stanton, Elizabeth Cady. *Eighty Years and More: Reminiscences 1815-1897*. New York: T. Fisher Unwin, 1898.

Stanton, Elizabeth Ccady and Susan B. Anthony. *Selected papers of Elizabeth Cady Stanton and Susan B. Anthony, 1866-1873*. Edited by. Ann D. Gordon. New Brunswick, NJ: Rutgers University Press, 2000.

Starret, Helen. *After College What?* Boston: Thomas Crowell and Co., 1896

Strasser, Susan. *Never Done: A History of American Housework*, New York: Pantheon, 1982.

   –Waste and Want: A Social History of Trash. New York: Metropolitan Books, 1999.

Steele Valerie. *The Corset: A Cultural History*. New Haven: Yale University Press, 2001.

Stephenson, O.W. *Ann Arbor: The First Hundred Years*. Ann Arbor: Ann Arbor Chamber of Commerce, 1927.

Stevens, Mrs. Mark. *Six Months at the World's Fair*. Detroit: Detroit Free Press Printing Co., 1895.

Stevens, Wystan. *Northfield Harvest*. Whitmore Lake, MI: Northfield Township Historical Society, 1999.

Stockham, Alice. *Tokology.* rev. ed. Chicago: Alice Stockham and Co., 1889.

Tarolli, Janet. "First Ladies in Medicine at Michigan" *Medicine at Michigan*. Ann Arbor: University of Michigan Medical School, Fall, 2000.

Tentler, Leslie Woodcock. *Wage-Earning Women*. New York: Oxford University Press, 1979.

Theriot, Nancy M. "The 'Green Sickness' Among Nineteenth Century Adolescent Girls." In *The Girl's History and Culture Reader*, edited by. Miriam Forman-Brunell, and Leslie Paris, 179-198. Urbana: University of Illinois Press, 2011.

Tobias, Tomas, et al. *Ypsilanti Area Sesquicentennial, 1823-1973*. Ypsilanti, MI: Sesquicentennial Committee, 1973.

Tocqueville, Alexis de. *Democracy in America*. Edited by J.P.Mayer. Translated by George Lawrence. New York: Harper Row, 1988.

Trollop, Frances *Domestic Manners of the Americans.* London: Whitaker, Treacher and Co, 1832.

Turner, Frank N.,ed. *An Account of Ingham County.* Dayton, OH: National Historical Association, Inc., 1924.

Ulrich, Laurel Thatcher. *A Midwife's Tale: The Life of Martha Ballard based on her Diary 1785-1812.* New York: Alfred Knopf, 1990.

　　–*Well Behaved Women Seldom Make History.* New York: Vintage Books, 2008.

Van Der Werker, Nettie. *History of Earliest Ann Arbor.* Ann Arbor: Van Der Werker, 1919.

Van Hoosen, Bertha. *Petticoat Surgeon.* Chicago: Pellegrini and Cudahy, 1947.

Vare, Ethlie Ann and Gred Ptacek. *Patently Female.* New York: John Wiley and Sons, 2002.

Verbrugge, Martha. *Able-Bodied Womanhood.* New York: Oxford University Press, 1988.

Vertinsky, Patricia. *The Eternally Wounded Woman: Women Doctors and Exercise in the Late Nineteenth Century.* Urbana: University of Illinois Press, 1994.

Walker, Dale. *Mary Edwards Walker.* New York: Tom Doherty Associates, 2005.

Walsh Mary Roth. *Doctors Wanted: No Women Need Apply.* New Haven: Yale University Press, 1977.

Warren Joyce W. Ed. *Ruth Hall and Other Writings.* New Burnswick, NJ: Rutgers University Press, 1986.

Waugh, Norah and Margaret Woodward. *The Cut of Women's Clothes, 1600-1930.* New York: Theatre Arts Books, 1968.

Welter, Barbara. "Cult of True Womanhod" *Our American Sisters.* edited by Jane Friedman, and William Shade. Boston: Allyn and Bacon, 1973.

　　–*The Woman Question in American History.* Hinsdale, IL: Dryden Press, 1973.

　　–*Dimity Convictions: The American Woman in the Nineteenth Century.* Athens, OH,: Ohio University Press, 1976.

Wertheimer, Barbara M. *We Were There: The Story of Working Women in Amercia.* New York: Pantheon Books, 1977.

Whorton, James. *Nature Cures: The History of Alternative Medicine in America.* New York: Oxford University Press, 2002.

Willard, Frances E. *Occupations for Women.* New York: The Success Co., 1897.

Willard, Frances and Mary Livermore. *Great American Women of the Nineteenth Century.* Amhearst, MA: Humanity Books, , 2005.

Wineberg, Susan. *Lost Ann Arbor.* Chicago: Arcadia Publishers. 2004.

Wolff, Cynthia G. *Emily Dickinson.* New York: A.A. Knopf, 1986.

Wood-Allen, Mary. *Almost a Woman.* Cooperstown, NY: Arthur H. Christ Co., 1907

Woodruff, Ann D. "Fashionable Diseases" in *Clio's Consciousness* edited by Mary Hartman and Lois Banner, 1-22. New York: Harper Row, 1974.

Woody, Thomas. *A History of Women's Education in the United States.* New York: Octagon Books, 1974.

Woolson, Abba ed. *Dress Reform.* New York: Arno Press, 1974.

Woolston, Howard B. *Prostitution in the United States prior to WWI.* Montclair, NJ: Patterson Smith, 1969.

Zeinert, Karen. *Those Courageous Women of the Civil War.* Brookfield, CT: Millbrook Press, 1998.

Index

Abortion 177
Adams, Edith 147
Adams, Lois Bryan 237
Administratices 78-79
Allmendinger, Amanda 53-55
          Sophie 53-55
          Elizabeth 113-114
Amaden, Addie 191
Anderson-Taylor, Christine 184-185
Anderson, Olive San Louis   163-164
Andrews, Wealthy 52, 66
Anthony, Susan B. 121, 197-198, 218, 248
Aprill, Magdalena 76-77
Art teachers 129
Artists 130
Atwood, Phoebe 232
Automobiles 248-249

Babbitt, Alice and Nan 155, 248
          Florence 16-18, 254
Bach, Anna B. 240
Bacon, Minerva 29-30
backlash 187-188 249-252
Barnegat, MI 57
Bell, Mary E. 36
Beers, Mrs. 20
Bender, Helen H.   182
Burger, Sarah - see Stearns
Berry, Maggie 144-5
Bicycles 247-248
Bigalke, Mary 80-81
Birth Control 177-178
Birth Rate 250
Blackwell, Elizabeth 173
Bliss, Martha 43
Blosser, Margaret 236
Boise, Alice 120-121
Bookbinders 235
Botsford, Eliza Copeland 112-113
          Eliza Smith 113
Bower, Emma 239-240
Bradwell, Myra 196-197
Brogan, Eliza Hall 219-220
Boyd, Mrs. 215
Brundage, Mrs. N. 86
Bryan, Sarah 11, 237
Bucholz, Marianna 207
Burton, Fannie Cheever 182-183
Butterick Patterns 34, 40

Campbell, Elizabeth 129
Carleton, Grace 201
Carpenter, Maude 226
Case, Eva 233

Caspary, Catherine 84-85, 216
          Frances 85, 127-128
Chapin, Lucy 154
Chlorosis 161
Civil War 61, 74, 77, 79, 81, 85, 138, 152, 188-189, 206
clairvoyant medicine 90-91
Clapp, Hannah Keziah 118-11925
Clark, Lucy 25
Clark sisters and school 103-104
Cleary College 155-156
Clinton, Anna 114-115
Coe, Olive 17-19, 23, 26
Co-education 101-102, 110-111, 117-118, 158
Commercial education 153-156
Cooley, Ora 89
Cooper, Mrs. F. L. 218
Corselius, Cornelia 103-104, 115, 134-135
Correctional facilities for women 73, 243-245
Cory, Jennie 36
          Ratie 36
Cox, Susan C. 88
Craine, A. M. 24
Crandall, Phoebe 22
Crane, Lucy 56
Crawford, Katherine -186-187
Crippen, Harriet 213
Cross-dressing 26,148, 152-153
Curtis, Esther 31
Cutcheon, Anna   107
          Harriet   107

Dancer, Elizabeth H. 219
dating 251
day care 251
Demorest, Nell 34
DeRyke, Lucille Johnson 236
Dewell, A. 20-21
De Witt, Lydia 185-186
Dieterle, Anna, 195
Dimick, Emma 195-196
Dimick, Harriet 195-196
Disderide, Katherine 77-78
Divorce 37-39, 250
Dodge, Helen 225
Dodge, Almira Pray 78, 225
Doty, Charlotte 131-132
Doty Clara 131-132
Draper, Emma 219
Dunlap, Aurilla Cook 46

Eamon, Nancy see Nutting
Eastman, Anna 114
Eaton, Lottie 145
Edmonds, Sarah Emma 148

Exposition of 1876 152
Exposition of 1893 142, 237

Fair, Susan 100
Fairbrother, Elsada 95
Fairbanks, Mary Rice 99, 168
Farmer, Julia 87-88
Farrand, Elizabeth 135-136
Felch, Eliza 57-58
Fitzgerald, Charlotte 185
Follett, Elvira Norris 62
Forbes, Matilda 29
Fortune Tellers 204
Foster, Clyde 127
   Eva and Mary 24
   Mary Lowry 198-199
Freeman, Julia Wheelock 188-189
French, Ruth 176
Friend, Olive 74-75
Fuller, Esther 72-73

Gardner, Nanette 239-240
Garretson sisters 130
Gauntlett, Sarah 215-216
Gay, Susan M. 219
Gerry, Ruth 175-176
Gerstner, Christine 80-81
Gibson, May Clark 141-142
Giles, Daphne S, 133
Gillett, Lucretia 139-140
   Anne
Glasier, Ella 29-30
Goddard, Mary 170
Goodell, Aurilla Stevens 51
Goodison, Bertha
Gorton, Olive 96-97
Gott, Julia Ann 105
Graves, Hannah 29
Gray, Frances E. 115
   Ida 194
Gregory, Hannah 46
Griffin, Mrs. Henry O. 104-105
   Miss 105
Groomes, Katherine 27-28

Hall, Emma Amelia 242-246
   Olivia B. 217-218
   Samantha 12
Hallock, Elsie A. 194
Hamilton, Mary L. 228-229
Hangsterfer, Catherine 79-80
   Elizabeth 80
Hartley, Sophia 183-184
Hathaway, Louise McMath see McMath
Hatten, Elizabeth 155-156
Haviland, Laura 86-87
Hawkings, Emma 226
Hayes, Abby Smith 109-110
   Louise and Mayme 142-143

Higgins, Hannah 224
Hilton, Hattie 176-177
Hoban, Mrs. 218-219
Hollister, Emily 46, 189-190, 207
   Martha 190-191
Holmes, Lettice Smith 106
Homeopathy 185
Hooker Katherine 30
   Phoebe 30
Hoover, Mary 191-192
Hoppin, Ruth 169-170
Hunt, Alice 166
   Nora Crane 129
   Phoebe 11

Jenter, Cora Grossman 216
Johnson, Hope 96-97
Jones, Emeline Roberts
Jordon, Myra 212
Journalists 236-238

Keal, Nellie 81-82
Keays, Hersilia 136
Kellogg, Martha 35,37
Killgore, Sarah 197-198
Kimmel, Sovengire 192--193
Kempf, Pauline 127
King, Julia Ann 167
Kinne, Jennie B. 240
Kirchofer, Marie 115-116
Kirkland, Caroline 45, 143
Knight, Electra and Harriet 209

Ladd, Martha 104-104
Langdon, Fanny 160
Larzelere, Harriet W. 60
Latham, Vida 194
Layton, Mrs. John 46-47
Lehman, Adena 224
Liesemer, Emma Helber 238-139
Lodholz, Henrica Spathelf 83
   Mary 83
Love, Mrs. 20-22
Lovell, Almira F. 223-224
Loving, Nellie 149-150

Madary, Elsie 55-56
Magoffin, Eliza 125
manicurists/pedicurists 146
marriage 76, 184, 196, 250
McAndrew, Helen 174-5
McArthur, Helen Dodge 27
McComber, Betsey A. 87
McCormick, Mary 89-90
McMath, Maribelle 97
   Mrs. 22, 86
   Louisa 22, 36
Merrylees, Sarah 112
Merrill family 101-102

Michigan, settlement of 10-11, 19, 204-205

Midwives 177
Miley, Mary 32
Mills, Vesta 125-6
Miner, Martha 47
Minor, Eusebia 98
Mize, Abbie 149
Moore, Jennie 222
Morse, Elba 191
       Ellen 216-217
Morton, Alzina 116
Mosher, Eliza 179-181, 184
Muehlig, Amelia Volz 89
       Bertha 221
Murray, Ellen B. 187-188

"New Woman" 247-252
Noble, Harriet 10
Nordman, Irene Smith 98
Norris Helen 116
Norris, Roccena 51,102
Norris, "Roccie" 130
Norton, Ada A. 115, 168
      Sarah 22, 56
Nute, Marion 166
Nutting, Nancy Eamons 77

Octagon Houses 174-175
Osband, Lucy A. 110-111
      Marna 166 , 237, 246
Osborne, Harriet 014

Padfield, Alice 190-191
Page -sisters and school 105-106
Palmer, Alice Freeman 13
      Blanche C. 37
      Fidelia Randall 97
      Ida May 219
      Mary 25
      Mattie 157
      Sarah 25
Parker, Mary E. 225
Parson, Olive 43
Parsons, Harriet 96-97
      Mary E. 141
Paton, Annie 42
Pearce, Abigail 171
Peterson sisters 30
Petrie, Marie Allmendinger Baur 54-55
Physical Education 169 181-183
Pierce, Adella 188
      Sophia 90-91, 132-134
Porter, Alice 114
Postmasters 240-242
Price, Mrs. 85
Prisons and reformatories for women 73
Professional women 201, 250
Public Speaking 199

Queen Sill 71

Randall, Cora B. 59
Rapelje, Mrs. 70
Rayne, Martha. Louise 14, 237-238
Remington, Emily 28
Rentschler, Christine 28
Restaurants 214-216
Restell, Madame 177
Richards, Louisa 221
Robinson, Lillian 71
Roehm, Ernestina 221
Rogers, Abigail 116-119
Rogers, Katie 81
Rominger, Marie 156-7
Roosevelt, Alice 249
      Theodore 250-251
Root, Mrs. Charles 34
Roper, Mary 143-144
Roth, Caroline 83-84
Rowley, Louisa 35
Ruch, Flora 176
Rumsey, Mrs. Elisha 19, 106
Ryan, Catherine 27
      Hannah 27
      Joanna 52
      Sue P. 226

Saloons 84
Schlimmer,Lana 48
Schneider, Barbara 71
Seances 91, 204
Sessions, Eunice 86
Sewing machines 25-26
Shade, Kunigunda 82
      Rosa 82-83
Shadford, Jennie 32
      Lizzy32-33
Sharp, Margaret 233-234
Shaw, Anna Howard 26, 119
      Mary 130-131
Sherman, Julia 228
Sherrill, Minnie Davis 128
Shewcraft, Elizabeth 144
Silk, Julia 91-92
Smith, Flora 227-8
Smith, Mrs. George 177
Solis, Jeanne 160
Snyder, Alice 181-182
      Minnie 227-228
Spathelf Anna 223
Speechley, Susan 140
Spooner, Bertha 35
Stark, Ella Josephine 215
Stanley, Elsa 128
Stanton, Elizabeth Cady 110, 121, 178, 197-8
Stearns, Sarah Burger 119-120
Stebbins, Miss 22
      Mr. and Mrs. Charles 215
      Mr. and Mrs. Henry 214

Stereotype 19, 84-85, 102, 160-161
Stevens, Julia 33
       Mrs. Stanley 24
Stewart Carrie Marsden 194-195

     Eliza 222, 242
     Frances 242
     Mrs. Isa 208
     Sarah 242
Stockwell, Madelon 162-163
Stone, Lucinda 106, 121, 124, 165
Storms, Eliza 26
Stowell, Louise Reed 165-166

Tarbell, Ida 252
Taverns and inns 205-206
Teachers' salaries 98-100
Temperance 133-4
Ten Brook, Emma 49-50
      Sarah 43
Thumm, Ida Mae 192
Tickner, Louisa   88
Todd, Electra 34
Trojanowski, Minnie 145-146
Trask, Frances 252-253
Trim, Nellie 225
Tyler, Mrs. H. 20-21

Unterkircher, Fannie 126

Van Hoosen, Bertha 178-179
Visal, Elvira C. 220
Vogel, Mary 208
Volland, Sophia 184

Wagner,Henrietta 31-32
Wakeman Sarah Rosetta 26-27
Waldron, Louisa   108
Walker, Esther 207-208
     Mary 162
     Selina 207-208
Wallace, Laura Ripley 50
Walton, Genevieve 150-151
Ward, Rebecca L. 45-6
Warner, Belle 176
Washburn, Lucy   38
Waterbury, Elvira 88
     Jeanette 88
Watson, Catherine 195
Watt, Rachel 51
Wellwood, Ella 100
Wertman, Sarah see Killgore
Whiting, Mary C. 199-200, 219
Widowhood 79
Wilbur, Bethiah Hiscock 212-213
Willcox, Mary Ann 87
Willcoxson, Abigail 204
Williams, Arvilla 28
     Emma 108
Wilson, Julia 25

Wines family 100-101
Women's exchanges 226-227
      health 158-162, 169, 171
      proper sphere 10-13, 79, 102, 124, 159, 163-164, 196-197, 229, 226
      suffrage 121, 239-240, 252
Wood-Allen, Mary A. 184
Woodard, Gertrude 248-249
Woodruff, Mrs. 19, 51
Worthington, Ruth Parker 109

YWCA 213